P9-ARL-031

Education

Reference Sources in the Social Sciences Series
Lubomyr R. Wynar, Series Editor

No. 1 *Sociology: A Guide to Reference and Information Sources.* By Stephen H. Aby.

No. 2 *Education: A Guide to Reference and Information Sources.* By Lois J. Buttlar.

No. 3 *Public Relations in Business, Government, and Society: A Bibliographic Guide.* By Anne B. Passarelli.

EDUCATION
A Guide to Reference and Information Sources

LOIS J. BUTTLAR

1989

LIBRARIES UNLIMITED, INC.

Englewood, Colorado

LIBRARIES UNLIMITED, INC.
P.O. Box 3988
Englewood, CO 80155-3988

Library of Congress Cataloging-in-Publication Data

Buttlar, Lois, 1934-
    Education : a guide to reference and information sources / Lois J.
Buttlar.
    xiv, 258 p. 17x25 cm. -- (Reference sources in the social sciences series ;
no. 2)
    Includes index.
    ISBN 0-87287-619-5
    1. Reference books--Education--Bibliography.   2. Education-
-Bibliography.   3. Reference books--Social sciences--Bibliography.
4. Social sciences--Bibliography.   I. Title.   II. Series.
Z5811.B89
[LB15]
011'.02--dc20   89-2651
                                                                   CIP

Contents

v

Foreword

This new series, Reference Sources in the Social Sciences, is intended to introduce librarians, researchers, and students to major sources within the social sciences disciplines. The series will cover the following disciplines: sociology, history, economics and business, political science, anthropology, education, psychology, and general social science reference sources.

The organization and content of each volume are shaped by bibliographic forms and subject structures of the individual disciplines. Since many subject areas within the social sciences are interrelated, some reference sections in the various volumes will have certain features in common (e.g., a section on general social science sources). Each volume in the series constitutes a unique reference handbook, stressing the informational subject structure of the discipline, major reference publications, databases, and other relevant sources, including serials, major professional organizations, and research centers.

It is hoped that *Education: A Guide to Reference and Information Sources* will fill an important gap in the professional social sciences literature, and provide useful tools for research in education. The volume is divided into twenty chapters and covers all major reference sources on educational disciplines, including over 900 titles.

Dr. Lois Buttlar is assistant professor of library science at Kent State University, School of Library Science, where she teaches courses in social sciences information sources and services, as well as those related to librarianship in school media centers, among others. Previously she served as acting director in the Instructional Resources Center of the College of Education at KSU, and director of the Curriculum Materials Library. She has compiled a number of published bibliographies related to education and reference librarianship.

L. R. Wynar
Series Editor

Introduction

PURPOSE AND SCOPE

The purpose of this guide is to provide descriptions of the major sources of information in education and fields related to it. Over 900 titles in 676 entries, including major guides, bibliographies, indexes, abstracts, and other reference sources are provided. In addition to these traditional print sources, databases that can be searched online, major research centers and organizations, and major periodical titles are also indicated. Almost all works selected were published after 1980 and are still available for purchase. Some exceptions are made for a limited number of important works, for example, unique bibliographies that still serve a worthwhile purpose to educational researchers.

Sources included are in the English language, with a few exceptions. The emphasis is on American works and, to a lesser extent, those published in Great Britain. Multilingual sources are, for the most part, sponsored by UNESCO or similar international organizations. Entries follow the bibliographic format of those in *American Reference Books Annual* (*ARBA*) and annotations are descriptive and, in some cases, evaluative in nature.

ORGANIZATION

This guide is divided into twenty chapters. The first is a selected listing of general reference sources that also are relevant to education. Since education is one of the subdisciplines of the social sciences, the second chapter covers selected general social science reference sources that pertain to education, while chapter 3 covers sources in specific social science disciplines (that is, sociology, psychology, history, political science, and social work). In the fourth chapter, general education reference sources, or those applicable to all the individual subfields of education, including online databases and services, are described.

In chapters 5 through 20, sources are organized in fourteen categories representing specific areas of education. Entries in "Educational Foundations" are related to the historical, philosophical, and psychological foundations of education, including two works that are major general historical treatises. Those in "Curriculum and Instruction" cover materials on curricular content (further subdivided by disciplines, for example, reading, science, social studies) and on teaching and teaching methodologies. Other chapters cover administration, evaluation, elementary and secondary education, higher education, special education, educational media and technology, career and vocational education, adult and nontraditional education (including correspondence or distance education), bilingual and multicultural education, international and comparative education, women's studies and feminist education, and religion and religious education.

Some fields of education have well-developed bodies of literature; therefore, these larger chapters have been subdivided into more specific topics. For example, the large number of directories in the higher education chapter are subdivided into general directories, and general and specialized college guides. Although entries in the chapter on special education cover all aspects of exceptionality (that is, gifted, learning disabled, physically handicapped, mentally retarded, and emotionally handicapped), subject subdivision was not employed because so many sources cover more than one aspect of special education, and neat subdivisions are not possible. Sources in the vocational education chapter cover vocational guidance and counseling, as well as career education. The broad field of educational media and technology suffers somewhat from a terminology problem. Sources were divided into those related to instructional design (including a systematic approach to instruction) and educational technology, sources related to school media specialists and media centers, and those related to the use of microcomputers in education.

Chapter 19 contains selected listings of research centers and organizations that sponsor and/or conduct research and other activities or provide professional services related to education. In chapter 20, major periodicals that report and disseminate research findings and information related to current trends and developments in education are described. Within each chapter and subject area, entries are arranged first by type of relevance format, and then alphabetically by author or, in some cases, title.

Information in each entry includes a complete bibliographic citation, consisting of author, title, edition, place of publication, publisher, date, number of pages (or volumes), series, price (if in print), and LC and ISBN numbers. For serial publications, an ISSN number is provided; the inception date and frequency are also indicated. In cases of government documents, Superintendent of Documents numbers are provided, when available.

Vendor prices are indicated for database connect time and telecommunication costs. This information was taken from the most recent edition of *Data Base Directory*. Most book prices were taken from the latest edition of *Books in Print*. Prices of serial titles were taken from *Ulrich's International Periodicals Directory* and *Irregular Serials and Annuals*. Obviously information on prices is outdated very quickly, but it gives the reader some idea of the price of an information source relative to others of the same nature.

Subheadings are consistent from one section to the next. For example, for the sake of consistency, the subheading "Dictionaries and Encyclopedias" is used for each subject category, whether there are both dictionaries and encyclopedias or just encyclopedias or just dictionaries in that category. In addition to accessing materials by the subject arrangement, an author/title/subject index is provided. Titles annotated, almost without exception, were examined personally by the author.

1

General Reference Sources
Relevant to Education

BIBLIOGRAPHIES

American Reference Books Annual. Edited by Bohdan S. Wynar. Littleton, Colo.:
Libraries Unlimited, 1970- . Annual. $75.00. ISSN 0065-9959.
This annual publication provides reviews of all major reference books published in the
United States during the previous year. This comprehensive and major reviewing service
provides critical and evaluative descriptions of new and reprinted works with annotations
prepared by experts in the subject field. Reviews are arranged in over forty subject
categories with sections subdivided by type of reference tool; for example, bibliographies,
encyclopedias, directories, handbooks and yearbooks, and indexes. Annual volumes begin
with a list of journals cited and a list of contributors. Author, title, and subject indexes are
provided.

Reynolds, Michael M. **Guide to Theses and Dissertations: An International Bibliography
of Bibliographies**. Rev. and enl. ed. Phoenix, Ariz.: Oryx Press, 1985. 263p. $125.00.
LC 85-43094. ISBN 0-89774-149-8.
Research reported in a thesis or dissertation represents a significant, although often
unpublished and hard to trace, portion of the literature of any discipline. This guide
covers a much broader subject area than education, and is useful to any researcher
interested in identifying retrospective bibliographies (up to 1984) of theses and dissertations in many subjects including area studies, special/racial groups, education, library
and information services, social sciences, and others.
The work begins with a list of universal titles, followed by national listings which are
arranged alphabetically by country from Algeria to Yugoslavia, and then by broad subject
categories. Entry format usually follows that of Library of Congress with transliterations
provided for non-Romance languages. Annotations include the level of the work, number
of items, years covered by materials, institution, subject coverage, arrangement, and index
access. Indexes to the work include institutions, names and journal titles, and subject.

Sheehy, Eugene P., ed. **Guide to Reference Books**. 10th ed. Chicago: American Library
Association, 1986. 1,560p. $50.00. LC 85-11208. ISBN 0-8389-0390-8.
This guide is the accepted standard for identifying reference books in all subject areas.
Prior to being edited by Sheehy, it was most recently edited by Constance Winchell
and Isadore Mudge, and first begun in 1902. It incorporates both generalized works
basic to research in all major fields, as well as specialized titles in the humanities,
social and behavioral sciences, history and area studies, and science, technology, and
medicine. Entries are arranged by subject and include complete bibliographic

citations, plus concise descriptive annotations. One volume in the British publication that is a counterpart to this guide is edited by A.J. Walford, *Walford's Guide to Reference Material: Volume 2, Social & Historical Sciences, Philosophy & Religion* (4th ed., Library Association; distr., ALA 1982).

Subject Guide to Books in Print. New York: Bowker, 1957- . Annual. 4v. $159.95. ISSN 0000-0159.

This guide constitutes the subject index to the major bibliography of books that are still in print and available for purchase. Other volume titles provide access by title and author. Library of Congress subject headings are used, and information provided in the entries includes author, title, publisher, date, pages, price, series, edition, and LC and ISBN numbers.

Indexes and Abstracts

Bibliographic Index. New York: H. W. Wilson, 1937- . Semiannual, with annual cumulations. Service basis. ISSN 0006-1255.

Citations are given to major bibliographies on a subject. This work is subtitled *A Cumulative Bibliography of Bibliographies*, and it is international in coverage with emphasis on modern and Romance languages. Each year approximately 2,500 publications are analyzed for bibliographies and listings contained in books and periodicals. This index database is available online through WILSONLINE.

Book Review Digest. New York: H. W. Wilson, 1906- . Monthly, with quarterly and annual cumulations. Service basis. ISSN 0006-7326.

This index to book reviews includes brief excerpts of the reviews, which is a very useful feature. Titles included in it have been reviewed in at least two journals. Reviews are selected from about seventy-five English and American periodicals, and are arranged alphabetically by author of the book reviewed. Entries include complete bibliographic citation (author, title, publisher, date, price, LC and ISBN numbers). In addition to a Dewey Decimal classification number, subject headings and a reference to the source of the review are provided.

Book Review Index. Detroit: Gale, 1965- . Bimonthly, with quarterly and annual cumulations. $170.00/yr. ISSN 0524-0581.

Reviews published in newspapers, magazines, and journal periodicals are covered in this index. Excerpts from the review are not available, but in some cases a code abbreviation indicates the type of work that is being reviewed (e.g., reference book, serial, children's book, young adult book). Approximately 450 publications are analyzed and review citations are listed by author of the book reviewed. A source of retrospective reviews is *Combined Retrospective Index to Book Reviews in Scholarly Journals, 1886-1974*, edited by Evan Ira Farber (Research Publications, 1979, 15v.).

Comprehensive Dissertation Index. Supplement. Ann Arbor, Mich.: University Microfilms International, 1973- . Annual. Price varies. ISSN 0361-6657.

Dissertations can be located by author or subjects in the social sciences, including education. Citations provide information related to author of the dissertation, title, date completed, university awarding the degree, pages, order number, and citation in

DAI (*Dissertations Abstracts International*). Cumulated volumes for 1861 to 1972 (University Microfilms International, 1973) have separate volumes for specific disciplines. The supplements are arranged in two categories: "Social Sciences and Humanities" or "Sciences." Author index provided.

Dissertation Abstracts International. Ann Arbor, Mich.: University Microfilms International, 1938- . Monthly, with annual author index. $175.00. ISSN 0419-4209.

Abstracts to dissertations are located by author. They are organized into volumes as follows: *Part A: The Humanities and Social Sciences*; *Part B: Sciences and Engineering*; and *Part C: European Abstracts*. Within each volume abstracts are further subdivided first by subject and then arranged by author. Complete bibliographic citations provide author, title, date of completion, degree granting institution, pages, director of the dissertation and order number. Access is also available by keyword title index. *DAI* is also available online through DIALOG.

Monthly Catalog of United States Government Publications. Washington, D.C.: Government Printing Office, 1895- . Monthly, with semiannual and annual indexes. $45.00. ISSN 0362-6830.

This is an extensive major index to publications of all branches of the federal government. Instructions for ordering documents are also included. AACR and Library of Congress form is used for main entries; subject headings are those of Library of Congress. Access to information is available by author, title, subject, keyword, series/report number, contract number, and stock number. *Monthly Catalog* is also available online through the database service of DIALOG.

DIRECTORIES

Annual Register of Grant Support. Chicago: Marquis Academic Media, Marquis Who's Who, 1969- . Annual. $69.50. ISSN 0066-4049.

This annual publication is a comprehensive guide to grant monies and fellowships provided by government agencies, foundations, labor unions, business and professional organizations, and community trusts. Information is well organized, arranged alphabetically in major subject categories. Each entry provides the name, address, and telephone number of the granting organization; name of the program; type of grant; eligibility requirements; amount and duration of award; application instructions and deadline; and number of applicants for, and recipients of, awards.

Information is indexed by subject, organization and program, geographic regions, and personnel officers. Data for the *Annual Register* are obtained directly from the funding sources and annual revisions make this reference guide an accurate and valuable tool for researchers in education and other disciplines.

DRG: Directory of Research Grants. Phoenix, Ariz.: Oryx Press, 1975- . Annual. $110.00. ISSN 0146-7336.

Approximately 5,800 grant programs related to educational research or other "creative endeavors" are listed in this annual directory. Funded conferences, fellowships, and scholarships are also covered. The 1987 edition is 981 pages long and lists 1,700 organizations, associations, and agencies as grant funding sources. The book begins with a discussion of how to apply for a grant and how to prepare a proposal requesting funds.

Entries are arranged alphabetically by grant title in broad academic subject categories, and information included in each covers requirements and restrictions of the grant, amount, due and renewal dates, and name of sponsoring organization or agency, as well as a brief description of the grant. Grants can be identified by a subject index, a sponsor index, or by type of agency. Although this directory is international in scope, emphasis is on educational research grants in the United States.

Encyclopedia of Associations. 23rd ed. Detroit: Gale, 1988. 3v. with supplements. Price varies. ISSN 0071-0202.

This major reference source to national and international nonprofit organizations and associations contains over 2,000 entries under keywords related to education alone. Entries provide name, address, and telephone number of the organization; officers; contact person; date established; aim or purposes (included in a brief paragraph annotation); research interests (if any); and names of official organs, newsletters, periodicals, or other publications. Volume titles in the series include volume 1 (Pt. 1-2), *National Organizations of the U.S.*; 1, (Pt. 3), *Name and Keyword Index*; 2, *Geographic and Executive Indexes*; 3, *New Associations and Projects*; "Companion" volumes include *International Organizations*; *Regional, State, and Local Organizations*; and *Association Periodicals*.

The Foundation Directory. New York: The Foundation Center, 1982- . Biennial with annual suppls. $85.00. ISSN 0071-8092.

Over 3,000 nongovernmental foundations that grant external funds for research and activities in many disciplines, including education, are arranged alphabetically by state. Each entry provides information on the foundation name, address, date of establishment, staff, aims and objectives, and amount funded. Access to information about grant foundations is by field or subject; geographic location; donors, trustees and/or administrators; and foundation name. *The Foundation Directory* is also available online via DIALOG.

The Foundation Center also publishes a yearly publication called *The Foundation Center Source Book* (1975-) which provides detailed information on the major grant foundations in the United States; *Grants for Higher Education* (1986); *Grants for Elementary and Secondary Education* (1984); *Grants for Religion and Religious Education* (1984); and *Foundation Fundamentals: A Guide for Grantseekers* (3d ed., 1985), edited by Patricia Read.

The Foundation Grants Index. New York: The Foundation Center, 1970- . Annual. $44.00. LC 72-76081.

This cumulative listing of foundation grants provides access to what is funded by major foundations. The fifteenth edition is edited by Elan Garonzik. Foundations can be identified by subject area, geographic focus, types of support, and/or the grant recipients. Grants are funded by 460 different foundations representing 40 percent of private monies awarded. A foundation is described here as a "nongovernmental, nonprofit organization with funds (usually from a single individual, family, or corporation) and program managed by its own trustees or directions," along with main educational and other activities.

Limitations of this index include the fact that smaller or mini-grants (anything under $5,000) are not indicated. Also, the quality of information varies since it is obtained primarily by voluntary reporting by foundations. Otherwise, this tool provides the grant seeker with a fairly representative overview of foundation giving. Introductory material outlines the general characteristics of foundation types, trends in giving, and key publications of the Foundation Center. The index is fairly easy to use, with clearly presented instructions. The main listing is alphabetical by state, but access is possible through six different listings.

The Grants Register. New York: St. Martin's Press, 1969- . Biennial. $59.95. LC 77-12055. ISSN 1140-7055.

This directory to scholarships, fellowships, grants, special awards, and other sources of financial aid available for graduate students or postgraduate scholars is international in scope. Included are over one million awards offered from over 2,000 sources, including government agencies, national organizations, and private corporations. Arrangement of entries is alphabetical by awarding agency, and information in each includes award name, purpose, amount, eligibility, application procedure, address, and duration of award. Grants range from travel money to attend a professional conference, to funds to conduct research, to fellowships for study that extends over several years.

Because most financial aid directories are aimed at undergraduates and limited to study or research in American institutions, *The Grants Register* makes a unique contribution to the reference literature.

STATISTICS SOURCES

American Statistics Index: A Comprehensive Guide and Index to the Statistical Publications of the U.S. Government. Washington, D.C.: Congressional Information Service, 1973- . Monthly, with quarterly and annual cumulations. Price varies. ISSN 0091-1658.

This reference tool indexes publications of all agencies of the U.S. government. Entries are arranged by government department or agency with a separate volume of subject headings, titles, or report numbers. It indexes over 700 periodicals and approximately 7,000 titles for statistical references. Related titles include *Statistical Reference Index: A Selective Guide to American Statistical Publications in Other Than the U.S. Government* (1980- , bimonthly) and *Index to International Statistics* (1983- , monthly), both published by Congressional Information Service.

Statistical Abstract of the United States. U.S. Bureau of the Census. Washington, D.C.: Bureau of the Census; distr., Government Printing Office, 1878- . Annual. Price Varies. ISSN 0081-4741.

This is a source of summary statistics on the political, economic, and social conditions of life in the United States. Included are population and demographic statistics, vital statistics, information related to immigration and naturalization, health, education, law enforcement, and international concerns. Further international statistics are available in *Statistical Yearbook* (UNESCO; distr., New York: UNIPUB, 1963- , annual).

Statistical Yearbook (UNESCO). United Nations, Department of International Economic and Social Affairs, Statistical Office. New York: UNIPUB, 1949- . Annual. $74.75. ISSN 0082-7541.

This international compendium of socioeconomic data allows comparisons by major factors related to the world's economy. Statistics compiled cover a wide variety of topics, including general economic growth; current status of developing countries and assistance to them; world populations; employment, inflation, and distribution of income; energy production, development, and sources; world trade; hunger and food supplies; world finances; education and literacy; and living conditions and housing.

Tables of statistical data are grouped in three major parts: world summary (principal trends in world economy overall); general socioeconomic statistics (economies of individual countries); and statistics of basic economic activities (agriculture, industry, construction, trade, energy, tourism, commerce, etc.).

Statistics Sources: A Subject Guide to Data on Industrial, Business, Social, Educational, Financial, and Other Topics for the United States and Internationally. 11th ed. Edited by Jacqueline Wasserman O'Brien, Steven R. Wasserman, and Kenneth Clansky. Detroit: Gale, 1987. 2v. 2,700p. $280.00. LC 84-82356. ISBN 0-0103-4398-3.

This comprehensive subject index to statistics on a wide variety of subjects was first published in 1962 and includes references to statistics related to education of members of ethnic and minority groups, as well as sources of data on other population demographics of the world. Sources of numeric data related to education in the United States are found under the specific topic, but data related to education in foreign countries are typically entered under the name of the country.

ONLINE DATABASES

Biography Master Index. Detroit: Gale, 1984- . Irregular. DIALOG (file #287, 288); $63.00/connect hr.

Information on some two million personalities (including outstanding educators and scholars in related fields) can be located in *BMI*, which indexes 375 biographical dictionaries and directories, both current and retrospective. Each record gives biographee's name, birth and death dates, and titles of sources that contain a more detailed biographical sketch. Coverage is international in scope and includes all time periods.

Database of Databases. Urbana, Ill.: M. E. Williams, in collaboration with the Information Retrieval Research Lab, Coordinated Science Lab, University of Illinois at Urbana–Champaign, 1950- . Quarterly reload. DIALOG (file #230); $48.00/connect hr.

Publicly available databases available by either an online search service or a batch processor are described in this file. Coverage is international and multilingual. A corresponding print title is *Computer-Readable Databases: A Directory and Data Sourcebook–Science, Technology, Medicine,* and *Computer Readable Databases: A Directory and Sourcebook–Business, Law, Social Science, Humanities* (ALA and Elsevier Science Publishers). This file is useful for selecting databases to search or to purchase, or for bibliometric analyses.

Dissertation Abstracts Online. Ann Arbor, Mich.: University Microfilms International, 1980- . Monthly updates. DIALOG (file #35); $72.00/connect hr.

According to Dialog Information Service, 99 percent of all American dissertations are cited in this database file, with abstracts included for all records from July 1980 on. In addition, master's theses have also been analyzed on a selective basis since 1962. The period of coverage extends from 1861 to the present.

Facts on File. New York: Facts on File, Inc., 1982- . Weekly updates. DIALOG (file #264); $60.00/connect hr.

This file contains the complete text of the weekly *Facts on File World News Digest*. This news reference service summarizes current events and affairs as reported in the newspapers of some of the major cities of the United States, Canada, and Western Europe. Arrangement of information is in four sections: (1) "International Affairs," (2) "U.S. Affairs," (3) "World News," and (4) "Miscellaneous" (sports, medicine, obituaries, literature, art, etc.). Subjects covered include education, arts and culture, and many others.

Foundation Grants Index. New York: The Foundation Center, 1973- . Bimonthly updates. DIALOG (file #27); $60.00/connect hr.

Information about external grant funds provided by over 400 nongovernmental, non-profit American foundations is available in this database file which corresponds to the printed title by the same name. The goals of the foundations are to support activities in the fields of education, health, humanities and religion, and science. Data are provided by The Foundation Center. Other related DIALOG files include *Foundation Directory* (#26) and *National Foundations* (#78), both of which are produced by the Foundation Center.

GPO Monthly Catalog. Washington, D.C.: Government Printing Office, 1971- . Biweekly updates. DIALOG (file #66); $35.00/connect hr.

This online version of the *Monthly Catalog of United States Government Publications* provides access to public documents from all branches and agencies of the federal government. It includes congressional hearings, bills, reports, committee documents and laws, presidential statements, annual agency reports, statistical summaries, maps, treaties, and other periodical publications. A related file, *GPO Publications Reference File*, indexes government documents that are currently available for purchase. Topics in both of these files include many produced by the U.S. Department of Education.

Information Science Abstracts. Alexandria, Va.: IFI/Plenum Data, 1966- . Monthly updates. DIALOG (file #202); $70.00/connect hr.

This database provides indexing and abstracting service of information from books, articles, conference proceedings, research reports, and other materials on an international basis. Coverage emphasizes library and information science, and related areas, including education. The file is an online version of the printed reference tool by the same name. English translations are provided for non-English titles. A similar DIALOG file (#61) is *LISA (Library and Information Science Abstracts)* produced in London by the Library Association.

Magazine Index. Belmont, Calif.: Information Access, 1983- . Monthly updates. DIALOG (file #47); $90.00/connect hr.

Information related to the social sciences can be accessed through this comprehensive index to approximately 450 American and Canadian magazines. A full text display of over 100 titles is possible. All periodicals indexed by the *Readers' Guide to Periodical Literature* are covered, including articles, editorials, reviews, biographical sketches, literary pieces (poetry and short stories), and major news items. A related file that overlaps with this file is *Academic Index* (Information Access Company).

PAIS International. New York: Public Affairs Information Service, Inc., 1976- . Monthly updates. DIALOG (file #49); $75.00/connect hr.

The Public Affairs Information Service database is the online version that corresponds to two print reference titles, *PAIS Bulletin* and *PAIS Foreign Language Index* (FLI). Over 8,000 monographs and 1,200 journals, including government publications, are indexed annually. Emphasis is on current issues related to public policy and many subdivisions of the social sciences.

PsycInfo (Psychological Abstracts Information Service). Washington, D.C.: American Psychological Association, 1967- . Monthly updates. DIALOG (file #11); $55.00/connect hr.

This data file covers topics in psychology and related behavioral and other sciences. Examples of specific topics applicable to educators include applied psychology, communication systems, developmental psychology, educational psychology, physical and psychological disorders, and psychometrics. Coverage is on an international basis; materials analyzed include monographs, periodicals, technical reports, and materials from *Dissertation Abstracts International*.

Sociological Abstracts (SA). San Diego, Calif.: Sociological Abstracts, Inc., 1963- . 5/yr. DIALOG (file #37); $60.00/connect hr.

This international database emphasizes methodological or theoretical problems in sociology. Of more interest to the educator is its subfile, *SOPODA* (Social Planning/ Policy and Development Abstracts) which is more concerned with application to specific problems, including sociology of education. Both files correspond to the print tools by the same titles.

Social Scisearch. Philadelphia: Institute for Scientific Information, 1972- . Biweekly updates. DIALOG (file #7); $63/connect hr.

This international database covers all the social, behavioral, and related sciences (including, among other topics, anthropology, communication, education, research, ethnic groups studies, information/library science, psychology, statistics). It corresponds to its printed counterpart, *Social Science Citation Index*. It has the unique feature of selecting materials for inclusion on the basis of citation analysis and provides the capability of citation searching. Approximately 2,400 journals are analyzed for articles, reports, meetings, letters, and editorials.

2
General Social Science Reference Sources

GUIDES

Guide to Resources and Services. Inter-University Consortium for Political and Social Research. Ann Arbor, Mich.: ICPSR, 1977- . Annual. ISSN 0362-8736.

Social science data, including that pertaining to various aspects of education, available from the consortium's data archives are provided. The guide is organized by divisions of the social sciences, and within that division studies are arranged alphabetically by name of the author or investigator. Entries for each study include an ICPSR study number and description of the study. Information is provided for ordering data sets and the codebooks that correspond to them; access to information is available through title, investigator, and subject indexes.

Webb, William H., ed. **Sources of Information in the Social Sciences.** 3d ed. Chicago: American Library Association, 1986. 777p. $70.00. LC 84-20494. ISBN 0-8389-0405-X.

This guide to the social sciences breaks the literature into nine major divisions—social sciences, history, geography, economics and business administration, sociology, anthropology, psychology, education, and political science—with a section devoted to each. Within each appear the subdivisions "Scope and Purpose," "Survey of the Field," and "Survey of the Reference Works"; which, in turn, are further subdivided chronologically and by type of reference format. The education section includes an introduction; classics; introductory works; educational history; educational philosophy; educational sociology; comparative and international education; educational psychology, measurement, and guidance; curriculum and instruction; preschool and elementary education; secondary education; higher education; teacher education; adult education; special education; educational research; educational administration and supervision; and educational criticism and controversy. A less comprehensive and less current work is Tze-Chung Li's *Social Science Reference Sources: A Practical Guide* (Greenwood, 1980).

BIBLIOGRAPHIES

Bibliographie der Wirtschaftswissenschaften. Gottingen: Vandenhoeck & Ruprecht, v.1., 1905- . Annual. Price varies. ISSN 0340-6121.

Replaces *Bibliographie der Sozialwissenschaften*, an annual publication which has had several name changes from 1905 to 1967. It is a comprehensive subject bibliography of books and periodical articles in the field of economics and social sciences with author and subject indexes covering about 7,500 items per year. International in scope, it is a very valuable compilation for social science research.

International Bibliography of the Social Sciences. London: Tavistock, 1955- . Annual. $110.00. ISSN 0085-204X.

The UNESCO-sponsored International Committee for Social Science Documentation provides bibliographic control of four subdivisions of the social sciences. Four individual bibliographies are drawn from this one major compilation: *International Bibliography of Economics, International Bibliography of Social and Cultural Anthropology, International Bibliography of Sociology,* and *International Bibliography of Political Science.*

London Bibliography of the Social Sciences. Compiled under the direction of B. M. Headicar and C. Fuller. London: Mansell, 1931- . Annual. (London School of Economics. Studies in Economics and Political Science: Bibliographies, No. 8). $100.00. ISSN 0076-051X.

This major comprehensive bibliography in the social sciences lists books, pamphlets, and government documents with entries arranged by subjects. Started as the printed version of the subject catalog of nine libraries, it now constitutes the holdings of the British Library of Political and Economic Science and the Edward Fry Library of International Law at the London School of Economics. Updated by computer-produced supplements.

INDEXES AND ABSTRACTS

Current Contents: Social and Behavioral Sciences. Philadelphia: Institute for Scientific Information, V. 6, no. 2, 1974- . Weekly. $283.00. ISSN 0092-6361.

Continues, and assumes the numbering of, *Current Contents: Behavioral, Social & Educational Sciences.* This index reproduces the tables of contents of over 1,300 international journals and multiauthored books, which are arranged in thirteen subject categories from the social sciences. An author and address directory, subject index, and publisher's directory are provided in each weekly issue. A cumulative contents index is produced on a triennial basis.

Human Resources Abstracts: An International Information Service. Beverly Hills, Calif.: Sage, 1966- . Quarterly. $85.00, individuals; $110.00, institutions. ISSN 0099-2453.

Formerly known as *Poverty and Human Resources*, this service provides abstracts of articles, books, parts of books, government reports, and some unpublished materials. It also includes feature articles and special analytical synopses of current issues and problems. Emphasis is on social science research and issues in the United States. Author and subject indexes are provided. Cumulations are published on an annual basis.

Social Sciences Citation Index. Philadelphia: Institute for Scientific Information, 1973- . 3/yr. $3,100.00 including annual cum. ISSN 0091-3707.

Over 4,700 journals and a selected number of monographic series covering all disciplines on an international basis. Additional items covered include proceedings, editorials, letters, reports, and book reviews. Citation patterns and title keywords are used as criteria for selecting articles from *Science Citation Index.* Components of the work include the *Citation Index, Source Index, Permuterm Subject Index,* and the *Corporate Index.* According to the introduction the "SSCI Annual also includes the *Journal Citation Reports*, a bibliometric analysis of sources and cited journals in the SSCI" (p. 5). Headings related to education are many, including education, evaluation, measurement, objectives, planning, problems, psychology, reform, research, standards, technology, theory, thought, and educators.

Social Sciences Index (SSI). New York: H. W. Wilson, 1974- . Quarterly. Service basis. ISSN 0094-4920.

Author and subject entries to 353 international periodicals in the English language, covering various fields of the social sciences, are provided in this cumulative index. Items indexed are in the literature related to anthropology, area study, community health and medical care, economics, geography, international relations, law and criminology, police science and corrections, psychology, social work and public welfare, sociology, and urban studies. Included are feature articles on these subjects, review articles, biographies and obituaries, interviews, advertising, announcements of meetings, cartoons, and letters to the editor. Editorials are, for the most part, excluded.

A dictionary arrangement is employed; subject headings are those of the Wilson indexes, Library of Congress, or the literature itself. Entries include title of article, author, periodical citation (abbreviated title, volume, pages, month and year of publication).

Social Sciences Index is one of two indexes formerly published as *Social Sciences and Humanities Index* (1916-1974) and provides major access to the scholarly periodical literature for all social scientists, including educators. Over 100 subject headings are related to education in a recent issue.

DICTIONARIES AND ENCYCLOPEDIAS

Encyclopedia of the Social Sciences. Edited by Edwin R. A. Seligman. New York: Macmillan, 1930-1935. 15v. LC 39-3962.

As the first comprehensive encyclopedia in the field of social science, this set was prepared under the auspices of ten learned societies. It includes a lengthy discussion of the nature and extent of the social sciences, including a historical analysis and survey of countries. Although outdated, it presents a good overview of concepts in political science, economics, law, anthropology, sociology, penology, and social work. It is also a good source for information about prominent social scientists who are now deceased and their major contributions to the field.

International Encyclopedia of the Social Sciences. Edited by David L. Sills. New York: Macmillan, 1968. 17v. LC 68-10023. ISBN 0-02-895510-2; V. 18, *Biographical Supplement*, 1979. 820p. $90.00. LC 68-10023. ISBN 0-02-895510-2.

Signed articles by subject experts discuss concepts, theories, and methods associated with the following branches of the social sciences: anthropology, economics, geography, sociology, and statistics. Biographical sketches were limited in the first seventeen volumes, which were published in 1968, to about 600, while the classic *Encyclopedia of the Social Sciences* covered about 4,000. Therefore, the eighteenth supplementary volume incorporates later developments in the social sciences through 215 biographical portraits of social scientists in all areas who made major contributions to the field, whose work fostered growth of the discipline, or whose research was representative of new developments. Lists of works about the subject and by the subject follow the articles. The original seventeen volumes were reprinted in eight volumes in 1977 (Free Press, 1977, $310.00).

Kuper, Adam, and Jessica Kuper, eds. **The Social Science Encyclopedia**. Boston: Routledge & Kegan Paul, 1985. 916p. $75.00. LC 84-27736. ISBN 0-7102-0008-0.

Signed articles, written by over 500 experts in the field, discuss social science theories, theorists, terms, and subdisciplines of the field. Coverage of topics varies in length with some articles consisting of several paragraphs, and others constituting several pages. The language is aimed at the scholarly reader.

HANDBOOKS AND YEARBOOKS

Miller, Delbert, C. **Handbook of Research Design and Social Measurement**. 4th ed. New York: Longman, 1983. 678p. $23.95pa. LC 82-15287. ISBN 0-582-28326-4pa.

This handbook describes how to do social science research. It is organized in five main sections: (1) research design, including writing a grant proposal; (2) collecting data, whether in the library, laboratory, or field; (3) statistical techniques and analyses; (4) selection of sociometric scales or indexes; and (5) costing and budgeting research projects and reporting findings at professional confererences or in scholarly meetings.

3

Social Science Disciplines
Reference Sources

SOCIOLOGY

Guides

Aby, Stephen H. **Sociology: A Guide to Reference and Information Sources**. Littleton, Colo.: Libraries Unlimited, 1987. 231p. (Reference Sources in the Social Sciences Series). $36.00. LC 86-27573. ISBN 0-87287-498-2.

This guide is arranged in three main sections. Part 1 covers general social science reference sources; part 2 covers individual social science disciplines of education, economics, psychology, social work, anthropology, and history. Part 3, the largest section, covers general reference sources in sociology and in twenty-three separate subfields. In each part, and in each sociological subfield, entries are arranged by format under whichever of the following categories are applicable: guides, bibliographies, indexes and abstracts, handbooks and yearbooks, dictionaries and encyclopedias, statistics sources, directories, and biographies. In addition, included in part 3 under "General Reference Sources" are special categories devoted to journals, research centers, organizations, and publishers. Each entry includes complete bibliographic information, price, and LC and ISBN numbers for ease in further identification and for calling up citations online.

Mark, Charles. **Sociology of America: A Guide to Information Sources**. Detroit: Gale, 1976. 454p. index. (American Studies Information Guide Series, Vol. 1: Gale Information Guide Series). $65.00. LC 73-17560. ISBN 0-8103-1267-0.

This first volume in the Gale Information Guide Series emphasizes materials that focus on the sociological study of American life, culture, and society. Chapter 1 is an introductory overview of resources; chapter 2 covers reference works (including periodical and newspaper directories and guides; government documents, databases, statistics sources; theses, dissertations, and research in progress).

Subsequent chapters are devoted to the periodical literature and to sources arranged in subject categories. One chapter is devoted to education, where over 100 reference and general works cover the sociology of education, crisis and change in American education, urban education, integration, colleges and universities, students in higher education, graduate and professional education, and faculty and administration. Access is possible through the following indexes: author, periodical and serial title, title, and subject.

Bibliographies

The Combined Retrospective Index Set to Journals in Sociology, 1895-1975. Edited by Annadel N. Wile. Washington, D.C.: Carrollton Press, 1978. 6v. $1,155.00. LC 77-70347. ISBN 0-8408-0194-7.

The six volumes of this major listing of the retrospective periodical literature in sociology cover some 85,000 articles that appeared in 118 international sociology journals published in the English language. Contents include volume 1, "Anthropology," "Applied Sociology," "Culture," "Death and Death Rates," "Differentiation and Stratification," and "Group Interaction"; volumes 2-3, "Institutions: In General," "Bureaucratic Structures," "Family," "Formal Voluntary Organizations," "Health," "Medical Systems and Structures," "Industrial Systems and Structures," "Law and Legal Systems," "Military (Personnel) Systems and Structures," "Political Institutions," and "Religion"; volume 4, "Knowledge," "Research in Sociology," "Rural Systems and Structures," "Social Disorganization," "Social Ecology," "Sociology as a Profession," "Theorists," "Theory of Sociology," and "Urban Systems and Structures"; and volume 6, "Authors."

Citations are arranged alphabetically by title keyword. The additional information that follows includes a short title, author, journal number, year, volume, and page. The journal titles are listed on the inside (front and back) book covers.

Harvard University. Library. Sociology. Cambridge, Mass.: Harvard University Library; distr., Harvard University Press, 1973. 2v. (Widener Library Shelflist, Vol. 45-46). $85.00. LC 72-83391. ISBN 0-674-81625-0.

This edition of the shelflist of the Widener Library at Harvard University includes some 49,000 titles covering sociological history and theory, social groups and institutions (including academic institutions), social problems and reform, and social psychology. The catalog is arranged in four parts. The first is the classification schedule, the second is a presentation of entries in shelflist order, and parts 3 and 4 are chronological listings and alphabetical (by author and by title) listings, respectively. Educators can identify topics of relevance in the classification schedules, such as "Sociology of Knowledge," "Special Schools and Systems," "Children," "Youth," and other topics.

International Bibliography of Sociology. Prepared by the International Committee for Social Science Information and Documentation. Chicago: Aldine, 1952- . Annual International Bibliography of the Social Sciences). $108.00. ISSN 0085-2066.

Individual titles in the *International Bibliography of the Social Sciences* are devoted to sociology, economics, political sciences, and cultural anthropology, and they index the major primary publications of that particular field for the given year. Some publications missed during the previous year are also included. Materials in English and French are covered, and are arranged under subject headings used in the *Thesaurus for Information Processing in Sociology*. A list of periodicals consulted, an author index, and subject index are provided. The subject index reveals a large number of titles related to education; some selected subject headings include "Education" (by country), "Women's Education," "Educational Administration," "Educational Development," "Cost of Education," "Educational Guidance," "History of Education," "Educational Innovations," and "Teaching Aids." Other topics followed by "Educational" include "Needs," "Objectives," "Opportunities," "Output Planning," "Policy," "Psychology," "Research," "Sociology Systems," "Technology," and "Theory."

Social Reform and Reaction in America: An Annotated Bibliography. Santa Barbara, Calif.: ABC-Clio, 1984. 375p. (Clio Bibliography Series No. 13). $65.50. LC 82-24294. ISBN 0-87436-048-X.

Scholarly writings on social reform in the United States and Canada are covered in this compilation of 2,993 article abstracts published during the ten-year period 1973 to 1982. Abstracts were selected from the publisher's comprehensive history database. Entries are, for the most part, chronologically arranged in six chapters: (1) "The United States and Canada"; (2) "The Colonial Experience"; (3) "Crusades in the New Republic, 1783-1860"; (4) "Crises of Modernization, 1861-1900"; (5) "Struggles of the Twentieth Century"; and (6) "The Contemporary Scene." Chapter titles are alphabetical by author. The subject index lists entries under education, adult education, bilingual education, coeducation, colleges and universities, curricula, discrimination, elementary education, federal aid to education, higher education, illiteracy, industrial arts education, physical education, progressive education, religious education, scholarship, schools, secondary education, special education, teaching, textbooks, vocational education, and numerous other education-related topics.

Wepsiec, Jan. **Sociology: An International Bibliography of Serial Publications 1880-1980**. London: Mansell; distr., New York: H. W. Wilson, 1983. 183p. index. $57.00. ISBN 0-7201-1652-X.

According to the introduction, the aim of this bibliography is to provide researchers, teachers, historians, and students of sociology with information about serial publications that deal with the sociological aspects of a wide range of subfields in sociology. Serial publications included here are journals, monographic series, transactions (papers delivered at conferences), and selected directories. Entries are arranged alphabetically by serial title. Each entry includes title, or name of issuing agency and title; designation of first issue; date of first issue; frequency; place of publication; publisher; changes of title; and supplements. The subject index lists numerous titles under education, adolescence, children, delinquency, doctoral dissertations, schools, and other topics of interest to educators.

Indexes and Abstracts

Sociological Abstracts. San Diego, Calif.: Sociological Abstracts, Inc., 1953- . 5/yr. $180.00; $35.00/copy. ISSN 0038-0202.

This major abstracting service covers the periodical literature, papers presented at professional meetings, and some monographs in the field of sociology. Arrangement of abstracts is by subject with some thirty major categories (many of which are further subdivided) and a separate section reviews books on an international basis. This publisher also provides a reproduction service for articles and conference proceedings on a selected basis. Access to abstracts and citations is available via author, subject, source, and reviewer indexes.

Dictionaries and Encyclopedias

The Encyclopedic Dictionary of Sociology. 3d ed. Guilford, Conn.: Dushkin Publishing Group, 1986. 320p. $10.95pa. LC 85-072122. ISBN 0-87967-607-8pa.

Entries in this encyclopedic dictionary range from brief twenty-five-word definitions to multipage discussions arranged alphabetically. Cross-references refer the user to more specific sources of information. The dictionary includes some illustrations, maps, diagrams, charts, tables, cartoons, and photographs. For selected major subject areas, an alphabetic directory of articles on the subject is provided, and topic guides interspersed throughout point out specific relationships between individual articles. For example, a topic guide on "Education, Sociology of" points out articles covering specific educational institutions (Schools, Public; and Schools, Private; Indoctrination; Colleges; Education, Technical; and Education, Department of). It also identifies information on "Segregation"; "Busing"; "Brown v. Board of Education"; "Separate But Equal"; and the government report, "Racial Isolation in the Public Schools." For equality of educational opportunity, it lists "Compensatory Education"; Elementary and Secondary Education Act of 1965; and the *Coleman Report*.

Handbooks and Yearbooks

Bart, Pauline, and Linda Frankel. **The Student Sociologist's Handbook**. 4th ed. Glenview, Ill.: Scott, Foresman, 1986. 249p. Write for price info. LC 85-19399. ISBN 0-394-35109-6.

This handbook provides step-by-step procedures for writing about research in sociology or for preparing field work papers. It discusses relevant periodicals, abstract and indexing services, bibliographies, and statistics sources (federal and nonfederal), including those published by the U.S. Department of Education, ERIC, and the National Center for Education Statistics. A related title is *Materials and Methods for Sociology Research* by James Gruber, Judith Pryor, and Patricia Berge (Libraryworks, 1980).

PSYCHOLOGY

Guides

Borchardt, D. H., and R. D. Francis. **How to Find Out in Psychology: A Guide to the Literature and Methods of Research**. Oxford: Pergamon, 1984. 189p. $24.00. LC 84-2827. ISBN 0-08-031280-2.

This guide to information sources in psychology is divided into eleven chapters. The first two chapters provide an overview of the field, including major concepts and theories. Chapters 3 through 6 describe reference sources; chapters 7 through 10 discuss principles of research methodology, and chapter 11 covers professional organizations. Appendix materials provide advice and information on library searches and writing empirical psychological reports. An international listing of major psychological societies (with their addresses) is also included. A bibliography and subject index conclude the work. Coverage given to developmental psychology and educational psychology will be of interest to educators and school psychologists.

McInnis, Raymond G. **Research Guide for Psychology**. Westport, Conn.: Greenwood, 1982. 604p. index (Reference Sources for the Social Sciences and Humanities, No. 1). $49.95. LC 81-1377. ISBN 0-313-21399-2. ISSN 0730-3335.

This guide describes sources of information of importance to scholars conducting research related to psychology. The work begins with identification of major guides and bibliographies, abstracting services, indexes, major databases, and specialized sources of information. The latter include biographical dictionaries and directories, sources of book review citations; encyclopedias, dictionaries, and reviews of research; research handbooks and directories of associations; works related to psychological measurement and methodology; and statistics sources. Subsequent chapters describe sources in specific subfields of psychology. Almost all chapters are of interest to educators, for example, those on experimental psychology (covers research on perception and motor processes, cognitive processes, motivation and emotion, attention, and learning); communication systems (covers language and speech, literature, and art); and developmental psychology (covers development of children and adolescents, black children, cognitive and perceptual maturation, psychosocial and personality development). In addition, several entire chapters are of direct concern to special educators, for example, "Physical and Psychological Disorders, Treatment and Prevention," and "Educational Psychology." A sixty-nine-page bibliography lists sources as they appear in the text; an index concludes the work.

Bibliographies

Bibliographic Guide to Psychology. Boston: G. K. Hall, 1975- . Annual. LC 76-642687. ISSN 0360-277X.

This annual subject bibliography lists publications cataloged by the Research Libraries of the New York Public Library and the Library of Congress. Arrangement of entries is alphabetical by main entry and by subject. Prior to 1975, G. K. Hall published *Psychology Book Guide* which covered only the Library of Congress publications, and is continued by *Bibliographic Guide to Psychology*.

Wertheimer, Michael, and Marilyn Lou Wertheimer. **History of Psychology: A Guide to Information Sources**. Detroit: Gale, 1979. 502p. (Psychology Information Guide Series, Vol. 1). $65.00. LC 79-9044. ISBN 0-8103-1442-8.

Organization of this bibliography on the history of psychology allocates the 3,000-plus titles to five major categories. Section A covers "General References"; section B, "References in the History of Psychology," includes general works and discussions, major periodicals, books of readings, and materials on the history of psychology by geographic area. Section C covers materials devoted to specific systems and schools of psychology; section D is "Histories and Major Works in Selected Content Areas of Psychology"; and section E is "Histories of Related Fields." The latter two sections include materials on education, among which are subdivisions for educational psychology. The subject index lists a variety of materials related to education. Name and title indexes are also provided.

Indexes and Abstracts

Child Development Abstracts and Bibliography. Chicago: University of Chicago Press, 1927- . 3/yr. $50.00. ISSN 0009-3939.

Educators doing research concerned with developmental factors should be aware of these abstracts covering articles in the following six categories: (1) biology, health, medicine; (2) cognition, learning perception; (3) social psychological, cultural, and personality studies; (4) educational processes; (5) psychiatry and clinical psychology; and (6) history, theory, and methodology. Author and subject access is available.

Each issue also includes a section called "Book Notices," where new titles in the field are described and critically evaluated. Approximately 700 citations and/or abstracts are included in each issue.

Psychological Abstracts. Arlington, Va.: American Psychological Association, 1927- . Monthly. $750.00, institutions; $375.00, members. ISSN 0033-2887.

This major index and abstracting service for the literature in the field of psychology and related disciplines covers new books, approximately 1,000 journals, technical reports, and other documents of a scientific nature. Abstracts are descriptive in nature and are arranged in sixteen major subject categories, some of which are further subdivided. Some entries are not annotated; others have minimal annotations. Entries classified in educational psychology and related areas are of particular usefulness to educators.

Each monthly issue has an author and subject index, cumulated quarterly and annually. *Psychological Abstracts* continues the former *Psychological Index*. It is produced from the PsychINFO database and can be accessed via online searches.

Dictionaries and Encyclopedias

Corsini, Raymond, J. **Concise Encyclopedia of Psychology**. New York: Wiley, 1987. 1,242p. $89.95. LC 86-22392. ISBN 0-471-01068-5.

This new work compresses almost all of the contents (80%) of Corsini's previous four-volume encyclopedia, *Encyclopedia of Psychology* (1984) into a handy, yet comprehensive, one-volume work. Entries consist of brief articles which give an overview, rather than in-depth information, related to the topic. Many of the psychological theorists included also had major influence on the field of education. Many entries throughout the volume are concerned with various aspects of education. Some examples include "Academic Achievement Tests," "Academic Aptitude Tests," "Academic Success and Grouping," "Academic Underachievement," "Aphasia," "Approaches to Learning," "Attention Span," "Behavior Modification," "Bilingualism," "Classroom Discipline," "Cognitive Abilities," "Discovery Learning," "Early Childhood Development," "Educational Assessment," "Gifted and Talented Children," "Grading in Education," "Human Intelligence," "School Reading Disabilities," and "Learning."

Goldenson, Robert M., and Walter D. Glanze. **Longman Dictionary of Psychology and Psychiatry**. New York: Longman, 1984. 816p. LC 83-13591. ISBN 0-582-28257-8.

Terms related to educational psychology, mental disorders and mental retardation, psychometrics, evaluation research, and school psychologists are included among the many defined in this comprehensive dictionary. Definitions are quite brief, ranging from one or two lines to about fifteen lines in a half-page column. Altogether, over 21,000 entries defining terms in psychology, psychiatry, and interdisciplinary fields are provided.

A related title, compiled and edited by Benjamin B. Wolman, is *Dictionary of Behavioral Science* (2d ed., Van Nostrand Reinhold, 1988).

Harre, Rom, and Roger Lamb. **The Encyclopedic Dictionary of Psychology**. Cambridge, Mass.: MIT Press, 1983. 718p. $90.00. LC 83-920. ISBN 0-262-08135-0.

Sixteen authorities in psychology, philosophy, and physiology have prepared articles on a wide range of topics related to cognitive psychology, psycholinguistics, and neuro-psychology and their fields of application. Educators and educational researchers would be especially interested in the many entries under topics such as educational psychology, developmental psychology, human thought and behavior, educational attainment, educational aims and objectives, learning and learning theory, school alienation, truancy, and others.

Kristal, Leonard, ed. **The ABC of Psychology**. New York: Facts on File, 1982. 253p. $16.95; $9.95pa. LC 82-1524. ISBN 0-87196-678-6; 0-87196-844-4pa.

Psychological concepts and theories are defined in this dictionary of terms commonly found in the literature of the field. Types of neuroses and other disorders are described; other entries provide biographical information on prominent theorists and practitioners. Many of the entries have application to educators, particularly those concerned with cognition, intelligence, learning, and perception. Entries range from brief definitions to somewhat lengthy signed articles.

Related titles include *Dictionary of Key Words in Psychology* by Frank J. Bruno (Routledge & Kegan Paul/Methuen, 1986) and *Dictionary of Psychology*. 3d ed. Edited by J. P. Chaplin (Dell, 1985).

Thesaurus of Psychological Index Terms. 5th ed. Prepared by the staff of the Retrieval Services Unit, PsychINFO Department. Washington, D.C.: American Psychological Association, 1988. 290p. $45.00pa. LC 88-139115. ISBN 0-912704-68-3.

The APA developed this thesaurus as a hierarchically structured set of terms associated with concepts in psychology. Its purpose is to function as an "authoritative list which allows for precise content representation of psychological literature " (p. i) and facilitates retrieval of materials. The major section is a "Relationship Section" which shows the interrelationships of terms, followed by an "Alphabetic Section." The latter section indicates a relatively large number of terms related to education and areas that overlap in relevance to psychologists and educators. Selected samples include educational administration, educational audiovisual aids, educational counseling, educational incentives, educational program evaluation, educational psychology, aphasia, autistic children, behavior modification, child psychology, higher education, grading, special education, skill learning, school environment, school learning, and preschool education.

Wolman, Benjamin, ed. **International Encyclopedia of Psychiatry, Psychology, Psychoanalysis and Neurology**. New York: Van Nostrand Reinhold, 1977. 12v. $675.00/set. LC 76-54526. ISBN 0-918228-01-8.

This multivolume encyclopedia has a foreward written by Jean Piaget, noted Swiss psychologist, whose research and work have had a marked influence on education. In addition to a major article on education, many other related entries are of interest to the educator, for example, abilities, achievement, adolescence, aptitude, attention, behavior modification, cognition, counseling, creativity, delinquency, development, developmental psychology, intelligence, language, learning, measurement, mental tests, memory, mental retardation, problem solving, school psychologist, and school psychology.

Handbooks and Yearbooks

Gilgen, Albert R., and Carol K. Gilgen, eds. **International Handbook of Psychology**. Westport, Conn.: Greenwood, 1987. 629p. index. $75.00. LC 86-29457. ISBN 0-313-23832-4.

The history and development of psychology are discussed from an international perspective, with coverage of twenty-nine countries provided. The various professions in the field, the education and training of psychologists (including educational psychologists), major research institutions, and publications are emphasized. Arrangement of information is in thirty chapters, each of which has a list of bibliographic references included. Contributors are national authorities in the field.

Mussen, Paul H. **Handbook of Child Psychology**. 4th ed. New York: Wiley, 1983. 4v. $246.95/set. LC 83-3593. ISBN 0-471-09057-3 (v.1); 0-471-09055-7 (v.2); 0-471-09064-6 (v.3); 0-471-09065-4 (v.4).

Each volume of this work is an individual handbook prepared by specialists in child psychology, and each includes bibliographic references and an index. Collectively, they provide a sourcebook for psychologists, educational psychologists, and educators. Volume titles include v.1, *History, Theory and Methods*, edited by William Kessen; v. 2, *Infancy and Developmental Psychobiology*, edited by Marshall M. Harth and Joseph J. Campos; v. 3, *Cognitive Development*, edited by John H. Flavell and Ellen M. Markman; and v. 4, *Socialization, Personality, and Social Development*, edited by E. Mavis Hetherington.

Educators will find especially useful discussions related to cognitive development and cognitive processes; problem solving; ability testing, and other standardized types of assessment; psycholinguistics and the development of language and communications; as well as articles related to personality development and social maturation.

Reed, Jeffrey G., and Pam M. Baxter. **Library Use: A Handbook for Psychology**. Washington, D.C.: American Psychological Association, 1983. 138p. $15.00pa. LC 83-12296. ISBN 0-912704-76-4.

This handbook is aimed at college students and other researchers in psychology and educational psychology. The authors suggest that it be used as a supplement to the APA's *Publication Manual* or to a research methods textbook. Information is arranged in eleven chapters. The introductory ones explain how to get started in using the library and defining a research topic; subsequent chapters cover use of specific tools, such as *Psychological Abstracts, Education Index, Social Sciences Citation Index*, and the ERIC database, among many others. Also given is how to use specialized sources of information, including government documents, online databases, current awareness services, biographical directories, book reviews, and special services of the library such as ILL (interlibrary loan). Appendix A is "Additional Specialized Sources"; appendix B is "Brief Guide to Literature Searching." An index concludes the volume.

HISTORY

Guides

American Historical Association. Guide to Historical Literature. Edited by George Frederick Howe. New York: Macmillan, 1961. 962p. LC 61-7062.

Over 20,000 items are covered in this classic guide to publications related to the historical literature. Entries are organized into thirty-five major categories, some of which are subject divisions, and some of which are geographical divisions. In spite of the fact that it must be used in conjunction with more current guides, this publication does provide the historical researcher with information and tips on conducting historical research.

Furay, Conal, and Michael J. Salevouris. **The Methods and Skills of History: A Practical Guide**. Arlington Heights, Ill.: Harlan Davidson, 1988. 245p. $15.95pa. LC 86-16733. ISBN 0-88295-851-8.

This guide to research methodology and sources of information in history is unique in that it not only identifies and discusses the major sources related to a particular aspect of history, but includes practice workbook exercises regarding their content and use. The book is based on *History: A Workbook of Skill Development* published in 1979. The first chapter is an essay on the uses and nature of history. Subsequent chapters deal with using the library to conduct research, including basic reference tools, classification of historical information, interpretation of historical evidence, reporting history in writing, and historiography. The appendix, "History and the Disciplines," compares history and science, history and social sciences (anthropology, sociology, political science, economics, psychology), and history and art. A bibliography of references for further reading and an index conclude the work.

Prucha, Francis Paul. **Handbook for Research in American History: A Guide to Bibliographies and Other Reference Works**. Lincoln: University of Nebraska Press, 1987. 289p. $21.95; $9.95pa. LC 86-30871. ISBN 0-8032-3682-4; 0-8032-8719-4pa.

Researchers in all aspects of American history, including the history of education, will find this handbook of relevance. It is arranged in two major sections. Part 1 covers sources of various types, for example, library catalogs and guides; general bibliographies; book catalogs; guides to periodical literature, manuscripts and newspapers; and lists of dissertations and theses. It also describes how to access information in biographical guides, oral history sources, government documents, the national archives, state and local materials, legal sources, geographical materials, and databases.

The second part of the work is devoted to specialized reference sources on such topics as political, military, social and economic history, foreign affairs, ethnic groups, women, religion, education, science and technology, regional materials, and travel. The section on education covers, in addition to the history of education, curriculum, teachers, and administrators.

Tingley, Donald F. **Social History of the United States: A Guide to Information Sources**. Detroit: Gale, 1979. 260p. (American Government and History Information Guide Series, Vol. 3). $65.00. LC 78-13196. ISBN 0-8103-1366-9.

The opening chapter in this annotated bibliography is entitled "Social History: The State of the Art," followed by chapter 2, "The Nature and Practice of Social History." Subsequent chapters are devoted to major bibliographies in the field, important general works, and then to sources by historical period (colonial era, nineteenth century, twentieth century); and by specific subject (black Americans, ethnic groups; women and feminism; marriage, divorce, family, and sexuality; children; aging; poverty; rural, city, and suburban life; popular culture, the arts; health and medicine). One entire chapter is devoted to sources related to education. Author, title, and subject indexes are provided.

Bibliographies

Beers, Henry Putney. **Bibliographies in American History, 1942-78**. Edited by Research Publications Staff. Woodbridge, Conn.: Research Publications, Inc., 1982. 2v. $260.00. LC 81-68886. ISBN 0-89235-038-5.

This major reference tool, first published in 1938, provided bibliographic control of the vast number of bibliographies devoted to some aspect of American history. It covers over 11,000 bibliographies published in separate works, articles, manuscripts, government documents, and archival collections. Volume 1 is arranged by subject; volume 2 is a listing by state. Chapters are devoted to specific topics, such as "Colonial Period," "Diplomatic History," "Education," and "Social, Cultural, Scientific." One chapter is devoted to education, but the index indicates that other chapters also provide information related to various aspects of American education.

Combined Retrospective Index to Journals in History, 1838-1974. Edited by Annadel N. Wile. Washington, D.C.: Carrollton Press, 1977-1978. 11v. LC 77-70347. ISBN 0-8408-0175-0 (v.1).

This multivolume reference work indexes 243 English-language journals in history via computer analysis for the period 1838-1974. Volumes 1 through 4 are devoted to world history; volumes 5 through 9 cover U.S. history; and the last two volumes consist of an author index. Articles are arranged by key word and assigned subject headings. The front end papers of each volume list codes used to identify journal titles.

Czarra, Fred. **A Guide to Historical Reading: Non-Fiction**. 11th ed. Washington, D.C.: Heldref, 1983. 312p. (McKinley Bibliographies Volume). $20.00. LC 93-156409. ISBN 0-916882-03-9.

Subtitled *For the Use of Schools, Libraries and the General Reader*, this guide is useful in identification of books for public and school libraries that are on historical subjects. Entries are arranged by geographical areas covering the ancient world; Europe; Asia, Africa, and the Pacific; the United States; and Canada and Latin America. Textbooks are not included. Within each geographic division, entries are further subdivided by specific country, city, or chronological period, as well as a section designated "Juvenile" aimed at readers in grades 7 to 10.

Brief annotations are provided. A "List of Publishers," "Index of Authors," and "Index of Titles" conclude the work.

Freidel, Frank, ed., with the assistance of Richard F. Showman. **Harvard Guide to American History**. Rev. ed. Cambridge, Mass.: Belknap Press, 1974. 2v. index. $60.00; $20.00pa./vol. LC 72-81272. ISBN 0-674-37560-2; 0-674-37555-6pa.

This classic bibliography of reference sources in American history is a selective listing to books and periodical articles contained in the libraries at Harvard University. The first volume organizes materials by subject; the second chronologically by historical time periods. Volume 1 covers research methodologies, biographical sources, personal records, and special topical histories such as the history of immigration and ethnicity, and the history of education in America. Subject and name indexes provide access to information.

Fyfe, Janet, comp. **History Journals and Serials: An Analytical Guide**. Westport, Conn.: Greenwood, 1986. 351p. index. (Annotated Bibliographies of Serials: A Subject Approach, No. 8). $45.00. LC 86-9986. ISBN 0-313-23999-1.

Approximately 500 important serials devoted to some aspect of history (including the history of education) and published in the English language are described in this guide. Included are also major newsletters and specialized journals. The annotations are more informative than other sources listing the same titles. An introductory section explains how to use the book, indicates whether the journals and serials provide abstracts, and are available online. Information about publishers who provide microform formats and reprints is also included. A related title is David Henige's *Serial Bibliographies and Abstracts in History: An Annotated Guide* (Greenwood, 1986).

International Bibliography of Historical Sciences. V. 1, 1926- ; Paris: Colin, 1930- . Annual (International Bibliography of the Social Sciences). Price varies ($74.00, v. 51). ISSN 0074-2015.

Major published works of a historical nature, including books and journal articles, are described on an annual basis. Entries are arranged by subject and cover all time periods and geographic areas; annotations are not included. Emphasis is on European history. This title suffers from a publication lag. Educators can find citations to publications covering the history of education and related topics.

Wiltz, John E., and Nancy C. Cridland. **Books in American History: A Basic List for High Schools and Junior Colleges**. 2d ed. Bloomington: Indiana University Press, 1981. 113p. $15.00; $5.00pa. LC 80-8766. ISBN 0-253-15255-0; 0-253-20266-3pa.

This reading list for high school students focuses on historical fiction and nonfiction titles that are of interest and relevance to secondary students. Materials were selected for inclusion if they met the following criteria: titles were in print and available, they were inexpensive or moderately priced, and the content was deemed readable and enjoyable. Entries are arranged chronologically by historical period. Information in each includes a complete bibliographic citation plus an evaluative annotation which not only describes and criticizes the work, but often compares it to those of a similar nature.

Writings on American History. Washington, D.C.: American Historical Association, 1974- . Annual. $45.00. LC 75-22257. ISSN 0364-2887.

This bibliographic series provides citations to approximately 500 current article-length items in the American history literature appearing in publication between June of one year through May of the next. Over 4,000 journals are consulted for selection of entries. Completed doctoral dissertations reported to the American Historical Association are also included. Although international in scope, emphasis of coverage is on the United States.

Entries are arranged, for the most part, by subject, and a chronological subdivision is also included. The 1988 annual volume begins with a general section listing materials under "Bibliography," "Archives," "Libraries and Museums," "The Historical Profession," "Historiography and Methodology," "The Teaching of History," "Oral History," "Quantitative Studies," "and Comparative Studies." Topics related to education and educational institutions fall under the category of "Social History."

This bibliography has had various editors and publishers since it was first published in 1902. No bibliographies were published for 1904 to 1905, 1941 to 1947; and a four-volume set was published in 1976 that covers the years 1962-1973. From 1974 on the bibliography was published on an annual basis with the subtitle *A Subject Bibliography of Articles*.

Indexes and Abstracts

America: History and Life. Santa Barbara, Calif.: ABC-Clio, 1964- . 3/yr. with semiannual and annual cumulative indexes. Price varies. ISSN 0002-7065 (pt. A); ISSN 0097-6172 (pt. B).

This major index to U.S. and Canadian history periodical literature abstracts articles dealing with contemporary American life and customs in over 2,000 periodical titles. Part A covers article abstracts and citations, arranged geographically by country, historical period and subject; part B is devoted to book reviews and is issued semiannually. Parts C and D are an annual bibliography of books, dissertations, and articles in an annual cumulated index, respectively. Periodicals analyzed provide historical coverage of local, state, regional, and national items and events. Approximately 1,000 foreign periodicals are also analyzed. A companion volume to *America: History and Life* is a quarterly publication with cumulative indexes, *Historical Abstracts* (ABC-Clio, 1955- .).

Dictionaries and Encyclopedias

Carruth, Gordon, and Associates, eds. **The Encyclopedia of American Facts and Dates**. 8th ed. New York: Crowell, 1987. 1,008p. $29.45. LC 86-45645. ISBN 0-06-181143-2.

This encyclopedia is chronologically arranged and covers the period from 986 to 1978, with information presented in four categories: (1) politics and government, war, disasters, and vital statistics; (2) books, painting, dance, architecture, and sculpture; (3) science, industry, economics, education, religion, and philosophy; and (4) sports, fashion, popular entertainment, folklore, and society. Portraits of American life for just under a 1,000-year period are provided. An extensive list of events and dates related to education is provided in the index under "Education." Additional information can be identified by consulting headings such as "Public Schools," "Educators," "Teachers," "Teachers College," "Teacher Training," among others.

Dictionary of American History. Rev. ed. New York: Scribner's, 1976-1978. 8v. LC 76-6735. ISBN 0-684-15078-6.

This multivolume work contains approximately 7,200 articles on the economic, political, cultural, and social aspects of American history. Most terms and concepts are explained in brief and concise articles; longer signed articles also include bibliographies for reference to additional reading. The eighth volume is the index volume, and a perusal of topics related to education reflect the work's broad interpretation of American history. A few selected examples include academic freedom; academies; Carnegie Corporation; charity schools; chautauqua movement; coeducational; colleges and universities; dame school; denominational colleges; district school; federal aid; Franklin Institute; Fulbright grants; GI Bill of Rights; Granger movement; grants-in-aid; Harvard University; Health, Education, and Welfare Department; Institute for Advanced Study; integration; intelligence tests; land grants; Latin schools; lyceum movement; McGuffey's Readers; National Education Association; private schools; Progressive Movement; reformatories; school books; school lands; separate-but-equal doctrine; teachers; and teachers' loyalty oaths.

Morris, Richard B., ed., and Jeffrey B. Morris, assoc. ed. **Encyclopedia of American History**. 6th ed. New York: Harper & Row, 1982. 1,285p. $29.45. LC 81-47668. ISBN 0-06-181605-1.

This encyclopedia is divided into four major sections. The first is a basic chronology of outstanding political and military events in U.S. history. The second is a topical chronology; the third is a bibliographical section providing information on 500 notable Americans (including a subsection on educators). The fourth section is entitled "Structure of the Federal Government" and includes information on presidents and their cabinets, Congresses, and U.S. Supreme Court Justices throughout American history (through 1981). Copies of the Declaration of Independence and the Constitution of the United States conclude the text.

The index indicates numerous topics of interest to educators and, particularly, educational historians, namely: adult education, federal funding of education, medical schools, teaching methods, innovations, education for veterans, education of women, colleges and universities, schools, Educational Television Facilities Act, educational testing, Education Amendments Act, school segregation and integration, among other topics. Many of these topics are subdivided into further subjects related to education.

Ritter, Harry. **Dictionary of Concepts in History**. Westport, Conn.: Greenwood, 1986. 490p. $55.00. LC 85-27305. ISBN 0-313-22700-4. ISSN 0730-3335.

The etymological development and current usage of important concepts in the field of history are presented in this unique dictionary. The relatively lengthy entries also emphasize bibliographic information, as each one is followed by a list of references for further study. Philosophies, philosophers, and historians, with major influence on the field of education (e.g., Progressivism, Kant, neo-Kantianism) are discussed.

Wetterau, Bruce, comp. and ed. **Macmillan Concise Dictionary of World History**. New York: Macmillan, 1983. 867p. $18.95. LC 82-24952. ISBN 0-02-626110-3.

Two types of entries (textual and chronologies) are contained in this dictionary of terms related to world history. Over 10,000 textual entries define a specific topic or provide basic information about it. Some 7,000 chronologies, on the other hand, are provided for broad topics (e.g., countries and major wars). A specific entry approach provides information on a wide variety of names and events. Educators can identify names of significant leaders and movements in education, for example, Horace Mann, Maria Montessori, Jean Piaget, and the chautauqua and lyceum movements. *Dictionary of Historical Terms*, edited by Chris Cook, is a related title published by Macmillan (1983).

Directories

Directory of Historical Agencies in North America. 13th ed. Edited by Betty P. Smith. Nashville, Tenn.: American Association for State and Local History, 1986. 695p. $64.95pa. LC 85-30589. ISBN 0-910050-77-5.

Approximately 5,800 history-related agencies in the United States and Canada are described in this directory. Entries are arranged geographically by U.S. state or Canadian province, first, then by individual city or town. Each provides the following information: name of the organization, address, date founded, chief officer(s), membership, staff size, major programs sponsored, collections of materials, and significant publications. For the most part, libraries and museums are not included.

Historical Periodicals Directory. Edited by Eric H. Boehm, Barbara H. Pope, and Marie S. Ensign. Santa Barbara, Calif.: ABC-Clio, 1981-1985. 5v. LC 81-12892. ISBN 0-87436-018-8.

There are five volumes in this comprehensive guide to periodicals and selected serials in history. Individual volume titles include volume 1, *USA & Canada* ($87.50, ISBN 0-87436-018-8); 2, *Europe: West, North, Central & South* ($95.00, ISBN 0-87436-019-6); 3, *Europe: East & Southeast; USSR* ($89.00, ISBN 0-87436-020-X); 4, *Africa; Asia & Pacific Area; Latin America & West Indies* ($89.00, ISBN 087436-021-8); and 5, *International Organizations; Addenda; Indexes* ($89.00, ISBN 0-87436-022-6).

Included are journals dealing with the history of education and the teaching of history. Entries are arranged alphabetically by country, and each entry provides journal title, frequency, publisher, address, descriptive statement, language, where indexed, former titles, and ISSN number.

Almanacs

Schlesinger, Arthur M., Jr. **The Almanac of American History**. New York: Putnam, 1983. 623p. $24.95. LC 83-3435. ISBN 0-399-12853-0.

The contents of this almanac represent a chronology of significant events in American history. Arrangement is in five major time periods: "Founding a Nation, 986-1787"; "Testing a Union, 1788-1865"; "Forging a Nation, 1866-1900"; "Expanding Resources, 1901-1945"; and "Emerging as a World Power, 1946- ." The index lists forty-seven references to education, including entries on colonial education and early schools in America, and legislation relating to education (e.g., desegregation, public education, military learning).

POLITICAL SCIENCE

Guides

Englefield, Dermot, and Gavin Drewry, eds. **Information Sources in Politics and Political Science: A Survey Worldwide**. London, Boston: Butterworths, 1984. 509p. $80.00. LC 84-2819. ISBN 0-408-11470-3.

This guide to reference and information sources is international in scope but includes, almost exclusively, materials in the English language. Written as a bibliographical essay, emphasis is on countries in the United Kingdom; countries of Southeast Asia are excluded.

The book is organized into four major parts. Part 1, "Resources," covers library aids and bibliographical tools; part 2 is concerned with approaches to the study of politics and government; and part 3 lists sources related to various aspects of political science in the United Kingdom (political parties and elections, parliament and ministers, public administration, judiciary, and local government). The fourth and final part, "Politics and Government: Overseas," has a chapter on international reference works, one on the United States, and nine others by geographic regions. The last chapter is devoted to international organizations.

Holler, Frederick L. **The Information Sources of Political Science**. 4th ed. Santa Barbara, Calif.: ABC-Clio, 1986. 278p. $65.00. LC 85-11279. ISBN 0-87436-375-6.

Holler begins with an overview discussion of the tools for retrieving information in political science. He covers bibliographies of various types (library catalogs, trade bibliographies, general, regional, and bibliographies of periodicals); indexes and abstracting services; and other reference sources. In addition to political science, general reference sources in the social sciences are covered. Subdivisions of the social sciences covered include political theory, international relations, international organizations, public administration, political behavior, comparative government and politics, American government, state and local government, public law, history, and other related disciplines.

McCarrick, Earlean M. **U.S. Constitution: A Guide to Information Sources**. Detroit: Gale, 1980. 290p. (American Government and History Information Guide Series, No. 4). $65.00. LC 74-15403. ISBN 0-8103-1203-4.

This guide to information sources on the Constitution is arranged in twelve chapters. The first five cover broad general topics, bibliographies, and other materials, many of which are related to the pre-Constitutional period. Chapter 2 deals with the Continental Congresses, the Declaration of Independence, and the Articles of Confederation. Other chapters are devoted to the Philadelphia Convention, Article I and Congress, Article II and the executive branch, the judiciary, the first ten amendments, and the Civil War amendments. Entries include complete bibliographic descriptions and descriptive annotations. Subjects related to education include sources on racial imbalance in education, desegregation, federal funding, discrimination, equality, religion in education, busing, school law, and educational policy under various administrations.

Morehead, Joe. **Introduction to United States Public Documents**. 3d ed. Littleton, Colo.: Libraries Unlimited, 1983. 309p. $19.50pa. LC 82-22866. ISBN 0-87287-362-5pa.

Basic sources of information provided by federal government publications are described in this guide. The first five chapters provide an introductory overview of information in public documents, and describe the administrative and bibliographic systems involved in the production and distribution of them, including the National Technical Information Service and ERIC (Educational Resources Information Center). Chapters 6 through 10 describe major reference sources (guides, bibliographies, indexes, etc.), legislative branch materials, publications of the president's control and authority, executive branch and independent agency publications, and legal sources of information. Two appendixes include appendix A, "Selected Online Databases for Federal Government Information," and appendix B, "Abbreviations, Acronyms, and Citations Used in This Text." Two indexes provide access by selected title/series and subject/name.

Bibliographies

ABC Pol Sci. Lloyd W. Garrison, ed. Santa Barbara, Calif.: ABC-Clio, 1969- . 6/yr. Price Varies. ISSN 0001-0456.

This current awareness service is subtitled *A Bibliography of Contents: Political Science & Government*. It provides reproduced and edited tables of contents of journals in the field in alphabetical order by journal title. Citations are numbered consecutively, and each includes the author and title of the article and page numbers.

Non-English titles have a translated title in parentheses, when translations are provided by the journal in which the article appears. A subject profile index provides a very brief profile of each cited article plus two or more descriptors (subject, geographic, biographic). An author index and a list of contributing periodicals conclude the work.

Each issue has numerous entries under the subject of "Education," as well as under "Teachers," "Public Schools," and other headings related to education.

Combined Retrospective Index to Journals in Political Science, 1886-1974. Edited by Annadel N. Wile. Washington, D.C.: Carrollton Press, 1977. 8v. $880.00/set. LC 78-108375. ISBN 0-8408-0186-6(v. 1); 0-8408-0187-4(v. 2); 0-8408-0188-2(v. 3); 0-8408-0189-0(v. 4); 0-8408-0191-2(v. 5); 0-8408-0190-4(v. 6); 0-8408-0192-0(v. 7); 0-8408-0193-9(v. 8).

Retrospective selective coverage of the periodical literature in 179 English-language journals in political science from 1886 to 1974 is provided in this multivolume computer-produced index. The contents of volume 1 cover international law, international organizations, international relations, international trade, and economics. Volume 2 is devoted to methodology and theoretical approaches, political behavior and process, political ideologies, political systems, and political thought. Volume 3 covers administration in general, economics in general, financial administration, management in general, organization, departments, and functions; volumes 4, 5, and 6 continue coverage of organization, departments, and functions; and volume 7 also includes personnel and population. Volumes 7 and 8 contain the author indexes.

International Bibliography of Political Science. London: Tavistock; distr., Chicago: Aldine, 1953- . Annual (International Bibliography of the Social Sciences). $99.00. ISSN 0085-2058.

Major scholarly contributions in political science published each year are indexed in this compilation, which is one of the four subdivisions of the *International Bibliography of the Social Sciences* (London: Tavistock, 1953- . Annual. ISSN 0085-2058). Between 4,000 and 5,000 items are selected for inclusion. Citations are arranged by subject. Subjects of interest to the educator and/or educational administrator or educational researcher include education, cost of education, educational policy (subdivided by country), educational reforms, educational systems, and bilingualism.

Indexes and Abstracts

International Political Science Abstracts. Oxford: Blackwell, 1951-72; Paris: International Political Science Association, 1973- . Bimonthly. $170.00, institutions; $50.00, individuals. ISSN 0020-8345.

World coverage of political science and topics related to the field is provided by this abstracting service. Over 5,000 entries are provided annually in six major categories: political science, political thinkers and ideas, governmental and administrative institutions, political process, international relations, and national and area studies. Abstracts are in English or French. Author and subject indexes are cumulated annually.

This reference work is prepared with the cooperation of the International Committee for Social Sciences Documentation and support of UNESCO; publishers have varied since its inception.

Dictionaries and Encyclopedias

Encyclopedia of American Political History: Studies of the Principal Movements and Ideas. Edited by Jack P. Greene. New York: Scribner's, 1984. 3v. $200.00. LC 84-1355. ISBN 0-684-17003-5.

Intended for students and lay readers, the articles in this encyclopedia cover major political events in American history, significant documents (including the Constitution and the Declaration of Independence), and the most important "issues, themes, institutions, processes and developments" (p. vii). A comprehensive article by Carl F. Kaestle is devoted to education covering the systems and structure of education in the United States, curriculum, financing, professional training, and other topics, with emphasis on political history. The index indicates numerous educational topics subsumed under other articles, such as "Academic Freedom," "Colleges and Universities," "Elementary Schools," "Head Start," "National Defense Education Act," "Parochial Schools," and "Upward Bound."

Robertson, David. **A Dictionary of Modern Politics.** Philadelphia: Taylor & Francis, 1985. 340p. $34.00. LC 85-2728. ISBN 0-85066-320-2.

According to Robertson, terms defined in this dictionary emphasize political ideas that are a part of the professional vocabulary in the field of politics. Terms range from those that are technical and highly specialized to more subjective concepts, which may have many meanings. In the latter case, the definitions attempt to reflect a professional consensus on their meaning. Entries range from brief and concise definitions of approximately 100 words to lengthier 1½-page treatments. Some terms overlap with educational practice and theory, such as discussions related to civil rights, civil service, existentialism, minorities, pluralism, positivism, racism, Plato, and Rousseau. Another less current, but very popular and well-respected dictionary, is *Political Science Dictionary* by Jack C. Plano, Milton Greenberg, Roy Olton, and Robert E. Riggs (Dryden Press, 1973).

Handbooks and Yearbooks

Andrews, William G., ed. **International Handbook of Political Science.** Westport, Conn.: Greenwood, 1982. 464p. $55.00. LC 81-6245. ISBN 0-313-22889-2.

The development of political science and professional activities in the field, on an international basis, are presented in this handbook. Chapters have been contributed by leading political scientists in twenty-seven countries, each covering the status quo of political science in that country. The status at the end of World War II and its evolution since 1945 is reported. Particular attention is given to the intellectual structure of the discipline, the teaching of political science, research activities of professional associations, and political science and the world of politics.

Book of the States. Lexington, Ky.: Council of State Governments, 1935- . Biennial. $42.50. ISSN 0068-0125.

Information on each of the individual U.S. states is provided in essay and tabular form. Nine sections emphasize the various branches of the government and/or their functions, and include coverage of intergovernmental affairs, governors, the executive branch, the legislatures, the judiciary, elections, constitutions, administration, major state services, state capitols, zip codes, statistics, and historical data about the states. Many of the chapters cover education. The section "Major State Services" discusses education, including state support for education, in depth. Other aspects covered include aid per student, boards, enrollments, expenditures, revenues, teachers, graduation requirements, minimum competency testing, institutions, occupational programs, and student aid.

Political and Social Science Journals: A Handbook for Writers and Reviewers. Santa Barbara, Calif.: ABC-Clio, 1983. 236p. $24.85; $12.85pa. LC 82-18455. ISBN 0-87436-026-9; 0-87436-037-4pa.

The purpose of this handbook is to provide "prospective authors with specific and current information on the editorial policies and procedures of journals accepting and publishing articles and reviews in political science" (p. ix). Other introductory materials include "Advice on Articles"; "Authors and the Law"; "Advice on Book Reviewing"; and a list of abbreviations used. The major portion of the work is devoted to a directory of political and social science journals.

Educators could conceivably be interested in the interdisciplinary titles *American Studies, Behavioral Science, The Black Scholar, Centerpoint: A Journal of Interdisciplinary Studies, Ethics, Ethnic and Racial Studies, Feminist Studies, Human Relations, The Journal of Applied Behavioral Science, Journal of Black Studies, The Journal of Social Issue*, and other related titles.

United States Government Manual. Edited by Rachel L. Jeffries. Washington, D.C.: Office of the Federal Register, National Archives and Records Administration, 1935- . Annual. $20.00. ISSN 0092-1904.

Extensive information on the agencies of the legislative, judicial, and executive branches of the U.S. government is provided in this manual which is published as a special edition of the *Federal Register*. For each agency, information provided includes a list of principal officials, summary of the agency's purpose and governmental role, brief historical background, source of its authority, programs, activities, contracts and grants, employment, publications, and other data incorporated in a "Sources of Information" section. Copies of both the Declaration of Independence and the Constitution are also provided. A chapter covering the Department of Education lists the Secretary of Education and other officers, such as the Director of Bilingual Education, and Assistant Secretaries for Elementary Education, Secondary Education, Educational Research and Improvement, Vocational and Adult Education, Special Education and Rehabilitative Services, and Postsecondary Education. It also lists federally aided corporations funded from the budget of the Department of Education.

Directories

Guide to Graduate Study in Political Science. Washington, D.C.: American Political Science Association, 1972- . Annual. $20.00, nonmembers; $15.00, members. ISSN 0091-9632.

Graduate programs in political science at the master's and doctoral levels are described in this annual directory. While the emphasis is definitely on U.S. institutions, Canadian institutions are also included in a separate listing. Entries are arranged alphabetically by name of academic institution. Information provided in each includes school name, address, and telephone number; degree offered; tuition/academic year; application deadlines; requirements for admission; financial aid; degree requirements; program description; and faculty. At the conclusion of the alphabetical listing, information about graduate programs at both degree levels can be analyzed comparatively in a twelve-page chart. A faculty index and an institution index conclude the work.

Social Service Organizations and Agencies Directory: A Reference Guide to National and Regional Social Service Organizations Including Advocacy Groups, Voluntary Associations, Professional Societies, Federal and State Agencies, Clearinghouses and Information Centers. Compiled and edited by Anthony T. Kruzas. Detroit. Gale, 1982. 525p. $140.00. LC 82-206132. ISBN 0-8103-0329-9.

Almost 7,000 organizations and agencies involved with a broad range of social concerns are arranged by subject in this directory, which is of interest to educators as well as sociologists. Chapters are subdivided into national, state and regional, state government, federal government agencies; and clearinghouses and information centers. One chapter is devoted specifically to education and covers adult education, alternative education, higher education, international exchange, physical education, preschool, special education, and tests and testing. Other chapters listing agencies of concern to educators are those devoted to exceptional children, gifted children, disabled/rehabilitation, vocational education, and youth.

Worldwide Government Directory and International Organizations. 4th ed. Bethesda, Md.: Worldwide Government Directory, 1987. 902p. $295.00. LC 83-641103. ISBN 0-942189-50-7. ISSN 0894-1521.

This directory provides information arranged by countries and by international organizations. In the first section, names, titles, and addresses of heads of state, ministers (including ministers of education), department heads, and central banking officers are provided, as are data related to language(s) spoken, currency, elections, and political parties, and regional and international organizations to which the country belongs (including the United Nations). In the second part, many of the international organizations described are affiliated with the United Nations (e.g., UNESCO).

A related work, with extensive directory information, is *Political Handbook of the World: 1987: Government and Intergovernment Organizations as of March 15, 1987*, edited by Arthur S. Banks (published for the Center for Education and Social Research of the State University of New York at Binghamton and for the Council of Foreign Relations by CSA Publications, 1987, 850p.). A directory to U.S. government personnel, including those in education-related positions is *Federal Staff Directory: Containing in Convenient Arrangement, Accurate Information Concerning the Executive Branch of the U.S. Government*, edited by Charles B. Brownson and Anna L. Brownson (Congressional Staff Directory, 1987).

Almanacs

The Almanac of American Politics. Edited by Grant Ujifusa. Washington, D.C.: Barone, 1981- . Biennial. $42.95. ISSN 0362-076X.

Information in this almanac is arranged geographically by state. It emphasizes political figures — from the president, senators, representatives, governors, and big-city mayors to senators and representatives at the state and district levels. Within each state chapter, demographic information might cover such topics as people of the region, with respect to population, education, poverty, ancestry, households, voting age population, registered voters, federal tax burden, federal expenditures, the political lineup, presidential vote, and other related information. Also included are congressional rating statistics of eleven lobby groups, *National Journal*'s ratings, and a "Key Votes" section which attempts to illustrate a legislator's stance on important issues. Other sections cover "Election Results" and "Campaign Finance." Educational topics addressed include bilingual programs, Pell grants, activities of the Education and Labor Committee, Tennessee's Better Schools Program, school lunch program, school prayer amendment, and school tuition and credit resolution.

SOCIAL WORK

Bibliographies

Elliott, Martha W., comp. **Ethical Issues in Social Work: An Annotated Bibliography**. New York: Council on Social Work Education, 1984. 95p. $7.70pa. LC 84-4953. ISBN 0-87293-003-3.

The introduction states that this bibliographic compilation of books and articles should serve as a "practical aid to those social work students, teachers, and practitioners who are interested in approaching the ethical issues and dilemmas inherent in life and in practice in a more knowledgeable and systematic way" (p. v). Entries are arranged in two major categories in the first section and are devoted to the philosophical and theological literature associated with the expanding field of applied ethics and the teaching of ethics. The second section is divided into several major subheadings: "Ethical Theory for Social Work"; "General Issues"; "Social Administration"; "Social Work Research"; "Social Work Practice Areas"; and "Social Work Education." Some topics are of particular relevance to educators, such as sources listed on teaching, mental retardation, and social work education.

Poole, Dennis L. **Rural Social Welfare: An Annotated Bibliography for Educators and Practitioners**. New York: Praeger, 1981. 316p. index. $35.95. LC 80-28691. ISBN 0-03-059331-X.

This bibliography was compiled to provide educators, students, researchers, and conference planners with sources of information on the various topics associated with rural social welfare. Its ten chapters cover human behavior; research; social policy; human services; planning, administration, and community development in rural areas; health; mental health; children and youth; aging; and curriculum materials for rural social work education. The emphasis in all chapters, except the last one on curriculum materials, is on periodical literature. Entries are arranged alphabetically by title within the subject categories. Annotations are relatively brief, ranging in length from one or two lines to ten or twelve lines. An alphabetically arranged index of authors completes the work.

Trattner, Walter I., and W. Andrew Achenbaum, eds. **Social Welfare in America: An Annotated Bibliography**. Westport, Conn.: Greenwood, 1986. 324p. index. $35.00. LC 83-10855. ISBN 0-313-23002-1.

According to the editors, this bibliography is designed for students, instructors, and scholars concerned with American social welfare history. They claim that they have given preference to books over articles, and to articles or essays over dissertations on any given topic. Arrangement of entries is both thematic and temporal within six chapters, which are "The Process and Progress of Social Welfare," "Caring for the Infant and Child," "Addressing the Problems of Youth," "Relieving the Domestic Crises of Adulthood," "Dealing with the Economic Woes of Adulthood," and "Coping with the Difficulties of Old Age." A total of 1,410 entries are included, although there is some duplication where items have been included in more than one category. The index directs the user interested in education to materials listed under education, adolescence, child care, childhood, children, children's rights, juvenile delinquency, mentally retarded, playgrounds, pluralism, state public school for dependent and neglected children, truant officer, and other relevant entries.

Indexes and Abstracts

Social Work Research and Abstracts. New York: National Association of Social Workers, 1965- . Quarterly. $75.00, institutions; $40.00, nonmembers. ISSN 0148-0847.

This reference tool abstracts publications of research in the field of social welfare, in combination with the types of material included in a previous journal that it continues, *Abstracts for Social Workers*. Emphasis is given to writings about social work technology, research strategies, and methods of research related to both theoretical and practical concerns of social workers.

Each issue contains a list of the approximately seventy journals reviewed. Many of these are of direct relevance to educators, for example, *Adolescence; Children Today; Child Welfare; Deaf Americans; Educational Gerontology; Journal of Continuing Social Work Education; Journal of Social Work Education;* and *Social Work in Education*.

Dictionaries and Encyclopedias

Encyclopedia of Social Work. 18th ed. Washington, D.C.: National Association of Social Workers, 1987. 3v. $75.00. LC 30-30948. ISBN 0-87101-141-7.

This major encyclopedic work covers various aspects of social work, and attempts to link them to social theories and to their social context. Social welfare is also emphasized in the articles that make up these volumes, as is biographical information about well-known scholars and practitioners in the field of social work.

Volume 1 provides an alphabetical list of articles indicating several topics of interest to educators, such as adult education, child welfare, preschool programs, and education for social work. In addition, index entries indicate education topics subsumed under other article titles covering, among numerous others, education of native Americans, Asian Americans, blacks, and Chicanos; education of the handicapped; and education of migrants and of minorities.

This encyclopedia began as successor to the *Social Work Year Book* published irregularly from 1929 to 1960. The fifteenth edition was the first publication under the title *Encyclopedia of Social Work* (1965), followed by the sixteenth and seventeenth editions (1971 and 1977) and a supplement to the latter in 1983.

Timms, Noel, and Rita Timms. **Dictionary of Social Welfare**. Boston: Routledge & Kegan Paul, 1982. 217p. $21.95. LC 82-5385. ISBN 0-7100-9084-6.

The purpose of this dictionary is, according to the introduction, "to introduce users to the study of social work and of social policy" (p. iii). The definitions range in length from one or two sentences to a page and a half. Many of the explanations would be of significance to educators and educational researchers; selected examples are accreditation, action research, adolescence, alienation, assessment, behavior modification, Central Council for Education and Training in Social Work, delinquency, deviance, and diagnosis, among others. British spellings, such as *centre* versus *center* and *organisations* versus *organizations* are used throughout; social welfare agencies described are typically British in nature.

Trattner, Walter, I., ed. **Biographical Dictionary of Social Welfare in America**. New York: Greenwood, 1986. 897p. $75.00. LC 85-9831. ISBN 0-313-23001-3.

Information on those individuals who have made significant contributions to American social welfare is included in this biographical dictionary. Approximately 130 contributors have prepared approximately 300 essays covering the biographees of this work. Coverage is not given to individuals living at the time of publication, elected public officials (unless primarily known of other reasons related to social welfare), philanthropists, abolitionists, feminists, labor union leaders, and intellectuals who were theoretical as opposed to activists in their orientation. Many of the subjects were also educators or were involved in work related to education.

4

General Education
Reference Sources

GUIDES

Berry, Dorothea M. **A Bibliographic Guide to Educatonal Research**. 2d ed. Metuchen, N.J.: Scarecrow Press, 1980. 215p. $17.50. LC 80-20191. ISBN 0-8208-1351-3.

In this second edition of her guide (first published in 1975), Berry has increased the number of entries describing educational sources from 504 to 772. She begins by introducing the reader to the initial stage of research from information about using the card catalog (already out-of-date in many large public and academic libraries) and providing an overview of the structure of education as it appears in both the Dewey Decimal and Library of Congress classification systems. This is followed by major generic catalogs and trade bibliographies, and then subject-specific titles related to reference work in education.

Entries are arranged alphabetically by author in broad format catagories, for example, bibliographies, directories, ERIC tools, research studies, government publications, and periodicals. Annotations are very brief and limited to descriptive comments. Author, title, and subject indexes conclude the work.

Berry's work needs updating, as is evident in the exclusion of any references to online catalogs and databases. Her annotations are quite brief and bibliographic entries lack indication of page numbers, information that readers find helpful in determining the extent of a reference source.

Durnin, Richard G. **American Education: A Guide to Information Sources**. Detroit: Gale, 1982. 247p. (American Studies Information Guide Series, Vol. 14; Information Guide Library). $65.00. LC 82-15387. ISBN 0-8103-1265-4.

This is a subject-arranged listing of reference and general works related to American schooling and the field of education. A total of 107 subject categories are arranged alphabetically, and within each subject category entries are arranged by format with reference works presented before general works or further subdivisions of the subject categories. Emphasis is given to the philosophical, historical, political, and sociological backgrounds of American schooling, including references to educators who played prominent roles in any level of education, from preschool to postgraduate.

The volume begins with an excellent bibliographic essay which is a chronological summary of American education from the seventeenth century to 1981. Other major sections include "Criticism, Issues, and Reforms of Education"; "Educators of Note"; "History of American Education"; "Methodology, Principles of Teaching"; "Secondary Education"; "Special Education"; "State and City Education Systems"; and "Women, Education of." In the extensive section "Higher Education," entries are subdivided chronologically by period and geographically by state. Histories of many American universities and colleges are identified here as well.

Although many annotations attempt to appraise the work with respect to its significance in the field, the annotations are, for the most part, quite brief. Durnin has provided a name index of all authors or persons treated as subjects. Separate title, author, and subject indexes, as provided in other titles in this Information Guide Series, would have been useful, as perusal of the table of contents is necessary for identifying specific topics. With respect to organization of materials, Woodbury's *A Guide to Sources of Educational Information* (Information Resources Press, 1982) is superior; however Durnin has described over 1,300 titles, making this a major reference tool for scholars in the field of education.

Woodbury, Marda. **A Guide to Sources of Educational Information**. 2d ed. Arlington, Va.: Information Resources Press, 1982. 430p. $39.95. LC 82-80549. ISBN 0-87815-041-2.

Woodbury lists the major sources of information needed to seek information related to American education. The work begins with a discussion of what constitutes effective research and a categorization of the various types of information sources, such as bibliographies, dictionaries, encyclopedias, as well as periodicals; abstracting, indexing, and current-awareness services; newsletters and news services; government documents; statistical sources; instructional and curricular materials; microfiche collections; ERIC sources and centers; computerized retrieval sources; and state library services to educators.

The annotated entries are arranged in four sections. Woodbury also outlines, in part 1, the step-by-step research process for systematic use of the information sources. Part 2 covers general reference sources; part 3 covers sources limited to a particular subject (e.g., special education). Part 4 lists databases available through commercial vendors and organizations, information brokers and clearinghouses, assessment instruments, library services, and other nonprint sources of information. The concluding chapter lists guides for writers, particularly those relevant to educators.

Each entry provides bibliographic information and an annotation of 100 to 150 words, typically, although a few are longer. Because page numbers are not provided the user cannot judge the scope or extent of a reference work; LC numbers and ISBN numbers are also lacking. Annotations are comprehensive, yet concise, and provide helpful information about how each source can be utilized. There is an introductory paragraph to each of the twenty chapters providing an overview of that category of sources. Educators and researchers should find this a very useful guide to information sources available up to 1982.

BIBLIOGRAPHIES

An American Federation of Teachers Bibliography. Archives of Labor & Urban Affairs, Wayne State University. Detroit: Wayne State University Press, 1980. 223p. $12.95; $6.95pa. ISBN 0-686-86864-1; 0-8143-1600-3pa.

Entries in this bibliography consist of sources related to the history of the AFT from its founding in 1916 to 1979. Arrangement is alphabetical in five sections, by format: books, articles, dissertations and theses, selected AFT documents and pamphlets, and archival materials. The periodical article section is also broken down into chronological divisions and constitutes 1,185 of the 1,475 entries. The annotations are descriptive and often consist of one line or one sentence.

In spite of the brevity of information, this listing is an important reference for researchers in the area of unions and arbitration. It also gives an overview of issues and concerns relevant to educators over the sixty-three years covered. In addition to selected records and papers from the Archives of Labor and Urban Affairs at Wayne State University, about twenty other archival repositories are described. A subject index is provided.

ARBA Guide to Education. Compiled and edited by Deborah J. Brewer. Littleton, Colo.: Libraries Unlimited, 1985. 232p. $23.50. LC 85-23150. ISBN 0-87287-490-7.

Brewer has compiled over 450 of the major reference sources in the field of education that have been reviewed in *ARBA* (*American Reference Books Annual*) since its inception in 1970. Arrangement of entries is in three sections. The first part focuses on sources providing bibliographic coverage, such as important bibliographies, indexes, and catalogs of established library collections. The second part covers dictionaries, encyclopedias, handbooks, yearbooks, directories, biographies, and other sources of ready reference-type information. Part 3 covers five additional categories: bilingual and minority education, dissertations and theses, instructional media, reading, and special education.

Although this bibliography lacks the special attention to additional information sources in education, such as periodicals, research organizations, and databases found in a guide such as Woodbury's *A Guide to Sources of Educational Information* (Information Resources Press, 1982), it does update this tool somewhat and is a convenient fifteen-year bibliography of major education reference sources. A good retrospective source of bibliographies is Theodore Besterman's *Education: A Bibliography of Bibliographies* (Rowman and Littlefield, 1971).

Bibliographic Guide to Education. Boston: G. K. Hall, 1979- . Annual. $230.00. LC 79-643170. ISSN 0147-6505.

This is an annual listing of titles relating to education that were cataloged the previous year and owned by the library of the Columbia University's Teachers College and the New York Public Library. It supplements the *Dictionary Catalog of the Teachers' College Library* (G. K. Hall, 1970) which is comprised of thirty-six volumes covering 400,000 items plus three supplements (1971, 5v.); (1973, 2v.); and (1977, 10v.). Entries cover children's books, government documents, monographs, and nonprint materials on titles, as well as some foreign publications and theses; serials are not included. Titles cover education from the preschool through adult levels.

Since it is a computer-produced publication made from OCLC tapes, complete bibliographic information is provided, including tracings, call numbers, LC and ISBN numbers.

Clarke, John L. **Educational Development: A Select Bibliography with Particular Reference to Further and Higher Education**. London: Kogan Page; New York: Nichols, 1981. 207p. LC 80-15563. ISBN 0-89397-092-1.

Educational development, as it is used in this reference work, is concerned with improvement of facilities for teaching and learning, provision of information and consultancy services on teaching strategies, evaluation methods, and curriculum development. Criteria for selecting entries for inclusion in this listing are not identified, but entries are arranged alphabetically by author in the following subject chapters: (1) "Educational Technology, Development and Innovation"; (2) "Curriculum Development"; (3) "Educational Objectives"; (4) "Strategies for Learning"; (5) "Educational Media"; (6) "The Evaluation of Teaching and Learning"; (7) "Staff Development"; (8) "The Student in Further and Higher Education"; (9) "Studies and Research in Further and Higher Education"; and (10) "Educational Theory." An additional chapter identifies American and British periodicals on educational development, including frequency, publisher and address, and ISSN. Entries are not annotated, nor is the work indexed—two serious limitations to the usefulness of this bibliography.

Cordasco, Francesco, and David N. Alloway. **Sociology of Education: A Guide to Information Sources**. Detroit: Gale, 1979. 266p. index. (Education Information Guide Series, Vol. 2; Gale Information Guide Library). $65.00. LC 78-10310. ISBN 0-8103-1436-3.

Cordasco is well known for his reference guides in the social sciences area, and particularly with regard to ethnic and other minorities. This bibliography, compiled in conjunction with David Alloway, lists major reference tools and bibliographies, textbooks, monographs, articles, and reports on the sociological aspects of schools and education.

Over 2,500 entries are arranged alphabetically by subject and are concerned with all levels of education and the curriculum. For example, topics listed under "Special Aspects of Education" include adult education, education of the disadvantaged, education of exceptional children, education of minorities, religion and education, vocational education, education and politics, and desegregation. Each citation in this useful compilation has complete bibliographic information, but annotations are minimal, with descriptions one or two sentences long.

Drazan, Joseph Gerald, comp. **An Annotated Bibliography of ERIC Bibliographies, 1966-1980**. Westport, Conn.: Greenwood, 1982. 520p. $49.95. LC 82-6151. ISBN 0-313-22688-1.

This bibliography is a comprehensive collection of over 3,200 individual bibliographies stored in the ERIC (Educational Resources Information Center) information system's microfiche files, about 75 percent of which are directly related to education. Entries are arranged in about 600 subject categories with cross-references to additional related citations. Each entry provides full title, compiler and imprint, if available, number of pages, and ED accession number. The annotations are quite brief, often limited to the scope of the work.

Drazan searched every issue of *RIE (Resources in Education)*, from its inception in 1966 through September 1980, under three headings: bibliographies, annotated bibliographies, and reference materials. The bibliography titles identified are all available for purchase in full text from EDRS (ERIC Document Reproduction Service) in either paper copy or microfiche. While researchers who have access to online searching could retrieve an even more comprehensive list on any specific topic, Drazan's compilation is still a very useful tool. The work is well organized; it includes a section on how to order an ERIC bibliography (or other document) and author and subject indexes.

Fifteenth to Eighteenth Century Rare Books on Education: A Catalog of the Titles Held by the Educational Research Library. Washington, D.C.: National Institute of Education; distr., Government Printing Office, 1976. 66p. $3.00pa. S/N 017-080-01605-2.

A publication compiled as part of the American bicentennial celebration, this illustrated catalog describes 383 rare books published prior to 1800. Titles include early textbooks, rules and regulations of the first colleges and universities, encyclopedias, and general treatises on education. A large number of titles are in Latin or other foreign languages. Entries are arranged chronologically in three major time periods and alphabetically by author within each section. Scholars interested in the history of education can access this volume by subject, language, and country of printer/publisher indexes.

Hall, G. Stanley, and John M. Mansfield. **Hints toward a Select and Descriptive Bibliography of Education**. Boston: D.C. Heath, 1886; republished Detroit: Gale, 1973; reprint of 1886 ed. 135p. $48.00. LC 72-10907. ISBN 0-8103-3176-4.

This republication of an 1886 bibliography will be of immense interest to education historians. Scholars in comparative or international education programs might also find useful historical information with respect to education in European countries. A detailed subject index precedes the actual list of selected monographs and journal articles in English, French, and German, and presents the user with the major encyclopedias, histories, curriculum guides, surveys, general works, and periodicals available in the latter part of the nineteenth century. All the disciplines are covered, as are topics such as "Moral Education," "Female Education," "General Aesthetics," and "The School and the Family."

While many of the educational concerns represented are interesting because they are unique to the historical period, many others are still issues of contemporary interest.

Hamilton, Malcolm, ed. **Education Literature, 1907-1932**. New York: Garland, 1979. 25v. in 12. $40.00/vol. LC 79-12425. ISBN 0-8240-3700-6 (v. 1).

This reprinted bibliography was originally published as 126 bulletins prepared by the staff of the Bureau of Education from 1907 to 1932. (The Bureau of Education became the U.S. Office in 1929.) Books, pamphlets, conference proceedings, and over 700 periodical titles were analyzed throughout this period, most of which are American titles, but others represent journals from Europe and other countries. Originally an index made up of twenty-five volumes, it was reprinted in eleven volumes with an additional twelfth volume being a newly developed cumulative index.

This publication is essential in an educational research library for providing access to the historical literature prior to the development of ERIC, *Education Index*, and other indexing tools and services.

Klein, Barry T., ed. **Guide to American Educational Directories: A Guide to the Major Educational Directories of the United States**. 5th ed. Rye, N.Y.: Todd Publications, 1980. 202p. $30.00. LC 63-14270. ISBN 0-915344-02-5.

Major educational directories in the United States are described in this annotated guide which has been published since 1963. Titles are arranged alphabetically under a wide variety of subject headings, which also appear in alphabetical order. Each entry provides a synopsis of the type of information the directory contains, the frequency of its publication, name and address of the publisher, and price. The directories included represent categories of information ranging from directories to schools and colleges (private, public, vocational, correspondence, adult, and evening) to various types of school administrators, from aeronautics and aviation to zoology. The designation *educational directories* must be considered in the broadest sense, as directories to subjects normally thought of as outside the realm of education are also included, such as advertising, marketing, and public relations; banking and investments; book dealers; military and minority groups; publishing; and retailing. Since criteria for selection are not included, it is difficult to ascertain on what basis titles have been excluded or included.

Master's Theses in Education. Edited by H. M. Silvey. Cedar Falls, Iowa: Research Publications, 1951- . Annual. $30.00. LC 53-62892. ISSN 0076-5112.

Organized research efforts of master's degree students related to education in the United States and Canada are listed in this annual subject-arranged bibliography. Only research that each institution accepts and classifies as meeting these standards is included. Research papers accepted in lieu of a thesis are excluded. Some theses are in a subject field (e.g., science, mathematics, social science, English, language arts, music), but are included if the writer is a candidate in a teacher education program. Also, all theses included are available on interlibrary loan.

Each entry includes the name of the author, thesis title, and institution number, which allows identification of the school at which the thesis was written in the institution index. Tables indicate the distribution of theses written on various topics and distribution of theses among the states and institutions granting master's degrees in education. Length in pages is not included, so the user cannot be sure of the extent of a title. Also a large number of institutions did not report any information for the period covered by the volume, limiting the usefulness of this reference tool.

A title that provides coverage of Canadian theses is by Denis Robitaille and Joan Waiser, *Theses in Canada: A Bibliographic Guide (Theses au Canada: Guide Bibliographique)* (National Library of Canada, 1986).

Moussavi, Fakhreddin, comp. **Guide to the Hanna Collection and Related Archival Materials at the Hoover Institution on War, Revolution and Peace on the Role of Education in Twentieth-Century Society**. Stanford, Calif.: Hoover Institution Press, 1982. 250p. (Hoover Press Bibliographical Series, No. 64). $19.95. LC 82-12131. ISBN 0-8179-2641-0.

The Hanna Collection on the Role of Education in Twentieth-Century Society was established in 1976 at the Hoover Institution with the purpose of alerting scholars to its wealth of education-related archival materials. Included in this collection guide are 600 archival and manuscript collections covering American educational policy, peace efforts promoted via education, propaganda and education in wartime, international and comparative education programs, education in developing nations, and other related topics.

The collection is named for Dr. Paul Hanna, founder and first director of the Stanford (University) International Development Education Center and Jean Hanna, English teacher and coauthor and editor (with her husband) of numerous textbooks. Educational historians, in particular, will be interested in the documents described here.

Parks, Arnold G. **Urban Education: An Annotated Bibliography**. Saratoga, Calif.: Century Twenty-One Publishing, 1981. 90p. $9.50. LC 80-69234. ISBN 0-86548-053-2.

Because the majority of Americans tend to live in large urban areas, educators are faced with difficult sociological problems in inner-city classrooms. Entries in this bibliography describe books published primarily in the 1970s, with the exception of major significant titles prior to that date. Arrangement is alphabetical by author. Although these citations lack complete bibliographic information (pages, prices, and ISBN numbers are not included), the annotations are helpful. However, some type of subject indexing is needed. Although there is a list entitled "Alphabetical Listing by Subject," the list is merely an alphabetical list of titles. The bibliography contains 325 titles about counseling, language development, preschool teaching, economic deprivation, cultural deprivation, segregation, racism, political issues, reading, education excellence, and many other topics that are part of urban education. If authors and titles are not known, the user must browse through the book to identify items on particular subjects. An earlier, somewhat more comprehensive, publication is *Urban Education: A Guide to Information Sources* (Gale, 1978) by George E. Spear and Donald W. Mocker.

Rosentiel, Annette. **Education and Anthropology: An Annotated Bibliography**. New York: Garland, 1977. 646p. (Reference Library of Social Science, Vol. 20). $75.00. LC 75-24100. ISBN 0-8240-9969-9.

This annotated bibliography of 3,435 entries identifies materials related to the historical influences, current trends, theory, and practical methodology related to the intersection of education and anthropology. Materials included cover the period from 1689 to 1976, and consist of books, articles, papers, and unpublished manuscripts, as well as selected novels.

Many items have been selected for their relevance to multicultural education. Some foreign language (French, Spanish, German, Italian, Portuguese) titles are included, but compilers have conveniently included an English translation as well as the original language title.

INDEXES AND ABSTRACTS

Canadian Education Index. Toronto: Canadian Education Association, 1965- . 3/yr. $184.00/yr. ISSN 0008-3453.

This index analyzes approximately 200 periodicals, books, reports, and other documents related to Canadian education. The work is in French and English (whichever language was used in the work cited), but the subject headings are in French. Prefatory material includes a key to abbreviations, instructions for consulting the index, and a list of the periodicals indexed. The index uses an author/subject approach. A list of monographs covered is provided at the back of each volume.

Contents Pages in Education. Hopkinton, Mass.: Carfax Publishing, 1986- . Monthly. $205.00/vol. ISSN 0265-92290.

This relatively new index to the international literature in education periodicals provides access by author/title/subject. The emphasis is on American and British titles, but there are many more foreign titles here than in *CIJE (Current Index to Journals in Education)*. Of the 580 education journals analyzed, approximately 50 percent are also covered in *CIJE*. Since information is available in a computerized database, maintaining currency is easily possible. The cover title is *Monthly Access to the World's Education Periodicals*.

Current Index to Journals in Education (CIJE). Phoenix, Ariz.: Oryx Press, March 1979- . Monthly (Published by Macmillan, 1969-February 1979). Monthly index plus semiannual cumulations. $207.00/yr. ISSN 0011-3565.

CIJE, sponsored by ERIC (Educational Resources Information Center) and NIE (National Institute of Education), is a guide to current periodical literature in education which is published monthly and cumulated semiannually and annually. Almost 2,000 articles per month from approximately 780 education journals are indexed. Some (approximately 100) foreign journals are also indexed and abstracted. Reprints of articles included in about two-thirds of the journals covered are available from University Microfilms International.

The main entry section is arranged by ERIC Clearinghouse and sequential EJ (ERIC accession) numbers. (Clearinghouses are Adult, Career, and Vocational Education; Counseling and Personnel Services; Reading and Communication Skills; Educational Management; Handicapped and Gifted Children; Languages and Linguistics; Higher Education; Information Resources; Junior Colleges; Elementary and Early Childhood Education; Rural Education and Small Schools; Science, Mathematics, and Environmental Education; Social Studies/Social Science Education; Teacher Education; Tests, Measurement, and Evaluation; and Urban Education.) Subject and author indexes provide access to information.

Each entry contains a brief summary with subject and author indexes to the EJ number. The reader has to search back and forth from index terms to locate information on a subject. The index terms come from the *Thesaurus of ERIC Descriptors*. Names and addresses of journal publishers, as well as prices, are also provided. While *CIJE* is not as convenient to use, or as current, as *Education Index*, it has the advantage of being able to be computer searched via DIALOG, ORBIT, or BRS retrieval systems.

Education Index: A Cumulative Subject Index to a Selected List of Educational Periodicals and Yearbooks. New York: H. W. Wilson, 1929- . Quarterly, with annual cumulations. Subscription service. $105.00/vol. ISSN 0013-1385.

As the major indexing service in the field, *Education Index* analyzes over 350 English-language periodicals, yearbooks, and monographs in series for all aspects and subdivisions of the field of education. Citations are in an integrated author and subject arrangement, with citations to book reviews presented in a separate section at the end of each volume. Each volume lists periodical abbreviations used and a list of all journals indexed.

The 1986 annual compilation is edited by Marylouise Hewitt and Barbara Berry and is 1,484 pages in length. As of 1984, *Education Index* has been available in machine-readable format, online through WILSONLINE or on CD-ROM through WILSONDISC, with coverage extending from September 1983 to date. A software package entitled WILSEARCH allows microcomputer access to WILSONLINE.

Resources in Education. Washington, D.C.: Educational Resources Information Center, 1966- . Monthly. $70.00. ISSN 0098-0897.

Resources in Education (RIE) abstracts ERIC documents and is a complementary tool to *Current Index to Journals in Education* (Oryx Press, 1979-) which is a monthly index to the periodical literature in education. Documents are alphabetized letter-by-letter and are indexed by author, subject, and institution name. Annual cumulations are in *Resources In Education Annual Cumulation* (1979- , annual, ISSN 0197-9973), also published by Oryx Press. ERIC Document Reproduction Service can provide issues on microfiche. *RIE* was published as *Research in Education* from 1966 through 1974.

State Education Journal Index and Educators' Guide to Periodicals Research Strategies. Westminster, Colo.: L. Stanley Ratliff, 1962- . Semiannual. $75.00/yr. ISSN 0039-0046.

SEJI indexes all titles published by state departments of education, many of which are only brief newsletters and are not covered by other standard indexes. It is edited by L. Stanley Ratliff. The index is arranged alphabetically by broad subject headings and cross-references. Titles that are not self-explanatory have succinct annotations. The prefatory material includes a guide to abbreviations used.

DICTIONARIES AND ENCYCLOPEDIAS

Barrow, Robin, and Geoffrey Milburn. **A Critical Dictionary of Educational Concepts**. New York: St. Martin's Press, 1986. 274p. $35.00. LC 86-21953. ISBN 0-312-00229-7.

Subtitled *An Appraisal of Selected Ideas in Educational Theory and Practice*, this dictionary is unique in that it attempts to define and assess broad concepts rather than specific terms. Issues and ideas that are part of the everyday discourse and language of classroom teachers and higher education faculty are discussed, as well as those that comprise educational theory or are mainly of interest to researchers or theoreticians. Although many conventional terms are included, the compilers have selected terms that have a definite educational philosophy orientation.

Collins, Carol C., and Tracey Dewart, eds. **America's Schools: Passing the Test of the '80s?** New York: Facts on File, 1985. 231p. (An Editorials on File Book). $24.95. LC 85-20412. ISBN 0-8160-1203-2.

Since the controversial report of the National Commission on Education in 1981, *A Nation at Risk*, there have been many items in the news in response and reaction to that work. Collins and Dewart have combed the major newspapers for the five-year period from 1981 to 1985 and collected editorials related to the topic. Reprinted in their original typeface, these editorials are arranged in seven subject categories. "The Current State of Education"; "Curricular Issues"; "Special Education"; "Religion and the Classroom"; and "The Alternative—Private Schools." Within these sections the editorials are subdivided with each subsection introduced by a very brief overview essay. A list of further references and a topical index conclude the work.

Dale, Edgar. **The Educator's Quotebook**. Bloomington, Ind.: Phi Delta Kappa Educational Foundation, 1984. 107p. $4.00pa. LC 83-63095. ISBN 0-87367-429-4.

This compilation of quotations by prominent educators and writers was prepared by an Ohio State University emeritus professor in the field of education. Dale developed the well-known Dale-Chall readability formula. The quotations are arranged alphabetically by subject categories, some of which include adolescence, books, censors, change, committees, discipline, education, intelligence, learning, professors, teaching, and thinking.

Although authorship of most quotations is indicated, citations are not provided that would indicate the context in which the quotation was made. Educational speakers might find this quotebook particularly useful. A similar source is a well-indexed collection, *Quotable Quotes on Education*, by August Kerber (Wayne State University Press, 1968), with quotations dating from ancient Greece to the 1960s. In spite of its extensive coverage, literary quotes are not documented and the 1968 copyright date also limits its use.

Deighton, Lee C., ed. in chief. **The Encyclopedia of Education**. New York: Macmillan and Free Press, 1971. 10v. $199.00/set. LC 70-133143. ISBN 0-02-893300-2.

This comprehensive work deals not only with the historical, theoretical, and philosophical issues of education, but also emphasizes institutions, people, processes, and products related to educational practice and training. In over 1,000 articles signed by contributing scholars, content is directed at teachers, administrators, guidance counselors, training directors in industry, legislators, and leaders involved in educational decision making. Some more technical articles are available for graduate scholars and researchers.

Articles are arranged alphabetically in the first nine volumes and are of varying lengths. Volume 10 includes the directory of contributors, a guide to articles, and an extensive index. *The Encyclopedia of Education* is particularly useful for articles on school administration, comparative education, curriculum, history of education, teacher training, and career education. Less attention is given to biographical information.

Another early multivolume set first published between 1911 and 1913 and reprinted in 1968 is *A Cyclopedia of Education*, edited by Paul Monroe (Macmillan, 1911-13, 5v.). *Teacher's Encyclopedia* (Prentice-Hall, 1966) is a one-volume work focusing on practical learning and teaching experiences in the classroom.

Dejnoska, Edward L., and David E. Kapel. **American Educators' Encyclopedia**. Westport, Conn.: Greenwood, 1982. 634p. index. $75.00. LC 81-6664. ISBN 0-313-20954-5.

This one-volume encyclopedia provides brief (100-200 word) entries covering elementary, secondary, and higher education. Entries are arranged alphabetically and each is concluded by a brief list of related titles for further reference. A "User's Guide" and a list of "Abbreviations and Acronyms" precede the main body of entries. According to the editors, subject content of the encyclopedia could be divided into twenty-two broad areas which include the various curricular disciplines, as well as such topics as administration and supervision, audiovisual education and library science, biographies, educational organizations, federal programs and legislation, minority education, school law, and other miscellaneous topics. A series of appendixes include important documents related to education (e.g., Declaration of the Rights of the Child, Caldecott and Newbery Award winners in children's literature, past presidents of major education associations, regional accrediting associations, land-grant colleges and universities, ERIC clearinghouses). As the only one-volume encyclopedia in the United States, this is a very convenient and ready reference for educators, librarians, and other scholars.

Encyclopedia of Educational Research. 5th ed. Edited by Harold E. Mitzel. New York: Free Press, 1982. 4v. index. $315.00/set. LC 82-2332. ISBN 0-02-900450-0.

Because of the thirteen years between the one-volume fourth and four-volume fifth editions, revisions are striking. An example of extensive reorganization of information is an article "Research Integration" in this edition which replaces two articles in the fourth. Topics new to the fifth edition are "Computer-Based Education," "Drug Abuse Education," and "Equity Issues in Education," among others. Some topics appear under new terminology: "Correspondence Study" replaced by "Distance Education" and "Independent Study," for example. A spot check of references would indicate consistent updating. These references represent the scholarly literature of the field, including ERIC documents.

A total of 317 subject specialists have prepared 256 signed articles under twenty-nine broad subject categories. New information has been provided on statistical design of research, multicultural and bilingual education, computers in education, nontraditional education and, for the first time, systems design in instruction receives fairly lengthy treatment.

Volume 4 concludes with a "Directory of Contributors" which lists the affiliation and article(s) contributed by authors. A name and subject index is provided. Sponsored by AERA (American Educational Research Association), this encyclopedia provides a valuable service to scholars by presenting critical and well-reported interpretations of research in the field of education. Because of its 1982 publication date, it must be used with more current indexes to identify the most recent research.

Farber, Bernard E., comp. **A Teacher's Treasury of Quotations**. Jefferson, N.C.: McFarland, 1985. 370p. $39.95. LC 84-43218. ISBN 0-89950-150-8.

This comprehensive source of quotations related to the field of education will be of interest to educators, particularly historians and public speakers. The author, himself a former educator, has compiled a wide variety of quotable sayings which span a long historical period and originate from people from many nations and many walks of life. Arrangement of material is in 450 subject categories, which are identified through the table of contents. The work is well organized and quotations are documented.

Gatti, Richard D., and Daniel J. Gatti. **New Encyclopedic Dictionary of School Law**. West Nyack, N.J.: Parker Publishing, 1983. 400p. $34.95. LC 83-3956. ISBN 0-13-612580-8.

New terms related to school case law are included in this second dictionary compiled by the authors. Their previous version was entitled *Encyclopedic Dictionary of School Law* and was published in 1975. While coverage of many of the previous subject categories is continued, many new categories are introduced and more emphasis is given to terms related to multiethnic education (bilingual and bicultural education) and those related to more recent social issues, such as the battered child, accountability, and competency testing. A total of 287 new cases are cited in tabular form preceding the alphabetical list of terms.

Gieber, Robert L. **An English-French Glossary of Educational Terminology**. Washington, D.C.: University Press of America, 1981. 206p. o.p. LC 80-5652. ISBN 0-8191-1344-1; 0-8191-1345-Xpa.

This glossary provides English and French equivalents of terms commonly used in education. French-speaking students from France, Belgium, Switzerland, Canada, and other French-speaking countries might find it useful, but since definitions are not included, its usefulness is rather limited. Gieber selected terms from school catalogs and other sources which are included in a bibliography. Many of the terms included need not have been, as the French and English words are so close (or even identical) in spelling that listing them is unnecessary. Any standard French-English dictionary, or even an illustrated title such as *The Oxford-Duden Pictorial French-English Dictionary* (Clarendon Press/Oxford University Press, 1983) would probably be more helpful to students and educators.

Good, Carter V., ed. **Dictionary of Education**. 3d ed. Prepared under the auspices of Phi Delta Kappa. New York: McGraw-Hill, 1973. 681p. LC 73-4784. ISBN 0-07-023720-4.

First published in 1945, this comprehensive work has long been the authoritative source of professional terms in education. The 33,000 terms cover the entire area of education from theoretical concepts to practical methods, movements, and technologies in education.

Each edition has substantially increased the number of terms from the original 19,000, and as a result of this breadth of coverage, definitions are concise (about fifty words) and the typeface is quite small. Foreign terms no longer appear in the third edition, but separate brief sections list terms particularly relevant to education in Canada, England, and Wales. A separate section lists associates and reviewers. This title has become a classic reference for educational terminology.

Gordon, Peter, and Dennis Lawton. **A Guide to English Educational Terms**. New York: Schocken Books, 1985. 238p. $16.00. LC 84-5305. ISBN 0-8052-3922-7.

This dictionary attempts to define terms that are commonly used in the educational systems of England and Wales, and, to some extent, Scotland. Most terms still reflect contemporary usage, but some terms of historical significance are included. In some cases, definitions are followed by a reference source directing the reader to a deeper explanation of a topic. Entries for prominent individuals in British education are not included. Acronyms must be looked up in a list that follows the main body of the work to determine the phrase they represent, as the acronyms themselves do not appear in the main dictionary with cross-references. A brief "List of Useful Reference Books" (twenty-eight titles) and a list of the current ministers of education conclude the work.

While there is a certain degree of overlap between the British and American term usage (e.g., *nature-nurture controversy, longitudinal study, taxonomy),* this tool is particularly useful to the educator/scholar who needs to identify specific British reports, cases, associations, and organizations that might not appear in other more generic sources.

Hawes, Gene R., and Lynne Salop Hawes. **The Concise Dictionary of Education**. New York: Van Nostrand Reinhold, 1982. 249p. LC 82-26-5. ISBN 0-442-26298-1.

The purpose of this education dictionary is to cover terms that affect the entire breadth of education, including newer words and concepts (e.g., *creationism, preppy, Pell Grants*). Entries are arranged in a strict letter-by-letter alphabetical listing and typically consist of only three to five lines or one or two sentences of definition. Phrase terms, such as *distributive education* or *deductive reasoning*, appear without inversion, rather than as *education, distributive* or *reasoning, deductive*. When terms have more than one meaning (as do grade and program) the most important, or predominately used, one is given first.

These simplified definitions are written in layperson's language and, therefore, this education dictionary would be current and useful in a public, academic, corporate, or large high school library.

Hills, Philip James. **A Dictionary of Education**. Boston: Routledge & Kegan Paul, 1982. 284p. $30.00. LC 81-22718. ISBN 0-7100-0871-6.

The most important terms related to three broad concepts of education are included in this selected compilation. The editor has defined terms related to (1) the setting for the process of education, (2) the process itself, and (3) the methods and techniques for application. Settings would include terms related to comparative education, administration, organizations, economics, and education in the business/industrial sector. Process terms are concerned with the history, philosophy, psychology, and sociology of education. Methods and techniques include curriculum development, educational technology, research, and measurement. Entries are arranged alphabetically, but category chapters are preceded by a brief essay on each of the above subjects with a list of references for further reading at the end of each.

First published in London, its spellings, organizations listed, and educational emphases are definitely British. The educational scholar reading the international literature in education would find this dictionary very useful.

Houston, James E. **Thesaurus of ERIC Descriptors.** 11th ed. Phoenix, Ariz.: Oryx Press, 1986. 640p. $65.00. LC 86-42555. ISBN 0-89774-159-5.

The controlled vocabulary of educational terms used in the information system produced and operated by the National Institute of Education, U.S. Department of Education, is listed here. Citations for all materials processed by ERIC (Educational Resources Information Center) appear in *Resources in Education (RIE)* or *Current Index to Journals in Education (CIJE)* and can be identified using terms from the *Thesaurus* to search these indexes. Terms that have been introduced since the previous edition are listed in a section called "New Descriptors." Other sections list descriptors downgraded to USE references (terms used to refer an indexer or searcher from a nonindexable term to the preferred indexable term), "dead" or no longer valid descriptors, and deleted descriptors. Indexing and retrieval in the system are explained, as is the *Thesaurus* construction and format.

Arrangement of entries in the "Alphabetical Descriptor Display" is alphabetical, including the complete records of all categories of *Thesaurus* terms interfiled word-by-word. The "Rotated Descriptor Display" is a permuted alphabetical index of all words that form *Thesaurus* terms and the "Two-Way Hierarchical Term Display" lists families (generic trees) of descriptors with both broader and narrower terms related to class membership indicated. The final section, "Descriptor Groups and Descriptor Group Display," acts as a table of contents with scope notes provided for each of the forty-one descriptor groups, followed by an alphabetical list of all descriptors to that group.

Husen, Torsten, and T. Neville Postlethwaite, eds. **The International Encyclopedia of Education: Research and Studies.** Elmsford, N.Y.: Pergamon Press, 1985. 10v. $1,750/set. LC 84-20750. ISBN 0-08-028119-2.

The editorial board responsible for this encyclopedia is truly an international body of prominent educators. The editors-in-chief, Torsten Husen and T. Neville Postlethwaite, are from the University of Stockholm and the University of Hamburg, respectively. A total of 1,448 articles signed by 1,300 contributors from over 100 countries are organized in twenty-five broad categories which cover administration; adult education; comparative and international education; counseling; curriculum; developing countries; discipline; early childhood; economics; educational institutes, organizations, and societies; policy and planning; higher education; educational technology; evaluation; human development; motivation; national systems; research; sex roles; social stratification; special education; teacher education; vocational education; and women in education. Systems of education in 160 countries are discussed with demographic data in charts and tabular form.

Page, G. Terry, and J. B. Thomas. **International Dictionary of Education.** London: Kogan Page; New York: Nichols, 1980. 381p. $13.95. LC 77-4868. ISBN 0-262-66043-1.

Over 10,000 concisely defined terms are included in this dictionary providing worldwide coverage to the particular language of the field of education. Major national and international organizations and honor societies are also included, as are slang, foreign, and other terms (e.g., *lararhogskolor*, or Swedish higher education institutions) not covered by standard educational works such as *Good's Dictionary of Education* or others limited to usage in American works.

Some entries cover biographical data for nationally and internationally prominent educators, such as Jean Piaget, Maria Montessori, and J.H. Pestalozzi.

Palmer, James C., and Anita Y. Colby, comps. and eds. **Dictionary of Educational Acronyms, Abbreviations, and Initialisms**. 2d ed. Phoenix, Ariz.: Oryx Press, 1985. 97p. $27.50. LC 84-42814. ISBN 0-89774-165-X.

Various ERIC sources, newsletters of educational organizations, *The Encyclopedia of Associations* (Gale, 1983), and many educational journals were the sources for information identifying 4,011 acronyms and abbreviated forms included in this dictionary. A total of 1,995 forms were added to this second edition. Entries are arranged alphabetically in two lists. In the first, terms are alphabetical by the acronym form. In the second listing they are arranged by unabbreviated form. In most cases, only the acronym and the words it represents are provided, but in a few cases a modifier is included in parentheses which either identifies a geographic location or a parent organization, for example, "OLPR—Office for Library Personnel Resources (American Library Association)." Sometimes an entry begins with the phrase "Not an acronym," to indicate the form of a program, agency, or software package name.

Since every scholar has probably experienced the frustration of reading discussions where acronyms are used with the assumption that the reader knows their reference terms, this dictionary is an essential and welcome reference tool in the field of education.

Psacharopoulos, George, ed. **Economics of Education: Research and Studies**. Elmsford, N.Y.: Pergamon Press, 1987. 482p. $85.00. LC 86-9498. ISBN 0-08-033379-6.

As a relative latecomer to economic theory, the branch of economics of education as it is described in this work is covered in twelve main chapter categories: (1) "The Formation of Human Capital," (2) "Educational Production," (3) "The Benefits of Education," (4) "Education and Employment," (5) "The Analysis of Earnings," (6) "The Distribution of Educational Outcomes," (7) "Ability and Screening," (8) "Education and Manpower Planning," (9) "Planning Models," (10) "Longitudinal Analysis in Education," (11) "Educational Costs," and (12) "The Financing of Education." Articles in each part are, mostly, reprints from *The International Encyclopedia of Education: Research and Studies*, and have all been prepared by specialists in the field. Access is available through contributor name, subject and title indexes.

Rowntree, Derek. **A Dictionary of Education**. Totowa, N.J.: Barnes & Noble Books, 1982. 354p. LC 82-206311. ISBN 0-389-20263-0.

In this dictionary of over 3,000 terms, Rowntree has focused on educational terms that have different meanings for English-speaking persons from different countries. Vocabulary terms that might differ from one country to another are immediately followed by a symbol for the country, either (UK) or (US), associated with the definition or interpretation given. Terms such as *public school, grammar school,* and *gymnasium* are some good examples. Although entries for some internationally known theorists (e.g., Jerome Bruner, Jean Piaget, Maria Montessori) are included, in general, biographies of educators are not. Societies and associations are also excluded.

Although it does not compare in scope to Good's *Dictionary of Education* (McGraw-Hill, 1973), this work performs a unique function in its attempt to bridge the gap between cultural interpretations of educational terms.

HANDBOOKS AND YEARBOOKS

Levin, Joel. **Getting Published: The Educators' Resource Book**. New York: Arco, 1983. 281p. $16.95; $11.95pa. LC 83-10042. ISBN 0-668-05477-8; 0-668-05481-6pa.

This handbook for educators and professional personnel gives tips on getting published in the scholarly educational journals. Information is arranged in three major sections. Part 1 provides an overview of publishing opportunities and advice on how to go about getting an article published. Part 2 includes educational publishers arranged alphabetically, and Part 3 is a subject-arranged list of 274 educational periodicals.

Mauch, James E., and Jack W. Birch. **Guide to the Successful Thesis and Dissertation: A Handbook for Students and Faculty**. New York: Marcel Dekker, 1983. 234p. (Books in Library and Information Science). $25.00. LC 83-2112. ISBN 0-8247-1800-3.

This handbook is aimed at both master's and doctoral level graduate students, who must write a thesis or dissertation for their advanced degrees, and their academic advisers who supervise and evaluate this research requirement. The authors have outlined the critical steps in conceptualizing, conducting, and reporting a research study, including timetable and checklist for proposal writing, data collecting, and hypothesis testing, through the final draft stages and submission and defense of the research. Emphasis is on research methodologies in education and other social sciences, with typical methods of investigation (case study, survey, etc.) and some popular basic means of statistical analysis described.

McCall, Chester Hayden, Jr. **Sampling and Statistics Handbook for Research**. Washington, D.C.: National Education Association, 1980. 366p. $15.00. LC 82-15290. ISBN 0-8138-1628-9.

This work is subtitled *A Technical Reference for Members of the Research Staff of the National Education Association and its State and Local Affiliated Associations*, and its foreword indicates that it "has been designed for researchers who are responsible for studying and solving educational problems" (p. 3). Basic statistical concepts for generic application in studies requiring statistical analysis are covered, with the intent that the novice can develop an understanding of both descriptive and inferential statistics. Contents emphasize the sampling process and survey sampling, descriptive measures of central tendency, variation, and association. Inferential statistics topics include concepts of randomness, estimation, hypothesis testing, multivariate and nonparametric techniques, and various sampling plans. There is a major emphasis on sampling, and McCall incorporates much information from a handbook developed during a NEA-sponsored experimental program, the Sampling Project, and a preliminary handbook, *Sampling and Statistics Handbook for Surveys in Education* (1965).

Appendix materials include a glossary of terms, references, discussions of arithmetic operations and probability, an index to descriptive formulas, methodology, computer programs, and various statistical tables. A subject index concludes the work.

NEA Handbook. Washington, D.C.: National Education Association, 1945- . Annual. $10.00. LC 87-6420809. ISSN 8755-1829.

This annual handbook provides basic information on this major professional association union and its key elected officials and staff members. Included are policy documents, organizational structure and governing bodies, goals and objectives, programs and administration, historical development, and directory information (names, addresses, and telephone numbers) of the board of directors and executive committee. Also described are the various NEA committees, state affiliates, UniServ Council and urban directory, membership data, the NEA constitution and bylaws, standing rules, resolutions, legislative program for the Congress, new business, and other actions adopted by the current representative assembly. It also provides a copy of the "Bill of Teacher Rights," "Code of Ethics of the Education Profession," past NEA presidents and convention sites, and a schedule of governance meetings for the calendar year. Name and subject indexes conclude the wealth of information presented in this handbook.

Requirements for Certification of Teachers, Counselors, Librarians, Administrators for Secondary School, Junior Colleges. Edited by Mary P. Burks. Chicago: University of Chicago Press, 1935- . Annual. $29.00. LC A43-1905.

Because state and regional certification requirements change frequently, this guide is constantly updated to reflect these revisions. The book opens with recommendations of regional and national associations (Middle States Association, North Central Association of Colleges and Schools, Northwest Association of Schools and Colleges, Southern Association of Colleges and Schools Commission on Secondary Schools, and American Association of Community and Junior Colleges) followed by information about applying for teaching positions in the United States and territories. The certification requirements are arranged alphabetically by state and cover regular certification for secondary teachers, as well as administrative, special services, vocational trades, early childhood, temporary and provisional special services, guidance counselor, school media specialist/librarian, and other certificates.

This long-standing authoritative source on certification for teachers and other school personnel is now in its fifty-first edition.

DIRECTORIES

Allen, G. G., and K. Deubert. **Guide to the Availability of Theses. II: Non-University Institutions.** Munich, New York: K. G. Saur, 1985. 124p. (IFLA Publications, 29). $17.50. ISBN 3-598-20394-2.

The IFLA committee which prepared this directory identified 1,090 institutions in fifty countries which offer postgraduate degrees at both the master's and doctoral levels, but are not designated as universities. Questionnaires were mailed to each of these institutions, but only 199 institutions responded with enough information and in time to be included in this publication. Arrangement of entries is by country and each provides information about the availability of theses, access to libraries, and opportunities for reproducing, purchasing, or loaning materials, if any. Access to information can be obtained through institution name, geographic, and subject indexes.

Cabell, David W. E., ed. **Cabell's Directory of Publishing Opportunities in Education.** Beaumont, Tex.: Cabell Publishing, 1985. 490p. $29.95pa. ISBN 0-911753-01-X.

Cabell describes publishing opportunities for prospective authors in 234 educational journals. Information was obtained by questionnaire responses, limiting coverage to those periodicals for which a response was obtained, with some important titles being omitted.

Entries are arranged alphabetically by title and provide coverage of review information including criteria for evaluation, circulation information, guidelines for submitting a manuscript (often reprinted verbatim from the journal), and address to which to send manuscripts.

Although this is a typewritten, offset publication, it has fairly detailed information. It should be used in conjunction with other works of its type for coverage of publishing opportunities in journals excluded here.

Directory of State Education Agencies. Washington, D.C.: Council of Chief State School Officers, 1983- . Annual.

State and national agencies related to education are combined in a single one-volume listing in this convenient directory. Information is arranged geographically (by state) and, for each state, the departments of education and officials associated with it are indicated. Also included are NEA (National Education Association) offices, and Council of Chief State School Officers directors, committees, and networks. A number of U.S. congressional committees are identified.

Hamilton, Malcolm C. **Directory of Educational Statistics: A Guide to Sources**. Ann Arbor, Mich.: Pierian Press, 1974. 71p. $19.50. LC 74-24673. ISBN 0-87650-054-8.

Sources of statistics relevant to education are identified as far back as the 1870 annual report of the U.S. commissioner of education to the early 1970s. Contents include data compiled from general surveys and summaries compiled from state and local areas and cover public and elementary schools, including salaries and other expenditures and revenues; nonpublic schools; institutions of higher education including degrees, enrollment, and salaries; international education; education in Great Britain; and other miscellaneous topics such as education of blacks, native Americans, and adults, and illiteracy in the United States. Title and subject indexes conclude the work.

Although this directory must be supplemented with more current information, it is of use to the researcher requiring sources of historical statistics in education.

Mooney, Edward D. **Directory of Federal Agency Education Data Tapes**. 2d ed. Washington, D.C.: National Center for Education Statistics, 1979. $6.00 (Limited copies available from NCES). NCES 79-426.

Even though this directory has not been updated since 1979, it provides the researcher with improved access to federal education data. When the National Center for Education Statistics was mandated by Congress, it organized the Federal Interagency Consortium of Users of Education Statistics. The thirty member agencies involved compiled these database abstracts, identifying and describing education databases available on computer tape from federal agencies conducting educational research and maintaining data systems. The databases described are available on magnetic tape.

Arrangement of entries is in the following categories: "Elementary and Secondary Education"; "Postsecondary Education" (including postsecondary, higher education, adult continuing, and vocational/technical education); "Demographic, Vital, Health, and Welfare"; "Manpower Supply and Demand"; "Libraries"; and "Federal Outlays for Education." Each entry provides the following information: contact person, date of the collection, frequency, methodology of collection, description of universe or sample size, major variables and purpose of collection, costs, data characteristics, and auxiliary services. Appendix A lists the agencies belonging to the Federal Interagency Consortium; appendix B provides screening criteria for inclusion in the directory. The work is not indexed, so subject access is limited to organizational categories.

National Education Directory. Rockville, Md.: Aspen Systems, 1982- . Annual. LC 82-22199.

This directory provides the names of major organizations and personnel related to the field of education. It identifies congressional committees and committee members; federal agencies; state officials, employees, agencies, and associations; national and regional associations; and honorary and professional associations that have a major relationship to education in general, or a particular aspect of it. Name indexes are provided.

Porter, Joanell. **Education Directory: State Education Agency Officials**. Washington, D.C.: National Center for Education Statistics, 1981. 81p. NCES 82-107.

This annual directory has been compiled from data collected by the National Center for Education Statistics. It provides a list of the principal officials, managers, and supervisors employed by the Department of Education office of each state. Agency officials of the seven vocational-technical education departments are also included. Arrangement of information is alphabetical by state. The official name of each state's education department is listed, followed by its address, telephone number, and indication of time zone. The name of the top official for each state (most commonly the state superintendent of education, superintendent of public instruction, or commissioner of education) is also provided, followed by an alphabetical listing of additional state agency officials, which gives their full names and appropriate titles. An alphabetical "Index of State Education Agency Personnel" concludes this convenient and useful compilation.

STATISTICS SOURCES

The Condition of Education: Statistical Report. Washington, D.C.: U.S. Department of Education, Office of Educational Research and Improvement, Center for Education Statistics; for sale by the Supt. of Docs., Government Printing Offices, 1974- . Annual. $13.00pa. S/N 065-000-00276-1.

This annual statistical summary of American education emphasizes current conditions, issues, trends, and developments at all levels of education from preschool through higher education. Special attention is given to finances, vocational education, and education for special groups. The edition published in 1987 is edited by Joyce D. Stern and Mary Frase Williams.

Special issues have been issued, such as *The Condition of Education for Hispanic Americans* (1980) and *The Condition of Bilingual Education in the Nation: Executive Summary* (1984). Numerous charts interspersed with narrative highlight educational issues of prime interest each year. Typically information covers enrollments, resources, student performance, degrees conferred, teacher supply and demand, and the teacher certification.

Digest of Education Statistics. National Center for Education Statistics. Washington, D.C.: Government Printing Office, 1962- . Annual. $18.00. S/N 065-000-00293-1.

Prior to 1975, when it made a slight name change, the *Digest* was known as *Digest of Educational Statistics*. The purpose of this annual publication is to abstract statistical information about American education on all levels from preschool through graduate programs. The National Center for Education Statistics is a major source of data, but other governmental and nongovernmental surveys and information sources are also used. Statistical information is included on enrollment in all types and levels of education institutions; number of schools, colleges, teachers, and graduates; finances; federal funds for education; employment and income of graduates; and collections, staff, and operating expenses of public school and large academic libraries. In addition, estimates about education of populations in selected countries of the world are also included. A comprehensive subject index directs the user to the appropriate statistical tables. Footnotes to tables give exact date and source of information.

BIOGRAPHICAL SOURCES

Directory of American Scholars. 8th ed. Edited by Jaques Collett Press. New York: Bowker, 1982. 4v. $295.00. LC 57-9125. ISBN 0-8352-1476-1 (set). ISSN 0070-5150.

Biographical sketches of approximately 3,750 U.S. and Canadian scholars actively teaching, researching, and publishing in the humanities are contained in this comprehensive biographical directory first published in 1942. Information contained in the entries was obtained from questionnaires sent to nominees and is arranged as follows: Volume 1, *History* (including art history, musicology, and archaeology); 2, *English, Speech, and Drama*; 3, *Foreign Languages, Linguistics, and Philology*; and 4, *Philosophy, Religion, and Law*. Entries include scholar's name, place and date of birth, date of marriage, number of children, primary discipline(s), education, honorary degrees, past and present professional experience, memberships, honors and awards, research interest, publications, and mailing address.

Kay, Ernest, ed. **International Who's Who in Education**. 3d ed. Cambridge, England: International Biographical Center, 1987. 715p. Price varies. ISBN 0-900332-87-5.

College and university teachers, administrators, and other professionals who are outstanding leaders in education in various countries of the world are included in this international biographical dictionary. Entries are arranged alphabetically, and include the biographee's complete name, date and place of birth, education, and earned degrees, professional experience and/or outstanding leadership roles, current position, and publications, if any. Previous editions were entitled *Who's Who in Education*.

Nauman, Ann K. **A Biographical Handbook of Education: Five Hundred Contributors to the Field**. New York: Irvington, 1985. 237p. $14.95pa. LC 82-6528. ISBN 0-8290-0722-9.

This collection of biographical sketches covers educators from all periods of history, including the classic Plato and Aristotle and such contemporaries as Illich, McLuhan, Broudy, Gagne, and Mager. Individuals were included because of their "reputation as a scholar and contributor to the overall body of knowledge" (p. vii). Some significant omissions, among others, include names such as those of Lawrence Cremin, John Goodlad, and Maxine Greene.

Entries are typically about 100 words in length and are arranged in strict alphabetical order. Brief lists of further references on the biographer conclude each sketch. In spite of some questions about criteria for selection and inclusion, this biographical dictionary is a relatively up-to-date tool serving as a place to start in compiling biographical information in the field of education.

Ohles, John F., ed. **Biographical Dictionary of American Educators**. 2d ed. Westport, Conn.: Greenwood, 1978. 3v. $150.00. LC 77-84750. ISBN 0-8371-9893-3.

Biographical sketches of 1,665 influential American educators from colonial days to America's bicentennial were prepared by Ohles and 465 other contributors primarily from the field of education. Identifying biographees for inclusion was done by consulting *Leaders in Education* (5th ed., 1974) and other biographical reference sources and by requesting state departments of education, historical societies, major educational and professional associations, and academic institutions to nominate eminent educators.

Sketches are arranged alphabetically and vary in length depending on the number of institutions attended by the subject, positions held, publications, and affiliations with professional associations. Information provided in each sketch includes place and date of birth, names of parents, spouse and date of marriage, number of children and names of eminent ones, date and place of death.

Since one of the criteria for inclusion was an age requirement where the educator had to be age 60, retired, or deceased as of January 1, 1975, this work is limited with respect to current prominent educators; but the editor made an effort to represent women and minority educators, and the fairly lengthy sketches (1-1½ pages) provide a substantial amount of information for historical biographers and researchers.

Princetonians 1776-1783: A Biographical Dictionary. Edited by Richard A. Harrison. Princeton, N.J.: Princeton University Press, 1981. 576p. $58.00. LC 80-7526. ISBN 0-69105-33607.

This series of biographical dictionaries of Princetonians provides a record of the alumni of the College of New Jersey from the classes of 1748 to 1783. (The first volume, by James McLachlan, covers the years 1748 to 1776 (1976) and the second and third, both by Richard A. Harrison, cover the years 1769 to 1775 (1980) and 1776 to 1783 (1981).

The following facts are incorporated into each biographical narrative: place and date of birth, father's name, mother's maiden name, date entered and left college, awards and organizations, further education and/or degrees, positions held, military service, political and governmental activities, religious affiliation, wife's (wives') maiden name(s), date of marriage(s), children, date and place of death, value of estate, slaves held, and publications. Sources of data on which the biographical sketch was prepared are also indicated, as are the initials of the biographer, if other than the book author.

These biographical sketches were compiled from various historical records of the school, including the personal files of former president, Aaron Burr, and many other well-known figures. Although some of the information overlaps with that found in *Dictionary of American Biography* and other similar sources, it provides much unique information about higher education in the eighteenth century, in general, and at Princeton, in particular.

Who's Who among American High School Students: Honoring Tomorrow's Leaders Today. 21st ed. Lake Forest, Ill.: Educational Communications, 1986-1987. 12v. $28.50/vol. LC 68-43796. ISBN 0-930315-27-8 (set).

High school juniors and seniors who are leaders in their schools, and who participated in extracurricular activities while maintaining excellent academic records, are included in this biographical reference source. Students were nominated by their schools and then selected by an external advisory council.

Introductory material provides high school students with advice on preparing for the SAT exam, selecting a major for college study, and how to go about securing financial aid. One section is devoted to identifying scholarship winners. Biographical entries list student's name, school and address, class rank, data related to academic and extracurricular achievements, and proposed college major and college.

Who's Who in America College Alumni Directory. Chicago: Marquis Who's Who, 1983. 1,188p. $375.00 ISBN 0-8379-6201-3.

This directory was compiled from the forty-second edition of the online edition of *Who's Who in America*. It lists 1,700 colleges and universities from countries all over the world, providing they had been included in the education section of at least five *Who's Who* biographees. So, in actuality, many biographees mention schools they attended, or from which they received an honorary degree, but from which they did not, in fact, graduate.

ONLINE DATABASES IN EDUCATION

Directories

Data Base Directory (DBD). Edited by Barbara Miller. White Plains, N.Y.: Knowledge Industry Publications, 1984- . Semiannual. $215.00. ISSN 0749-6680.

This directory, while international in scope, includes "all identified databases that are technically accessible in North America" (p. vii). According to the editors, over 35 percent of the listings are produced outside of the United States. The latest edition extends the coverage to over 3,000 individual files. Major database services which include databases that can be searched individually are described collectively and by individual database components. The database is updated monthly through *Data Base Alert*. It is available online through BRS.

Encyclopedia of Information Systems and Services. 7th ed. Edited by Amy F. Lucas and Kathleen Young Marcaccio. Detroit: Gale, 1987. 3v. $185.00(v.1); $210.00(v.2); $370.00(v.3). LC 78-14575. ISBN 0-81032492X (set).

Subtitled *A Guide to Information Storage and Retrieval Services, Data Base Producers and Publishers, Online Vendors, Computer Service Companies, Computerized Retrieval Systems, Micrographic Firms, Libraries, Government Agencies, Networks and Consortia, Information Centers, Data Banks, Clearinghouses, Research Centers, Associations, and Consultants*, this encyclopedic work contains recorded information from some form of raw numeric or graphic data to bibliographic citations; much of the material is available by online computer. Arrangement is alphabetical by parent organization, and each entry provides name, address and telephone, data, head of unit, staff, related organizations, description of system or services, scope and/or subject matter, input sources, holdings and storage media, publications, and products and services. A series of eighteen indexes, including a subject index, facilitates access to information. Over twenty headings are devoted to education.

Hall, James L., and Marjorie J. Brown. **Online Bibliographic Databases: A Directory and Sourcebook.** 4th ed. London, Aslib; distr., Detroit: Gale, 1986. 509p. $95.00. ISBN 0-8103-2080-0.

A total of 179 major databases are described in this directory to online resources. Entries provide information on the database name, supplier, subjects covered, corresponding print works, sample online record, time span of database, type of database (bibliographic, directory, full text, etc.); number of records; frequency of updating; documentation; and services by which it is available.

Lesko Matthew. **The Computer Data and Data Base Source Book.** New York: Avon Books, 1984. 768p. $14.95. LC 84-45219. ISBN 0-380-36942-X.

Over 1,000 databases on a wide variety of subjects are described, ranging from public and governmental databases to commercial ones that are international in scope. Many of the public databases include those related to education and may be accessed free of charge. Entries are arranged in subject categories. Topics under education include "Adult and Continuing Education," "Bilingual Education," "Community and Junior Colleges," "Educational Trends and Projections," "Elementary and Secondary Education," and "International Education." Information provided includes subject, source, contents, producer, data systems containing the data files, and hourly cost of connect time.

Databases

A-V ONLINE. Albuquerque, N.M.: Access Innovations, Inc., 1978- . Continuous updates.
DIALOG (file #416); $1.17/min. plus $8.00-$11.00/hr. telecommunications cost.

This major database to educational audiovisual materials covers information on topics
from preschool to postgraduate. Materials can also be retrieved by media formats: 16mm
films, 35mm filmstrips, overhead transparencies; videotapes and cassettes; audio
recordings; slides; and 8mm motion picture cartridges. A series of annual print tools
known as the *NICEM Indexes* are also prepared from this database.

AVLine Audiovisuals Online. Bethesda, Md.: National Library of Medicine MEDLARS,
U.S. Dept. of Health and Human Services, 1975- . Weekly updates. MEDLARS;
$7.50/hr. prime time; $4.50/hr. non-prime time.

Over 14,800 mediated instructional packages in the various health sciences can be
identified in this bibliographic/reference database. Some of the older records (1975-1982)
contain information about audience level, reviewer's ratings, and instructional design.
About 1,200 new records are added per year. Available through Tymnet, Telenet, and
direct dial.

Bilingual Education Bibliographic Abstracts. Arlington, Va.: National Clearinghouse
for Bilingual Education (NCEB), InterAmerica Research Associates, 1975- . Monthly
updates. BRS (BEBA); $16.00-$35.00/hr. plus $10.00 royalty fee and $3.00-$9.00/hr.
telecommunication cost.

Citations and abstracts related to bilingual education of minority children are
available in this bibliographic database. Also covers the history of bilingual education and
different categories of bilingual students, such as students in special education and vocational education. Other topics are language testing and evaluation, international education, English as a second language, and bilingual education for adults. This database is
available through Telenet, Tymnet, and direct dial.

College Entrance Examination Board (CEEB). New York: College Board, 1975- . Semiannual updates. CompuServe; $12.50-$15.00/hr. prime time; $6.00-$12.50/hr. non-
prime time.

Information available from print reference sources, *The College Handbook* and *The
College Cost Book*, is compiled from this online database providing data for prospective
college students covering admissions, credit-by-exam possibilities, and continuing education. Articles, bibliography, glossary of terms, and an interactive program, "Estimating
Your Eligibility," are available for determining college costs and required financial
resources. Records can be accessed through Telenet, Tymnet, CompuServe, and direct dial.

College Press Service (CPS): National Campus Classifieds. Denver, Colo.: College Press
Service, Interrobang, Inc., 1983- . Weekly updates. CompuServe, $12.50-$15.00/hr.
prime time; $6.00-$12.50/hr. non-prime time.

National trends, major developments, and news items related to students, administration, legislation, and court decisions that affect higher education are covered in this full-
text database. Records include government documents and reports, newspaper articles,
and periodicals, and are available through Telenet, Tymnet, CompuServe, direct dial, or
NewsNet subscription.

Current Index to Journals in Education (CIJE). Bethesda, Md.: ERIC Processing & Reference Facility, Educational Resources Information Center (ERIC), 1969- . Monthly updates. DIALOG; $4.50/min. plus $8.00-$11.00/hr. telecommunication cost; BRS (ERIC); $16.00-$35.00/hr. plus $3.00-$9.00/hr. telecommunication cost.

ERIC is a national database sponsored by the U.S. Department of Education from which *CIJE* is a subset. The monthly periodical index by the same name is compiled from this source. It provides bibliographic citations to education sources covering all levels from preschool to postgraduate. A wide range of areas of education and subjects related to it are covered, including, for example, all areas of the curriculum, special education, vocational education, bilingual education, adult education, child development, learning, teaching, guidance and counseling, teacher education, and other topics covered in over 750 periodicals related to education. It is available through Tymnet, Telenet, Dialnet, and direct dial.

D&B: Dun's Electronic Directory of Education. Mountain Lakes, N.J.: Dun's Marketing Services, 1984- . Semiannual updates. DIALOG (file #511); $1.00/min. plus $8.00-$11.00/hr. telecommunication cost.

This database contains directory-type demographic information on colleges and universities and public libraries in the United States. It covers school enrollments, budgets, names of administrators, counselors and librarians, and microcomputer facilities. Files are more current and complete than the corresponding print source, *CIC School Directories*, which provide demographic data and statistics about schools in each state. It is accessed through Tymnet, Telenet, and Dialnet.

Education Daily Online. Arlington, Va.: Capitol Publications, 1988- . Daily updates. Special Net; $13.00/hr. prime time; $7.00/hr. non-prime time; $200.00/yr. subscription fee.

Federal education policy, congressional activities, and critical court cases and decisions are covered in this abbreviated online version of *Education Daily*. Records include information from press conferences, press releases, and government publications, including congressional hearings. Particular attention is given to federally funded projects from the proposal requesting funds to the final appropriations bill. This database is updated daily and back issues for approximately one month may be retrieved. It is accessed through Telenet.

Education Index. New York: H. W. Wilson, 1983- . Twice weekly updates. WILSONLINE; $25.00-$40.00/hr. plus $8.00/hr. telecommunication cost; $300.00-$2,400.00/yr. subscription fee.

Over 350 major international educational periodicals in the English language are covered in this major bibliographic database. The print version has been available since 1929; online sources input from September 1983 on. All levels of education and all aspects of it are covered, including curricular subjects, teaching and teacher education, special education, vocation education, adult education, multicultural and bilingual education, classroom computing, school prayer, literacy, and federal funding. The database may be accessed by subject, author, title, language, year of publication, title of periodical, type of article, among other ways. Records are very current; it is accessed through Telenet and Tymnet.

Educational Research Forum (ED R&D). Washington, D.C.: American Educational Research Association, 1983- . Updated as files submitted. CompuServe; $12.50-$22.50/hr. prime time; $6.00-$19.00/hr. non-prime time.

This AERA database provides access to user-submitted conference papers and articles, article abstracts from the various AERA journals, and reviews of statistical software programs for analyzing research data. Topics cover a wide range of subjects related to education, special education, learning and other aspects of educational psychology, and use of microcomputers for both administrative and instructional purposes. It is accessed through Tymnet, Telenet, Datapac, and CompuServe.

Educational Testing Service Test Collection Database (ETSF). Princeton, N.J.: Educational Testing Service, 1950- . Quarterly updates. BRS (ETSF); $16.00-$35.00/hr. plus $3.00-$9.00/hr. telecommunication cost.

This bibliographic database includes descriptions of tests that measure achievement, aptitude, attitudes and personal interests, personality, sensory-motor skills, and vocational (occupational) affinity. Tests are, for the most part, published in the United States; others are from England, Canada, and Australia. In addition to formally administered tests, the database includes diagnostic and assessment evaluation instruments and questionnaires. It is accessed through Telenet, Tymnet, and direct dial.

The Electric Pages. Austin, Tex.: National Information Systems, 1983- . Daily updates. National Information Systems; $15.00/hr. plus $12.00/hr. telecommunication cost prime time; $6.00/hr. non-prime time.

This online database provides electronic mail service, electronic conference capabilities, directory information, bibliographic information, and abstracts of books, theses and dissertations, and articles and newsletters about services and resources of interest to educators. The Texas Computer Education Association, sponsored by Apple Computer, also contributes data. The corresponding print source is *The Electric Pages Newsletter*, which describes the contents of the databases and available services. The database is accessed through direct dial (Southwestern Bell).

EPIE On-Line. Water Mill, N.Y.: EPIE Institute, 1980- . Bimonthly updates. CompuServe; $12.50-$22.50/hr. prime time; $6.00-$19.00/hr. non-prime time.

Microcomputer software packages used in educational settings (for both management and instructional purposes) are described. Information includes program or package name, subject classification, suggested grade level usage, program type, function, components, network version, whether or not program is copy protected, required hardware configuration, producer and/or distributor, and sources of evaluative reviews and review abstracts. Policies regarding sales, backups, and warranties are also indicated. It includes information provided in *TESS: The Educational Software Selector* and various EPIE publications, *EPIE Micro-PRO/FILES*, and *EPIEgram*. The database is accessed through Telenet, Tymnet, and direct dial.

EUDISED R&D. Strasbourg, France: Council of Europe, 1976- . Quarterly updates. ESA-IRS; AU $61/hr. plus ca. AU $10/hr. telecommunication cost.

Abstracts to unpublished ongoing educational research projects conducted in the European countries of Austria, Belgium, Cyprus, Denmark, Finland, France, Federal Republic of Germany, Greece, Ireland, Italy, Luxembourg, Netherlands, Norway, Portugal, Spain, Sweden, Switzerland, Great Britain, and Yugoslavia are available in this bibliographic database. Data are contributed by the individual countries. Records can be accessed by keywords in a multilingual thesaurus. Access is possible through Tymnet, Datapac, Telex, Itapac, Esanet, PSS, and Transpac.

Exceptional Child Education Resources. Reston, Va.: Council for Exceptional Children, 1966-1986. BRS (ECER); $16.00-$35.00/hr. plus $3.00-$9.00/hr. telecommunication cost; DIALOG (file #54); $.58/min. plus $8.00-$11.00/hr. telecommunication cost.

The Council for Exceptional Children maintains this bibliographic database to literature on all aspects of special education. It publishes, in print form, *Exceptional Child Education Resources*. Materials covered include books, monographs, theses and dissertations, journal articles, government documents, and conference proceedings. Subject access is possible using subject headings from the *ERIC Thesaurus*. The database covers records for the twenty-one years from 1966 to 1986. It is accessed through Telenet, Tymnet, Dialnet, and direct dial.

GRADLINE. Princeton, N.J.: Peterson's Guides, 1976- . Annual updates. DIALOG; $1.00/min. plus $8.00-$11.00/hr. telecommunication cost.

Peterson's Guides maintains an extensive and comprehensive database of information related to programs and services available in accredited colleges and universities in the United States and Canada. Institutional profiles provide demographic information and descriptions of academic offerings at the graduate level. Three types of records can be accessed: institution, unit, and directory. Online access to information is provided in the five volumes that are annual guides to graduate study by Peterson's Guides. The corresponding print source is *Peterson's Graduate and Professional Programs: An Overview*. Records are updated every academic year; accessed through Telenet, Tymnet, Dialnet, and direct dial.

Guidance Information System (GIS). Hanover, N.H.: Houghton Mifflin, 1969- . Semi-annual updates. Houghton Mifflin Co., TSC Div.; $2,500.00 annual lease.

Information in full-text form is available in six files related to career education and guidance; occupations (over 1,000); two-year colleges (1,798); four-year colleges (1,775); graduate and professional schools (1,550); military service occupations (113); and financial aid (600). Information is obtained from statistics provided by the government and from the institutions and associations themselves. It is accessed through Telenet and direct dial.

Mental Measurements Yearbook (MMYD). Lincoln, Nebr.: Buros Institute of Mental Measurements, University of Nebraska, 1974- . Monthly updates. BRS (MMYD); $16.00-$35.00/hr. plus $3.00-$9.00/hr. telecommunication cost.

Reviews of educational tests and measurement instruments published in the English language are available in this online version of Buros' *Mental Measurements Yearbook* (8th and 9th eds.). Records cover tests related to mental ability or intelligence, achievement, proficiency in reading, language, science, mathematics, personality, and other subject-oriented and sociometric assessment. It is accessed through Telenet and Tymnet.

Microcomputers in Education. Darien, Conn.: Microcomputers in Education, 1986- . Monthly updates. NewsNet; $48.00/hr.; $15.00/mo. subscription fee.

New software products, techniques, and strategies for using microcomputers in instruction are covered in this relatively new online database. It includes records from 1986 to the present and monthly updates that advise NewsNet subscribers of public domain software useful for classroom instruction.

Peterson's College Database. Princeton, N.J.: Peterson's Guides, 1976- . Annual updates. BRS (PETE); $16.00-$35.00/hr. plus $3.00-$9.00/hr. telecommunication cost; DIALOG; $.90/min. plus $8.00-$11.00/hr. telecommunication cost.

This Peterson's Guides database provides access to information about accredited undergraduate colleges and universities. It corresponds to printed volumes published by Peterson's Guides. School descriptions can be retrieved by type or other specific characteristics and provide data on demographic information, faculty, majors offered, selectivity and admissions requirements, tuition, fees, and housing. It is accessed through Telenet, Tymnet, Dialnet, and direct dial from BRS and DIALOG.

Resources in Computer Education (RICE). Portland, Oreg.: Computer Technology Program, Northwest Regional Educational Lab, 1979- . Quarterly updates. BRS (RICE); $16.00-$35.00/hr. plus $3.00-$9.00/hr. telecommunication cost.

Descriptive and evaluative information about computer software programs appropriate for use in elementary and secondary school classrooms is available in this bibliographic database. Information provided includes program name, producer, price, hardware and software requirements, and ordering information. Database records can be accessed through Telenet, Tymnet, and direct dial.

Resources in Education (RIE). Bethesda, Md.: ERIC Processing & Reference Facility, Educational Resources Information Center (ERIC), ORI, Information Systems Division, 1966- . Monthly updates. DIALOG; $.50/min. plus $8.00-$11.00/hr. telecommunication cost.

This section of the comprehensive ERIC database provides, for the most part, bibliographic coverage of unpublished materials that are hard to find in *Education Index* or other indexing periodicals. They include conference proceedings, reports of research studies, curriculum materials, bibliographies, program descriptions and evaluations, and government documents, as well as books, theses, and dissertations. A large share of the online database is printed as a monthly abstracting journal, *Resources in Education (RIE)*. The database covers all education subjects and, although American education is emphasized, is international in content.

Resources in Vocational Education (RIVE). Columbus, Ohio: National Center for Research in Vocational Education, 1978- . Quarterly updates. BRS (RIVE); $16.00-$35.00/hr. plus $3.00-$9.00/hr. telecommunication cost.

Descriptions of research studies recently completed and research in progress are described in this database which provides bibliographic information related to vocational education. It also contains curriculum development projects, descriptions of career education projects administered by state and federal agencies, and by-products of these projects. It is accessed through Telenet, Tymnet, and direct dial.

VOC Education Curriculum Materials (VECM). Columbus, Ohio: National Center for Research in Vocational Education, Ohio State University, 1979- . Quarterly. BRS (*VECM*); $16.00-$35.00/hr. plus $3.00-$9.00/hr. telecommunication cost.

Access to information about print and nonprint materials appropriate for use in vocational education curricula is provided in this bibliographic database. Abstracts/summaries and directory information (contact names, addresses, availability) are also provided. It is available through Telenet, Tymnet, and direct dial.

5
Educational Foundations (Historical, Philosophical, and Psychological) Reference Sources

HISTORY

General Works

Brubacher, John Seiler, and Willis Rudy. **Higher Education in Transition: A History of American Colleges and Universities, 1636-1976**. 3d ed. New York: Harper & Row, 1976. 536p. $32.45. LC 75-6331. ISBN 0-06-010548-8.

Brubacher and Rudy have chronicled the evolution of higher education in America for a period of nearly three-and-one-half centuries. The book is divided into five sections. Part 1 is concerned with the beginnings of the colonial colleges, their organization and administration, and early student life. Part 2 deals with nineteenth-century innovations in the colonial college and early methods of instruction. Part 3 covers the rise of universities, including state schools, graduate schools, professional education, and the role of the federal government in higher education. Part 4 deals with issues related to secondary and postsecondary curricula, methods, philosophy; and part 5 is a summary of the distinguishing features of American higher education, including its democratization, broad scope, dedication to community service, diversity, voluntary setting of standards, and corporate structure.

Almost 100 pages of reference notes, a bibliography of American college and university histories published between 1871 and the 1970s, and an index conclude the work.

Cremin, Lawrence. **American Education: The National Experience, 1783-1896. Vol. II**. New York: Harper & Row, 1982. 607p. $34.50; $11.50pa. LC 79-3387. ISBN 0-06-090921-8pa.; 0-06-010912-2.

Lawrence Cremin is a well-known scholar of American educational history. This volume is a continuation of a previous one, *The Colonial Experience, 1607-1783* (Harper & Row, 1970) in which Cremin traced the origins of American education to the European Renaissance, with particular emphasis on the transplanting of educational institutions from the old world to the new. He describes how these European systems and traditions were modified under new social and economic conditions and the role of the new knowledge that developed in a cohesive new society. Volume 2 provides a comprehensive portrayal of American education from the American Revolution through the first 100 years of the new nation. A third volume is planned to bring this major history up-to-date.

Bibliographies

Beach, Mark, comp. **A Subject Bibliography of the History of American Higher Education**. Westport, Conn.: Greenwood, 1984. 165p. $29.95. LC 83-22565. ISBN 0-313-23276-8.

Beach has compiled 1,325 citations to major books, articles, and dissertations in a topical arrangement of sources of information related to the history of education in America. As a former professor of history and education, Beach would have been well qualified to provide annotations for entries, which he did not — a factor that limits the usefulness of a work that represents one of the most current listings of its kind available. Beach has also omitted some of the subtitles to dissertations which are often quite self-explanatory, and especially useful when annotations are not included. He has only included recent references to works related to the history of particular American colleges and universities, as these were covered in his earlier publication, *A Bibliographic Guide to American Colleges and Universities from Colonial Times to the Present* (Greenwood, 1975). In spite of these limitations, Beach's work is a useful compilation and fills a gap in the bibliographic literature on the topic.

Other related bibliographies on the history of education in America include Cordasco, Alloway, and Friedman's *The History of American Education: A Guide to Information Sources* (Gale, 1979); *An International List of Articles on the History of Education Published in Non-Educational Serials, 1965-1974* by Joseph M. McCarthy (Garland, 1977); *The Rise of American Education: An Annotated Bibliography* by Joe Park (Northwestern University Press, 1965); and *The Progressive Education Movement: An Annotated Bibliography* by Mariann P. Winick (Garland, 1978).

Beauchamp, Edward R. **Dissertations in the History of Education 1970-1980**. Metuchen, N.J.: Scarecrow Press, 1984. 259p. $24.00. LC 84-14125. ISBN 0-8108-1742-X.

Beauchamp personally searched *Dissertations Abstracts International* from 1970 to 1980 to identify titles in any way related to the history of education. Although *DAI* has a section on history, over 50 percent of the titles included here were listed under other categories, such as American studies, sociology, political science, literature, and science. According to the author, computer searches were also inadequate because titles did not contain the key words necessary to retrieve them.

Arrangement of entries is primarily geographical as each of the eight chapters covers the history of education in a specific country or region: United States, Canada, Europe, Asia, Africa, Middle East, Latin America, and Australasia. Within these chapters, materials are further subdivided by topic and/or chronological events. Information in each entry includes author, title, degree, institution, degree date, pages, *DAI* volume and number, *DAI* date, page number, and order number. Since annotations are not included, the abstract in *DAI* must be consulted to determine whether the user would find a particular title pertinent.

Cordasco, Francesco, and William W. Brickman, eds. **A Bibliography of American Educational History: An Annotated and Classified Guide**. New York: AMS Press, 1975. 394p. $47.50. LC 74-29140. ISBN 0-404-12661-8.

Some 3,000 books and periodicals related to the history of American education, ranging from early compilations to those of the early 1970s, are described in this comprehensive list of general and specialized materials. Entries are arranged in three parts; part 1 is "Bibliographies, Source Collections, Historiography and Comprehensive Histories."

Part 2, "Subject Fields and Miscellaneous," includes chapters on elementary, secondary, and vocational education; higher education; instructional materials; teaching; church, state, and education; the federal government; the education of women; biographies of American educators; foreign influences; and contemporary issues. Part 3, "Chronological Tableaux," lists sources that are particularly related to a particular time in American history from the seventeenth into the twentieth century. Because of the nature of these various subdivisions, some titles will be listed more than once as they fit more than one category.

Entries are, for the most part, quite briefly annotated; some are not annotated at all. An author index is provided; subject access is available only through the categorical chapter subdivisions, a serious limitation to the usefulness of this work. For example, if one wished to examine the impact of Jean Piaget on American education, one would have to consult a section entitled, "Individual and Specific Influences" under the chapter on foreign influences and read through a list. (The latter chapter includes references on Jane Addams, Thomas Jefferson, George Peabody, etc. — names usually not traced under "foreign influences.") This work needs updating (particularly sections such as "Contemporary Issues") but the sources on historical information would be very valuable to the educational researcher and/or historian.

King, Cornelia S., comp. **American Education 1672-1860: Printed Works in the Collections of the American Philosophical Society, the Historical Society of Pennsylvania, the Library Company of Philadelphia**. New York: Garland, 1984. 354p. (Americana to 1860, Vol. 3). $64.50. LC 83-49301. ISBN 0-8240-8966-9.

Educational historians would be interested in this catalog of print materials on American education from three major collections that document American history and thought, namely those of the American Philosophical Society, the Historical Society of Pennsylvania, and the Library Company of Philadelphia. Coverage is given to all aspects of education, both formal and informal, and includes books; serials; publications of professional educational associations, educational institutions and organizations; speeches and public addresses. Excluded are textbooks, dissertations, library catalogs, and materials on professional schools, including divinity and theological schools.

Entries are arranged alphabetically by author; the appendix lists institutions of public education, schools and orphan houses, colleges and universities, educational societies and conventions — all subdivided by geographic location. Early special education attempts for the blind, deaf, and mentally retarded are also documented.

Sedlak, Michael W., and Timothy Walch, eds. **American Educational History: A Guide to Information Sources**. Detroit: Gale, 1981. 265p. (American Government and History Information Guide Series, Vol. 10; Gale Information Library). $65.00. LC 80-19646. ISBN 0-8103-1478-9.

Books, articles, and dissertations on the history of American education are included in this bibliography. Entries are arranged in nine sections: "American Educational Development (1632-1965)," "Pedagogy," "Higher Education," "Outsiders," "Race and Education," "Families and Delinquents," "Cities," "Schooling and the Workplace," and "Guides to Further Research." Each chapter begins with an introductory historiographic essay. Most entries are briefly annotated and access to titles is available in both subject and author indexes.

Directories

Seybolt, Robert Francis. **The Private Schools of Colonial Boston**. Salem, N.H.: Ayer Co., 1935; reprinted Westport, Conn.: Greenwood, 1970. 106p. (American Education: Its Men, Institutions and Ideas, Series 1). $9.00. LC 70-100838. ISBN 0-405-01468-6.

Educational historians would be interested in this list of private schools of the seventeenth century. Arranged chronologically, this work lists schools, teachers, and subjects. School announcements of the eighteenth century are also included. Chapter titles are "The Schools," "Masters and Ushers of the Grammar Schools," "Masters and Ushers of the Writing Schools," "Appointments and Qualifications," "Support," "Salaries and Allowances," "Supervision," and "Studies." A series of appendixes list other information related to the early history of education in America. A related title is *Source Studies in American Colonial Education: The Private School* (Arno Press, 1971) also by Robert Seybolt.

Sourcebooks

Cohen, Sol, ed. **Education in the United States: A Documentary History**. Westport, Conn.: Greenwood, 1974. 5v. $225.00. LC 73-3099. ISSN 0-313-20141-2.

This five-volume reference work is a comprehensive compilation of over 1,300 of the most significant documents in the history of American education from the beginning of the sixteenth century until 1973. The work is arranged in three books spread over five volumes. Book 1 is *The Planting, 1607-1789*. Book 2 is *The Shaping of American Education, 1789-1895*, and book 3, *The Transformation of American Education, 1895-1973*. The documents consist of letters, legislation, essays, and reports which have been arranged chronologically within subject chapters. A comprehensive bibliographic citation for each document is also provided. Some of the themes include political issues, outstanding educators, major reforms and movements, education for minority and multicultural groups, and the history of teaching. Any student of the broad educational issues and movements in education would want to consult this documentary history.

PHILOSOPHY

Bibliographies

Blyth, Dale A., and Elizabeth Leuder Karnes. **Philosophy, Policies and Programs for Early Adolescent Education: An Annotated Bibliography**. Westport, Conn.: Greenwood, 1981. 789p. $55.00. LC 81-4237. ISBN 0-313-22687-3.

Books, articles, dissertations, and reports related to early adolescent education are arranged alphabetically by author in twelve chapters, each of which represents an issue central to the field. Topics covered include philosophy and theory, prescriptions and descriptions of middle schools and junior high schools, guidance programs, school design and renovation, internal organization of schools, development and implementation of curriculum, cocurricular and extracurricular activities, school policy, research, teacher training, and discipline and behavior problems. Annotations vary from one sentence to one-half page in length, and are primarily a summary of contents, rather than a critical evaluation of the title. Author and subject indexes are provided.

Boydston, Jo Ann, and Kathleen Poulos. **Checklist of Writings about John Dewey, 1887-1977**. 2d ed. Carbondale, Ill.: Southern Illinois University Press, 1978. 488p. $19.95. LC 77-17136. ISBN 0-8093-0842-8.

This extensive checklist of writings related to John Dewey includes published and unpublished works about Dewey himself as well as reviews of Dewey's works and reviews of works about Dewey. The authors have used basic reference sources, including M. H. Thomas's *John Dewey: A Centennial Bibliography* (University of Chicago Press, 1962) and information about unpublished materials from librarians and readers of *The Dewey Newsletter*. The work covers eight-five years.

Who's Who entries and encyclopedia articles have not been included and only newspaper and news magazine articles accessible through major indexes are listed. Rather than integrate the additional entries of the enlarged second edition into the main body of the work, the first 294 pages are a repeat of the first edition published in 1974. The three-page agenda section was expanded to a fifty-five-page supplement to the first edition. This inconvenience is minor in comparison to the assistance that this guide supplies to the student, scholar, or researcher interested in this major name and influence in American education.

Leming, James S. **Contemporary Approaches to Moral Education: An Annotated Bibliography and Guide to Research**. New York: Garland, 1983. 451p. $53.00. LC 81-48422. ISBN 0-8240-9389-5.

The renewed interest in moral education and the plethora of writing on the subject in the late 1970s make this a timely reference tool for teachers and teacher educators. The intent of this bibliography, according to the compiler, is to present the practical aspects of the moral education movement. Most of the sources were published after 1965, with the exception of a few seminal works. It is not a guide to moral education curriculum materials, although, when consulting the subject index under that topic, the user can find items that would lead to sources of curriculum materials.

Entries are numbered and are arranged alphabetically by author under broad topic areas, such as "General Analyses, Issues and Approaches"; "Values Clarification"; "Humanistic/Affective Education"; and "Directive Moral Education." In addition, some chapters treat moral education in subject areas and others list materials that compare various approaches to it. This bibliography presents very thorough coverage of the practice of moral education, including titles of special editions and sections of periodical literature on the topic. While the bibliographic information is complete, including ERIC numbers when appropriate, the annotations are brief, averaging about twenty-five words in length. Author and subject indexes are provided.

The author has also compiled *Foundations of Moral Education: An Annotated Bibliography* (Greenwood, 1983).

Simpson, Elizabeth Leonie. **Humanistic Education: An Interpretation**, with Gray, Mary Anne. *A Comprehensive Annotated Bibliography of Humanistic Education*. Cambridge, Mass.: Ballinger, 1976. 328p. LC 76-15280. ISBN 0-88410-168-1.

This report to the Ford Foundation is a state-of-the-art report on humanistic education in the United States. The initial chapters define the movement and character-istics of humanistic teacher training and curriculum development. The second part is an annotated bibliography of over 1,000 reference books, monographs, articles, and reports on various aspects of humanistic education. Materials are arranged first by broad subject, and then alphabetically by author under format divisions. Some of the subjects covered include rationale, theory, research reports related to curriculum, teacher-training programs, student and teacher attitudes, instructional technology, and evaluation and measurement. Because of the major sociological impact of humanism in America from the 1960s on, this work, though dated, should not be ignored by educational philosophers and historians.

PSYCHOLOGY

General Works

Glaser, Robert, ed. **Advances in Instructional Psychology**. V.3. Hillsdale, N.J.: Lawrence Erlbaum, 1987. 357p. $29.95. ISBN 0-89859-706-4.

Current research in instructional psychology, a relatively new subfield in education, is presented in a series of articles. Various learning theories and their applications are represented, and research studies cover a variety of developmental aspects of learning and instruction. The first volume, also edited by Glaser, was published four years prior to this one (Lawrence Erlbaum, 1978).

Modgil, Sohan, and Celia Modgil. **Piagetian Research: Compilation and Commentary**. Windsor, England: NFER Publishing; distr., Atlantic Highlands, N.J. Humanities Press, 1976. 8v. $124.00/set. LC 76-378105. ISBN 0-85633-089-2.

These eight volumes provide a unique compilation of Piagetian research studies that include published and unpublished pieces of research, including heavy use of theses and articles in fifteen major aspects of Piaget's work. Each of the individual volumes address one or two main areas with an integrated review of the range of studies with abstracts of researches following in alphabetical order. Individual volumes were all published in 1976: (V.1, Pt.1) *Jean Piaget, An Appreciation—Piaget's Major Works;* (Pt.2) *The Theory of Cognitive Development*; Pt.3 *Sensory Motor Intelligence*; (V.2, Pt.1) *Experimental Validation of Conservation*; (Pt.2) *The Child's Concept of Space*; (V.3, Pt.1) *The Early Growth of Logic*; (Pt.2) *The Construction of Formal Operational Structures*; (V.4, Pt.1) *School Curriculum*; (Pt.2) *Test Development*; (V.5, Pt.1) *Personality, Socialization and Emotionality*; (Pt.2) *Reasoning among Handicapped Children*; (V.6) *The Cognitive-Development Approach to Morality*; (V.7) *Training Techniques*; and (V.8) *Cross-Cultural Studies*.

In spite of the fact that the research conducted by Swiss psychologist Jean Piaget has had a major influence on American education, in general, and teacher education, in particular, the findings and conclusions of much of his research have been misinterpreted, misrepresented, or not clearly understood by teachers, students, administrators, and scholars conducting educational research.

Bibliographies

Baatz, Olga K., and Charles Albert Baatz. **The Psychological Foundations of Education**. Detroit: Gale, 1981. 440p. $65.00. LC 81-2832. ISBN 0-8103-1467-3.

This husband-and-wife team compiled an annotated bibliography of sources related to the psychological foundations of education including moral, emotional, aesthetic, and self-actualization considerations. Selection of materials is not inclusive or systematic, but is a start at gaining bibliographic control of a field with some relatively new approaches and areas of focus. Emphasis is on research that studies "the education of human beings as free persons" (p. 12) as opposed to animal or experimental research.

All items are in English. Arrangement of books and articles is in six chapters, each devoted to a broad subject category: "Education and Psychology," "Intellectual Education," "Moral Education," "Affective Education," "Poetic (Aesthetic) Education," and "The Acting Person." Each chapter lists resources on the structure and design of the curriculum, teaching and learning processes and methods, teacher education and preparation, and other topics. Information is inconsistent, as only about 50 percent of the titles have a descriptive annotation. Access is convenient through author, title, and subject indexes. The excellent indexing, fairly comprehensive coverage (over 3,000 entries) and unique content make this a useful guide for academic libraries, scholars, and researchers in the field.

A related title by the same author is *The Philosophy of Education: A Guide to Information Sources* (Gale, 1980).

Handbooks and Yearbooks

Reynolds, Cecil R., and Terry B. Gutkin, eds. **The Handbook of School Psychology**. New York: Wiley, 1982. xviii, 1,284, 30p. $61.95. LC 81-3375. ISBN 0-471-05869-6.

This handbook is aimed at teachers, practitioners, and researchers in the realm of school psychology. Its coverage is comprehensive, including sections on assessment problems, (including test bias) and methodologies, interventions, evaluation and training, medical problems, legal issues, federal and other regulations, school psychology in other countries of the world, ethical concerns (including the ethical guidelines of the American Psychological Association and the National Association of School Psychologists), and the role of the school psychologist. Overviews of major therapies used by school psychologists, such as group counseling, music and art therapy, family therapy, and short-term dynamic therapy, are also included.

Directories

Brown, Douglas T., and Kathleen M. Minke. **Directory of School Psychology Training Programs**. Stratford, Conn.: National Association of School Psychologists, 1984. 427p.

The compilers state in their introduction that the "99 percent of the known programs in school psychology who meet the criteria for inclusion" (p. 11) are included in this directory which is a publication of the National Association of School Psychologists in cooperation with James Madison University in Harrisburg, Virginia. Lists of programs accredited in school psychology were submitted by each state department of education. These programs were then mailed a questionnaire, from which data were obtained.

Entries are arranged alphabetically by state and include information about the contact person (or training program director) and address, accreditation, degree enrollment, students graduated, degree program offered, admission requirements, required courses/competency areas, financial aid, program philosophy, and faculty. An institute name index concludes the work.

6

Curriculum and Instruction Reference Sources

CURRICULUM

Bibliographies

Kraus Curriculum Development Library. Millwood, N.Y.: Kraus International Publications, 1983- . Annual. Prices vary. LC 86-642753.

This series was begun as the Pitman Curriculum Development Library (which was bought out by Kraus) and consists of annual collections from 1978 to 1984, with some years combined. From 1983 on the plan was to select approximately 300 of the most outstanding and innovative curriculum guides developed in schools across the United States for inclusion in this collection. The documents cover twenty-two subject areas from school districts, state education agencies, and private curriculum development companies in the United States and Canada. The guides are in microfiche format with a printed *Cumulative Subject Index*.

This is a useful collection for instructional resources or educational learning centers connected with teacher education programs to own. There are, however, two major drawbacks: the format and the price. The core collection for 1978 to 1982, for example, costs over $12,000, a steep price for an academic library, let alone a smaller-budgeted resource center, to afford. Then, also, most students and faculty object to examining all of the guides via a microfiche reader. Instructors want to be able to use the materials in class; users want to have the convenience of reading curriculum guides in book format.

Schubert, William Henry, with special assistance from Ann Lynn Lopez Schubert. **Curriculum Books: The First Eighty Years**. Lanham, Md.: University Press of America, 1980. 389p. $33.75; $17.75pa. LC 80-8275. ISBN 0-8191-1261-5; 0-8191-1261-3pa.

Educators and other scholars who are interested in the study of curriculum in American schools will find this bibliography and bibliographic essay, in chronological form, a source of references to curriculum books from 1900 to 1979. Entries are arranged by year in nine chapters, each covering a decade, and subdivided in four parts: "Contextual Reminders" (background and setting), "Curriculum Thought and Literature" (bibliographic essay), "Notes," and "Bibliography of Curriculum Books" (for the particular decade). An index of authors and subjects is provided.

ART

Bibliographies

Bunch, Clarence. **Art Education: A Guide to Information Sources**. Detroit: Gale, 1978. 331p. (Art and Architecture Information Guide Series, Vol. 6; Gale Information Guide Library). $65.00. LC 73-17518. ISBN 0-8103-1373-7.

This bibliography covers a wide range of sources in art education. Chapter topics include general reference sources; periodicals and serials; organizations and publishers; history of art education; art schools; philosophy and methods (at elementary, middle school, and secondary levels); higher education; continuing education; museum art education; interdisciplinary art education; international art education; research; measurement; curriculum building; art appreciation, art and religion; examinations for art teachers and career guidance; student teaching in art education; resource materials and facilities for teaching art; financing art education; textbooks; and children's art books.

Entries in each chapter are arranged alphabetically by author and many include brief annotations. In describing a criterion for inclusion, Bunch stated that books about art or art methods where the authors emphasized use of the books' content with children and/or adults were favored. Although this compilation is limited to English-language sources and needs to be updated, it is the only guide available that deals with almost all aspects of art education and, thus, provides a useful tool for researchers and practitioners in the field of art education.

Related titles include *The Art Teacher's Resource Book* by Leslie A. Baker (Reston Publishing, 1979) and *The Elementary Teacher's Art Handbook* by Kenneth M. Lansing and Arlene E. Richards (Holt, Rinehart and Winston, 1981).

Clark, Gilbert A., and Enid D. Zimmerman. **Resources for Educating Artistically Talented Students**. Syracuse, N.Y.: Syracuse University Press, 1987. 176p. $22.00. LC 86-023183. ISBN 0-8156-2401-8.

This reference work will direct teachers, administrators, and parents to resources that will be useful in working with creative youngsters with special talents in the arts. The compilers have identified people, agencies, materials, models, and federal, state, and local policies that are relevant to education of such students. It also includes diagnostic instruments for identifying the artistically talented. A bibliography of outstanding instructional resources and a bibliography of further references on the subject are included.

Handbooks and Yearbooks

Holden, Donald. **Art Career Guide: A Guidance Handbook for Art Students, Teachers, Vocational Counselors, and Job Hunters**. 4th ed. New York: Watson-Guptil, 1983. 320p. $16.95. LC 82-24701. ISBN 0-8230-0252-7.

The author's purpose is to help prospective artists identify possible career opportunities where art talent could be utilized. This fourth edition of this handbook should be particularly useful for students, teachers, vocational guidance counselors, and librarians, as it is a major update of information since the last edition in 1973. Arrangement is in four parts: "Planning Your Education," "Choosing a Career," "Finding a Job," and "Schools and Professional Organizations."

Part 1 includes information on choosing an art school; in part 2, individual chapters address career options in the fine arts, illustration, graphic design, fabric design, interior design, architecture, industrial design, photography, art teaching, art museums, and crafts. Other chapters in parts 2 and 3 cover job prospects, tips on writing a resume, planning an art portfolio, and job hunting and interviewing. Part 4 contains a directory to degree-granting schools that will help students, parents, and counselors identify art education possibilities.

Wankelman, Willard, and Philip Wigg. **A Handbook of Arts & Crafts for Elementary and Junior High School Teachers**. 6th ed. Dubuque, Iowa: W.C. Brown, 1985. 348p. Write for price info. LC 84-70993. ISBN 0-697-03606-5pa.

The sixth edition of this handbook for elementary and junior high school art programs incorporates new suggestions and new projects not included in previous editions. The work begins with a discussion of the basic concepts of art instruction and then gives guidelines for creative art teaching in a wide range of media, including ceramics, chalk, crayon, paint, ink, sculpture, stencils, and textiles. Other chapters cover effective use of bulletin boards, various crafts, lettering, using paper and cardboard, printing, and other techniques. A related title is Jane Bryant's *Why Art, How Art: A Comprehensive Guide* (Special Child Publications, 1983).

HEALTH AND PHYSICAL EDUCATION

Bibliographies

Educators Guide to Free Health, Physical Education and Recreation Materials. Randolph, Wis.: Educators Progress Service, 1968- . Annual. $24.75. ISSN 0424-6241.

This twentieth edition (1987) is compiled and edited by Patricia Horkheimer. Arrangement of the free materials available in this guide is by media format and subject, covering health, physical education, and recreation in films; filmstrips and slides; tapes, scripts and transcriptions; and printed materials. Within each section, entries are alphabetical by title. Most bibliographic information is provided, but production dates are sometimes missing, so that currency of materials is not always easy to determine. Annotations are aimed at the teacher and provide useful information for lesson planning.

Complete directions are provided for attaining materials, including a sample letter of request, and sections on how to cooperate with sponsors and evaluation of industry-sponsored educational materials. Title, subject, source, and availability indexes are provided.

Indexes and Abstracts

Physical Education Index. Edited by Ronald F. Kirby. Cape Girardeau, Mo.: Ben Oak Publishing, 1978- . Quarterly, with annual cumulations. $150.00. ISSN 0191-9292.

This subject index accesses foreign and domestic English-language materials related to physical education, dance, health, physical therapy, recreation, sports, and sports medicine in 189 professional journals. Coverage is given to national and international association conferences, biographical sketches and obituaries, and legislation pertaining to any of the above topics. Specific topics analyzed concern administration, biomechanics, kinesiology, coaching, curriculum, facilities, history, measurement/evaluation, motor learning, perception, philosophy, physical fitness, research, sport psychology, sport sociology, teaching methods, training, and all sports activities. For each article indexed, the following information is provided: title, author, periodical name and volume, pages, and date of article publication. Names of the editorial staff, abbreviations used, periodicals indexed, and a "Book Reviews" section are also included.

Dictionaries and Encyclopedias

Encyclopedia of Physical Education, Fitness and Sports. Edited by Thomas Kirk Cureton, Jr. Sponsored by the American Alliance for Health, Physical Education, and Recreation. Salt Lake City, Utah: Brighton, 1977-1985. 4v. (Vol. 3 has imprint: Reading, Mass.: Addison-Wesley, 1977). Prices vary. LC 76-45508.

In each volume individual chapters are written by contributors who are experts in their fields. They include background information and coverage of the historical development of the particular aspect of physical education. Individual volume titles include volume 1, *Philosophy, Programs, and History*, edited by J.S. Bosco and M.A. Turner (1981); 2, *Training, Environment, Nutrition and Fitness*, edited by G. Alan Stull (1980); 3, *Sports, Dance, and Related Activities*, edited by Reuben B. Frost (Addison-Wesley, 1977); and 4, *Human Performance: Efficiency and Improvement in Sports, Exercise and Fitness*, edited by Thomas K. Cureton, Jr. (1985).

Handbooks and Yearbooks

Physical Education Handbook. Edited by Neil Schmottlach, and Irene Clayton. 7th ed. Englewood Cliffs, N.J.: Prentice-Hall, 1983. 381p. $31.00. LC 82-12215. ISBN 0-13-667535-2.

This handbook was first published in 1951 with the intention of providing brief information about sports and activities included in physical education programs. The various editions have included coverage that provides, for each sport, history, nature of the game, selection and maintenance of necessary equipment, rules, playing techniques and strategies, and selected bibliographic references. Over the years, new sports have become popular and have been included in subsequent editions. This handbook is a useful reference for teachers and administrators involved in physical education curricula and instruction. Another related title is *A Teacher's Guide to Elementary School Physical Education* by Norman A. Cochran (Kendall/Hunt, 1982).

LANGUAGE ARTS

Bibliographies

Fagan, William T., and Charles R. Cooper, and Julie M. Jensen. **Measures for Research and Evaluation in the English Language Arts, Volume 2**. Urbana, Ill.: ERIC Clearinghouse on Reading and Communication Skills and National Council of Teachers of English, 1985. 245p. $17.00pa. ISBN 0-8141-3101-8.

Educators in the area of English-language arts have made a shift in the last ten or more years from product-oriented instruction to a process-oriented approach. The authors have compiled descriptions of eighty measures for assessing performance in English and language arts. Each assessment instrument is cataloged by the type of language process it measures. Information in each entry provides bibliographic information, age range for which the instrument is appropriate, construction date, purpose, methodology, validity and reliability measures, normative data, and ordering information.

Matthias, Margaret, and Diane Thiessen. **Children's Mathematics Books: A Critical Bibliography**. Chicago: American Library Association, 1979. 61p. $6.00pa. LC 79-11896. ISBN 0-8389-0285-5.

The compilers used *Children's Books in Print* to identify, review, and evaluate mathematics books written for children. The entries in this bibliography describe the content of the book, illustrations, writing style, whether or not reader activities are included, and judgments on its accuracy and appropriateness for children. Entries are arranged under the following subject categories: "Counting," "Geometry," "Measurement," "Number Concepts," "Time," and "Miscellaneous." Evaluative ratings are assigned from "not recommended" to "highly recommended." Grade levels are also indicated.

McDonald, Bruce, Leslie Orsini, and Thomas J. Wagner. **Creative Writing through Films: An Instructional Program for Secondary Students**. Littleton, Colo.: Libraries Unlimited, 1984. 224p. $23.50. LC 84-10077. ISBN 0-87287-432-X.

High school English and language arts teachers and others who teach creative writing skills would find this volume relevant and helpful. It is divided into two major sections covering (1) elementary skills (e.g., development of the story idea, characterization); and (2) advanced skills (e.g. theme, setting, image). Examples that illustrate each skill to be learned are included with a list of approximately five films that also exemplify each skill. A total of sixty-five films in all are described, all of which have been carefully selected not only for their usefulness in teaching creative writing skills, but for their freedom from sexual and racial biases, their appropriateness with respect to length, their interest level and vocabulary.

McDonald, Bruce, Leslie Orsini, Thomas J. Wagner, and Lynn Birlem. **Basic Language Skills through Films: An Instructional Program for Secondary Students**. Littleton, Colo.: Libraries Unlimited, 1983. 313p. $23.50. LC 83-14901. ISBN 0-87287-368-4.

A total of 166 educational films in the areas of social sciences, science, and language arts that can be used to teach reading, creative writing, library research, and other basic communication skills are described with suggested use activities. The films are arranged in the following skill categories: "Writing Skills," "Persuasion," "Refining the Message," "Reading Comprehension" (SAT skills), and "Research Skills." Each skill is briefly introduced, explained, and/or illustrated. For each film discussed, the film title, producer, length in minutes, black-and-white or color designation, and production date are provided. The content of the film is then described and its applications to the particular language arts skill are explained, followed by student and teacher instructional activities. Two indexes provide access to information on film titles and language skills terms. Although most high school English teachers and school media specialists are not in a position to purchase films, those that have some input into film selection would find this a very useful resource.

MUSIC

Bibliographies

Harris, Ernest E. **Music Education: A Guide to Information Sources**. Detroit: Gale, 1978. 566p. (Education Information Guide Series, Vol. 1). $65.00. LC 74-11560. ISBN 0-8103-1309-7.

Compiled by a professor of music education, this bibliography lists sources of information in five broad categories: (1) general reference sources, (2) music education, (3) subject matter areas, (4) uses of music, and (5) multimedia and equipment. Entries are arranged in seventy-four sections within these five areas. Annotated bibliographies and other sources included cover national music fraternities, music for the handicapped, music for the gifted, music therapy, and ethnic music education in urban and culturally disadvantaged areas. In addition to reference books, this guide also lists library collections, indexing and abstracting journals, sources (producers, distributors, etc.) for musical equipment, and multimedia resources.

READING

Bibliographies

Boehnlein, Mary Maher, and Beth Haines Hager, comps. **Children, Parents, and Reading: An Annotated Bibliography**. Newark, Del.: International Reading Association, 1985. 138p. $5.75pa. LC 85-167. ISBN 0-87207-341-6.

This bibliography includes books, articles, reports, research, bibliographies, and reviews of the literature that are concerned with parental involvement with reading. Materials are arranged in four sectons: "Parents and Reading," "Professional and Home/School Involvement," "Booklets and Pamphlets for Parents," and "Miscellaneous." Approximately 900 entries are included and each provides complete bibliographic description, plus an annotation which summarizes the material. Particular attention is given to materials that are related to home/school partnership or cooperation, have relevance to professionals in the reading field as well as parents, and provide a balance of items reflecting theoretical and practically oriented contents.

Brooks, Ellen J. **Learning to Read and Write: The Role of Language Acquisition and Aesthetic Development. A Resourcebook**. New York: Garland, 1986. 157p. (Garland Reference Library of Social Science, Vol. 278). $35.00. LC 84-48392. ISBN 0-8240-8800-X.

This brief bibliography of 245 citations to textbooks, monographs, research reports, and periodical articles on the subject of developmental and other aspects of reading would be of benefit to researchers studying reading instruction, teachers of language arts and reading, as well as parents and other professionals involved with the care and education of primary students. Much attention is also given to early writing, artistic, and play activity.

Arrangement of entries is in four subject categories: parallel processes in oral language development, connections to cognitive development in artistic expression, reading and writing processes, and applications for instruction for curricular planning.

Carlsen, G. Robert. **Books and the Teenage Reader: A Guide for Teachers**. 2d rev. ed. New York: Harper & Row, 1980. 290p. $16.45. LC 78-2117. ISBN 0-06-0106-26-3.

Carlsen answers the question, What is adolescent literature? by saying "The best definition is simple: it is that literature which adolescents read." This guide is a collection of annotated bibliographies on books that teenage readers (ages twelve to twenty) like to read. The introductory chapters, "Teenage Books," "Adult Books Read by Teenagers," and "The Teenager's Worlds," present an overview discussion of adolescent literature as it meets the developmental needs of teenagers, as well as educators' roles in selecting and utilizing reading materials.

Each topic chapter begins with a discussion of the particular topic followed by a bibliography. Some chapter topics include "The Adolescent Novel," "The Popular Adult Book," "Reading Rights (Censorship)," "Significant Modern Literature Classics," and an interesting coverage of "Subliterature" (comics, romances, books made into films, etc.). Since only a subject index is provided, an integrated list would enhance the convenience of this bibliography for the user. This is an important title for teachers, librarians, and counselors who work with this age group.

Dechant, Emerald. **Teacher's Directory of Reading Skill Aids and Materials**. West Nyack, N.Y.: Parker Publishing, 1981. 274p. $14.95. LC 81-405. ISBN 0-13-888255-X.

Instructional aids chosen to provide remediation in specific reading skills are included in this subject (skill) arrangement. The five major parts cover materials for developing (1) enabling skills (e.g., auditory and visual perception, listening, letter discrimination; (2) word identification and word recognition; (3) word meaning and vocabulary; (4) comprehension and functional reading; and (5) comprehensive reading programs. In each section, definitions of the types of skills covered and background information precede the listing of materials. Bibliographic information is limited to title, distributor, grade level, and brief statement of instructional purpose. A list of publishers is appended and a topical index concludes the work.

Flemming, Carolyn, and Donna Schatt, eds. **Choices: A Core Collection for Young Reluctant Readers**. Evanston, Ill.: John Gordon Burke Publishers, 1983. 554p. ISBN 0-934272-10-7. ISSN 0735-6358.

A total of 360 books are evaluated and/or summarized in this list of books selected from children's literature collections, basal reading series, and major reviewing sources. Selection criteria are explained and include readability assessment, relevance of subjects for grades 1 through 6, and availability to readers. Entries are arranged by subject. Each entry includes a complete bibliographic citation and an annotation of 150 to 250 words describing the plot and main characters. Access to books is available by either author or subject.

Friedlander, Janet, comp., with Elizabeth Hunter-Grundin and Hans U. Grundin. **Early Reading Development: A Bibliography**. New York: Harper & Row, 1981. 446p. (Harper Reference). ISBN 0-06-318161-4.

Titles published from 1920 to 1976 in the field of language and reading for children up to age seven are covered in this subject-arranged international bibliography. Some of the topics covered more extensively include artificial alphabets, beginning reading instruction and theory, ethnic-cultural factors, language development, and reading readiness. Each chapter opens with a brief introductory overview of the topic (prepared by Elizabeth Hunter-Grundin and Hans U. Grundin). Entries are not annotated; author and subject indexes are provided. Since a major share of the bibliography represents the periodical literature, an international list of periodical titles and their abbreviations precedes the bibliography. The foreword indicates that the majority of sources were identified in *British Education Index, Current Index to Journals in Education, Education Index, Resources in Education,* and *Sociology of Education Abstracts.*

Goodman, Kenneth S., and Yetta M. Goodman, comps. **Linguistics, Psycholinguistics, and the Teaching of Reading: An Annotated Bibliography.** 3d ed. Newark, Del.: International Reading Association, 1980. 77p. $20.00pa. LC 80-16364. ISBN 0-87207-312-2.

This annotated bibliography of the professional literature in reading instruction was first published in 1967, with a second edition in 1971. The arrangement of entries is alphabetical by subject and each title deals with a significant aspect of the reading process, learning, or instruction. Some major subjects covered include beginning reading, comprehension, reading curricula, language differences/dialects, bilingualism, reading testing and evaluation, discourse analysis, and theories of reading, among others. Annotations are quite brief (one or two sentences). This is an important research tool, but its usefulness would be enhanced by inclusion of an index.

Heiser, Jane-Carol, comp. **Literacy Resources: An Annotated Check List for Tutors and Librarians.** Baltimore, Md.: Enoch Pratt Free Library, 1983. 144p. $5.00pa. ISBN 0-910556-19-9.

Materials in this bibliography have been assigned levels of reading difficulty from level 1, a reading level of grade 3 and below; level 2 (grades 4-7); level 3 (grades 8-12); to level 4 (grades 12 and above). The items are those found to be most successful as instructional materials in the Literacy Program of the Enoch Pratt Free Library. Materials at the third level have been found appropriate for use with persons preparing for the GED exam. The majority of the citations are classified into the lower levels around major topics as follows: basic English and study skills; life skills, such as jobs and child care; leisure reading; instructional materials (teaching guides, manuals, reference tools, textbooks); and adult education.

High Interest Easy Reading for Junior and Senior High School Students. 5th rev. ed. Edited by Dorothy Matthews and the Committee to Revise High Interest-Easy Reading. Urbana, Ill.: National Council of Teachers of English, 1988. 115p. $6.25pa. LC 88-1430. ISBN 0-8141-2096-2.

Almost 300 titles are selected for students whose chronological ages exceed their reading levels. Suitable for junior and senior high school students, the titles are annotated and arranged alphabetically by author. Fiction stories predominate, but a large number of nonfiction titles are included for students who are interested in real people and real-life problems, animals, and factual events. This list should be extremely helpful to reading teachers, tutors, counselors, and school and public librarians. A related title is *Easy Reading: Book Series and Periodicals for Less Able Readers,* by Michael F. Graves, Judith A. Boetteker, and Randall A. Ryder (Newark Del.: International Reading Association, 1979).

LiBretto, Ellen V., comp. and ed. **High/Low Handbook: Books, Materials, and Services for the Teenage Problem Reader.** 2d ed. New York: Bowker, 1985. 286p. $29.95. LC 85-17514. ISBN 0-8352-2133-4.

In this selection tool, contributors share experiences in identifying problem readers at the junior and senior high school levels, and in helping them become interested in books, periodicals, and other materials they can read independently. Titles are arranged in sections dealing with the characteristics of the high/low reader/selection and evaluation of appropriate materials; titles that constitute a core collection. Entries are annotated and listed alphabetically by author. Reading and interest level designations are provided. Subject and title indexes and two appendixes are included. Appendixes include supplementary titles, and sources of current reviews.

Schantz, Maria E., and Joseph F. Brunner, eds. **Reading in American Schools: A Guide to Information Sources**. Detroit: Gale, 1980. 266p. (Education Information Guide Series, Vol. 5; Gale Information Guide Library). $65.00. LC 79-23770. ISBN 0-8103-1456-8.

The compilers of this bibliography are well qualified to identify sources on reading for teachers and reading tutors. Both are professors in education and have had extensive experiences with administration and teaching in reading programs. They have annotated over 1,000 titles on reading theory, teaching methodologies, reading programs, bilingualism, children's and adolescents' literature, diagnosis and remediation of reading problems, legislation affecting education and reading, literacy, and other topics.

The sections on theory, teaching of reading, and basal and remedial reading programs are particularly solid. Criteria for inclusion are not consistently spelled out in every section, but the appendix contains a list of journals which are thoroughly described. Access to entries by author, title, and subject indexes is provided. A related reference source is *Early Reading: An Annotated Bibliography*, compiled by William H. Teale (Newark, Del.: International Reading Association, 1980).

Weintraub, Sam, and associates. **Summary of Investigations Relating to Reading**. Newark, Del.: International Reading Association, 1979- . Annual. $91.60. ISSN 0197-5129.

Each year 1,000 or more research studies related to reading and reported in the periodical literature are summarized. Arrangement of entries is in major subject chapters covering the sociology, physiology, and psychology of reading and various aspects of teaching it. Complete bibliographic information is provided for each citation plus a summary of the research study including objectives, methodology, significant effects, and other findings. Scholars in the field of teaching reading will find this compilation useful in identifying research studies in particular aspects of reading.

Your Reading: A Booklist for Junior High and Middle School Students. New ed. Edited by Booklist Committee and Jane Christensen. Urbana, Ill.: National Council of Teachers of English, 1983. 764p. $14.50pa. LC 83-17426. ISBN 0-8141-5938-9.

This bibliography of over 3,000 recommended titles for reading by junior high and middle school students includes many annotations written by students themselves, and covers both fiction and nonfiction. Teachers and school media specialists should find it particularly helpful in providing young people with relevant books, as well as useful as a checklist in evaluating school collections. Books are arranged alphabetically by author, first by form (fiction, humor and satire, poetry, plays, short story collections, nonfiction), then by subject.

Language Teaching: The International Abstracting Journal for Language Teachers and Applied Linguistics. Cambridge, England: Cambridge University Press, 1968- . Quarterly. $65.00 U.S. and Canada. ISSN 0261-4448.

This abstracting periodical was formerly known as *Language Teaching Abstracts*. It is compiled at the Centre for Information on Language Teaching and Research (CILT) and the English Language and Literature Division of The British Council. Each issue contains approximately 150 abstracts in the following categories: "Language Learning and Teaching—Theory and Practice," "Teaching Particular Languages," "Research in the Supporting Sciences," and "Language Description and Use."

Some 400 journals are analyzed for significant articles in language teaching that introduce new issues, clarify a problem area, review earlier work, report major research findings, or provide useful and/or new instructional methods or materials. Additional sections are devoted to reviews and listings of new books, current research in Europe, lists of periodicals and abstractors, and subject and author indexes.

Dictionaries and Encyclopedias

Harris, Theodore L., and Richard E. Hodges, eds. **A Dictionary of Reading and Related Terms**. Newark, Del.: International Reading Association, 1983. 381p. $27.50; $18.00pa. LC 81-12392. ISBN 0-87207-944-9.

Approximately 7,500 terms in 4,780 entries in the vocabulary of reading pedagogy and related disciplines are defined in this dictionary. An editorial advisory board of experts in reading was established to rate terms for exclusion or inclusion. Related fields include sociology, psychology, physiology, pedagogy, language, and supporting areas of media and technology, library science, statistics, and evaluation (including tests and measurement). A special group of entries not typically found in a dictionary of reading is devoted to sixty Piagetian terms. English words for about 150 ambiguous or controversial terms are given in conjunction with their corresponding meanings in French, Spanish, German, Danish, and Swedish (appendix A). Illustrative sentences and phrases are used to help clarify terms. Personal names and reading test names are excluded; only a highly selective group of readability formulas are included. Although a large number of British terms are defined, British spellings are not used. Pronunciation immediately follows the boldface main entry and the most popular definition is given first. Sources used to compile the dictionary are provided in appendix B.

Handbooks and Yearbooks

IRA Desktop Reference 87. Newark, Del.: International Reading Association, 1972- . Annual. 224p. $12.00pa. ISBN 0-87207-781-0. ISSN 0090-8975.

The International Reading Association (IRA) and all of its affiliated agencies and councils all over the world are listed in this reference tool. All kinds of information related to the activities of the association are described here arranged in a monthly calendar listing all local and national events in sequence.

Special funds and services provided by the IRA, awards, special projects, membership information, committees, publications, and officers are all included. Reading teachers who are members of the IRA, and those who are not, would find the services and activities provided by this professional association of interest and use.

Malmquist, Eve, comp. **Handbook on Comparative Reading: An Annotated Bibliography and Some Viewpoints on University Courses in Comparative Reading.** Newark, Del.: International Reading Association, 1982. 78p. LC 81-19320. ISBN 0-87207-338-6.

Malmquist, as chairman of the IRA Comparative Reading Committee, states that the purpose of this bibliography is "to locate studies from various cultures and nations that would provide useful sources for university courses in comparative reading." The studies are arranged in three categories: "Methodology of Comparative Education and Comparative Reading," "Studies and Descriptive Reports," and "Reviews and Descriptions of the State of the Art Regarding Research and/or the Teaching of Reading."

Each entry provides complete bibliographic description plus a brief (75-100 word) annotation summarizing the study reported. Many of the annotations were written at the University of Linkoping, Sweden. Three prominent scholars in the field, John Downing of the University of Victoria, H. Alan Robinson of Hofstra University, and Eve Malmquist of the University of Linkoping, have also contributed articles expressing their insights into the field.

Miller, Harry, and others. **Teacher's Kaleidoscope of Reading Activities.** Lanham, Md.: University Press of America, 1985. 254p. $26.75; $12.50pa. LC 85-7384. ISBN 0-8191-4693-5; 0-8191-4694-3pa.

This collection of approximately 200 learning activities for the teaching of reading is arranged around reading skills in seven areas: readiness, word recognition, word analysis, word meaning, comprehension, content subject areas, and special reading skills. Activities are written for large groups, small groups, and individuals, and may be duplicated for classroom use. Within each chapter, activities are, for the most part, in alphabetical order, and each entry includes grade level, objective, time needed, materials needed, preparation (including examples), activity directions, and evaluation methods. Reading teachers will welcome this comprehensive source of teaching/learning activities.

Mosse, Hilda L. **The Complete Handbook of Children's Reading Disorders: A Critical Evaluation of Their Clinical, Educational, and Social Dimensions.** New York: Human Sciences Press, 1982. 2v. $80.00. LC 81-132. ISBN 0-89885-077-0.

The purpose of this two-volume handbook is to provide the methodology for appropriate clinical examination of children with reading disorders. According to Mosse, an M.D., clinical associate professor in psychology (New York Medical College), and school psychiatrist (New York City Board of Education), the clinical method should involve a thorough psychiatric examination, the components of which he describes. He also presents major sections on reading disorders that have an organic basis; symptoms associated with reading, writing, and arithmetic disorders; psychogenic and sociogenic reading disorders; and treatments. Many related topics are included, such as speech disorders, attention disorders, hyperactivity, hypoactivity, and mood disorders.

The volumes are illustrated (mostly with examples of children's perceptual skill development). Almost 500 references document this reference source; each volume is indexed. These volumes represent very thorough and authoritative coverage of the medical, educational, and social concerns related to children with reading disorders.

Thomas, James L., and Ruth M. Loring, eds. **Motivating Children and Young Adults to Read, Vol. 2.** Phoenix, Ariz.: Oryx Press, 1983. 189p. $30.00pa. LC 82-42924. ISBN 0-897740-46-7.

The editors, professors at North State University, have gathered in one volume articles from American and British journals written by reading teachers and school library media specialists. All of the materials emphasize the importance of encouraging reading among children. Thomas and Loring feel this is a positive step toward decreasing functional illiteracy in American society.

Titles are arranged in four sections: "Methodology" (how to motivate), "Interests," "Programs," and "Nonprint" (includes students producing their own filmstrips). This title should provide many suggestions to teachers and librarians. The editors produced a previous compilation (Oryx Press, 1979) which is also still in print ($30.00).

SCIENCE

Bibliographies

Educators Guide to Free Science Materials. Randolph, Wis.: Educators Progress Service, 1960- . Annual. $24.75. LC 61-919. ISSN 0070-9425.

Now in its twenty-eighth edition (August 1987), this guide provides an ongoing listing of educational materials in various fields of science that are available free of charge or for minimal loan fees to teachers and other educators. Types of materials covered include films (617), filmstrips and slides (14), tapes (32), printed materials for reference and the professional section (146), charts, posters and periodicals. Subjects emphasized include aerospace, education, biology, chemistry, environmental education, general science, nature study, and physics. Arrangement is alphabetical by color-coded subject sections, and each entry provides title, date, medium, length, descriptive annotation, producer and/or distributor, and whether information may be duplicated for class handouts. The address of the issuing agency is provided in the source index. Title and subject indexes are also included. Directions to obtaining materials and significant features of the year's edition are indicated preceding the listing of materials. Science instructors should find this a helpful and reliable resource. Another title in this series is *Science and Computer Literacy Audiovisuals: A Teacher's Sourcebook* (1986).

Schroeder, Eileen E., and David A. Tyckoson, comps. **Science Education**. Phoenix, Ariz.: Oryx Press, 1986. 103p. (Oryx Science Bibliographies, Vol. 6). $16.00pa. LC 86-42578. ISBN 0-89774-227-3.

Science education at the K-12 level is the subject of this annotated bibliography of 337 citations. Entries are arranged in subject chapters and include sources of elementary and secondary education, specific disciplines in the sciences (e.g., physical science, biology). Emphasis is on journal articles published in the 1980s.

An introductory review of research summarizes some of the major trends and issues covered in the bibliographic citations. Teacher educators who provide instruction in science methodology would find this a useful resource.

Science and Computer Literacy Audiovisuals: A Teacher's Source Book. National Information Center for Educational Media. Albuquerque, N. Mex.: Access Innovations, 1986. 266p. $49.95. ISBN 090320-101-4.

This title represents one of several curriculum-oriented indexes initiated by NICEM in 1986. Teachers and school media specialists in various areas will be able to identify nonprint materials for classroom use related to specific subject areas. Annotations are brief and nonevaluative, but the listing is very comprehensive. As all NICEM indexes, these reference tools are available in both print and online formats (through DIALOG). Other titles in the series include *Coaches' Guide to Sports Audiovisuals; Foreign Language Audiovisuals: A Teacher's Source Book; Index to Health and Safety Education; Language Arts Audiovisuals; Social Studies Audiovisuals; Vocational and Technical Audiovisuals;* and *Wellness Media.*

Wilms, Denise, ed. **Science Books for Children: Selections from Booklist, 1976-1983.** Chicago: American Library Association, 1985. 183p. $15.00pa. LC 84-12421. ISBN 0-8389-3312-2.

Children's science books that have received favorable reviews in *Booklist* are described here. Titles are arranged in fourteen broad subject categories and cover a wide range of subdivisions of science. Grade levels are indicated (from preschool to grade 9). Author/title and subject indexes are provided. Related titles are *Best Science Books for Children* and *Best Science Films, Filmstrips and Videocassettes for Children*, both of which were compiled by Kathryn Wolff and published by American Association for the Advancement of Science in 1983.

SEX EDUCATION

Bibliographies

Campbell, Patricia J. **Sex Education Books for Young Adults, 1892-1979.** New York: Bowker, 1979. 169p. $19.95. LC 79-1535. ISBN 0-8352-1157-6.

Campbell traces the historical development of books written for adolescents from the Victorian era through the 1970s, and she emphasizes how they have reflected societal attitudes and values. Arrangement of information is in chronological chapters, each covering approximately one decade. Annotated entries conclude the narrative discussions. Emphasis is on a frank and open approach to sex education, with availability of all kinds of information for children and young people. A list of evaluation sources is also provided. Campbell has also compiled *Sex Guides: Books and Films about Sexuality for Young Adults* (Garland, 1986).

SOCIAL STUDIES

Bibliographies

Data Book of Social Studies Materials and Resources. Boulder, Colo.: Social Science Education Consortium, 1971- . Annual. $10.00. LC 82-20089. ISSN 0747-4857.

Textbooks, curriculum guides, teacher resource materials, and a variety of audiovisual materials for teaching social studies at the K-12 level are described in this resource guide. Evaluations are organized by grade level and type of material. In addition, curriculum guides indentified through ERIC are evaluated in another section, and another one describes and discusses materials that are concerned with new approaches to teaching and learning and other professional concerns of teachers.

This guide should be of interest at institutions of higher education. The first three volumes in this series were published between 1971 and 1978, and with the fourth volume in 1979 it became an annual publication. Earlier issues are known as *Social Studies Curriculum Materials Data Book*.

Educators Guide to Free Social Studies Materials. Randolph, Wis.: Educators Progress Service, 1961- . Annual. $26.50. LC 61-65910. ISSN 0070-9433.

Free materials to support the social studies curriculum, primarily at the K-12 level, are listed in this annual guide. The twenty-seventh edition (1987) describes 2,511 selected items as follows: 922 films, 84 filmstrips, 183 slide sets, 1 set of transparencies, 400 audiorecordings, 263 videotapes, 3 scripts, and 585 printed materials. A limited number of audiovisual materials may be retained by the educator; others are available for free loan.

The materials are arranged in color-coded sections by subject and media format covering communications and transportation, geography, history, social problems, citizenship, world affairs, and teacher reference and professional growth. Annotations list title, date, producer and/or distributor, medium and length, and brief description. Grade level is not indicated. Title, subject, and source indexes conclude the work.

Hepburn, Mary A., and Alfred Dahler. **Social Studies Dissertations 1977-1982**. Boulder, Colo.: Social Science Education Consortium, 1983. 268p. $14.95pa. ISBN 0-89994-283-0.

Social science dissertations were extracted from *Dissertation Abstracts International* from January 1977 to mid-1982. A total of 394 titles were included in this fourth volume of its kind, extending the coverage of the previous three from 1963 to 1982 inclusive. All of these compilations are a part of the ERIC database as follows: 1963 to 1969 (ED 098 085); 1969 to 1973 (ED 063 202); and 1973 to 1976 (ED 164 361). Entries are arranged in five broad categories of research. The type of research methodology employed in each dissertation is also noted. Annotations represent summaries of the abstracts written for inclusion in *Dissertation Abstracts International*.

Handbooks and Yearbooks

Barth, James L. **Elementary and Junior High/Middle School Social Studies Curriculum, Activities, and Materials**. 2d ed. Lanham, Md.: University Press of America, 1983. 311p. $15.25. LC 83-155687. ISBN 0-8191-3197-0.

This compilation of instructional activities and resources is intended for teachers, prospective teachers, teacher education faculty, curriculum supervisors, and other educators involved in the development and implementation of social studies programs at the elementary and junior high/middle school levels. Information is arranged by grade level (K-8). A chapter for each grade is introduced by discussion of topics typically taught and national trends, followed by course objectives, basic content, and examples of programs with activities. A similar resource is available by the author for social studies at the high school level, *Secondary Social Studies Curriculum, Activities and Materials* (1984). A related title is *A Handbook for the Teaching of Social Studies*, edited by William S. Dobkin (University Press of America, 1983).

INSTRUCTION (TEACHERS AND TEACHING)

Bibliographies

Karnes, Elizabeth Lueder, and Donald D. Black, comps. **Teacher Evaluation and Merit Pay: An Annotated Bibliography**. Westport, Conn.: Greenwood, 1986. 400p. (Bibliographies and Indexes in Education, No. 2). $45.00. LC 85-27226. ISBN 0-313-24557-6.

The literature documenting attempts to pay teachers and administrators based on performance rather than seniority is described in this annotated bibliography. It covers books, journal articles, dissertations, published papers, and a few nonprint items that appeared in print primarily from 1980 through 1984. Arrangement is in chapters by type of publication. Bibliographic description varies somewhat; annotations are descriptive in nature. The emphasis of the content is on various evaluative procedures used in the teaching profession, merit pay, master teacher concept, and performance incentives. A separate chapter contains samples of evaluation forms and instruments that have been used by some of the larger public school districts.

Karnes, Elizabeth Lueder, Donald D. Black, and John Downs. **Discipline in Our Schools: An Annotated Bibliography**. Westport, Conn.: Greenwood, 1983. 700p. $55.00. LC 84-32091. ISBN 0-313-23521-X.

Classroom management and control received increased attention in education literature and research in recent years. This compilation describes over 4,200 books, dissertations, journal articles, and school district reports published in the 1970s and 1980s that cover strategies for teachers and administrators, and other aspects of school discipline. Entries are arranged alphabetically by type of publication, and each entry provides complete bibliographic description and an annotation summarizing contents of the item.

Powell, Marjorie, and Joseph W. Beard. **Teacher Attitudes: An Annotated Bibliography and Guide to Research**. New York: Garland, 1986. 457p. (Garland Bibliographies in Contemporary Education, Vol. 4; Garland Reference Library of Social Science, Vol. 199). $66.00 LC 83-48213. ISBN 0-8240-9053-5.

Approximately 2,000 entries are included in this annotated bibliography of the periodical literature on studies dealing with teacher attitudes toward teaching, other teachers, students, the curriculum, and teaching environment. The compilers analyzed *Education Index, Dissertation Abstracts, Current Index to Journals in Education* and *Resources in Education* for citations covering attitudes of teachers at the K-12 level. Two major types of studies are described, namely (1) teacher attitudes defined by subject area taught, and (2) attitudes organized by teacher characteristics (e.g., age, sex, experience). Entries are arranged in seven subject chapters describing teachers' attitudes and influences on them, and reviews of research. While full bibliographic citations are provided, the entries are not annotated. Access is available through author, title, and subject indexes.

This title is a companion volume to a previous publication by the author, *Teacher Effectiveness: An Annotated Bibliography and Guide to the Research Literature* (Garland, 1984).

Dictionaries and Encyclopedias

Dunkin, Michael J., ed. **The International Encyclopedia of Teaching and Teacher Education**. Elmsford, N.Y.: Pergamon Press, 1987. 878p. $90.00. LC 86-9325. ISBN 0-08-030852-X.

This encyclopedia presents articles reprinted from *The International Encyclopedia of Education: Research and Studies* (Pergamon Press, 1985). Arrangement is in six sections devoted to (1) concepts and methods, (2) methods and paradigms for research, (3) teaching methods and techniques, (4) classroom procedures, (5) contextual factors, (6) teacher education. All sections begin with an introductory summary by the editor. This work should be of interest to both the researcher/theorist and the practitioner, and, in fact, should strengthen the link between the two.

Handbooks and Yearbooks

Harris, Sherwood, and Lorna B. Harris, eds. **The Teacher's Almanac, 1987-1988**. New York: Facts on File, 1987. 320p. $29.95. ISBN 0-8160-1807-3. ISSN 0889-079X.

Statistics and other data related to teachers and teaching are brought together in this one-volume reference source. Arrangement of information is in eleven sections: (1) "The Teacher's Year" (significant events, activities of the year, obituaries, etc.); (2) "State Rankings" (NEA enrollment statistics, per capita expenditures, etc.); (3) "Teacher Salaries and Jobs"; (4) "Profile of the Teaching Profession" (demographic characteristics of teachers); (5) "Student Performance"; (6) "Awards and Achievements" (including school receiving awards or special recognition); (7) "Issues and Challenges"; (8) "Books, Periodicals, Tests, and Computers"; (9) "School Districts and Enrollment"; (10) "Finances"; and (11) "Higher Education."

Hoover, Kenneth H. **The Professional Teacher's Handbook: A Guide for Improving Instruction in Today's Middle and Secondary Schools**. 3d ed. Boston: Allyn and Bacon, 1982. 672p. LC 81-19093. ISBN 0205077242.

Teaching methods, techniques, and activities for instructing the individual, small group, or total class are discussed. The book also covers affective learning concepts and strategies, different techniques and instruments for diagnosis and assessment for all learners, and information for dealing with special learners as well.

Sample evaluation forms for student teachers, an instructional unit, a learning activity package, and a list of audiovisual resources are included in the appendix.

Petreshene, Susan S. **A Complete Guide to Learning Centers**. Rev. ed. Palo Alto, Calif.: Pendragon House, 1982. 309p. (Educational Series). $12.95pa. LC 76-49794. ISBN 0-916988-08-2.

This guide not only lists a wealth of learning center activities in the basic skills, particularly language arts and mathematics, but provides the learner with a guide to development of a sequential individualized instruction program. Materials and activities presented here were field tested in classrooms and workshops and include step-by-step instructions on how to determine individual student needs, prescribe for those needs, prepare materials, and establish a sound record-keeping system that provides essential information without endless paperwork.

Tiedt, Iris McClellan, and Sidney Willis Tiedt. **Elementary Teacher's New Complete Ideas Handbook**. Englewood Cliffs, N.J.: Prentice-Hall, 1983. 308p. $18.95. LC 83-8611. ISBN 0-13-26095-X.

Teacher-tested ideas, sources, and strategies for instruction at the K-8 level in all areas of the curriculum are incorporated in this well-organized handbook. Contents are arranged in chapters targeting specific skills and/or subject matter (e.g., oral language; writing; spelling, dictionaries and handwriting; reading; mathematics; science; social studies; music; art; and games). The first chapter is devoted to dealing with students in general, promoting their self-esteem, and handling problems. Hints on daily classroom routines, interacting with parents, preparing the classroom, and calendar events are also included. The work concludes with a briefly annotated bibliography of resources for teaching and an index. All teachers should find some new ideas and strategies here, but beginning teachers, especially, should find these curriculum-related activities helpful and time saving. A related title that is still available is *Encyclopedic Deskbook of Teaching Ideas and Classroom Activities* by Harold I. Cotler (Parker Publishing, 1977).

Wittrock, Merlin C., ed. **Handbook of Research on Teaching**. 3d ed. New York: Macmillan, 1986. 1,037p. $55.00. LC 85-4866. ISBN 0-02-900310-5.

Sponsored by the American Educational Research Association, the third edition of this major handbook has expanded and updated its coverage of all fields of educational research from preschool to professional education, and from theory to practice. New chapters are devoted to "Teachers' Thought Processes" and "Students' Thought Processes" and their effect on motivation, reinforcement, and attribution theory. New research in many other areas, including "The Teaching of Learning Strategies" and studies conducted in the military services on intelligent computer-assisted instruction, is introduced.

The handbook is arranged in five major parts which report and summarize research findings in (1) "Theory and Method of Research on Teaching," (2) "Research on Teaching and Teachers," (3) "The Social and Institutional Context of Teaching," (4) "Adapting Teaching to Differences among Learners," and (5) "Research on the Teaching of Subjects and Grade Levels." Each of the thirty-five chapters is written by one or more educational researchers, many of which are noted scholars (e.g., Maxine Green, E. Paul Torrence, Richard E. Snow, Thomas L. Good, Jere E. Brophy). Each entry concludes with a lengthy list of references on the subject. *Handbook of Research on Teaching* is a scholarly treatise on the state of the art of educational research, and its quality is typical of projects associated with AERA.

7
Educational Administration Reference Sources

BIBLIOGRAPHIES

Rowland, A. Westley. **Key Resources on Institutional Advancement**. San Francisco: Jossey-Bass, 1986. 251p. (Jossey-Bass Higher Education Series). $27.95. LC 86-10296. ISBN 1-55542-014-1.

Editor of *Handbook of Institutional Advancement* (2d ed., Jossey-Bass, 1986), Rowland has also provided a bibliography to resources on institutional advancement, including academic development, public relations, alumni relations, fund raising, publicity, and marketing. He describes 523 books and periodical articles, and annotations, which, for the most part, summarize rather than evaluate the item. Over sixty periodicals related to institutional advancement are also listed. Academic administrators and development personnel, in particular, would find this an up-to-date and relevant resource tool.

INDEXES AND ABSTRACTS

Educational Administration Abstracts. Beverly Hills, Calif.: Sage, 1966- . Quarterly. $45.00/yr.; $110.00/yr., institutions. ISSN 0013-1601.

Produced by the University Council for Educational Administration in cooperation with Washington State University, this periodical reviews over 160 titles for abstracting. It covers major journals in educational management and administrative sciences. Doctoral dissertations related to educational administration are also included in a separate section. Main headings for subject access are as follows: (1) "Tasks of Administrators," (2) "Administrative Processes and Organizational Variables," (3) "Societal Factors Influencing Education," (4) "Programs for Educational Administrators," (5) "Theory and Research," and (6) "Planning and Futurology."

DICTIONARIES AND ENCYCLOPEDIAS

Dejnoska, Edward L. **Educational Administration Glossary**. Westport, Conn.: Greenwood, 1984. 247p. LC 83-5719. ISBN 0-313-23301-2.

As a professor of educational administration and author in the field, Dejnoska is well qualified to define the terms within each of the areas related to educational administration (e.g., personnel, finances, law, management, accounting). Definitions were validated and critiqued by a panel of reviewers with expertise in the field. The 1,400 terms emphasize administration in elementary and secondary schools. The definitions are followed by a bibliography and a useful series of appendixes which include a statement of ethics for school administrators, relevant national and regional organizations, state school board associations, national PTA state offices, state departments of education, regional accrediting associations, ERIC clearinghouses, educational administration periodicals, abstracting and reviewing journals, member universities of the University Council for Educational Administration and partnership school districts, regional offices of the U.S. Department of Education, area offices of the Bureau of Indian Affairs, NCATE-accredited programs, and key governmental and intergovernmental offices.

Deskbook Encyclopedia of American School Law. Rosemount, Minn.: Data Research, 1980-81- . Annual. $45.00. LC 86-657590.

Entries in this encyclopedia are based on decisions made in federal and state appellate courts in education-related cases. The cases are arranged in major subject categories, some of which cover accidents, injuries, and deaths; faculty promotion and tenure; freedom of speech and religion; termination/dismissal/resignation; students' rights; and collective bargaining. The subject index helps indentify cases on various topics, such as home study programs, library materials (selection freedom), and national teacher exams. Although the subject index has a category on homosexuality, it does not have one on cases related to AIDS.

The biggest advantage to this publication is that it provides—for school administrators, teachers, and other professionals, including lawyers concerned with legal cases in education—a one-volume access to major litigation. The encyclopedia was published under the name *Informational Research Systems* until the 1986 edition. The editorial staff of Data Research also publishes a monthly newsletter service, *Legal Notes for Education*.

Fehrman, Cherie. **School Secretary's Encyclopedic Dictionary**. Englewood Cliffs, N.J.: Prentice-Hall, 1984. 300p. $24.95. LC 84-3185. ISBN 0-13-794446-2.

Terms defined here are all related to the topic of the school secretary in everyday job performance. The compiler is, herself, a school secretary and is able to write clear, understandable brief articles which help paint a realistic view of school office management with a hands-on and practical orientation.

The 1,300 entries are arranged alphabetically and cover a wide range of procedures, services, and functions associated with a school secretary's job description.

Mamchak, P. Susan, and Steven R. Mamchak. **School Administrator's Encyclopedia**. West Nyack, N.Y.: Parker Publishing, 1982. 414p. $27.50. LC 81-22492. ISBN 0-13-792390-2.

The authors' attempt was to combine in a single source "definitions, observations, laws, references, and commentary on educational topics that are a vital part of every administrator's existence" (p.7). Approximately 500 entries on all aspects of education are arranged alphabetically by topic. Topics indirectly related to school administration are also included; e.g., an entry on Christian Scientists explains when treatment is permissible, and when it is not, for a child who becomes ill or injured on school property. Other entries provide information on a wide variety of issues from dress codes, prayer, drinking, self-defense (of teachers and administrators), and strikes, to what is meant by such terms as *privileged communications, reasonable and prudent* and *reduction in force (RIF)*.

The school administrator will find clearly defined information related to the office or position, particularly with respect to the ramifications and interpretation of educational and civil law, budget, the physical plant, and relationships with students, faculty, and the community. The Mamchaks have also authored the *Complete School Communications Manual: With Sample Letters, Forms, Bulletins, Policies and Memos* (Prentice-Hall, 1984) which covers communications related to absenteeism, academic freedom, budget, child abuse, dismissal, due process, and medical and other forms; and *Teacher's Communication Resource Book* (Prentice-Hall, 1985).

HANDBOOKS AND YEARBOOKS

De Roche, Edward F. **An Administrator's Guide for Evaluating Programs and Personnel: An Effective Schools Approach**. 2d ed. Boston: Allyn and Bacon, 1987. 319p. Write for price info. LC 87-1400. ISBN 0-205-10512-1.

Examples, ideas, illustrations, and suggestions are included for school administrators to use in evaluating programs and personnel. This work also includes guidelines for conducting assessments and self-evaluations and descriptions of evaluation instruments that the author has found useful, reliable, and valid. It is aimed at building level principals, but superintendents, curriculum specialists, school board members, and other professionals concerned with evaluation would also be interested in this guide. Specific program evaluations covered include instructional leadership and supervision; teaching and teachers; curriculum programs and materials; school and classroom climate, in addition to office, food, and transportation services; plant and facilities; student activities; and pupil personnel services (school counselors, health services, psychological services).

Rowland, A. Westley, ed. **Handbook of Institutional Advancement: A Practical Guide to College and University Relations, Fund Raising, Alumni Relations, Government Relations, Publications and Executive Management for Continued Advancement**. 2d ed. San Francisco: Jossey-Bass, 1986. 796p. $45.00. LC 85-45912. ISBN 0-87589-689-8.

Rowland uses institutional advancement to describe all institutional activity under-taken "to develop understanding and support from all its constituencies in order to achieve its goals in securing such resources as students, faculty, and dollars" (p. xiii). This handbook is a practical resource for a broad audience—advancement professionals, volunteers, and others doing promotional work—that needs help with everything from overall planning to designing and producing press releases and other publications to fund raising.

The fifty-nine chapters are arranged in major categories including managerial strategies, strengthening institutional relations, fund raising, alumni support, government relations, promotional communications, periodical publications, enrollment planning and management, and special topics (e.g., legal issues).

Another title in this Jossey-Bass Series in Higher Education is also aimed at institutional development officers and provides an in-depth treatment of educational fund raising. Francis C. Pray has edited *Handbook for Educational Fund Raising* (Jossey-Bass, 1981).

Stoops, Emery, Max Rafferty, and Russell E. Johnson. **Handbook of Educational Administration: A Guide for the Practitioner**. 2d ed. Boston: Allyn and Bacon, 1981. 499p. $44.95. LC 80-17118. ISBN 0-205-07133-3.

American school leadership and administrative operations and procedures are addressed in this handbook. Over 100 trends are described, and research reported is a balance of theoretical elements and practical application. Information is organized around defining and evaluating administration, issues and problems related to control and governing agencies, financial support and fiscal management, physical plant, special services and programs (e.g., health services), personnel, and instruction.

School administrators, as well as students in school administration courses, would find this handbook very helpful as it deals with every aspect pertaining to the operation of a school district. A related title is *Leadership in Higher Education: A Handbook for Practicing Administrators*, edited by Bob W. Miller and associates (Greenwood, 1983).

Walling, Donovan R. **Complete Book of School Public Relations: An Administrator's Manual and Guide**. Englewood Cliffs, N.J.: Prentice-Hall, 1982. 222p. $18.95. LC 82-12340. ISBN 0-13-158337-9.

Step-by-step guidelines, checklists, and examples of techniques for planning and/or improving school public relations programs are included in this manual. It also describes the A.I.M. planning model (assessing, involving, making a commitment) for developing improved cooperation between teachers and administrators and communication with the community. Tips on composing letters and flyers, dealing with the news media, and making audiovisual presentations and visual displays are included. *Administration of Public Education* (4th ed., Harper & Row, 1984) by Stephen J. Knezevich is a related title for educational administrators.

Yearbook of School Law. Topeka, Kans.: National Organization on Legal Problems of Education, 1933- . Annual. Price varies. LC 52-2403.

Editors and publishers of this yearbook have varied since it was first published in 1933. It provides a summary and analysis of all court decisions that affected schools and education during the previous calendar year. State appellate and federal courts records related to school laws are documented and a table of cases is provided. Topics covered include litigation concerning school administration; property; finances; faculty, staff and other employees; collective bargaining; segregation; desegregation; busing; discipline; and other issues. A similar work by the same publisher at the higher education level is *Yearbook of Higher Education Law*.

DIRECTORIES

Who's Who in Educational Administration. Arlington, Va.: American Association of School Administrators, 1976- . Annual. $700.00; free to members.

The 1987-1988 edition of this directory represents the roster of current members of the American Association of School Administrators (AASA), a national professional association founded in 1865. Names of members are arranged alphabetically by state, followed by listings in Canada, other countries, and territories. Each entry lists, in addition to the member's name, his/her position, address, and highest earned degree. Retired members are listed as such in the space designated for position. Administrators included represent positions from elementary school to institutions of higher education.

The range of members includes those in the following positions: superintendent, assistant and associate superintendent, and deputy superintendent; professor of educational administration; curriculum director; principal; director of special education; director of secondary education; supervisor of gifted programs; administrative assistant; director of management and personnel services, among others. Superintendents account for the majority of administrators who are members of AASA. An alphabetical list of all members (individuals and institutions) concludes the directory.

8

Evaluation in Education
Reference Sources

BIBLIOGRAPHIES

The ETS Test Collection Catalog, Volume 1: Achievement Tests and Measurement Devices. Compiled by Test Collection, Educational Testing Service. Phoenix, Ariz.: Oryx Press, 1986. 286p. $49.50pa. LC 86-678. ISBN 0-89774-248-6.

This work covers over 2,000 assessment instruments selected from the comprehensive collection in the database of the Educational Testing Service that are available for purchase or use. The compiling staff claims that, unlike the *Mental Measurements Yearbook* series, *The ETS Test Collection Catalog* includes many unpublished instruments that would otherwise escape the attention of school psychologists or other diagnosticians and researchers, or be very difficult to trace. They also claim that the subject access is superior, although the *ERIC* descriptors employed are difficult to search without the inclusion of an accompanying thesaurus. In spite of this problem, however, the information provided in this catalog is well worth the money. Career-oriented instruments are covered in *Volume 2: Vocational Tests & Measurement Devices* (1987, 288p., $49.50pa., ISBN 0-89774-439-X).

Educational Testing Service also publishes *Tests in Microfiche* (1986, $1,300.00/set), but buying the complete set is probably out of the question for many libraries.

Ninth Mental Measurements Yearbook. Edited by James V. Mitchell, Jr. Lincoln, Nebr.: Buros Institute of Mental Measurements; distr., University of Nebraska Press, 1985. 2,002p. $175.00. LC 39-3422. ISBN 0-910674-29-9.

This series of yearbooks provides detailed descriptive listings and evaluative reviews of commercially published diagnostic and assessment instruments available in the English language. Tests are arranged alphabetically by title, and information for each test includes title, age group for which intended, date of publication, what the test measures, availability of manuals, instructions for administration, price of score sheets, scoring services, normative data, and publisher and distributor. This information is followed by test references and reviews of the test.

These yearbooks were compiled and edited by Oscar Krisen Buros at the Buros Institute of Mental Measurements until his death in 1978. The institute also publishes the *Tests in Print* series, also edited by Mitchell, (*Tests in Print III, 1985*), which is an extensive bibliography of English-language tests that are commercially available, as well as a bibliography of references related to test development, construction, validity, and administration. It also publishes a title index that covers all tests, both in-print and out-of-print. Other separate monographs published by the institute cover all tests and reviews on a specific subject (e.g., intelligence tests, social studies tests, vocational tests).

A wide variety of professionals, particularly teachers and school psychologists, have found this comprehensive tool an indispensable and reliable reference in making educational assessments and decisions.

Sweetland, Richard C., and Daniel J. Keyser, eds. **TESTS: A Comprehensive Reference for Assessments in Psychology, Education, and Business**. 2d ed. Kansas City, Mo.: Test Corporation of America; distr., Detroit: Gale, 1983. 890p. $49.00. LC 86-14416. ISBN 0-933701-05-5.

While not as comprehensive as Buros's *Mental Measurement Yearbook*, this work attempts to identify, categorize, and describe assessment tests used in diagnosis in the regular classroom, special education, clinical assessment, and the business world. Information provided in each entry includes the test purpose and intended audience, description, implementation needs, publisher, and cost. Another directory to a specialized type of test which provides illustrations and sample items from the tests is John Eliot and Ian Macfarland Smith's *An International Directory of Spatial Tests* (Humanities Press, 1983).

DICTIONARIES AND ENCYCLOPEDIAS

Anderson, Scarvia B., Samuel Ball, Richard T. Murphy, and associates. **Encyclopedia of Educational Evaluation: Concepts and Techniques for Evaluating Education and Training Programs**. San Francisco: Jossey-Bass, 1975. 515p. $27.95. LC 74-6736. ISBN 0-87589-238-8.

This well-designed work combines the features of a research handbook with those of an encyclopedia in that it describes measurement approaches and provides essential details about program evaluation. It includes approximately 150 well-written brief reference essays (3 to 4 pages each) which contain cross-references and well-selected annotated bibliographies. Many provide supporting examples, graphs, and tables.

A separate classification guide provides an overview of eleven major subject areas by listing pertinent entries under such broad topics as program objectives and standards, techniques, and measurement approaches. These categorized entries, which could almost substitute for brief courses in the topics addressed, are made up of initialed essays, written by authorities in the field. Emphasis is on program objectives and standards, systems techniques and measurement approaches, the social context of evaluation, and types of variables. A twenty-six-page bibliography is included along with subject and author indexes.

Although in need of updating, this encyclopedia fulfills a definite need in the reference literature in the field of educational evaluation. Its emphasis on research in evaluation adds to its overall usefulness.

HANDBOOKS AND YEARBOOKS

Standards for Educational and Psychological Testing. Prepared by the Committee to Develop Standards for Educational and Psychological Testing of the American Educational Research Association, the American Psychological Association, and the National Council on Measurement in Education. Washington, D.C.: American Psychological Association, 1985. 100p. $23.00pa. LC 85-071493. ISBN 0-912704-95-0.

These criteria for evaluating tests used for educational purposes, testing practices, and the effects of test use should be of interest to scholars interested in test construction, and in utilizing test results, as well as those persons who are taking such tests.

In part 1, technical standards cover test validity; reliability and errors of measurement; test development and revision; and scaling, norming, and test publication. Part 2 covers general principles of test use; testing in clinical, school, counseling, and employment settings; licensing and certification; and program evaluation. Special cases of testing linguistic minorities and the handicapped and standards for administrative procedures are covered in parts 3 and 4. A bibliography and index are provided.

Weaver, S. Joseph, ed. **Testing Children: A Reference Guide for Effective Clinical and Psychoeducational Assessments**. Kansas City, Mo.: Test Corporation of America, 1984. 304p. $40.00. LC 84-8882. ISBN 0-9611286-2-3.

School psychologists, clinical practitioners, and students preparing for a career in school assessment will find this volume an essential reference source. Information is arranged by type of diagnosis, with chapters on autism, learning disabilities, hearing impairment, visual disabilities, and emotional disorders. For each group of children the physical, intellectual, emotional, educational, and social factors of assessment are covered. Legal aspects are also addressed in separate chapters. The appendixes list and describe the most popular tests used in clinical and diagnostic procedures.

DIRECTORIES

Directory of Selected National Testing Programs. Compiled by Test Collection, Educational Testing Service. Phoenix, Ariz.: Oryx Press, 1987. 280p. $35.00pa. LC 86-43112. ISBN 0-89774-386-5.

According to Educational Testing Service, this directory is a modified version of the *DANTES Directory of Selected National Testing Programs* published in 1975 and revised in 1985. It was sent to military education centers under a DANTES (Defense Activity for Nontraditional Education Support) grant. Information has been updated for this 1987 edition. The testing programs described here are arranged in three categories: selection/admission, academic credit/advanced standing, and certification/licensing. Entries in each category include name of testing program, purpose of the test, description, fees, and test dates. Three indexes provide access to testing programs by program name, program sponsor, and subject.

9

Elementary and Secondary Education Reference Sources

BIBLIOGRAPHIES

Elementary Teachers Guide to Free Curriculum Materials. Edited by Kathleen Suttles Nehmer. Randolph, Wis.: Educators Progress Service, 1944- . Annual. $22.75. LC 44-52255. ISSN 0070-9980.

Almost 2,000 references representing free teaching aids and other materials that support K-12 curricula are described in this annual compilation. Items described are donated or loaned free of charge by private agencies, organizations, and business corporations. Entries are arranged in fourteen subject categories, plus sections for nonprint and audio-visual materials and for materials designed for teachers and other personnel that would be included in a school's professional collection. Each entry provides a bibliographic description and annotation summarizing the instructional materials. Access to materials is available through several indexes, and complete instructions for ordering are provided.

Karnes, Elizabeth Lueder, Donald D. Black, and John Downs. **Discipline in Our Schools: An Annotated Bibliography**. Westport, Conn.: Greenwood, 1983. 700p. $55.00. LC 83-12847. ISBN 0-313-23521-X.

Classroom management and control has received increased attention in education literature and research in recent years. This compilation describes over 4,200 books, dissertations, journal articles, and school district reports published in the 1970s and 1980s that cover strategies for teachers and administrators, and other aspects of school discipline. Entries are arranged alphabetically by type of publication, and each entry provides complete bibliographic description and an annotation summarizing contents of the item.

Scheffler, Hannah Nuba, Bernice Cullinan, Dorothy Strickland, and Renee Queen. **Resources for Early Childhood: An Annotated Bibliography and Guide for Educators, Librarians, Health Care Professionals and Parents**. New York: Garland, 1985, c1983. 584p. (Garland Reference Library of Social Science, Vol. 118). $61.00; $20.00pa. LC 81-48421. ISBN 0-8240-9390-0; 0-8240-8769-0pa.

The emphasis of this bibliography is on major works published in the field of early childhood education during the 1970s and 1980s. Entries are arranged in sixteen subject chapters, each dealing with a particular area prominent in the early childhood literature for the period covered; for example, child development, the family, health, nutrition, expressive arts, multicultural education, and nonsexist education.

Songe, Alice H. **Private School Education in the U.S.: An Annotated Bibliography, 1950-1980**. Jefferson, N.C.: McFarland, 1982. 89p. index. $15.95pa. LC 81-20884. ISBN 0-89950-045-5.

Because of the attacks in recent years on public education in the United States, and suggestions from some authors that private school education is superior to that received in the public schools, this bibliography is of major interest to educators. Songe has selected 421 books, articles, government documents, and dissertations dealing with private elementary and secondary education for the years 1950 to 1980. Issues and concerns of the period are emphasized. Arrangement is by type of publication. Annotations are clear and concise (dissertations are not annotated) and a list of related state and federal associations is provided. A subject index provides access to the work.

HANDBOOKS AND YEARBOOKS

Spodek, Bernard, ed. **Handbook of Resources in Early Childhood Education**. New York: Free Press, 1982. 677p. LC 81-71152. ISBN 0-02-030570-5.
Reviews of research and theory in early childhood education are presented for beginning students, advanced scholars, teachers, administrators, policymakers in the field of early childhood education, day-care workers, early childhood educators, and child development specialists. Information is organized in five major sections, and articles in each are contributed by experts in the area.
Part 1, "Early Education and Child Development," covers cognitive, motor, and social development, and language acquisition. Part 2, "Developmental Theories and Early Education," covers curriculum models, psychodynamic theory, behavior analysis models, and Piagetian constructivism. Part 3, "Early Childhood Classroom Processes," covers play, written language acquisition, cognitive learning, and visual arts. Part 4 is "Public Policy and Early Childhood Education" and Part 5 is devoted to research methodologies. Name and subject indexes are included. A title for education at the secondary level is *A Resource Guide for Secondary School Teaching* by Eugene C. Kim and Richard D. Kellough (4th ed., Collier Macmillan, 1987).

DIRECTORIES

Georges, Christopher J., and James A. Messina, eds. **Harvard Independent Insider's Guide to Prep Schools**. New York: NAL Penguin, 1987. 453p. $9.95pa. LC 86-33121. ISBN 0-452-25920-7.
Two hundred preparatory schools are described here in an informal and subjective style. Schools were supposedly selected on the basis of whether or not they had "an interesting program of study" as well as a student body of 175 students or more. Information about schools includes some of the standard demographic data, tuition, dress code, enrollment, scholarships, as well as information about the most popular courses, most and least successful teams, and extracurricular activities. Entries are arranged alphabetically by state and many of the school descriptions are written by Harvard students. Emphasis is on eastern schools, and in spite of the subjective opinions offered, this directory does give the prospective student insights into a particular school's "personality" or "flavor."

Guide to Independent Secondary Schools. Princeton, N.J.: Peterson's Guides, 1980- . Annual. $17.95pa. LC 80-645111. ISSN 0196-7495.
Private college preparatory high schools in the United States, Canada, and abroad are described in this directory in the Peterson's Guide series. In the section "School Profiles and Announcements," schools are listed alphabetically with brief facts about each. For most schools, longer narrative summaries are provided in the "Descriptions" section. Data

are presented concisely in tabular form in the "General Register" arranged alphabetically by state. In this section, school offerings, faculty, enrollment, admissions data, and other features can be compared at a glance. Various directory lists group schools by type of school and program specialization. The eighth (1987-1988) edition is edited by Billy Christopher. The cover title is *Peterson's Guide to Independent Secondary Schools*.

The Guide to Summer Camps and Summer Schools. Boston: Porter Sargent, 1936- . Biennial. $26.00; $21.00pa. LC 37-4715. ISSN 0072-8705.

This biennial directory comparatively describes selected summer education programs available from primary to college level. The range of programs available runs from camping and other recreational programs, including specialized sports, to academic programs in music and arts, computer studies, marine biology, special tutoring and/or enrichment programs, programs in areas of special education, as well as programs of study abroad.

In order for parents and educators to identify available programs by geographic region, the guide is arranged by state. Canadian listings appear in a separate section. Each entry includes information about the name, location, and objectives of the program; age groups accepted; tuition and/or fees; average class size, program duration, and so on. A section entitled "Features Classified" precedes the listings and identifies by geographic location programs in specific categories, some of which include tutoring, postgraduate courses, developmental reading, mathematics, languages, remedial work, natural science, specialized studies, wilderness campus, and scuba diving. The work is indexed.

The Handbook of Private Schools: An Annual Descriptive Survey of Independent Education. Boston: Porter Sargent, 1915- . Annual. $45.00. LC 15-12869. ISSN 0072-9884.

This annual directory, now in its sixty-eighth edition, describes over 1,800 independent private schools at the elementary and secondary levels in the United States. School descriptions are arranged first geographically by regions and then alphabetically by city. This allows for comparative analysis of schools in the same or adjacent areas.

The first category lists leading private schools of international and historic reputation. Other sections include "Schools Classified," a section listing names and geographic locations of schools arranged in categories that represent specific needs (e.g., schools offering a postgraduate year, schools offering English as a second language); "Private Schools Illustrated"; and "Select Directory of Summer Academic Programs and Summer Camps." (The latter two sections are comprised of announcements by the schools and camps in their own words, with illustrative photographs.) Another section, "Concise Listing of Schools," presents information about boarding schools and day schools. Information provided in each description includes entry number; school name and category; address and telephone number; academic head of school; curriculum and grade levels offered (college preparatory, general, classical, commercial, vocational, secretarial); new admissions; enrollment; faculty; graduates; tuition; calendar; association membership; history and development of the school. An alphabetical index of schools concludes the work.

Pinnell, Gay Su, and associates. **Directory of Schools Reported to Have Exemplary Discipline**. Bloomington, Ind.: Phi Delta Kappa Educational Foundation, 1982. 121p. (Report of Phi Delta Kappa Commission on Discipline Series). $6.00pa. LC 81-84895. ISBN 0-87367-779-Xpa.

Discipline in American schools has recently received much attention in the media as an impediment to excellence in education. Strategies, procedures, and techniques that have been reported as successful for maintaining good classroom management are included in this directory. Categories of discipline activities in the index direct the user to specific schools' reports of their use. The directory was designed to be used as a companion volume to *PDK Handbook for Developing Schools with Good Discipline* (Phi Delta Kappa, 1982).

Private Independent Schools: The Bunting and Lyon Blue Book. 40th ed. Wallingford, Conn.: Bunting and Lyon; distr., New York: Bowker, 1943- . Annual. $49.00. LC 72-122324. ISSN 0079-5399.

Profiles of private schools and descriptive articles in this annual directory are aimed primarily at parents seeking alternative academic programs for their children, although teachers, guidance counselors, and other education professionals might find it useful. Private schools subscribe to a place in the main section where descriptive articles elaborate on each school's history and background and facts about the campus, faculty, student body, academic program, student activities, admission, and costs. This section is followed by brief profiles of all the private schools at no cost to the schools.

All schools profiled are accredited, or are accepted by (or members of) national and regional associations. They are arranged alphabetically by American states, followed by other countries and territories, in each section. The three indexes are an alphabetical "Index of Educational Associations," an "Index of Schools," and a "Geographical and Classified Index of Schools." The latter index makes distribution of private schools by state or country very easy to discern.

Bunting and Lyon have been compiling and publishing information about private independent schools since 1939 and are an established and reliable source of data about private boarding schools, day schools, religious schools, secular schools, military schools, and elementary, secondary, and college preparatory academic programs.

Utterback, Ann S., and Shirley Levin, comps. and eds. **Summer on Campus: College Experiences for High School Students**. Washington, D.C.: Transemantics, 1985. 98p. $7.95pa. LC 85-090272. ISBN 0-9613816-1-2.

This directory identifies colleges and universities in the United States that offer a total of 111 residential summer programs. Senior high school students in grades 10 through 12 who would like to spend a summer on a college campus in some kind of enrichment instruction should consult this directory. It is similar to one in the Peterson's Guides series, *Summer Opportunities for Kids and Teenagers 1988* (1987), but the latter also lists programs in other countries and summer camps.

Programs are arranged by academic institution, and each entry provides program name, institution name and address, costs, dates, eligibility, admissions, housing, credit, and other programs available.

STATISTICS SOURCES

Gardner, Randolyn Kay. **Kindergarten Programs and Practices in Public Schools**. Arlington, Va.: Educational Research Service, 1986. 123p. (ERS Report). $32.00pa./yr.

Demographic and other data related to kindergarten classes in American schools have been compiled from reports of the Educational Research Service. Charts and graphs present information on transportation of kindergarten pupils, instructional approaches, curricula, evaluation of the child's progress and achievements, and other questions and issues of concern to teachers, administrators, parents, and professional personnel associated with teacher education programs in the area of early childhood education.

Ranking of the States. West Haven, Conn.: NEA Professional Library, 1957- . Annual. ISSN 0077-4332.

This research publication from the collection of the NEA Professional Library provides information about public school education ranked by state (and the District of Columbia) on a variety of topics. Tables are included on the following topics: population, enrollment and attendance, faculty, general financial resources, governmental revenue, school revenue, government expenditures, and school expenditures. Each table is preceded by several introductory and explanatory paragraphs. The NEA obtains data from individual state departments of education.

BIOGRAPHICAL SOURCES

Who's Who among American High School Students: Honoring Tomorrow's Leaders Today. 21st ed. Lake Forest, Ill.: Educational Communications, 1986-1987. 12v. $28.50/vol. LC 68-43796. ISBN 0-930315-27-8 (set).

High school juniors and seniors who are leaders in their schools, and who participated in extracurricular activities while maintaining excellent academic records, are included in this biographical reference source. Students were nominated by their schools and then selected by an external advisory council.

Introductory material provides high school students with advice on preparing for the SAT exam, selecting a major for college study, and securing financial aid. One section is devoted to identifying scholarship winners. Biographical entries list student's name, school and address, class rank, data related to academic and extracurricular achievements, and proposed college major and college.

CURRICULUM GUIDES

A Child Goes Forth: A Curriculum Guide for Preschool Children. 6th ed. Edited by Barbara J. Taylor. Minneapolis, Minn.: Burgess Publishing, 1985. 329p. LC 84-23087. ISBN 0-8087-3663-9.

This curriculum guide, a welcomed source of ideas, lessons, and activities for designing and implementing a stimulating and carefully planned preschool learning environment, is now in its sixth edition. It includes chapters on overall preschool curriculum planning with suggestions for topics, creative expression, language arts and children's literature, music, art, science, math, field trips, and many other topics encouraging physical, social, emotional, and cognitive development. Values for children are emphasized throughout. Each chapter includes a bibliography of relevant books and other materials. A subject index is provided.

Cooper, Grace C. **Guide to Teaching Early Child Development: A Comprehensive Curriculum**. 3d ed. New York: Child Welfare League of America, 1983. 321p. $19.95. LC 75-15336. ISBN 0-87868-154-X.

This curriculum for early childhood programs was first published in 1975. The package was prepared by the Child Welfare League's Consortium on Early Childbearing and Childrearing and was designed to teach basic information about child development to adolescent parents or prospective parents.

Information is arranged in sections covering physical, social and emotional, and cognitive development in different developmental periods. The curriculum guide includes information to be covered with a subject-arranged bibliography on various aspects of child development, sample lesson plans and organization of topics covered in an eighteen-week semester or course, vocabulary lists, discussion questions, tests, worksheets, role-playing and other teaching methods and activities, and recommended films and audiovisual aids. Appendix materials cover child development theorists, a discussion of adolescence and adolescent pregnancy, birth control, language development, and language and other characteristics of ethnic subcultures.

Eliason, Claudia Fuhriman, and Loa Thomson Jenkins. **A Practical Guide to Early Childhood Curriculum**. 3d ed. Columbus, Ohio: Merrill, 1986. 425p. $21.95. LC 85-29844. ISBN 06752-0607-3.

This curriculum guide is designed to provide qualitative concrete learning experiences that meet the developmental needs of children aged three to six. It includes an overview of early childhood education and planning curricula for it. Lesson plans are arranged by concepts and subjects (music, language arts, number recognition, temperature and weather, color discrimination, etc.). Goals and objectives are stated, followed by activities spelled out on a daily basis for individuals, and both small and large groups. Means of evaluation conclude each unit.

10
Higher Education Reference Sources

GUIDES

Willingham, Warren W. in association with Elsie P. Begle, Richard I. Ferrin, Judith M. Gray, Katherine Keleman, and James C. Stam. **The Source Book for Higher Education: A Critical Guide to Literature and Information on Access to Higher Education**. New York: College Entrance Examination Board, 1973. 481p. LC 72-97458.

In addition to being an extensive annotated bibliography of material in books, articles, government documents, reports, and newsletters, this reference work has true guide features of providing access to the literature of the field. An overview chapter outlines the important characteristics of the process of access to the field, including a taxonomy of theory and practice, and sources of information in journals, newsletters, report series, statistical series, proceedings and yearbooks, data sources, information centers, general references, catalogs, and biographical directories. Under what Willingham has categorized as access agents, he lists organizations and programs.

BIBLIOGRAPHIES

Cohen, Arthur M., James C. Palmer, and K. Diane Zwemer. **Key Resources on Community Colleges**. San Francisco: Jossey-Bass, 1986. 522p. (Jossey-Bass Higher Education Series). $35.00. LC 86-45628. ISBN 1-55542-020-6.

Almost 700 books, articles, and research reports on community colleges and community college education are described in this selected bibliography. The authors emphasized materials that depict major themes, research findings reported in the literature, and developments that influenced the role of two-year colleges, as well as some of the more important or best-known publications on the subject.

Arrangement of entries is in subject chapters, including students, vocational and career education, and other aspects of community college education. Each entry includes bibliographic information and an ERIC document number. All entries are from ERIC sources and are available in the libraries of the University of California, Los Angeles.

Collective Bargaining in Higher Education and the Professions. New York: National Center for the Study of Collective Bargaining in Higher Education and the Professions, Baruch College, City University of New York, 1973- . Annual. $25.00. ISSN 0738-1913.

This is the fourteenth bibliography in the series; the 1986 issue is edited by Joel M. Douglas with Mary Donovan and Beth Hillman. Arrangement is in six parts: Part 1 is not annotated, but lists sources covering faculty bargaining on a wide variety of issues, such as fringe benefits and workload. The sources in part 2 are related to collective bargaining among the medical and other professions. Part 3 covers major court cases and decisions made by the National Labor Relations Board. Part 4 lists bibliographies and other general reference sources related to bargaining in higher education. Parts 5 and 6 are indexes providing access by author, subject, and court case. A list of acronyms and abbreviations is also provided.

The first edition of this bibliography appeared in 1973 and this publication expands and updates the coverage provided by previous editions available as ERIC documents. The National Center for the Study of Collective Bargaining in Higher Education and the Professions also publishes an annual *Directory of Faculty Contracts and Bargaining Agents in Institutions of Higher Education* (1975-).

Cordasco, Francesco, and David N. Alloway. **Medical Education in the United States: A Guide to Information Sources**. Detroit: Gale, 1980. 393p. (Education Information Guide Series, Vol. 8; Gale Information Guide Library). $65.00. LC 79-24030. ISBN 0-8103-1458-4.

The 2,364 sources related to medical education in the United States included in this bibliography are arranged in nine subject categories as follows: (1) bibliographies, dictionaries, directories, and general information; (2) history of medicine; (3) medical school admissions; (4) medical education; (5) health policy; (6) women's medical education; (7) hospitals; (8) autobiographies, biographies, reminiscences, and related materials; and (9) miscellaneous. Obviously, with these category divisions, coverage is broader than medical education, as the title indicates. A list of American medical schools is provided in the appendix.

Halstead, D. Kent, ed. **Higher Education Planning: A Bibliographic Handbook. Vol. II**. Washington, D.C.: National Institute of Education, Educational Policy & Organization Group; distr., Government Printing Office, 1984. 750p. $14.00. LC 78-24104.

This is the second of a two-volume series. The first *Higher Education Planning: A Bibliographic Handbook* was published in 1981. In the introduction to this work Halstead writes that, in light of the volume of literature published in the field of higher education, this reference work attempts to provide bibliographic control to selected sources chosen by experts in their fields who have "attempted to select only substantial and distinctive works, with emphasis on practical value" (p. x).

Coverage is broad, including all aspects of higher education from students to faculty, teaching to administration, history to mission. Some individual chapter titles include "Comparative National Systems," "Philosophy," "Resource Allocation and Budgeting," "Curriculum," "Libraries," and "Lifelong Learning," among thirty-eight chapter topics. The focus of the first volume is that of a national perspective. Volume 2 concentrates on issues of concern at the individual institution level.

Within the topical chapters entries are numbered according to the federal government's taxonomy system and year of publication. Annotations are fairly detailed and give good coverage of the intent, scope, and adequacy of each title.

In spite of its purposeful selectivity, this bibliography is a major comprehensive compilation of higher education sources.

Hines, Edward R., and John R. McCarthy. **Higher Education Finance: An Annotated Bibliography and Guide to Research**. New York: Garland, 1985. 357p. (Garland Bibliographies in Contemporary Education, Vol. 4; Garland Reference Library of Social Science, Vol, 198). $50.00. LC 83-48212. ISBN 0-8240-9054-3.

Approximately 1,000 briefly annotated entries comprise this bibliography on the research and other literature on fiscal issues in higher education. Coverage is provided for the years 1970 to mid-1983. Materials included are books, articles, essays, reports, government documents that have appeared in ERIC, bibliographies, and reference lists. Arrangement of entries is in eight subject chapters covering external grant fundings; student fellowships, grants, loans, and other forms of financial aid; reduction in student enrollment and staff; retrenchment; financial aid from government sources; and budgets and fiscal planning. Author and subject indexes provide access to the contents.

Parker, Franklin, and Betty June Parker. **U.S. Higher Education: A Guide to Information Sources**. Detroit: Gale, 1980. 675p. (Gale Information Guide Library: Education Information Guide Series, Vol. 9) $65.00. LC 80-21959. ISBN 0-8103-2476-2.

This annotated bibliography of 3,194 books and reports covers all aspects of higher education in the United States. A selective approach was used for determining inclusion of nineteenth-century materials; the goal was to be comprehensive with respect to the twentieth century.

Arrangement of entries is strictly alphabetical by author, so the subject index must be used extensively to indentify materials by topic. Major topics identified in the preface include educational history, philosophy, administration, finance, governance, curriculum, student life, library and audiovisual services, government relations at various levels, innovations, and the needs of women, minorities, students, faculty, and staff. Author and title indexes are also provided.

While the usefulness of the Parkers' work might have been enhanced by use of a subject arrangement, it is still a reliable and comprehensive analysis of the higher education literature up to 1980.

Quay, Richard H. **Research in Higher Education: A Guide to Source Bibliographies**. 2d ed. Phoenix, Ariz.: Oryx Press, 1985. 133p. $32.00. LC 85-45510. ISBN 0-89774-194-3.

This bibliography of bibliographies to sources of research in higher education includes 932 compilations arranged alphabetically by author in broad subject category chapters. Higher education from community colleges to graduate programs in major universities are covered in chapter titles as follows: "Comprehensive Sources"; "History and Philosophy of Higher Education"; "Four-Year Institutions"; "Two-Year Institutions"; "Students"; "Faculty"; "Administrators and Support Staff"; "Curriculum and Instruction"; "Financial Management"; "Administrative Behavior"; "Research, Planning, and Policy Development"; "Social and Political Issues"; "Physical Plant Management"; "Comparative Higher Education"; and "Adult and Lifelong Education."

Only a very few entries are annotated, and page numbers are not included, so it is hard to determine the extent of any particular bibliography. However, the second edition of this work updates and expands the 1976 edition by 360 entries. ERIC document numbers are provided for bibliographies available through the Educational Resources Information Center. Books and articles on higher education as a field of study are in appendix A; "Directory of Higher Education Research Centers and Advanced Programs," arranged alphabetically by state, constitutes appendix B. Both an author and a subject index are included, with the subject index based on the *Thesaurus of ERIC Descriptors*.

Researchers in the field of educational history would also be interested in Quay's *Index to Anthologies on Postsecondary Education, 1960-1978* (Greenwood, 1980).

Quay, Richard H. and Peter P. Olevnik. **The Financing of American Higher Education: A Bibliographic Handbook**. Phoenix, Ariz.: Oryx Press, 1984. 142p. $36.00. LC 83-13192. ISBN 0-89774-047-5.

The problem of financing over 3,000 institutions of higher education in the United States is increasingly complicated, especially when there are ever more demands for research, instruction, and public service and, at the same time, fewer sources of income. This comprehensive bibliography covers over twenty years of the major trends, issues, and legislation in the literature on higher education finance, including the influence of demographic, economic, political, and social forces.

The 1,117 entries are arranged by subject in nineteen chapters which have been grouped in four clusters: "Political Economy of American Higher Education"; "Institutions, Programs, and Coalitions"; "Human Resources"; and "Research, Planning, and Policy Development." Some individual chapters are concerned with federal, state, and private support; graduate and professional education; faculty salaries, benefits, productivity, and collective bargaining; enrollment projections; price indexes; and retrenchment and reallocation of resources. Complete bibliographic information is provided for each title, as well as descriptive and, sometimes, evaluative annotation.

Appendix A is devoted to related listings covering financing of higher education; appendix B lists higher education financial data and statistical sources. Author and subject indexes conclude this well-prepared handbook compiled by two experienced bibliographers and librarians.

Ryans, Cynthia C., and William L. Shanklin. **Strategic Planning, Marketing & Public Relations, and Fund-Raising in Higher Education: Perspectives, Readings, and Annotated Bibliography**. Metuchen, N.J.: Scarecrow Press, 1986. 266p. $20.00. LC 86-3871. ISBN 0-8108-1891-4.

College and university administrators must deal with diminished financial resources and changes in curricular emphases from liberal arts and humanities to business and technological interests. According to the authors, strategic planning is a management process that will help them to anticipate future changes and identify options for responding to them.

This reference tool is divided into three major sections. The first one contains three reprinted journal articles on different aspects of strategic planning, followed by a fifty-item annotated bibliography on the subject. Section 2 is concerned with marketing and public relations and includes four articles and a bibliography of 113 citations; section 3, on fund raising again has three reprinted articles and a 140-item bibliography. In addition, each section is prefaced with an introductory overview essay by the authors. Access to individual items is available through author, title, and subject indexes.

Swanson, Kathryn. **Affirmative Action and Preferential Admissions in Higher Education: An Annotated Bibliography**. Metuchen, N.J.: Scarecrow Press, 1981. 336p. $22.50. LC 81-45. ISBN 0-8108-1411-0.

Bibliographic control of the literature on affirmative action and preferential treatment to minorities and women is attempted in this compilation of 1,180 annotated entries. Materials cited include books, periodical and newspaper articles, ERIC documents, and selected chapters from monographic works from 1970-1981. Arrangement of materials is in three sections, each of which begins with an introductory essay.

Section 1 covers materials related to legal aspects, "The Law and the Courts," and includes coverage of some landmark court cases, such as the *University of California v. Allan Bakke*. The reaction of higher education institutions is covered in the second part, "The Academic Community Response," and philosophical issues of debate are also included.

Access is available only through the name and title index; a subject index would make this tool more useful. Even though the cut-off date is 1980, these entries can provide the researcher with information on the historical development of affirmative action in higher education.

A related title that provides information about affirmative action programs and includes a twenty-five page bibliography is *Affirmative Action in Higher Education* by Lois Vanderwaerdt (Garland, 1982).

White, Jane N., and Collins W. Burnett, eds. **Higher Education Literature: An Annotated Bibliography**. Phoenix, Ariz.: Oryx Press, 1981. 177p. index. $60.50. LC 81-11206. ISBN 0-912700-80-7.

Although this bibliography is already somewhat dated, it is of value to the educational researcher and, particularly, the educational historian. Emphasis is on topics and issues of the 1970s. The first section is devoted to 236 citations to books and articles in the category entitled "Historical Backgrounds and Scope of Higher Education." Other aspects of higher education are covered in additional broad category sections: "Teaching-Learning Environment," "Organization and Administration," "Community and Junior Colleges," "Comparative Systems of Higher Education," and "Higher Education as a Specialized Field of Study."

There are 1,618 entries arranged in subject subdivisions within these categories. In addition, another twenty-five entries describe selected reference sources and another forty describe major professional journals in the field of higher education in the appendix material. The eleven appendixes provide useful information related to higher education, such as definitions of terminology, higher education programs and centers, national professional associations, accrediting associations, publishers, federal legislation related to higher education, and land grant colleges and universities.

Titles can be accessed through both author and subject indexes.

INDEXES AND ABSTRACTS

Quay, Richard H., comp. **Index to Anthologies on Postsecondary Education, 1960-1978**. Westport, Conn.: Greenwood, 1980. 342p. $39.95. LC 79-8286. ISBN 0-313-21272-4.

Quay claims that a large portion of articles and essays written on higher education appear in anthologies not typically covered by periodical indexes. Therefore, this index to the anthology literature for the period 1960 to 1978 provides access to a large number of additional resources. Over 3,600 entries are arranged alphabetically in subject categories. Almost all of the entries are unannotated, but each entry indicates the anthology in which the item was found and whether it was an original or reprint. Author and subject indexes are included, with the subject index using ERIC descriptors. In spite of the absence of annotations, this index fills a gap in the reference literature, as it provides access to all aspects of postsecondary education. It should be of great interest to educational historians, doctoral candidates, and other researchers in the field, especially since, according to Quay, 87 percent of the essays indexed here are not identified in standard sources.

DICTIONARIES AND ENCYCLOPEDIAS

The International Encyclopedia of Higher Education. Edited by Asa S. Knowles. San Francisco: Jossey-Bass, 1977. 10v. $650.00. LC 77-73646. ISBN 0-87589-323-6 (set).

A total of 588 scholars from sixty-nine countries of the world have contributed 1,300 signed articles on various topics related to contemporary higher education. Volume 1 of this comprehensive set lists all contributors, their affiliations, and titles of articles they prepared. It also includes an alphabetical listing of all entries by volume, a list of acronyms, and glossary of terms. Volumes 2 through 9 contain the articles, which are fairly comprehensive, typically covering about seven pages. Although some articles are as brief as one-half page, others are much longer, for example, a discussion of "Academic Dress and Insignia" covers seventeen pages of text and illustrations. Appended bibliographies vary in currency and comprehensiveness.

Although entries are arranged alphabetically, they can be organized categorically to cover national systems of education, topical essays, fields of study, educational associations, research centers and institutes, reports on higher education, and documentation centers. Biographical entries are excluded. An extensive indexing system and cross-references direct the user to nonalphabetical entries.

Some major educational libraries of the world are described in detail, but educational institutions are not included. Print size is large, headings are bold, and the liberal use of space make it very readable, while, undoubtedly, adding to its expense. This encyclopedia provides the only comprehensive coverage of its kind directed to various aspects of higher education from national, international, and comparative perspectives of analysis.

Ohles, John F., and Shirley M. Ohles. **Public Colleges and Universities**. Westport, Conn.: Greenwood, 1986. 1,014p. $95.00. (Greenwood Encyclopedia of American Institutions). LC 85-17725. ISBN 0-313-23257-1.

This reference work provides 578 sketches covering the historical background and current status of public institutions offering undergraduate and/or graduate programs. All of the public colleges and universities included were listed in the *Higher Education Directory 1983* (Higher Education Publications, 1983) *Yearbook of Higher Education, 1982-83* (14th ed., Marquis Professional Publications, 1982), which represent institutions that are accredited or candidates for accreditation by regional or national accrediting agencies.

Entries are arranged alphabetically by institution name and include the following: institution name, address, enrollment, faculty size, library holdings, academic calendars, contributors of information, and sources for further reference. A running chronology of the founding of public schools in the United States can be found in appendix 1, "Years Founded"; 2, "Location by State"; 3, "Land-Grant Institutions"; and 4, "Specialized Institutions." An index concludes the work.

Although the sketches of institutions vary in length, most provide more detail than those found in standard guides or directories. As a part of the *Greenwood Encyclopedia of American Institutions* series, this work indeed provides information that is encyclopedic in nature with emphasis given to the institution's historical background, as opposed to the type of data that would help a prospective college student select a particular school (e.g., financial aid or scholarships available, faculty credentials, SAT score ranges, tuition and fees). The Ohles' have compiled a unique and valuable tool for educational researchers and historians in this guide and a previous publication, *Private Colleges and Universities* (Greenwood, 1982).

HANDBOOKS AND YEARBOOKS

Barron's How to Prepare for the Advanced Placement Examination in Biology. 3d rev. ed. Edited by Gabrielle Edwards and Marion Cimmino. Woodbury, N.Y.: Barron's Educational Series, 1987. 352p. $9.95pa. ISBN 0-8120-3875-4.

Students who are getting ready to take the Advanced Placement Examination in biology can find sample tests and questions. Included as well are tips on how to study and how to compete with other test takers. Barrons has also prepared similar titles for those who wish to take the same type of placement exam in other subjects, such as mathematics, English, or the CPA exam.

Barron's How to Prepare for the SAT (Scholastic Aptitude Test). 14th rev. ed. Woodbury, N.Y.: Barron's Educational Series, 1987. 672p. $9.95pa. LC 87-18845. ISBN 0-8120-3844-4.

High school students who want to compete for admission to selective colleges want to attain the highest SAT score possible. Barron's has developed a study guide to help them prepare for this exam. There are many other titles in this publisher's series of the same nature, for example, *Barron's How to Prepare for the American College Testing Program (ACT)* (1985); *Barron's How to Prepare for the CLEP General Examinations* (1986); *Barron's How to Prepare for the Graduate Record Exam* (7th ed., 1985); *Barron's How to Prepare for the High School Equivalency Exam (GED)* (rev. 6th ed., 1984); *Barron's How to Prepare for the MAT (Miller Analogies Test)* (4th ed., 1986); *Barron's How to Prepare for the National Teachers Examinations—Common Exam: Education in the Elementary School* (1984); *Barron's How to Prepare for the Regent's Competency Examination: Writing* (1983); *Barron's How to Prepare for the Test of English as a Foreign Language* (5th ed., 1986); and *Barron's How to Prepare for the Graduate Management Admission Test (GMAT)*(7th ed., 1987). Other "how to prepare" guides cover high school proficiency exams; College Board Achievement Tests In Latin, European History and World Culture, Spanish, Biology, English, Mathematics; the GED in specific subjects; and the regent's exams in other subjects.

Fact Book on Higher Education. Compiled by Cecilia A. Ottinger. New York: American Council on Higher Education/Macmillan, 1987. 209p. (American Council on Education/Macmillan Series on Higher Education). $39.95. ISBN 0-02-909680-4. ISSN 0363-6720.

This reference source condenses data from over thirty documentary sources including the National Center for Education Statistics, the U.S. Bureau of the Census, the Office of Civil Rights, the Bureau of Labor Statistics of the U.S. Department of Labor, the U.S. Department of Commerce, the National Science Foundations, and congressional committees. It also contains unpublished tabulations of government data. *Fact Book on Higher Education* is arranged in seven sections: (1) "Demographic and Economic Data," (2) "Enrollment data," (3) "Data on Institutions," (4) "Data on Faculty and Staff," (5) "Student Data," (6) "Earned Degrees Data," and (7) "Student Aid Data." Detailed highlights are compiled at the beginning of each section. Data are current and well organized in clearly presented charts, graphs, tables, and maps. This title was first published in 1958.

McCarthy, Jane E., Irving Ladimer, and Josef P. Sirefman. **Managing Faculty Disputes: A Guide to Issues, Procedures and Practices.** San Francisco: Jossey-Bass, 1984. 270p. (Higher Education Series). $25.95. LC 84-47991. ISBN 0-87589-623-5.

This reference manual is aimed at administrators at the college and university level who are involved in faculty governance and/or the resolution of faculty disputes. The authors present a wide variety of problems related to promotion and tenure, discipline, retrenchment and reorganization, and other issues. Information is arranged in three parts related to grievances and policy disputes, with an emphasis on the management process rather than specific problems solutions. Part 1 is "Recurring Disputes"; parts 2 and 3 are "Procedures for Resolving Recurring Disputes" and "Special Issues and Institutional Practices." Descriptions of disputes come from accounts published in the media (e.g., *Chronicle of Higher Education*), and, according to the authors, the book came about as a result of their experiences and workshops at the Center for Mediation in Higher Education at the American Arbitration Association.

Miller, Jerry W., and Eugene J. Sullivan, eds. **Guide to the Evaluation of Educational Experiences in the Armed Services**. Washington, D.C.: American Council on Education, 1986. 3v. $50.00/set; $19.95/vol. ISBN 0-02-897540-5(set); 0-02-897510-3(v.1); 0-02-897520-0(v.2); 0-02-897530-8(v.3).

This three-volume work is designed to assist administrative personnel in postsecondary institutions evaluate and award appropriate credit for course work taken by those serving in the armed services. Volume 1 lists course exhibits for U.S. Air Force personnel; volume 2 covers the U.S. Army and volume 3 the Coast Guard, Marine Corps, and Navy.

The American Council on Education has cooperated with the Department of Defense since the first edition of this reference work in 1946 in helping servicemen and women get degree-related credit for programs of learning undertaken while in the military.

Formal course offerings in each volume are arranged by OECC (Office on Educational Credit and Credentials) ID number. In addition, each entry includes the official military course title and number, length of course, dates, location, objectives or purpose of the course, brief description of the instructional methods, credit recommendations, and evaluation date (when the credit recommendation was established).

Phifer, Paul. **College Majors and Careers: A Resource Guide for Effective Life Planning**. Garrett Park, Md.: Garrett Park Press, 1987. 166p. $15.00pa. LC 87-80226. ISBN 0-912048-46-8.

The unique feature of this reference source is that it attempts to help college students identify courses of study or college majors that are most relevant to, and will lead to work opportunities related to, their individual interests. It might also be of interest to someone who needs help and direction in making a career change.

Sixty broad interest areas (e.g., communications or social work) are arranged alphabetically and discussed briefly. Under each interest are provided lists of related occupations and activities. Major skills, qualities, and characteristics that are necessary and/or beneficial for pursuing careers related to the interest area are also indicated. The appendixes contain brief job descriptions, definitions of skills and attitudes, a bibliography of references on the subject, and a list of degree fields. Another handbook related to college selection is Louis Mazzari's four-volume *Admissions Data Handbook* (Orchard House, 1986).

Whitney, Douglas R., and Andrew G. Malizio. **Guide to Educational Credit by Examination**. 2d ed. New York: American Council on Education/Macmillan, 1987. 172p. $25.00. LC 86-16177. ISBN 0-02-901580-4.

How do postsecondary academic institutions determine how credit for extrainstitutional learning should be awarded? The Center for Adult Learning and Educational Credentials has a Credit-by-Examination Program directed toward helping schools establish policies and procedures for making such decisions based upon ACE (American Council on Education) evaluations. The center also helps adult learners obtain credit for external learning tests or learning experiences.

Eleven chapters discuss various credit-by-examination tests and programs; for example, CLEP (College Level Examination Program), GED (General Education Development), the test review process and reporting, followed by several specific programs. Some of the latter include American Chemical Society (ACS) Examinations, American College Testing Program Proficiency Examination Program (ACT PEP), The California State University (CSU) English Equivalency Examinations, and Certified Professional Secretary (CPS) Examination. Appendixes cover tests no longer available or not evaluated by the ACE and sample test review forms.

DIRECTORIES

Bricker's International Directory: University Executive Programs. Woodside, Calif.: Bricker Executive Education Service, 1969- . Annual. $110.00. LC 73-110249. ISSN 0361-1108.

Programs for university executives at higher levels of administration are compiled and organized in this directory. Over 300 programs offered in the English language on a worldwide basis are described, and arrangement of entries is in four major parts. Part 1 includes general management programs; part 2 is devoted to functional management programs. Part 3 provides descriptions of the institutions where the programs are located, and part 4 includes appendix material. The latter includes information on dates when programs begin and end and other relevant information for those interested in enrolling in a management program.

Beginning with the twelfth edition in 1981, the publication became an annual directory. Recent editions have been edited by Samuel A. Pond.

Directory of Faculty Contracts and Bargaining Agents in Institutions of Higher Education. New York: National Center for the Study of Collective Bargaining in Higher Education and the Professions, Baruch College, City University of New York, 1975- . Annual. $20.00pa. ISSN 0276-7805.

This annual directory covers all faculty bargaining activities, elections held, and contracts negotiated between faculty unions and the college of university administrations for the previous year. Unionized institutions in the United States and Canada are listed alphabetically by state or province. A separate list of contracts for adjunct faculty is also included. Entries include the following: institution name, bargaining agent, size of unit, date of election of current agent, date of initial contract, type of institution (public, private, two-year, four-year, etc.), number of campuses, and contract expiration date. Tabular data depict how bargaining units are distributed geographically, and summarize legislation related to collective bargaining and other concepts associated with negotiation.

Directory of the College Student Press in America. 6th ed. Edited by Dario Politella. New York: Oxbridge Communications, 1986. 300p. $75.00. LC 78-120744. ISBN 0-917460-14-6.

One purpose of this directory is to provide a comprehensive guide to all formats of college student media—newspapers; magazines (devoted to art, literature, humor, etc.); handbooks; and yearbooks. Over 3,500 institutions of higher education were contacted by mail and telephone to gather information about college student publications. Entries are arranged alphabetically first by state and then by school, and provide: college or university name, address, and telephone number; president's name; Director of Student Activities (DSA); type of college (public/private, two-year/four-year, coed or other); enrollment;

title and type of publication; publication advisor; year established; frequency; subscription rate; circulation; average pages/issue; advertising; physical format features; and budget and means of financing. A title index is not provided, so a reader would be unable to locate the school affiliated with a known title. Otherwise this guide performs a unique and very useful function.

Faculty Directory of Higher Education 1988: A Twelve-Volume Subject-Classified Directory Providing Names, Addresses, and Titles of Courses Taught for More than 600,000 Teaching Faculty. Edited by GMG Information Services Staff. Detroit: Gale 1988. 12v. $785.00/set. ISBN 0-8103-2750-3. ISSN 0894-9476.

Eleven of the volumes in this set contain names and addresses of over 600,000 faculty members teaching in over 3,100 two-year community colleges, four-year colleges, and universities in the United States. Selected coverage is also given to faculty in 220 Canadian schools. Arrangement of entries is in broad academic subjects and then alphabetically within subject volumes. Information in each entry covers institution, department, address, and titles of courses taught. The broad subject arrangement makes it hard to identify faculty members and courses taught in smaller subdivisions of the broad category. A two-volume index lists faculty alphabetically. Faculty names are obtained from mailing lists compiled by GMG Publishing Company for companies that market to academic faculty at the higher education level. Considering how soon this multivolume work will be out-of-date, the price is very steep.

The National Dean's List. 10th ed. Lake Forest, Ill.: Educational Communications, 1987. 2v. $333.50/set. LC 79-642835. ISBN 0-930315-39-1.

This annual reference guide lists students in 2,500 American colleges and universities who have earned grades high enough to be recognized by the deans, academic vice presidents, or registrars of their schools for their academic achievement. Brief biographical sketches of students are arranged alphabetically by student name. Each entry includes student's name, college or university, city and state where school is located, academic year, degree sought, accomplishments, major field of study, career plans, and indication of whether student is included in previous edition. The directory also includes photographs of the year's *National Dean's List* scholarship winners, a glossary of abbreviations that appear in the biographical sketches, lists of professional and social fraternities/sororities, honor societies, and recognition and service societies. Photographs available on some of the students follow the main body of entries.

The National Faculty Directory: An Alphabetical List, with Addresses, of Approximately 650,000 Members of Teaching Faculties at Junior Colleges, Colleges, and Universities in the United States and at Selected Canadian Institutions. Detroit: Gale, 1970- . Annual. $500.00. ISSN 0077-4472.

In its eighteenth edition, this four-volume directory lists the names and departmental and institutional affiliations of about 660,000 faculty members at approximately 3,200 American and 120 Canadian colleges and universities. Librarians and other nonteaching staff members are not included. Information for the directory is obtained from surveys sent to faculty members listed in academic catalogs and course lists, and does not cover nonteaching personnel who hold faculty rank, such as librarians in academic institutions.

The list of faculty is preceded by a table that lists abbreviated terms used to indicate geographic location, type of program, institution, and so on. This is followed by a list of all schools covered in the directory arranged alphabetically first by states in the United States, then territories, and Canadian provinces.

Although this is the most comprehensive directory of its kind, there are still gaps where current catalogs have not been available to the publisher.

Visiting Fulbright Scholars & Occasional Lecturers. Washington, D.C.: Council for International Exchange of Scholars, 1984- . Annual. LC 84-649184. ISSN 0888-3386.

This directory was originally known as *Directory of Visiting Fulbright Scholars & Occasional Lecturers*. Volume 1 of this new annual is a listing of about 900 recent postgraduate recipients of Fulbright Awards. This scholarship program, named after U.S. Senator J. William Fulbright, was established to promote and increase "mutual understanding between the people of the United States and the people of other countries" (p. 4). These awards can be won by Americans for overseas scholarship, and by foreign scholars who wish to do advanced research, university teaching, or graduate study in the United States. Entries are arranged alphabetically by subject discipline and include the award recipient's name, position, and address in native country; nature of Fulbright appointment and location of institution; duration of scholarship period; and name of sponsoring or contact person.

Access to visiting scholars is possible by: Home Country Index; Host State Index; and Alphabetical Index.

COLLEGE GUIDES (GENERAL)

AACJC Directory of Community, Technical and Junior College Directory. Washington, D.C.: American Association of Community and Junior Colleges, 1987- . Annual. $30.00. LC 87-641565. ISSN 0884-7169.

Produced by the national organization that represents two-year colleges (AACJC), this annual directory provides current data about community, technical, and junior colleges in the United States. The organization has published this directory under various titles from 1930 on. From 1975 to 1982 it was known as *Community, Junior, and Technical College Directory*, after which it became *Community, Technical and Junior College Directory, A Statistical Analysis*. Entries are arranged alphabetically by state and include institution name, location, chief executive officer, telephone number, date of establishment, control or affiliation, AACJC membership, recognition or accreditation, academic year, enrollment, professional staff, administration, and tuition and fees.

In addition to the schools, this directory provides information (including photos) about the AACJC Board of Directors, the association's mission and goals, affiliated councils, international members, associates, corporate members, and executive officers. The directory is preceded by several pages discussing interpretation of the data, including summary statistics on enrollments in private/public two-year institutions; definitions of terms; key to abbreviations; and deletions and additions since the previous year's directory. This directory is a must in high school libraries where school administrators, media specialists, and guidance counselors can direct students to educational opportunities in two-year programs.

Accredited Institutions of Postsecondary Education. Edited by Sherry S. Harris. Washington, D.C.: American Council on Education, 1976- . Annual. $22.50. ISSN 0270-1715.

This annual directory lists, by state, accredited institutions or those accepted for accreditation by the Council on Postsecondary Accreditation (COPA). Entries are arranged in categories of colleges or universities already accredited and those that are candidates for accreditation. Information in each entry includes date when the institution was first accredited, or the date when admitted to candidacy for accreditation, renewal dates, name of accrediting association, academic calendar year, degrees, specialized accreditation, chief executive officer, enrollment, and telephone number. Specialized accreditations by professional bodies (53 professional agencies in 102 fields) are indicated.

American Universities and Colleges. 13th ed. Compiled and edited by American Council on Education. New York: De Gruyter, 1987. 2,024p. $119.50. LC 28-5598. ISBN 0-89925-179-X.

This comprehensive directory to institutions of higher education in the United States is published approximately every four years. It is divided into five sections. Part 1 covers the origin and development of higher education in the United States, its structure and an overview of the different types of institutions; characteristics of graduate and undergraduate students; the role of the federal government; and international students. Part 2 focuses on accreditation agencies and activities associated with thirty-nine different fields of professional specialization. Institutions that are accredited by each agency are listed (including degrees offered). Part 3 comprises the main body of the work, providing directory type information to 1,728 undergraduate and graduate institutions of higher education. Entries are arranged alphabetically by state and include information related to admission standards, degree requirements, student body composition, special educational programs, costs, financial aid, faculty, library resources, and school calendar. Parts 4 and 5 are made up of appendixes and indexes, respectively. Although this work is very comprehensive in scope, information about individual institutions and American higher education, in general, needs to be updated.

An Assessment of Research Doctorate Programs in the United States. National Academy of Sciences. Washington, D.C.: National Academy of Sciences Press, 1982, 5v. $52.50/set; $12.50(v.1); $11.50(v.2); $11.50(v.3); $11.50(v.4); $11.50(v.5). ISBN 0-309-03344-6.

Comparative data assessing the quality of doctoral programs offered at 228 universities in thirty-two disciplines are provided in this five-volume set. Information covered includes size of program and number of doctoral students enrolled, characteristics of graduates, institutional image as reflected by faculty survey results, and library holdings. The assessment, sponsored by the Conference Board of Associated Research Councils, is reported in five volumes: volume 1, *Humanities*; 2, *Social & Behavioral Sciences*; 3, *Biological Sciences*; 4, *Engineering*; and 5, *Mathematical & Physical Sciences*.

Barron's Profiles of American Colleges. Compiled and edited by the College Division of Barron's Educational Series. Woodbury, N.Y.: Barron's Educational Series, 1973- . Biennial. 2v. $12.95/vol. LC 86-14010. ISSN 0533-1072.

Accredited four-year colleges in the United States are described in individual profiles arranged alphabetically by state, and then institution. Each entry includes name, address, and telephone number of the college or university; tuition and costs; student enrollment data; faculty; admission requirements; campus life and extracurricular activities; transfer information; and programs of study. Schools can also be approached by major area of study where availability of specific undergraduate majors and required courses associated with them are indicated for individual schools.

Regional editions of this title have also been published for the Northeast, the Midwest, the South, and the West, as well as an abridged edition, *Barron's Compact Guide to Colleges* (5th ed., 1986). The Barron's guides are reliable and comprehensive. Other publications based on the data provided in *Profiles of American Colleges* are numerous and include, among others, *Barron's Guide to the Most Prestigious Colleges* (4th ed., 1986); Barron's Guide to the Two-Year Colleges (1981); and *Barron's Guide to the Best, Most Popular and Most Exciting Colleges* (4th ed., 1986). In addition, Barron's has prepared numerous guides to graduate study in various fields, such as *Barron's Guide to Graduate Schools, Vol. 5 Education* (1975); *Barron's Guide to Medical & Dental Schools* (2d ed., 1985); *Barron's Guide to Law Schools* (7th ed., 1986); and *Barron's Guide to Graduate Business Schools (1988)*.

Birnbach, Lisa. **Lisa Birnbach's College Book**. New York: Ballantine Books/Random House, 1986. 536p. $9.95pa. LC 84-90910. ISBN 0-345-30918-9.

The focus of this college guide is on the college atmosphere and student life-style. Birnbach is highly selective, choosing 186 schools to describe. Information was obtained via questionnaire, interviews, and visits to the campuses.

The writing style is humorous and informal, but depth of information is not always consistent from one entry to the next. While a prospective student might enjoy reading this inside information about favorite courses of study and faculty, about the "best" eating places, degree of acceptance for minorities and gays, the extent of drug and alcohol use, and so on, the scope of limitations necessitates that this directory be consulted in conjunction with one of the more comprehensive standard guides.

Cass, James, and Max Birnbaum. **Comparative Guide to American Colleges, for Students, Parents, and Counselors**. New York: Harper & Row, 1964- . Biennial. $34.50. LC 85-42557. ISBN 0-06-055090-2; ISSN 0893-1216.

The thirteenth edition, (1987) is a 777-page comprehensive directory to American colleges and universities. All accredited four-year schools are described with primary attention given to scholastic and academic achievements and opportunities and standard data related to controlling agency, founding date, accreditation, admission requrements, faculty, calendar, enrollment, transfer policy, and housing. An additional feature is that schools are compared with respect to the social life of the campus, religious affilation, and cultural environment. Entries are not equal in length for each institution, nor do they provide equal coverage of the criteria addressed. Information about institutions can be accessed through the indexes by state, admissions selectivity, religious affiliation, or academic majors.

Chronical Four-Year College Databook. Edited by Paul Downes. Moravia, N.Y.: Chronicle Guidance Publications, 1980- . Annual. $17.75pa. LC 79-644820. ISSN 0192-3670.

This annual college directory, published as *Chronicle College Charts* from 1978 to 1979, lists over 2,000 schools. Individual schools are organized under specific curricular areas of study, and only brief information, in tabular form, provides name and address of the school, telephone number, enrollment statistics, admissions policy, tuition costs and fees, and availability of financial aid. Other databooks in this series provide information about community, junior, and technical colleges, *Chronicle Two-Year College Databook* (1974-); and a total of 3,700 vocational schools are listed in *Chronicle Vocational School Manual* (1981-).

College Blue Book. 21st ed. New York: Macmillan, 1986. 5v. $200.00/set; $40.00/vol. LC 79-66191. ISBN 0-02-695960-7 (set).

The *College Blue Book* is a five-volume set covering postsecondary institutions and the various programs and opportunities they offer. The volumes may be purchased individually or as a set and include *Narrative Descriptions; Tabular Data; Degrees Offered by College and Subjects; Occupational Education;* and *Scholarships, Fellowships, Grants and Loans.* In each volume, entries are first arranged alphabetically by state or province.

Narrative Descriptions fully describes over 3,100 colleges in the United States and Canada. Each entry includes a paragraph providing background information about accreditation, enrollment, degrees granted, academic calendar, entrance requirements, costs, and collegiate and community environment. The *Tabular Data* volume lists information about institution type, characteristics of student body, accreditation, costs, enrollment, housing, student/faculty ratio, chief administrative officers, and so on. *Degrees Offered by College and Subject* helps guidance counselors by identifying degrees offered at each college and providing a subject listing to schools in each state or province offering a program in the various subjects. *Occupational Education* lists schools providing training in technical skills for paraprofessional or trade positions. Each entry provides information about the curriculum; whether or not a high school degree is required; whether job placement service is available; degrees or certificates awarded; as well as costs, term, and so on. The volume devoted to financial aid, *Scholarships, Fellowships, Grants and Loans* describes the various kinds of financial assistance programs available (from outright awards that do not have to be repaid to private and governmental loans). Specific dollar amount of information is probably dated, but the student can at least get a profile of the types of assistance possible.

As a set, the *College Blue Book* provides a very comprehensive guide to a wide variety of information about postsecondary education.

The College Handbook, 1987-88. 25th ed. New York: College Entrance Examination Board, 1985. 1,900p. $15.95pa. ISBN 0-87447-208-3.

First published in 1941, *The College Handbook,* a guide to colleges that are members of the College Entrance Examination Board, is now in its twenty-fifth edition. Its purpose is to provide detailed information about the more than 3,000 undergraduate college and university programs in the United States that lead to two-year associate degrees or four-year baccalaureate degrees. Introductory material will help prospective college students, parents, school librarians, and guidance counselors in narrowing choices of colleges; will help in determining how and when to apply; and provide financial sources (etc.), as well as a glossary of terms commonly found in college catalogs.

Arrangement of entries is alphabetical by state; American Samoa, Caroline Islands, Guam, and the Virgin Islands follow the alphabetical listing of states. Information is given about accreditation, enrollment, academic calendar, location, campus environment, special features, curriculum, admissions, student life, annual expenses, and address/telephone. This college guide's one-volume paperback format makes it attractive as a convenient and inexpensive addition to a school library collection.

De La Croix de Lafayette, Jean-Maximillien. **Directory of United States Traditional and Alternative Colleges and Universities 1984-1986**. Washington, D.C.: NASACU (National Association of State Approved Colleges and Universities), 1986. 476p. $30.00. LC 86-645312. ISSN 0082-7745.

This directory attempts to list all colleges and universities legally authorized to grant academic degrees including traditional accredited schools and alternative schools. The latter are defined as those schools which have high academic standards, but are relatively unknown despite outstanding offerings. The author says that his objectives include protecting the public from "fly-by-night" schools or "diploma mills" and "to inform various authorities (academic and governmental) about the existence of thousands of legitimate and good schools which were not listed in other directories" (p.xviii). Another feature which makes this directory unique is the listing of opportunities to receive credit for prior learning via life experiences as opposed to strict adherence to credit for formal course work only.

The book opens with a state-arranged list of authorities on higher education in the United States in chapter 1, followed by a list of colleges and universities legally empowered to grant academic degrees (also arranged alphabetically by state) in chapter 2. Chapter 3, "What Accreditation Is All About," discusses the difference between accredited and unaccredited institutions. Subsequent chapters cover alternative nontraditional education; nonresidential degree programs; independent study programs; external degree programs; programs requiring short attendance on campus; correspondence schools; degree programs via television, radio, newspapers, and telephone; honorary degrees; and others.

Appendix material includes objectives and membership criteria of NASACU. The work is indexed, with access by subject and institution name. Although students seeking a traditional education would want to consult more in-depth information in the standard college guides, this unusual reference tool provides very comprehensive lists of schools catering to learners with specific educational requirements or limitations (e.g., law school programs offered in evening sessions) as well as a wide assortment of information about higher education in general and higher education in particular settings.

Directory of Postsecondary Institutions. Washington, D.C.: National Center for Education Statistics; distr., Government Printing Office, 1986- . Annual. $16.00pa. S/N 065-000-00268-0.

This annual directory continues *Education Directory, Colleges and Universities* (1976-1986), which prior to 1976 was known as *Education Directory: Higher Education* (1912-1975). It lists colleges and universities in the United States and its outlying areas (American Samoa, Guam, Northern Mariana Islands, Puerto Rico, the Virgin Territory of the Pacific Islands) legally authorized to offer at least a one-year program leading toward a postsecondary degree. Institutions included must have submitted the required information and met nationally recognized accrediting agency criteria. A list of these accrediting agencies is provided in the introduction.

Entries for institutions are arranged alphabetically by state and information provided includes name of institution, address and telephone number, FICE (Federal Interagency Committee on Education) identification number, entity number, date of establishment, composition of student body, enrollment, undergraduate tuition and fees, control or affiliation, calendar system, CS classification structure, highest level of offering, and type of program.

Guide to American Graduate Schools. 5th ed. Edited by Harold R. Doughty. New York: Penguin Books, 1986. 605p. $14.95pa. LC 86-42541. ISBN 0-14-046725-4.

This directory covers graduate and professional study programs in the United States in over 900 accredited colleges and universities. Entries are alphabetically arranged by name of school, providing information on location, founding date, type of support/control, academic calendar, library and research facilities, costs, academic calendar, library and research facilities, admission requirements and standards, housing, enrollment, faculty, financial aid, degree requirements, and fields of study.

Because of the strict alphabetical format, if the user wishes to know, for example, library science programs in Ohio, he/she would have to check the "Location of Institutions, by State" to identify Ohio schools and then consult the "Index to Fields of Study" to see if there is an overlap of schools listed under "Library Science" with those in the Ohio list. This kind of information is available in *Peterson's Annual Guides to*

Graduate Study (Princeton, N.J.: Peterson's Guides, 1976- , annual) in more detail, but Doughty has provided a fairly comprehensive, inexpensive, one-volume work. An additional guide to graduate study is the four-volume *Directory of Graduate Programs* (Educational Testing Service, 1984).

The HEP Higher Education Directory. Washington, D.C.: Higher Education Publications, 1983- . Annual. $32.50pa. ISSN 0736-0797.

The unique feature of this geographically arranged directory to academic institutions of higher education is that it identifies major academic officers (presidents, vice-presidents, deans, directors, registrars, and other administrators). It was formerly known as *Educational Directory* (1912-1948), then *Education Directory* (1948-1969), after which it broke off into separate publications: *Education Directory: Public School Systems* (1969-70- ., irregular), *Education Directory: Higher Education* (1969-1975); and *Education Directory: Colleges and Universities* (1976-1982).

Entries in *HEP* include the following information: institution name, address, telephone number, county, congressional district, date established, enrollment, highest degree offered, programs offered, affiliation or control, undergraduate tuition and fees, academic calendar, and accreditation status. Personal name index and an institutional index are included; state agencies, higher education associations, and professional organizations are listed in the appendixes. This volume contains a wealth of information for a relatively modest price.

The Index of Majors. New York: College Entrance Examination Board, 1978- . Annual. $12.95pa. LC 80-648202.

The purpose of this handbook is to allow students and guidance personnel to identify which subject majors or particular programs are offered at various institutions of higher education. Earlier editions of this annual were known as the *College Handbook of Index Majors*. Descriptions of over 350 curricula and the accredited colleges offering majors in them are provided. Arrangement is alphabetical by state. Although the *College Blue Book* has more comprehensive coverage in this vein in the volume entitled *Degrees Offered by College and Subject*, this tenth edition is a welcomed reference guide and source of current information about available careers.

The Insider's Guide to the Colleges, 1987-1988: Students from Coast to Coast Tell What Their Colleges Are Really Like. 13th ed. Compiled and edited by the *Yale Daily News* staff. New York: St. Martin's Press, 1987. $10.95pa. LC 73-161139. ISBN 0-312-00136-0.

An informal, subjective, and sometimes entertaining, writing style makes this a popular college directory. The thirteenth edition (for 1987-1988) features a section that compares the advantages and disadvantages of schools from the standpoint of students. Since the descriptions of close to 300 colleges are written by students, the information is sometimes biased and emphasizes social and recreational activities, campus culture (including drug use), available housing, fraternities and sororities, and characteristics of the student body. Additional information covers standard data related to enrollment, applicants accepted, tuition, library holdings, ACT/SAT scores, financial aid, and faculty-student ratio. This directory should be used in conjunction with one of the more comprehensive standard guides.

Lovejoy's College Guide: A Complete Reference Book to Some 2,500 American Colleges and Universities for Use by Students, Parents, Teachers, Reference Libraries, Youth Agencies, Guidance Counselors, Industrial Corporations, Foundations, Army,Navy, Air Force Stations, Other Federal Services and by Foreign Governments and Agencies. 18th ed. Edited by Charles T. Straughn II and Barbarasue Lovejoy Straughn. New York: Monarch Press, 1987. 872p. $14.95pa. ISBN 0-671-64759-8.

The title, subtitle, and the publisher of this directory have varied over the years. Its aim has been to provide concise information to students, parents, teachers, and guidance counselors about American colleges and universities. Entries provide information on location, enrollment, type of school, faculty, academic programs, degrees offered, facilities, expenses, and availability of scholarships and financial aid. The introductory sections also give suggestions and insights on criteria to consider in choosing a school. Lovejoy has also compiled *Lovejoy's Prep and Private School Guide: Independent, Private, Nonpublic Institutions, Boarding and Day* (5th ed., Simon & Schuster, 1980).

Moll, Richard. **The Public Ivys: A Guide to America's Best Public Undergraduate Colleges and Universities**. New York: Viking Penguin, 1985. 289p. $18.95; $7.95pa. LC 83-40639; 86-4933pa. ISBN 0-670-38205-0; 0-14-009384-2pa.

Moll has described, in fairly extensive detail, seventeen public academic institutions of higher education that he considers the most prestigious. Criteria for inclusion were based on admissions selectivity, the quality of undergraduate programs available, and resources provided.

The school descriptions include demographic statistics, information about the institutions' historical background and development, faculty, staff, academic programs, admission requirements and procedures, composition of student body, and the general campus atmosphere. Although the number of schools covered is quite limited, as compared to the standard college guides, a prospective college student would find this guide useful, particularly if he/she were interested in one of these public colleges.

National College Databank: The College Book of Lists. 4th ed. Edited by Kim R. Kaye and Andrea E. Lehman. Princeton, N.J.: Peterson's Guides, 1987. 465p. $12.95pa. LC 87-7752. ISBN 0-87866-550-1.

Utililizing the computer's advantage to retrieve information in various category arrangements, this Peterson guide allows the user to obtain lists of all schools that fall into a particular category or meet certain requirements. Major categories of lists include (1) schools offering undergraduate work; (2) identification of types of colleges and degrees awarded (private, public, two-year, four-year, women's colleges, men's colleges, etc.); (3) undergraduate enrollment characteristics; (4) academic programs; (5) campus life; (6) admissions information; (7) entrance difficulty data (college's own assessment of entrance difficulty level); (8) expenses; (9) financial aid; and (10) intercollegiate athletics. It should be noted that a complete description of the school would need to be obtained from a standard college guide and used in conjunction with this list. For institutions that can afford the luxury of this secondary type of information, it will, as its cover states, answer questions about which colleges have "evening and weekend degree programs, open admissions, honors programs, study abroad, guaranteed freshman housing, ROTC programs, co-op programs, fraternities and sororities, skill-building programs, non-need scholarships, intercollegiate athletic teams for men and women by sport."

Patterson's American Education. Mount Prospect, Ill.: Educational Directories, 1904- .
Annual. $47.50. LC 04-12953. ISSN 0079-0230.

This authoritative guide to educational institutions in the United States and territories is divided into two major sections: secondary and postsecondary schools. The 1986 edition is the eighty-third volume and was edited by Douglas C. Moody. Part 1 is a comprehensive source of information on junior and senior high schools, and the major emphasis of the work. Over 32,000 approved public, private, and church-affiliated schools and 13,000 officials at state and local levels are identified.

Entries are arranged alphabetically by state first, and then city and county. Other information includes city population, school district name, enrollment, and name and address of superintendent and/or principal (or other official). Although part 1 covers secondary schools, names of postsecondary schools are listed along with those of private high schools and parochial high schools in the annotation for the city in which they are located. Part 2 is a separate renumbered section (273 pages) of entries devoted to information on over 6,500 accredited colleges, universities, and other institutions of higher education (for both graduate and undergraduate work). The index to schools is divided into the following sections: colleges and universities; junior colleges; vocational, technical, and trade schools; hospitals; and prep schools. *Patterson's Schools Classified*, edited by Douglas Moody (Educational Directories, 1986), includes this information in a separate publication with some special categories devoted to Bible colleges, schools for the handicapped, and others.

According to the introductory material, the majority of "users view the directory as a source of mailing addresses rather than visiting addresses" (p.4), so users who want further description of schools would need to consult directories published by individual state departments of education or guides with more detailed information such as *Barron's Profile of American Colleges* (Barron's Educational Series, 1964-) among others.

Peterson's Annual Guide to Four-Year Colleges. Princeton, N.J.: Peterson's Guides, 1976- . Annual. $15.95. LC 73-642965. ISSN 0737-3163.

This publication, formerly titled *Annual Guide to Undergraduate Study* (1971-1975), is now in its eighteenth edition. This publisher maintains a database of information on over 3,000 undergraduate institutions in the United States, its territories, and Canada. Each profile gives the name and address of the school, enrollment, characteristics of the student body, student/faculty ratio, library holdings, admission requirements, expenses, financial aids, housing, majors, and campus life. The information in this database is available online through various vendors.

Other titles by the same publisher include *Peterson's Annual Guide to Two-Year Colleges 1987* (1986); *Peterson's Guide to College Admissions: Getting into the College of Your Choice* (4th ed., 1987); and *Who Offers Part-Time Degree Programs?* (2d ed., 1985).

Peterson's Competitive Colleges. 6th ed. Edited by Karen C. Hegener. Princeton, N.J.: Peterson's Guides, 1987. 348p. $9.95pa. ISBN 0-87866-539-0. ISSN 0887-0152.

Whether or not a school is defined as "competitive" depends on the average student SAT or ACT scores and class rank of the freshmen. This compilation describes approximately 300 colleges and universities considered to meet the criteria for "competitive" or "selective" schools. The emphasis is on undergraduate programs. Since art and music schools have slightly different criteria for selection of students, the better schools in this category are listed in a separate section. The profiles include standard demographic information about the schools, in addition to special information about the composition of the student body with respect to test scores, percentage completing degrees, minority composition, and so on. Lists of majors, athletic programs, financial aid, and other pertinent information are also included.

Peterson's Graduate and Professional Programs. Edited by Theresa C. Moore. Princeton, N.J.: Peterson's Guides, 1966- . 5v. Annual. ISSN 0887-8366.

This comprehensive series provides extensive information about graduate programs in a wide variety of subject fields. It is a five-volume work, with the first volume providing an overview of graduate study and subsequent volumes providing detailed specific program descriptions (with information contributed by the academic institutions). The first volume is entitled *Peterson's Graduate and Undergraduate Professional Programs: An Overview*. Additional series titles are devoted to specific academic and professional fields: Book 2, *Graduate Programs in the Humanities and Social Sciences*; 3, *Graduate Programs in the Biological, Agricultural, and Health Sciences*; 4, *Graduate Programs in the Physical Sciences and Mathematics*; and 5, *Graduate Programs in Engineering and Applied Sciences*.

Entries provide information about program faculty, size, enrollment, financial costs, degrees awarded, entrance requirements, and accreditation.

In some cases professional associations provide similar types of directories to accredited graduate programs—an example being *Graduate Study in Psychology and Associated Fields* (American Psychological Association, 1987).

Peterson's Graduate Education Directory. Edited by Paul Miers and Amy J. Goldstein. Princeton, N.J.: Peterson's Guides, 1986. 637p. $29.95pa. LC 86-1386. ISBN 0-87866-445-9.

This new directory provides information about administrative and academic officers, and heads of graduate programs (with telephone numbers), listed in hierarchical order for each institution. About 1,439 accredited colleges and universities in the United States and Canada that grant graduate degrees are included. Access is available by subject and geographic indexes.

Randax Education Guide to Colleges Seeking Students 1986. Edited by Stephen E. Marshall. Randolph, Mass.: Education Guide, 1971- . Annual. $10.95pa. LC 84-4084. ISSN 0097-5206.

Two-year and four-year colleges that are actively recruiting college students are described in this highly selective listing. Entries for each type of college are arranged alphabetically by state, and information provided in each includes the typical demographic data found in the more comprehensive standard directories: address of institution, contact official, accreditation, tuition and fees, majors offered, and admission requirements. Health care and schools devoted to specific careers are handled in a special section. Narrative sections discuss various kinds of financial assistance and how to apply for them, among other topics. Indexes provide access to colleges, college majors, state, and institution name.

The Right College 1988. Edited by College Research Group of Concord, Massachusetts. New York: Arco/Simon & Schuster, 1987. 1,545p. $24.95. ISBN 0-13-044868-0.

This new addition to the numerous directories to colleges and universities is fairly comprehensive with respect to schools in the United States, but offers limited coverage of schools in Canada and countries abroad, without explaining the criteria for inclusion. It provides the usual demographic type of information (name and address of institution, enrollment, costs, majors and degree programs offered, availability of financial aid, etc.).

A series of articles is provided in a section called "What's New in American Colleges 1988" that discusses various aspects of college life including recruiting, colleges for women only, financing a college education, and other topics. Other information provided in various charts and tables identifies the number of graduates from a particular school who went on to professional graduate study, or attempts to establish the selectivity of a school with respect to socio-economic or academic criteria. A directory that singles out the least expensive accredited schools is *America's Lowest Colleges: A Comprehensive Directory of Fully Accredited Colleges and Universities with Tuition Costs of $1,500 or Less for an Entire Academic Year* by Nicholas A. Roes (Freundlich Books; distr., Scribner's, 1985).

Selective Guide to Colleges. 4th ed. Edited by Edward B. Fiske, with Amy Stuart Wells and Selective Guide to Colleges Staff. New York: Times Books, 1987. 646p. $10.95pa. LC 86-30102. ISBN 0-8129-1263-2.

Formerly titled *The New York Times Selective Guide to Colleges* (until the 1982-1983 edition), the editors of this college directory use a unique system of ranking institutions on the basis of academic strength, social life, extracurricular activities, housing, food, and the student body. As opposed to providing just the objective facts and statistics contained in the major standard comprehensive guides, or just the very subjective impressionistic views of the "confidential" type guides, the editors claim to have chosen the optimum features of each.

The journalistic style in these essays of 600-2,000 words is not only informative, but highly readable and entertaining. All discuss which academic departments are weak and which are outstanding, and whether or not dorms are coed. Other topics are treated on an optional basis, although fairly consistently, from one entry to the next (e.g., social life, composition of student body, local environment, drinking age, predominate political views, entertainment and recreational opportunities, dating, interaction with neighboring colleges, and the intellectual climate in general). While libraries could not provide adequate service without the standard comprehensive guides (those published by Barron's, Peterson's Guides, etc). a prospective college student would, undoubtedly, enjoy getting the flavor of a school with this type of inside information, in addition to data related to enrollment, SAT scores, financial aid, student employment, and expenses that they get in the standard directory.

COLLEGE GUIDES (SPECIALIZED)

Allied Health Education Directory. Chicago: American Medical Association, 1972- . Annual. $25.95. LC 72-626303. ISSN 0194-3776.

Educational programs in allied health occupations accredited by CAHEA (Committee on Allied Health Education and Accreditation) are described in this comprehensive directory. It also includes information on allied health professions and professional associations, a description of the general CAHEA accreditation process and review committees, statistical data, and a glossary of relevant terms. The 1,700 directory entries are arranged in alphabetical order by state. Information in each entry includes institution name and allied health educational programs sponsored; address; officials (e.g., program director, medical director, educational coordinator); class capacity; dates programs begin and end; tuition; next accreditation review date; and affiliates.

American Chemical Society Directory of Graduate Research 1985. Edited by the Committee on Professional Training. Washington, D.C.: American Chemical Society, 1985. 1,260p. $46.00. ISBN 0-8412-0935-9. ISSN 0193-5011.

Students interested in studying chemistry at the graduate level and researchers who want to keep abreast of the field and find out the kind of research being conducted by scholars in other locations would find this directory of interest. A total of 11,215 faculty members from 713 graduate departments in the United States and Canada are listed. Arrangement of entries is in six department sections: chemistry, chemical engineering, biochemistry, pharmaceutical/medicinal chemistry, clinical chemistry, and polymer chemistry. These sections are further subdivided by university name and then by faculty members. For each department, types of degrees granted and fields of specialization are included. Under the faculty member's name are listed date of birth; academic rank; degrees received and dates; postdoctoral appointments, if any; research fields; current research interests; telephone numbers; and research departments. A faculty name index is also provided.

Anderson, Marcia J., and Barbara A. Schmidt. **Directory of Degree Programs in Nursing: Baccalaureate, Master's, Doctoral**. New York: Arco, 1984. 280p. $29.95. LC 84-10968. ISBN 0-668-05757-2.

Anderson and Schmidt surveyed over 500 nursing schools in the United States and Puerto Rico to compile this first directory to baccalaureate, master's, and doctoral degree programs in nursing in one volume. Arrangement of entries is alphabetical by state, first, and then by name of the institution. Each entry includes school name, location, chairperson, telephone number, degrees offered, accreditation information, curricular content, admission requirements, application procedures, person to contact, and admission requirements. Students, parents, and guidance counselors will find this a useful reference tool.

AWP Catalogue of Writing Programs: A Descriptive Listing of College and University Workshops and Degree Programs in Creative Writing. 4th ed. Norfolk, Va.: Associated Writing Programs, 1983. 120p. $10.00. LC 80-67017. ISBN 0-936266-05-8.

This is a highly specialized college guide listing colleges and universities in the United States and Canada that offer writing programs in which both undergraduate and graduate degrees are awarded. Programs offered include "Studio Writing Programs" (writing workshops, independent writing projects, thesis preparation); "Studio/Academic Writing Programs" (emphasis on both creative writing and literature); and "Traditional Literature Study and Creative Writing" (with additional work in the department of English).

Arrangement of academic institutions is alphabetical by name. Each entry includes name of institution, nature of degrees offered, required courses of study, information about faculty members (including major publications), degree requirements, and admission requirements. An index lists entries geographically by state also. The information in this reference tool is concise and well organized. It should be noted that none of the programs described are self-instructional or distance education modules.

Bear, John. **Bear's Guide to Non-Traditional College Degrees**. Rev. 9th ed. Berkeley, Calif.: Ten Speed Press, 1985. 265p. $9.95pa. LC 82-50905. ISBN 0-89815-149-X.

Bear has prepared a very readable, yet carefully researched, directory to institutions of higher education that have nontraditional degree programs or offer alternative ways of acquiring college credit. One of his objectives is to make the reader aware of the pitfalls associated with "buying" degrees through so-called diploma mills, and to provide information on accredited programs that accommodate working adults and nonresidential students in flexible arrangements.

The major portion of the guide is comprised of the directory to schools, arranged alphabetically. Entries provide information about name and address, curricular emphases, degrees, accreditation, financial aid, and other demographic data. Other sections cover nontraditional professional education, such as medical schools, law schools, weekend degree programs, and programs offered in foreign schools. Colleges in the United States and Canada that offer parallel work/study courses can be identified in *Directory of Cooperative Education* (Cooperative Education Association, 1980- , biennial).

Crocker, John R. **The Student Guide to Catholic Colleges and Universities**. Wilmington, N.C.: McGrath Publishing, 1982. 468p. $9.95. LC 82-48923. ISBN 0-06-061602-4.

For educators, parents, and students who are only interested in a Catholic school, this directory to Catholic colleges and universities might be an interesting and helpful reference guide. However, other standard college guides (e.g., *Peterson's Guide to Four-Year Colleges, College Blue Book, Comparative Guide to American Colleges for Students, Parents and Counselors*, and other similar titles) would supply as much or more information on Catholic schools, as well as on many others. Since the information in the entries is taken from questionnaires and each school's own promotional publications, it is highly favorable as opposed to critical or comparatively analytical in nature.

Directory of Master's Programs in Foreign Languages, Foreign Literatures, and Linguistics. New York: Modern Language Association of America, 1987. 173p. $15.00pa. LC 87-11254. ISBN 0-87352-169-2.

Information about master's programs in linguistics and foreign language instruction available in the United States (including Puerto Rico) is provided in this alphabetically arranged directory. Over 500 departments offering such programs are included. Entries are arranged by institution and then by department and provide data on institution and address, master of arts programs offering the degree, number of credits required for the degree, core or required courses, and type of certificate, degree, diploma available. Access to information is obtained via six different indexes: (1) program (subdivided geographically by state), (2) state (subdivided by program), (3) special program, (4) certificate or diploma, (5) departments offering the master of arts in teaching degrees, (6) a comprehensive, integrated general index.

Fischgrund, Tom. **The Insider's Guide to the Top Ten Business Schools**. 3d rev. ed. Boston: Little, Brown, 1988. 297p. $9.95pa. LC 83-13567. ISBN 0-316-28383-5.

The top ten business schools in the country, according to Fischgrund, are Harvard, Stanford, Wharton (University of Pennsylvania), Chicago, Sloan (MIT), Northwestern, Michigan, UCLA, Columbia, and Amos Tuck (Dartmouth). Ten articles, each written by a graduate of these schools, describe them in light of seven topics: (1) the program and reputation of the school, (2) admission policies and standards, (3) the academic environment, (4) social life, (5) placement record and opportunities, (6) usefulness of the MBA, (7) an overview summary.

Several chapters are devoted to suggested strategies for applying and getting into business schools, and competing for school and career success. The appendix provides graphic information on student enrollment (e.g., male/female ratios), median age, ability levels, and facts about the schools (tuition, courses of study, job success rate, teaching methodologies, curricular requirements, etc.).

Jobst, Katherine, ed. **Internships: 35,000 On-the-Job Training Opportunities for College Students and Adults**. Cincinnati: Writer's Digest Books, 1981- . Annual. $18.95 pa. ISSN 0272-5460.

Students who wish to get practical work experience in the form of internships or other assignments related to a career would want to consult this directory to 35,000 such programs in approximately 1,700 sponsoring organizations. Many of these programs pay the student while they are being trained; others exist in cooperation with an academic institution where the student receives course credit and, in some cases, the student can receive monetary compensation and credit.

Entries are arranged in seven broad subject categories, each of which are preceded by an overview essay. Some of the annotations are written by former interns. Access to information is also available through geographic and sponsoring organization indexes.

Kurst, Charlotte, ed. **The Official Guide to MBA Programs, Admissions & Courses**. Princeton, N.J.: Graduate Management Admissions Council, 1986. 603p. $9.95pa. ISBN 0-446384-37-2.

Information about graduate management programs is arranged alphabetically by institution and also geographically (by country and state) in this international directory. Entries include data related to each institution's name, address, telephone number, course offerings, admissions criteria, tuition and other costs, enrollment, faculty, contact person, financial assistance, and placement services. A "Key Facts" section capsulizes data in chart form. Introductory material discusses careers in management and considerations for selecting an MBA program.

Newell, William H. **Interdisciplinary Undergraduate Programs: A Directory**. Oxford, Ohio: Association for Integrative Studies, Miami University, 1986. 277p. $34.95. LC 85-62972. ISBN 0-9615764-0-5.

In recent years there have been calls for stronger liberal arts curricula, a return to humanities courses, and less emphasis on practical professionally oriented programs. This directory lists 235 interdisciplinary programs, or those requiring courses in several departments. Entries include information on program location, contact person, type of program, length of program, enrollment, faculty, individual courses, brief history and summary of the program, program goals and objectives, and how it is administered between and within departments.

FINANCIAL AID GUIDES

The A's & B's: Your Guide to Academic Scholarships 1986-1987. 8th ed. Edited by Victoria A. Fabisch. Alexandria, Va.: Octameron Press; distr., Naperville, Ill.: Caroline House, 1985. 77p. $4.00pa. ISBN 0-917760-61-1.

An extensive use of tables makes available in compact form information about 100,000 scholarships offered by 1,200 colleges and universities, most of which are merit based. Organization is alphabetical by state first, and then by school. Individual entries provide scholarship program name, the number of awards given, amount, criteria for selection, fields of study, restrictions and limitations, type of scholarship (financial need or academic achievement), whether the scholarship is renewable, and other student qualifications. Scholarships listed are awarded by the government at state and federal levels, and private agencies and organizations. In spite of its size, this handy one-volume reference provides a lot of information to prospective college students about the availability of scholarship assistance.

Bailey, Robert L. **How and Where to Get Scholarships and Financial Aid for College**. New York: Arco/Simon & Schuster, 1986. 170p. $7.95pa. LC 85-15652. ISBN 0-668-06424-2.

Bailey, the director of admissions and records at the University of California, Berkeley, lists 900 scholarships that are awarded on the basis of merit rather than financial need. A major part of this work is devoted to a lengthy discussion of the recent use of merit awards. Some discussion is given to other sources of financial aid than scholarships, including student grants and scholarships, and to financial aid based on economic factors. This publication, with parts of it appearing to be offset typed pages, lacks a slick professional appearance and is somewhat selective in coverage.

Bauer, David. **The Complete Grants Sourcebook for Higher Education**. 2d ed. New York: American Council on Education. Macmillan, 1985. 465p. $85.00. LC 84-25030. ISBN 0-02-901950-8.

Since grant monies to higher education programs have been dropping in spite of an increase in foundation giving, this sourcebook should be of great help and interest to educational researchers. This second edition is completely redesigned and is a total revision of the earlier (1980) publication. It is now divided into four major sections dealing with (1) how to increase grant proposal success rates, (2) sources of private foundation funding, (3) sources of corporate funding, and (4) sources of government funding. Section 1 gives explicit tips on proposal preparation including sample inquiry letters to a funding source, sample letter proposals, checklist for proposal preparation, and so on. Each of the following three directory sections are preceded by tips on how to maximize success in writing the particular type of proposal, and information about the application process. Section 2 is an alphabetical directory of 146 private foundations, section 3 is an alphabetical listing of 200 corporate foundations, and section 4 provides information about 200 federal agencies arranged in numerical order by CFDA (Catalog of Federal Domestic Assistance) number. Individual entries designate foundation requirements for eligibility, foundation policy, financial profiles, deadlines, guidelines, previous funding history, sample grants, and so on.

The advantage of this guide over other major guides to grants and foundations such as *Annual Register of Grant Support* (Marquis), *The Grants Register* (St. Martin's Press), and others of that nature is that it singles out those foundations (whether private, corporate, or governmental agencies) that are most likely to fund research projects in higher education.

Cassidy, Daniel J., and Michael J. Alves. **The Scholarship Book: The Complete Guide to Private-Sector Scholarships, Grants and Loans for Undergraduates**. 2d ed. Englewood Cliffs, N.J.: Prentice-Hall, 1987. 373p. $29.95; $19.95pa. LC 84-11683. ISBN 0-13-792425-9; 0-13-792417-8pa.

Financial aid in the form of private sector scholarships, loans, grants, fellowships, and internships is listed in this directory. Since most financial aid programs are directed at students in a particular educational field, awards are arranged alphabetically by major academic field. To identify awards in a specific area one must consult an index called "Major and Specific Fields of Study," which precedes the main body of the work. For example, under "Business" are references to aid in accounting, actuarial science, banking, business administration, and so on.

Information contained in the entries was compiled from National Scholarship Research Service data based in San Rafael, California, and includes the following: scholarship name, address, and telephone number; amounts (or job assignments); application deadlines; distinctive areas; brief description of award and eligibility requirements; and other information about scholarship renewability, loan payment, and number of available awards.

A similar guide is *Chronicle Student Aid Annual 1* (Moravia, N.Y.: Chronicle Guidance Publications, 1987, 420p., $19.95pa., LC 79-640360, ISBN 1-55631-011-0), which focuses on regional or national financial aid programs sponsored by both public and private organizations.

The College Cost Book 1987-88. College Scholarship Service. 8th ed. New York: College Board, 1987. 280p. $10.95pa. LC 80-648095. ISBN 0-87447-288-1.

The major focus of this book is on identifying sources of financial aid for prospective college students, but it also provides information explaining the various components of college expenses, how to apply for aid, and how much students can expect to get. Information is arranged alphabetically by state, listing the current costs at each institution and options for attaining financial aid as well as the percentage of students that receive financial help. A bibliography of additional references on the topic, a glossary of terms, some sample aid application forms, a decision-making model, and a financial aid checklist are also included.

The College Money Handbook: The Complete Guide to Expenses, Scholarships, Loans, Jobs, and Special Aid Programs at Four-Year Colleges. Princeton, N.J.: Peterson's Guides, 1983- . Annual. $22.95; $17.95pa. ISSN 0883-5578.

The fifth edition of this guide is edited by Andrea Lehman. Its purpose is to help college students, parents, and counselors determine the overall costs of a college education at varying institutions, estimate how much financial aid they could expect, and how to apply for it. The information is arranged in three sections. The first describes types of aid available, conditions for eligibility, and application procedures. The second major part consists of approximately 1,750 profiles of accredited colleges and universities. (Institutions offering part-time, correspondence, or external study are excluded.) Information includes type of school; degrees awarded; enrollment; number of freshmen (etc.); annual total expenses; undergraduate financial awards summary; need-based freshman aid profile (percentages of students applying for, judged to have need of, and awarded aid); non-need freshman awards (merit or other scholarships); money-saving options available (also of interest to students who do not qualify for financial aid); supporting data to be submitted in applying for aid; and chief financial aid officer. The third section is "Directories": It lists colleges that offer scholarships for freshmen that are not based on financial need. Other features of the book include a glossary which defines terms and acronyms aid-seekers need to know, such as GSL (Guaranteed Student Loan) or CWS (College Work-Study).

This comprehensive reference tool allows students and parents to compare resources available and decide on an optimum school in light of their financial situation. It makes an excellent supplementary volume to guides that emphasize academic and other features in college selection.

Costs at U.S. Educational Institutions. New York: Institute of International Education, 1979- . Annual. $29.95pa. LC 80-123400. ISSN 0270-1413.

The unique feature of this handbook to college costs is that it provides a "monthly maintenance rate" or MMR. This monthly cost-of-living rate is based on room and board plus spending money for clothing and other incidentals, and is calcualted by using Consumer Price Index statistics, location, and personal income.

Information in this reference work is divided into three parts. In the first part, schools are listed alphabetically by state, with National Research Council code and the MMR included. Part 2 also lists schools by states with the MMR, plus information related to tuition and fees for the academic year, for summer school, and for out-of-state students; academic year calendar and dates; registration dates; and full-time credit loads for the academic year and summer school. The third part lists, by institution, special fees, if any, for international students.

Deutschman, Alan. **Winning Money for College: The High School Student's Guide to Scholarship Contests**. Princeton, N.J.: Peterson's Guides, 1984. 209p. $8.95. LC 83-22151. ISBN 0-87866-261-8.

Over fifty national scholarship contests open to high school students are described in this reference source. Awards are funded from private sources and are based on ability or talent in a particular area or achievement. For example, there are scholarships for piano performance, essay writing, and proficiency in a foreign language (determined by examination scores). Athletic scholarships are not included. Entries describing contests provide information on contest name, entrance rules and procedures, where to write for further details, and an annotation which summarizes the purpose and amount of the scholarship, including samples of test questions or examples of other successful contest entries.

Entries overlap to some extent with those in other directories listing scholarships, but also provide many unique entries. In a section called "Helpful Hints," the author, who has had experience applying for and winning scholarships contests, gives some guidelines to would-be contest winners.

Don't Miss Out: The Ambitious Student's Guide to Financial Aid 1988-89. Edited by Robert Leider and Anna Leider. Alexandria, Va.: Octameron Press; distr., Naperville, Ill.: Caroline House, 1976- . Annual. $5.00. ISSN 0277-6987.

The twelfth edition covers 1988 through 1989 and, as in previous editions, strategies and techniques for ascertaining financial aid for college are covered thoroughly. The first part addresses suggestions, tips, and trends, but also attempts to debunk some myths about sources of funding. A large part of the guide is comprised of descriptions of the major sources of aid, which are colleges and universities and federal and state governments. Scholarships and grants from business and industry and branches of the military are also indentified, with procedures for applying for and securing them. Other sources designated particularly for minority or female students, outstanding athletes, adults returning to the classroom, and other nontraditional students are also identified. Charts and tables concisely summarize information in this useful and well-organized work.

Federal Student Financial Aid Handbook. Department of Education. Office of Student Financial Assistance. Washington, D.C.: Department of Education, Office of Student Financial Assistance, 1982- . Annual. LC 82-640139. ISSN 0730-8922.

This handbook is really aimed at colleges and universities, as it helps administrative personnel understand the rules and regulations associated with each of the major federal student financial aid programs. A wide variety of financial assistance programs is covered, including Pell Grants, Supplemental Educational Opportunity Grants (SEOG), College Work Study (CWS), National Direct Student Loans (NDSL), Guaranteed Student Loans (GSL), State Student Incentive Grants (SSIG), and Parent Loans for Undergraduate

Students (PLUS). *Federal Student Financial Aid Handbook* is also useful in that parents, students, and guidance counselors can determine financial aid opportunities available.

Feingold, Norman, and Marie Feingold. **Scholarships, Fellowships and Loans: Volume VIII**. Arlington, Md.: Bellman, 1987. v, 484p. $80.00. LC 49-49180. ISBN 0-87442-008-3.

The Feingolds describe local, regional, and national funding sources of financial aid for undergraduate and graduate study, including the fields of law, medicine, dentistry, and veterinary medicine. Sources of aid indentified are both federal and private sector organizations, with entries arranged alphabetically by awarding agency/organization.

Volume 8 was designed to be used as a supplement to volume 7 published in 1981 and information replaces that found in volumes 1 through 6.

Access to data is made through the "Vocational Goals Index" which highlights, in chart format, eligibility requirements, the course of study for which monies will be awarded, the administering agency, level of study, and type of award. The entries themselves, which follow, provide more detailed information about qualifications, funds available, special fields of interest and information about the purpose of the award, and place of application.

According to the introduction, programs identified here are also available to researchers, so this work has a somewhat broader scope than other directories to student aid.

Fenske, Robert H., Robert P. Huff, and associates. **Handbook of Student Financial Aid**. San Francisco, Calif.: Jossey-Bass, 1983. 508p. $29.95. LC 83-11336. ISBN 0-87589-571-9.

This presents a history and overview of student financial aid and describes the objectives and functions of numerous financial aid programs in the first section. Subsequent chapters are each written by different authors and give information on how to get aid, effective administration of financial aid resources, and institutional policy questions. Fenske and Huff have prepared a brief introduction to each chapter, highlighting critical information. Emphasis is given to federal aid programs, but state, institutional and private sector sources are also covered.

Green, Alan, and Amy Holsapple Clark. **The Directory of Athletic Scholarships**. New York: Facts on File, 1987. 343p. $29.95; $15.95pa. LC 86-29377. ISBN 0-8160-1549-X; 0-8160-1550-3pa.

Students seeking scholarship aid for athletic ability can consult this directory either by individual school in the main body or by specific sport played, state, or name of athletic conference in the indexes. The first edition of this directory was compiled by Barry and Alan Green (Putnam, 1981). Scholarships at both two-year and four-year colleges are listed alphabetically by institution name. Entries include data about the institution (address, telephone numbers for athletic departments, and other demographic statistics). Some of the introductory information addresses procedures and guidelines for seeking scholarship monies established by the NCAA and other major organizations.

A similar title covering seventeen different sports is *Chronicle Sports Guide: Inter-Collegiate Athletics & Scholarships* (Chronicle Guidance Publications, 1987).

Keeslar, Oreon Pierre. **Financial Aids for Higher Education: A Catalog for Undergraduates.** 12th ed. Dubuque, Iowa: W. C. Brown, 1986. 748p. $34.00. LC 85-62777. ISBN 0-697-00773-1.

High school students, parents, and guidance counselors will find this reference tool helpful not only in explaining different types of financial aid available for financing college study, but also in identifying programs established to meet the needs of specific categories of student need and eligibility. Arrangement of entries is alphabetical by program title with special indexing that allows users to identify aid opportunities that match potential students' characteristics. The special feature of this work is its many nontraditional approaches to obtaining money for college expenses.

Leskes, Andrea, ed. **Grants for Graduate Students 1986-88.** Compiled by the Graduate School of the University of Massachusetts at Amherst. Princeton, N.J.: Peterson's Guides, 1986. 385p. $29.95pa. ISBN 0-87866-483-1. ISSN 0889-1613.

The major purpose of this directory of financial grants to graduate students is to identify programs that give awards based on merit rather than on financial need. Over 650 grant and fellowship opportunities are described with entries arranged alphabetically by name of sponsoring agency. Information in each entry includes an identification number; name, address, and telephone number of the sponsoring agency or organization; contact person; program description and overview; statement of eligibility requirements; and application procedure (including time deadlines). An annotated bibliography of sources of financial support is also included. Indexes provide access by subject and keyword, but an interdisciplinary index is also presented.

O'Neill, Joseph P. **Corporate Tuition Aid Programs: A Directory of College Financial Aid for Employees at America's Largest Corporations.** Princeton, N.J.: Conference University Press, 1984; distr., Princeton, N.J.: Peterson's Guides, 1985. 194p. LC 83-63528. ISBN 0-87866-338-X.

A questionnaire was sent to all *Fortune 1000* companies with 655 responses received. Of these companies, 631 said they provided scholarship aid for their employees and their families. The companies are listed alphabetically in this directory with data supplied with respect to eligibility requirements for financial aid, amounts funded, and special restrictions and limitations, if any. A summary article, "The Impact of Corporate Tuition Reimbursement Plans on Employee Persistence in Educational Programs," follows the main body of the volume. Ten tuition benefit plans are provided as samples or models. A bibliography of sources and tuition aid is also included.

STATISTICS SOURCES

Federal Support to Universities, Colleges, and Selected Nonprofit Institutions. Washington, D.C.: Government Printing Office, 1969- . Annual. $6.50. LC 85-19197. S/N 038-000-00508-1.

This annual statistical report to the president documents how federally funded monies were used to support scientific research in educational institutions and nonprofit organizations in the United States. The fifteen federal agencies submitting data represent all categories of direct federal support. Information is arranged in three major categories of federal support: "General Notes," "Technical Notes," and "Detailed Statistical Tables." It breaks down money spent by type of activity, by agency and subagency, by field, and is compared with other economic indicators. It also provides information on federal obligations to research and development centers in institutions of higher education.

Educational researchers, particularly those seeking external funds to support research projects, will find this information useful and interesting.

Gourman, Jack. **The Gourman Report: A Rating of Graduate and Professional Programs in American and International Universities**. 6th rev. ed. Los Angeles, Calif.: National Education Standards, 1987. 280p. $14.95. LC 86-63799. ISBN 0-918192-10-2.

The academic quality of programs of study at American colleges and universities is rated in this report. Some of the criteria for evaluation include the credentials of the faculty, the quality of the students (ability and achievement), admission standards, number of students enrolled, background of school, facilities, finances, research productivity, attainment of alumni, libraries, public relations programs, among other considerations.

Gourman's first report came out in 1967, and subsequent editions have published ratings of graduate and undergraduate programs in separate editions, including also *The Gourman Report: A Rating of Undergraduate Programs in American and International Universities*.

11

Special Education
Reference Sources

GUIDES

Davis, William E. **Resource Guide to Special Education: Terms/Laws/Assessment Procedures/Organizations.** 2d ed. Boston: Allyn and Bacon, 1986. 317p. $29.95. LC 85-18647. ISBN 0-205-08546-6.

This guide is aimed at all professional and other personnel who work with special education students, including students in teacher education programs, parents, and community agency personnel. Arranged in five sections, the first section defines terminology used in special education and related fields, and constitutes the major portion of the book. The vocabulary is aimed at the layperson, as well as at the professional. Section 2 is a selected list of commonly used acronyms and abbreviations; section 3 is a selected and annotated list of assessment tests, scales, and inventories. Arranged alphabetically by title under subject categories, each entry describes the purpose of the instrument, age level for which it is appropriate, date, and publisher. Section 4 is devoted to legal aspects of special education and includes brief summaries of federal legislation, and unique or outstanding litigations that have had significant impact on all handicapped individuals in general. Section 5 lists agencies and organizations, as well as all of the divisions of special education located within each of the departments of education for each state and U.S. territory. The glossary and descriptions of assessment instruments are valuable alone, but combined with the other features of this guide they make it a very convenient one-volume reference.

Dequin, Henry C. **Librarians Serving Disabled Children and Young People.** Littleton, Colo.: Libraries Unlimited, 1983. 303p. $22.50. LC 83-5381. ISBN 0-87287-364-1.

The purpose of this reference work is to assist school media specialists and public librarians who serve disabled youth from kindergarten through high school age. It emphasizes the general and special services, programs, materials, and other sources of information they can provide, as well as special equipment and devices available for the handicapped. The opening chapters cover steps in library service needs assessment, identify the categories that characterize the term *disabled*, and describe some major court cases related to the right to library and educational services. Attitudes of librarians and other educators and individualized instruction are also discussed.

Appendix A, "Standard Criteria for the Selection and Evaluation of Instructional Material," provides an extensive checklist prepared by the National Center on Educational Media and Materials for the Handicapped (NCEMMH). Appendix B, "Criteria for Media Selection," presents guidelines and special considerations in developing a library collection for the mentally retarded. A selected bibliography and an index conclude the work. This is a unique guide to approximately 500 important, and often neglected, relevant sources of information.

BIBLIOGRAPHIES

Clarkson, Mary Cervantes, comp. **Mainstreaming the Exceptional Child: A Bibliography**. San Antonio, Tex.: Trinity University Press, 1982. 240p. index. (Checklists in the Humanities and Education: A Series, No. 6) $25.00; $15.00pa. LC 81-84636. ISBN 0-911536-92-2; 0-939980-02-9pa.

Mainstreaming children with special needs was initiated in response to Public Law 94-142 mandating education of all handicapped children in the public schools. This bibliography includes 3,122 books, journal articles, ERIC documents, dissertations, government documents, and pamphlets published between 1964 and 1982. A helpful introduction defines the term *mainstreaming*. Entries are arranged in separate chapters by type of exceptionality: "General," "Gifted," "Hearing Impaired," "Learning Disabled and Emotionally Disturbed," "Mentally Handicapped," "Physically Handicapped," "Speech Handicapped," "Visually Handicapped," plus a section of supplementary materials.

Since citations concerned with three or fewer headings are not included in the chapter of general works, but are repeated in each chapter where applicable, there is some duplication of titles. The fact that these entries are not annotated limits its usefulness, but it is still a convenient compilation for educators, particuary teachers, administrators, and school media specialists, researchers, and other professionals.

Clendening, Corinne P., and Ruth Ann Davies. **Challenging the Gifted: Curriculum Enrichment and Acceleration Models**. New York: Bowker, 1983. 482p. $39.95. LC 82-20777. ISBN 0-8352-1682-9.

Alternative models of programming for the gifted are presented in a series of model programs. In describing the programs, over 7,400 instructional items, including books, documents, programmed instructional guides, periodicals, posters and prints, audio modules, cassette and disc recordings, charts and graphs, computer programs, films and filmstrips, maps, microforms, resource kits, and transparencies that lend themselves to creative use with the gifted are listed. The work is arranged in two parts. The first gives guidelines for designing and implementing programs. The major part of the work consists of the fifteen model programs in part 2. A directory to publishers, producers, and distributors and an index conclude the work. Anyone concerned with gifted education would find these models and media bibliographies extremely useful.

Compton, Carolyn. **A Guide to 75 Tests for Special Education**. Belmont, Calif.: Fearon Education, a division of Pitman Learning, 1984. 341p. $22.95pa. LC 83-62086. ISBN 0-8224-3583-7.

Teachers, administrators, school psychologists, and other diagnosticians will find this guide useful in planning and implementing a testing program, interpreting test results, and communicating them to the appropriate people. Media specialists and librarians would also find it a useful guide.

Tests are grouped according to the specific skills they are designed to assess (reading comprehension, math computation, as well as particular learning behaviors such as the ability to follow group instruction or to work independently). Each test review has a brief introductory narrative which describes the test's purpose, major areas tested, age or grade level for which it is intended, whether test is timed, and how much time is required for administration and scoring/interpretation. The test format is described and critical comments address its strengths and limitations, followed by guidelines for use of the text.

Gravitz, Ina. **The Gifted and Talented Student: An Annotated Guide for Parents, Educators and Students**. 2d ed. Centereach, N.Y.: Middle County Public Library, Adult Services Department, 1985. 53p.

Although this bibliography is quite brief, consisting of 194 annotated entries, professionals who teach in the area of gifted education, or provide support services for those who do, as well as parents of gifted children, often find the kind of information listed here to be limited. There are fifty more entries in this second edition than in the original 1983 edition. A third, expanded edition is planned for 1989. Materials included here are books, pamphlets, chapters in books, and periodicals which emphasize the definition and assessment of giftedness, characteristics of gifted and talented students, the role of intelligence tests, and career guidance. Some attention is also given to gifted students who are academic underachievers and how they can be motivated to develop their full potential.

Hagen, Dolores. **Microcomputer Resource Book for Special Education**. Reston, Va.: Council for Exceptional Children, 1984. 207p. $21.50; $18.50pa. LC 83-17651. ISBN 0-8359-4345-3; 0-8359-4344-5pa.

The emphasis of this resource book is not on programming or computer literacy, but on how special education students can use the microcomputer and software programs to meet specific needs. There are seven chapters and ten appendixes. The chapters discuss such topics as general rules to locating software, implementing microcomputer technology with special education students, advantages of the microcomputer for specific disabilities, and communication via online services. The appendixes provide a list of software publishers and distributors (with indication of education skills or subjects emphasized and microcomputer brands); a selected annotated list of software for special education; lists of software for specific disabilities (physically handicapped, blind, etc.); authoring systems to help create microcomputer lessons, and clinical and diagnostic software programs. One appendix discusses special hardware devices for use in special education; another discusses online services, Logo programming language, and reviewing periodicals. The work is indexed.

This guide is not very comprehensive (as far as number of references included), but its importance lies, rather, in the unique principles and information it provides for educators in selecting and designing microcomputer instruction. A related title which provides more emphasis on software products and titles is *The Specialware Directory: A Guide to Software Sources for Special Education* (2d ed., LINC Associates, 1986).

Mauser, August J. **Assessing the Learning Disabled: Selected Instruments, the Diagnostician's Handbook**. 3d ed. San Rafael, Calif.: Academic Therapy Publications, 1981. $20.00pa. LC 77-5099. ISBN 0-87879-279-1.

The third edition of this guide describes over 400 selected assessment instruments for evaluation of learning disabilities. Tests are arranged alphabetically in categories: intelligence tests; preschool readiness tests; motor, sensory, and language tests; diagnostic and other types of reading tests; creativity tests, and others. Information included in each entry includes test title, age/grade level, time required for administration, a brief annotation indicating what the test measures, subscales, information about scoring, test correlates, and a coded symbol indicating the test publishers. A directory of publishers and a list of "Selected Readings" conclude the work.

This is a highly selected list in comparison to the Buros series, *Personality Tests and Reviews, Mental Measurements Yearbook*, and *Tests in Print*, but it allows the users to have a quick overview of instruments appropriate for assessing learners in a specific category of exceptionality.

Polette, Nancy. **Books and Real Life: A Guide for Gifted Students and Teachers**. Jefferson, N.C.: McFarland, 1984. 125p. $15.95pa. LC 84-42607. ISBN 0-89950-119-2.

Since the majority of gifted students are accelerated readers it is important for educators, including school media specialists, to be aware of literature as a means of enriching the lives of gifted children. The titles selected in this bibliography represent real-life problems, losses, and other experiences where the characters deal with conflict with a psychologically sound approach. Some of the topics covered include dealing with divorce, death, anger, rejection, friendship, sibling rivalry, and handicaps.

A total of 130 entries are arranged alphabetically in two major categories: "Pre-School and Primary," and "Junior Novels." Each entry provides bibliographic information, a synopsis of the story, and suggested activities and discussion questions appropriate to each book. A subject index provides access through fifteen specific topics.

Polette has compiled another listing of titles for gifted children in early childhood programs, *Picture Books for Gifted Programs* (Scarecrow Press, 1981).

Special Education Index to Assessment Materials. Los Angeles: National Information Center for Educational Media (NICEM), University of Southern California, 1980. 127p. $10.00pa. LC 79-84457. ISBN 0-89320-026-3.

The entries in this volume represent a 1,500-item subsection of the NICSEM (National Information Center for Special Education Materials) database concerned with special diagnostic tests and instruments developed to assess, both formally and informally, skills, aptitude, and achievement of students with varying disabilities. Also described are professional materials on testing procedures, and test development, construction, and interpretation. Other guides developed from the NICSEM database include *Special Education Index to Learner Materials; Special Education Index to In-Service Training Materials; NICSEM Mini-Indexes to Special Education Materials: Family Life and Sex Education; Independent Living Skills for Moderately and Severely Handicapped Students; Functional Communication Skills; Personal and Social Development for Moderately and Severely Handicapped Students; Functional Communication Skills; Personal and Social Development for Moderately and Severely Handicapped Students; High Interest, Controlled Vocabulary, Supplementary Reading Materials for Adolescents and Young Adults; NICSEM Master Index to Special Education Materials; NICSEM Special Education Thesaurus* (2d ed.), and *NICSEM Source Directory*.

The SpecialWare Directory: A Guide to Software for Special Education. 2d ed. Columbus, Ohio: LINC Associates; distr., Phoenix, Ariz.: Oryx Press, 1986. 160p. $22.50pa. LC 85-23880. ISBN 0-89774-192-7.

Over 300 computer software programs for use with special education students are identified in this directory. Materials are current, since all titles bear copyrights after 1980, and represent software packages from more than one hundred publishers/producers. Arrangement of entries is alphabetical by title. Each entry provides data related to title, publisher/producer, date, address, format, version, catalog numbers, compatible hardware and peripherals, specific area of special education (e.g., hearing or visual impairment, learning disability, mental retardation), grade level, reading level, interest level, curricular area, and function (drill and practice, tutorial, simulation, game, etc.). A detailed annotation describes each software title; sources of critical reviews are also listed.

A series of indexes allow access by curriculum area, technique, type of exceptionality, hardware, input-output options (e.g., joystick, voice input), and grade level (preschool to adult). The appendix material provides information related to publishers/producers and distributors, warranties, preview availability, and other information of interest to special education teachers and school media specialists.

Stein, Morris I. **Gifted, Talented, and Creative Young People: A Guide to Theory, Teaching, and Research**. New York: Garland, 1986. 465p. (Garland Reference Library of Social Science, Vol. 120). $80.00. LC 81-48419. ISBN 0-8240-9392-5.

Books, articles in journals, newsletters, and other periodicals, and chapters in books are summarized in this annotated bibliography related to gifted, talented, and creative students. Emphasis of content covered is on theory, teaching (including curricular programs and instructional strategies and techniques), and research. Although publication dates cover a wide span of years during the twentieth century, emphasis is on gifted education literature of the 1970s.

Entries are arranged first in three broad categories: (1) identification and selection, (2) education and training, and (3) research, then alphabetically by author under more specific topical headings. An introduction provides an overview of present and future trends in the education of exceptional students who fall into these categories of special education.

Sternlicht, Manny, and George Windholz. **Social Behavior of the Mentally Retarded: An Annotated Bibliography**. New York: Garland, 1984. 226p. (Developmental Disabilities Series, Vol. 1). $42.00. LC 82-49140. ISBN 0-8240-9137-X.

This annotated bibliography includes 619 entries of books and articles arranged by subject in eleven chapters. The emphasis is on periodical literature and covers topics related to patterns of social development, interactions with family and peers, adjustments in the classroom, institutional settings, the community, and the work world, as well as emotional disturbances, leisure-time pursuits, and independent living.

An eighteen-page introduction provides an expository treatment of these aspects of the social development of the mentally retarded from birth to adulthood.

Annotations are in reality brief abstracts reporting subject, methodology, and results of many research studies. What this work lacks is a preface defining the scope of the work, types of periodical indexes searched, and so on. An author index concludes the work.

Sternlicht, Manny, with Madeline Sternlicht. **Special Education: A Source Book**. New York: Garland, 1987. 431p. (Source Books on Education, Vol. 7; Garland Reference Library of Social Science, Vol. 375). $50.00. LC 87-129. ISBN 0-8240-8524-8.

Books, articles, chapters from books, dissertations, and papers presented at professional meetings are included in this annotated bibliography of special education sources. A total of 1,001 citations are arranged in broad subject chapters: mental retardation, giftedness, visual and hearing impairments, learning disabilities, brain damage, speech and language impairments, orthopedic and other physical impairments, emotional and behavioral impairments, and mainstreaming, each of which is introduced by a brief overview of the topic. Each entry contains complete bibliographic description; annotations are descriptive in nature and range from very brief (50 words) to about 200 to 250 words. This is one of the more comprehensive works providing bibliographic control of the literature on special education for a period of over twenty-five years from 1960 to 1986.

INDEXES AND ABSTRACTS

Chicorel, Marietta, and Robert Lynn. **Chicorel Abstracts to Reading and Learning Disabilities**. New York: American Library, 1978- . Annual. (Chicorel Index Series). $95.00. LC 78-58455. ISSN 0149-533X.

Abstracts from different journals on reading and learning disabilities provide the scholar with concise information about in-depth special education research. Research studies cover the K-12 level and abstracts indicate level of language, research methodology, and intended audience. These guides are divided into two areas of reading disabilities and learning disabilities, each of which is further subdivided into over 100 subject headings. All information is from primary sources and gives the full journal citation, title, volume, issue number, date, and pages. Good use of cross-references directs the user to further sources.

Chicorel has also published annotated bibliographies which have evaluated a wide range of popular to scholarly books, with inconsistency in format and depth of coverage. A positive feature of the abstracts is a list of which types of professionals would find the articles beneficial. A list of periodicals surveyed is also included. The price is steep for a reference book of this size and type.

NICSEM Master Index to Special Education Materials. National Information Center for Special Education Materials (NICSEM). Los Angeles: University of Southern California, 1980. 3v. $106.00pa/set. LC 80-83854. ISBN 0-89320-049-2.

A subsection of the NICEM database is devoted to special education materials. Known as NICSEM, this database is a massive compilation of records describing print and nonprint resources for dealing with physical and mental disabilities. The master list is comprehensive in scope and covers all types of special education materials. Additional subject-specific indexes include *NICSEM Mini-Index to Special Education Materials: Functional Communication Skills* (1980); *NICSEM Mini-Index to Special Educational Materials: Family Life and Sex Education* (1980); *NICSEM Mini-Index to Special Education Materials: High Interest, Controlled Vocabulary Supplementary Reading Materials for Adolescents & Young Adults* (1980); *NICSEM Mini-Index to Special Education Materials: Independent Living Skills for Moderately and Severely Handicapped Students* (1980); *NICSEM Mini-Index to Special Education Materials: Personal & Social Development for Moderately and Severly Handicapped Students* (1980); *NICSEM Source Directory* (1980); *Special Education Index to Parent Materials* (1979); *NICSEM Index to Non-Print Special Education Materials: Multimedia (Professional Volume)* (1978); and *NICSEM Special Education Thesaurus* (2d ed., 1980). The indexes are available in print format or through DIALOG.

DICTIONARIES AND ENCYCLOPEDIAS

Bornstein, Harry, Karen L. Saulnier, and Lillian B. Hamilton, eds. **The Comprehensive Signed English Dictionary**. Washington, D.C.: Gallaudet College Press, 1983. 456p. $25.95. LC 82-82830. ISBN 0-913580-81-3.

Deaf students who are learning to sign the English language and special education teachers who teach them or are teaching in teacher education programs will be interested in this extensive dictionary. It contains over 3,100 sign language words and fourteen grammatical markers. Terms and concepts described are those that comprise the everyday language of children and young people, including some slang expressions. Terms are presented in alphabetical order with an illustration for each sign word, and written instructions for making the hand movements.

Hanson, David P., and David A. Penrod. **A Desk Reference of Legal Terms for School Psychologists and Special Educators**. Springfield, Ill.: Charles C Thomas, 1980. 210p. LC 79-26525. ISBN 0-398-04015-X.

This reference guide is intended for school personnel who are concerned with legal rights, issues, and problems related to the education of children with special needs. The book is arranged in three sections. Part 1 summarizes eight significant court cases which had major impact in the formulation of Public Law 94-142. Part 2 provides a historical overview of legislation and funding for the handicapped and topics such as the right to education, management of pupil records, assessment procedures, due process, IEPs (Individualized Educational Programs), and implications for school specialists. Part 3 contains the actual glossary of approximately 700 legal terms. More than half of the volume is devoted to the appendix which contains the complete text of P.L. 94-142, Education of Handicapped Children Act. The volume is concluded with a section entitled "Bibliography and Organizations," which also includes selected newsletters and periodicals, and a "Selected List of Organizations Serving the Handicapped." This is, indeed, a handy one-volume reference to the rationale, origin, implementation, and ramifications of P.L. 94-142.

Kelly, Leo J., and Glenn A. Vergason. **Dictionary of Special Education and Rehabilitation**. 2d ed. Denver, Colo.: Love Publishing, 1985. 207p. $14.95. LC 84-81939. ISBN 0-89108-168-2.

Approximately 2,500 terms in the fields of special education and rehabilitation are defined in this dictionary. Selection of entries for inclusion was based on currently used texts and professional books in the field, as well as on a previous publication by Kelly, *A Dictionary of Exceptional Children* (1977). This second edition represents an expansion of the 1978 edition, with many new terms in the jargon unique to the field added, some rewritten, and other definitions clarified.

Entries are alphabetized word by word and include phonetic pronunciations. Key terms used within a definition are printed in italics, so the user is aware that they are also defined. Definitions are limited to one or two sentences, in most cases. Materials provided at the end of the book include information on associations and national centers, periodicals and journals (English language), and sources of legal assistance. This information has also been revised and updated. The second edition also includes lists of major microcomputer clearinghouses and centers. A bilingual title is *The Bilingual Special Education Directory* by Richard H. Figueroa and Nadeen T. Ruiz (National Hispanic University Press, 1983).

Moore, Byron C., Willard Abraham, and Clarence R. Laing. **A Dictionary of Special Education Terms**. Springfield, Ill.: Charles C Thomas, 1980. 117p. $15.25. LC 79-23015. ISBN 0-398-04009-5.

The emphasis of this dictionary of terms related to education of exceptional children is on the changing concepts in special education, and the different disciplines (e.g., psychology, medicine, sociology) that have a vested interest in the field. Approximately 3,500 entries are included covering terms in such major areas as mental retardation, emotional handicaps, hearing, vision, learning disability, speech, physical handicaps, and giftedness. Because usage was determined from reference sources currently available on the market, these definitions should reflect current meanings and vocabulary. A pronunciation key is also provided.

Reynolds, Cecil R., and Lester Mann, eds. **Encyclopedia of Special Education: A Reference for the Education of the Handicapped and Other Exceptional Children and Adults**. New York: Wiley, 1987. 3v. $189.95/set. LC 86-33975. ISBN 0471-82858-0.

This three-volume encyclopedia contains over 2,000 articles about various aspects of special education aimed at "educators, psychologists, physicians, social workers, occupational and physical therapists, lawyers, and ministers." Arrangement of information is alphabetical, and articles are signed by international contributors who are known authorities in their fields. Many articles are followed by brief bibliographies that suggest sources for further study.

The Education for All Handicapped Children Act of 1975 (P.L. 94-142) is repeated verbatim in the appendix, along with a discussion of its development and the impact of its provision on special education and in the lives of children classified as exceptional.

HANDBOOKS AND YEARBOOKS

Chalfant, James C., and Margaret Van Dusen Pysh. **The Compliance Manual: A Guide to the Rules and Regulations of the Education for All Handicapped Act, Public Law 94-142: Questions, Answers and Recommended Practices**. Mount Kisco, N.Y.: PEM Press, 1980. 101p. illus. $9.95pa. LC 79-90320. ISBN 0-933922-01-9.

The purpose of this manual is to help parents, teachers, members of boards of education, and administrators interpret and understand the intent of Public Law 94-142, the first piece of national legislation attempting to provide educational opportunity for all handicapped children. The manual is written in a question-and-answer format addressing major issues raised over implementation of P.L. 94-142. Answers to questions include reference to specific sections of the rules and regulations, as well as recommended procedures for compliance. Some questions answered include (1) "Who are Handicapped Children?" (2) "How do states apply for P.L. 94-142 funds?" (3) "How do local educational agencies apply for P.L. 94-142 funds?" and (4) "What access rights do parents have to inspect and review educational records?" A brief listing entitled "Compliance Manual References" is also included.

This manual will be absolutely essential to parents and school personnel who are concerned with special education programs from diagnosis and evaluation, parental consent through placement, to writing IEPs (Individualized Education Programs) to impartial due process hearings.

Clendening, Corinne P., and Ruth Ann Davies. **Creating Programs for the Gifted: A Guide for Teachers, Librarians, and Students**. New York: Bowker, 1980. 574p. $29.95. LC 80-10544. ISBN 0-8352-1265-3.

This guide provides answers to questions asked by parents, school personnel, and school board members about special programs for gifted and talented children. It is arranged in two major sections: Part 1, "Educating the Gifted and Talented," answers questions such as (1) What are they like? (2) How are they identified? (3) How accurate are screening procedures and tests? and (4) What percentage of school children are gifted and talented? It also includes the characteristics of gifted children as defined by the Council for Exceptional Children, findings of the Marland Report (Report to the U.S. Congress by the U.S. Commissioner of Education, 1972), and an overview of the history of gifted and talented education in the United States.

Part 2 describes model instructional programs for a variety of subjects in the K-12 curriculum. Appendixes contain the text of the Marland Report, some diagnostic instruments used in identifying gifted children, and a list of basic reference tools, among other pertinent items. A bibliography is also included. This is a useful reference tool for all students, instructors, and administrators on an aspect of exceptionality that has been somewhat neglected in the literature.

Deiner, Penny L. **Resources for Teaching Young Children with Special Needs**. New York: Harcourt Brace Jovanovich, 1983. 564p. $21.95pa. LC 82-84254. ISBN 0-15-576627-9.

This reference tool is designed to be a source of programs for children with special physical, mental, and emotional needs who have been mainstreamed into the regular classroom. It provides suggestions for adapting the curriculum, and over 300 specific learning activities. Arrangement is in two parts. The first part provides information on developing the skills of working with parents, writing IEPs (Individualized Education Programs), and ten chapters on specific special needs (speech and language, hearing, visual, learning, physical, health problems, adjustment, culturally distinct, gifted and talented, intellectual). Part 2 presents activities organized by curriculum areas and by goals (e.g., to improve expressive language, to encourage creativity, to increase vocabulary, to improve self-concept). For each activity a behavioral objective is also included, as well as a list of materials required, specific procedures, and a paragraph commenting on special features, instructions for, or uses of each activity. All activities are listed in the general index and an index at the end of each special needs chapter lists activities particularly appropriate to meet that specific handicap.

This is a practical hands-on resource guide which, according to Deiner, "translates theory into practice" (p. v). The activities are designed to be used with all students in the classroom, while providing special benefits for special needs children.

Fadely, Jack L., and Virginia N. Hosler. **Developmental Psychometrics: A Resource Book for Mental Health Workers and Educators**. Springfield, Ill.: Charles C. Thomas, 1980. 158p. $21.75. LC 79-28746. ISBN 0-398-04056-7.

This resource book is aimed at helping medical and educational professionals screen and diagnose children with behavioral disorders. It includes an overview of a comprehensive screening process including materials, assessment instruments, and guidelines. The authors state that another intention of the book is to help diagnosticians gain "practical information that can immediately be translated into treatment objectives" (p. vii). Chapter headings provide an indication of the coverage: (1) "General Levels of Developmental Assessment"; (2) "Intelligence, Development, and Learning"; (3) "The School Community Interface"; (4) "The Preschool Child"; (5) "Perceptual Motor Development"; (6) "Learning Skills Assessment"; (7) "Personality Factors"; and (8) "Social Behavioral Assessments." The lists of additional references concluding each chapter are very brief and limited; the work is indexed.

Goldberg, Steven Selig. **Special Education Law**. New York: Plenum Press, 1982. 229p. (Critical Topics in Law & Society). $29.50. LC 82-13190. ISBN 0-3-6-40848-1.

As an important area of civil rights legislation, laws pertaining to special education are particularly relevant to educators and parents of exceptional children and to other professionals who work with them. This guide identifies all major national laws related to the field of special education. Special attention is given to the Education for All Handicapped Children Act of 1975 (Public Law 94-142) and Section 504 of the Rehabilitation Act of 1973. The introductory chapter provides the history of special education legislation, including landmark cases. One chapter deals entirely with the special education "placement" or "due process" hearings which are held to ascertain the proper program or special services demanded by the special needs of each particular child.

Such major issues as education extending beyond the normal school year, discipline problems, language and racial minorities, malpractice claims, and comparative laws with respect to gifted and talented children are also covered. The appendixes include the full text of P.L. 94-142, Section 504 and their regulations, as well as names and addresses of legal organizations. An index concludes the work.

Harrington, Thomas F., **Handbook of Career Planning for Special Needs Students**. Rockville, Md.: Aspen Systems, 1982. 358p. $34.00. LC 82-11419. ISBN 0-89443-661-9.

Although this handbook begins by addressing theories of career development and career planning in general, its unique focus is on providing vocational guidance for the handicapped. It is directed at individuals with cognitive, visual, hearing, physical, and emotional impairments from adolescence to young adulthood, or approximately ages 12 to 22. Arranged in three major sections with chapters in each authored by specialists in that area, the handbook covers part 1, "Career Planning Concepts, Goals, and Resources"; 2, "The Disabled Population: Unique Career Development Issues"; and 3, "Facilitating Strategies, Approaches, and Information." Contributors include experts in guidance counseling, handicapped program management, rehabilitation counseling, disabled student services, family therapy, behavioral disabilities, psychology, special education, and a pediatric physiatrist. The work is indexed.

Idol-Maestas, Lorna. **Special Educator's Consultation Handbook**. Rockville, Md.: Aspen Systems, 1983. 357p. $35.00. LC 82-18445. ISBN 0-89443-926-X.

The author of this handbook feels that the support or consultation provided in the elementary and secondary classroom for mildly handicapped students should be taught to preservice special education teachers. Elements from five preparation programs that provide instruction and practice for consulting teachers are reviewed here. All aspects of teacher consultation are covered and extensive reviews of research findings in the literature are included. A major share of the book is concerned with forty-one reports, done by resource/consulting teachers studying at the University of Illinois, of specific cases related to various issues related to providing resource support (e.g., transfer of skills learned to the regular classroom, academic problems, improving social behavior, reading instruction, teacher-parent consultations, inservice programs) dispersed throughout the chapters. The work is concluded with a bibliography of over 200 references and an index.

While this handbook is unique in the information that it provides, it lacks either a preface or an introduction that delineates the author's purpose, scope of information provided, and criteria for its selection for inclusion.

Jones, Philip R. **A Practical Guide to Federal Special Education Law: Understanding and Implementing PL 94-142**. New York: Holt, Rinehart and Winston, 1981. 220p. $27.95. LC 81-81212. ISBN 0-03-05551-5.

This guide for educational administrators provides information necessary for implementing federal laws regarding handicapped children, particularly Public Law

94-142. Other professionals, as well as parents, will find its contents helpful. Major coverage is given to the historical background of The Education for All Handicapped Children Act, why Congress passed the statute, reactions of parents and educators, and changes that have taken place since 1975. Due process procedures are outlined, as are implementation strategies and implementation challenges. Appendix A contains the text of P.L. 94-142; appendix B provides sample formats and policy papers of IEPs (Individual Education Programs). Other appendixes include a list of national centers for providing information on education of the handicapped, special education units within state departments of education, newsletters, and legal advocacy organizations related to special education. A subject index concludes this work. While the ramifications of this law are no longer current news in the field of special education, this reference guide provides the researcher with historical background information and copies of important documents related to special education legislation.

Karnes, Frances A., and Emily C. Collins. **Handbook of Instructional Resources and References for Teaching the Gifted**. 2d ed. Boston: Allyn and Bacon, 1984. 196p. $34.95pa. LC 83-22366. ISBN 0-205-08151-7.

The objectives of the compilers are twofold: (1) to provide a listing of commercially available materials that are especially appropriate for use with the gifted education curriculum, and (2) to provide an annotated list of books about the gifted and talented for use by those professionals who work with them. Materials have been selected to include those that encourage creativity, logical and critical thinking, leadership, and group dynamics and issues related to values clarification.

The book begins with a discussion of the nature and needs of the gifted, and considerations and criteria for selecting materials. Arrangement of titles is in a multipage chart providing analysis of 631 items. The name of the item, company distributing it, cost, suggested use level, dimensions of learning (skills, type of development, etc.), format, and components are described. Another chart is devoted to analysis of 208 games, puzzles, and brainteasers. In the bibliography of professional references, 425 titles are annotated and arranged in the curricular disciplines and other subjects. A list of publishers and their addresses follows. The appendix lists major organizations and national resources serving the gifted, as well as journals and magazines for gifted students, and their parents and teachers.

With increased attention to providing excellent education for the gifted, exceptional student, this is a comprehensive source of useful information about a wide variety of materials and programs. A related title is one by Sara Lake, *Gifted Education: A Special Interest Resource Guide in Education* (Oryx Press, 1981).

Kauffman, James M., and Daniel P. Hallahan, eds. **Handbook of Special Education**. Englewood Cliffs, N.J.: Prentice-Hall, 1981. 807p. LC 80-17390. ISBN 0-13-381756-3.

This comprehensive handbook provides basic information on all aspects of special education for parents, teachers, school psychologists, guidance counselors, curriculum specialists, and administrators. It includes information contributed by forty-nine experts in the field, arranged in thirty-four topical chapters and five major sections: (1) "Introduction," (2) "Conceptual Foundations," (3) "Service Delivery Systems," (4) "Curriculum and Methods," and (5) "Child and Environment Management." Bibliographies are included in the chapters. An index concludes the work. A handbook devoted specifically to research is *Handbook of Special Education: Research and Practice*, edited by Margaret C. Wang, Maynard C. Reynolds, and Herbert J. Walberg (Pergamon Press, 1987).

Learning Disabilities: A Reference Book. Guilford, Conn.: Special Learning, 1980. 599(24)p. (Special Education Series). LC 85-233785. ISBN 0-89568-116-1.

Although this reference book deals with all aspects of the education of learning disabled students, it is aimed at the regular classroom teacher. Learning problems outlined in Public Law 94-142 in reading comprehension; oral, written, and listening expression; basic reading skill; and mathematical calculation and reasoning are explained. Suggestions, techniques, and teaching methods related to specific disabilities in these areas are provided, with major emphasis given to perceptual disorders and disordered psychological processes. In addition, chapters are devoted to issues, classroom management, and parental counseling. A glossary of terms precedes the main body of the work. Major research studies and their findings are discussed throughout, with many reference lists included. Some attention is also given to the effects of medication. While the book is primarily concerned with the education of school-aged children, some attention is given to problems in infancy and adulthood.

The work is concluded by a learning disabilities checklist with questions in three categories: preschool age, grades 1 through 8, and high school. This is followed by a summary of behavioral characteristics of children with learning disabilities, a brief outline of legislation related to exceptional children, and an appendix listing special agencies and services. A subject index is provided.

Because of the breadth and scope of information included in this comprehensive source of information, it is a must for teachers, administrators, and parents involved with learning disabled children.

Mann, Philip H., and associates. **Handbook in Diagnostic-Prescriptive Teaching**. 3d ed. Boston: Longwood Division, Allyn and Bacon, 1987. 579p. $22.46. LC 87-925. ISBN 0-205-10322-7.

This handbook spells out specific procedures for assessing the learning needs of learning disabled children. Introductory chapters provide theoretical insights into individual differences and explanations for why children fail to learn. Individual chapters provide specific checklists for screening children with respect to spelling, reading, oral language development, and a variety of developmental tasks. Teachers and/or other professionals are instructed in how to record and observe all pertinent behaviors.

The suggested curricula designed for specific deficit levels and for specific task levels will undoubtedly be useful resources for educators of exceptional children. A glossary and bibliography conclude this very practical and essential handbook.

Mayer, C. Lamar. **Educational Administration and Special Education: A Handbook for School Administrators**. Boston: Allyn and Bacon, 1982. 383p. $24.00. LC 81-3586. ISBN 0-205-07555-X.

Directed at the practical needs of school administrators, this work begins by defining different types of exceptionality and characteristics of children associated with each. The second part covers laws, regulations, policies, hearings, court decisions, and various agencies related to special education programs. Part 3 provides models for programs/services and part 4 addresses a variety of daily concerns related to assessment, placement, working with parents and teachers, the special education curriculum, budgets, equipment, and program evaluation. The appendixes provide such useful items as checklists used by compliance review teams, local board policies, agencies providing services for the handicapped, sample questions for special education programs, sample letters to parents, as well as IEPs (Individualized Education Programs).

Meers, Gary, ed. **Handbook of Special Vocational Needs Education**. Rockville, Md.: Aspen Systems, 1980. 383p. $34.00. LC 80-17759. ISBN 0-89443-288-5.

Designed for educators, administrators, parents, and counselors of any type who are involved with special needs students, whether they are handicapped or in some way disadvantaged, this handbook covers each aspect of special vocational needs programs. It is arranged in three sections with emphases as follows: section 1, the foundations of special vocational needs programs; section 2, the basis for program development and implementation; and section 3, program evaluation, administration, and personnel requirements. This is a useful reference for those who have some concern in helping handicapped and disadvantaged students make vocational decisions that are fulfilling and within reach of their qualifications and needs. In addition to the glossary and a list of contributors with addresses, the appendixes contain very helpful information: A, "Directory of Organizations, Advocacy Groups, and Curriculum Centers Related to Serving Special Needs Populations"; and B, "Additional Special Needs Resources." The work is indexed.

Mori, Allen, A., and Jane Ellsworth Olive. **Handbook of Preschool Special Education: Programming, Curriculum, Training**. Rockville, Md.: Aspen Systems, 1980. 518p. $33.00. LC 80-14199. ISBN 0-89443-276-1.

This handbook is aimed at the parents of infants and toddlers with special needs and the practitioners who work with them. It is divided into two sections. Part 1 provides a balanced combination of materials on general developmental theory and assessment along with practical information on planning and implementing early intervention programs, planning and implementing paraprofessional training programs, and basic teaching goals and techniques (including behavior modification). In addition, part 1 contains chapters that explain the importance of early diagnosis, intervention, and stimulation; describe the development of the child from prenatal through perinatal, infancy, and early childhood stages; and identify and describe the screening instruments used in assessing a child's performance (including a complete developmental checklist).

Part 2 includes a collection of lesson plans and learning activities designed to achieve objectives related to reflex/gross motor development, perceptual/fine motor skills, sensory/cognitive development, language development, and personal/social self-help skills.

This handbook presents a wealth of information and lessons coordinated with specific developmental learning goals; it should prove to be a great time-saving tool for those involved with preschool children in a special education program.

Polette, Nancy, and Marjorie Hamlin. **Exploring Books with Gifted Children**. Littleton, Colo.: Libraries Unlimited, 1980. 214p. bibliog. index. $18.50. LC 80-23721. ISBN 0-87287-216-5.

This curriculum resource provides suggested techniques, strategies, questions, and model units for teaching various aspects of literature to gifted children. Each chapter provides a complete instructional outline on such topics as critical reading, plot construction, the study of setting and mood, character development, and dramatization, as well as specific author studies.

Appendix 1 is entitled "Selection Aids to Assist in the Development of Unit Models." Appendix 2 lists unit studies on various suggested topics at both primary and intermediate grade levels. An author/title/subject index concludes the work.

Because of the constant pressure of designing instruction for typical students as well as those who need remediation, the discussion guides, suggested learning and/or culminating activities, and highlighting of concepts are extremely helpful to the teacher providing for a group of gifted and creative learners who might otherwise be short changed.

Stowitschek, Joseph J., and associates. **Instructional Materials for Exceptional Children: Selection, Management and Adaptation**. Germantown, Md.: Aspen Systems, 1980. 379p. $34.00. LC 80-11730. ISBN 0-89443-277-X.

Because the Education of All Handicapped Children Act of 1975 requires a written Individualized Education Program outlining instructional objectives and the strategies designed to achieve them for each child, this guide will be of great assistance to educators.

Teachers have in this resource a wealth of objectives, specialized applications of media to children with handicaps, including how to select, utilize, and adapt instructional materials. Types of resources available at state agencies (with contact persons), are also identified. Also included are chapters on how to measure learner progress in various subjects and developmental tasks, and child-based materials evaluation. Numerous self-check exercises are included throughout the volume with sample responses provided. Sample forms used to record the educational history and progress of students are also included. The work is indexed, and includes additional references and a list of publishers of special education materials.

DIRECTORIES

The Directory for Exceptional Children: A Listing of Educational and Training Facilities. 11th ed. Boston: Porter Sargent, 1987. 1,472p. $45.00. LC 54-4975. ISBN 0-87558-116-1. ISSN 0070-5012.

This directory to a wide range of some 3,000 facilities, organizations, and programs for children with developmental, organic, and emotional handicaps is greatly expanded since its first ninety-six page edition in 1954. It is arranged in fourteen sections, covering the learning disabled, the emotionally disturbed and socially maladjusted, autistic, neurologically handicapped, mentally retarded, blind and partially sighted, deaf and hearing impaired, and speech handicapped. Some of the sections are devoted to psychiatric and guidance clinics; associations, societies, and foundations; and federal and state agencies and personnel. In each section, information is alphabetical by state. Parents, educators, and other professionals making placement decisions for handicapped children will find this comprehensive directory a reliable and essential source of information.

Directory of Facilities and Services for the Learning Disabled. Novato, Calif.: Academic Therapy Publications, 1967- . Annual. $1.50 (postage and handling). ISSN 0092-3257.

This publication was known as *Directory of Educational Facilities for the Learning Disabled* from 1967 through 1980, changing its name with the 1981-1982 edition. It lists over 500 specialized facilities and services, such as remedial teachers and tutors, counselors, psychologists, pediatricians and pediatric services, guidance/mental health services, speech and language therapists, vision and hearing specialists, vocational/career counselors, as well as all-day and residential schools.

Entries are arranged alphabetically by state and include name of person or organization offering service, address, telephone number, and data with respect to staff, type of services offered, fees, grade and age levels, and so on. A code key precedes the directory, providing help in interpreting the abbreviated form of information. A list of tests and assessment instruments, and a list of "Sources of Specialized Material in Learning Disabilities" and an index conclude the work.

Directory of National Information Sources on Handicapping Conditions and Related Services. Compiled by Clearinghouse on the Handicapped, Office of Human Development Services, Office for Handicapped Individuals. 4th ed. Washington, D.C.: Government Printing Office, 1986. 366p. $6.50pa; single copy free from clearinghouse. LC 86-602366. S/N 065-000-00254-0.

As the major reference tool of the National Clearinghouse on the Handicapped, this directory identifies and describes national organizations that provide information and services for the handicapped. Organizations are listed alphabetically in categories: "Advocacy, Consumer, Voluntary Health Organizations"; "Information/Data Banks/Research"; "Data Base Vendors"; "Federal Government Other than Information Units"; "Professional and Trade Organizations"; "Facilities, Schools, Clinics"; "Service Organizations"; "International Information."

Each entry provides information about the handicapping conditions served, an overview of the organization, a description of the information services provided, and publications (if any) of the organization. Although many of the organizations listed in this directory go beyond the scope of education, a large number fall into education-related categories, such as accreditation; audiovisual materials; career counseling; day care/head start; developmental disabilities, service personnel; educational media/materials; health education; learning disabilities; library services; postsecondary education, handicapped; preschool education; sex education; and sheltered workshops. The appendixes list religious and sports organizations, provide a briefly annotated list of national directories of services and resources for the handicapped, and alphabetically list all the organizations and federal agencies included in the directory. A subject index concludes this major overview of organizations providing help and information to the disabled.

Directory of Special Education. Repertoire de l'Educational Speciale. Repertorio de Educacion Especial. Paris: Special Education Section, UNESCO; distr., Lanham, Md.: UNIPUB, 1986. 104p. (IBEdata Series). $5.00pa. ISBN 92-3-002413-9.

The major governmental and nongovernmental agencies and research institutes associated with special education and rehabilitation services in nations that belong to UNESCO are listed in this directory. Information included in the entries came from questionnaires sent to the agencies and covers agency name and address, population served, programs, services, and publications. International organizations that provide services to the handicapped and other special education directories are listed in the appendixes.

Eckstein, Burton J., ed. **Handicapped Funding Directory: A Guide to Sources of Funding in the United States for Handicapped Programs, 1986.** 5th ed. Marina del Rey, Calif.: Research Grant Studies,1986. 189p. $20.50pa. LC 82-163843.

This guide provides current information for educators and other professionals who are seeking grant funds for programs and services for the handicapped. Associations are listed alphabetically by name. Addresses, telephone numbers, and a brief indication of the types of grants funded (e.g., research grants, training grants, rehabilitation and mental health grants, education and research grants, medical student fellowships, postdoctoral fellowships, special projects in occupational therapy).

Foundations are arranged alphabetically by state. Federal agencies are listed in numerical order. Information for the latter is detailed, providing full name of the federal agency, authorization, objectives, types of assistance, eligibility requirements, uses and restrictions, application and award process, assistance considerations, financial information, and previous program accomplishments.

Other features of the directory include a bibliography of further sources for grants research, regional and local federal offices, tips on grant proposal writing, and commonly used abbreviations and acronyms. There is a separate index for each type of funding source (associations, foundations, and federal agencies). The editor has listed the sources he consulted to compile this directory. Anyone seeking funds for services and/or research, and other programs for mentally retarded, speech impaired, emotionally disturbed, health impaired, hard of hearing, deaf, visually handicapped, orthopedically impaired, and learning disabled individuals, will benefit from this publication which provides in one volume information about relevant resources available for support to the handicapped.

Educators with Disabilities: A Resource Guide. Washington, D.C.: Government Printing Office, 1981. 153p. $6.50pa. S/N 065-000-00104-7.

This guide identifies over 900 educators who have various disabilities and who responded to a detailed questionnaire prepared by ASCTE (The American Association of Colleges for Teacher Education). The purpose of the guide is threefold: (1) to identify disabled educators and allow them to contact others in the field; (2) to allow schools, government, and organizations to locate handicapped experts in education; and (3) to allow disabled students to use it to identify role models for their own career development preparation. The volume is arranged in five parts: Part 1 focuses on career counseling with respect to the various teacher education components. Part 2 describes problems of disabled educators and how they coped with them. Problems include those related to blind/visually impaired, deaf/hard of hearing/neurological disabilities (cerebral and spinal cord), neuro-muscular disabilities, organic disorders, orthopedic handicaps, speech impaired, and mentally retarded. Part 3 describes the barriers faced by disabled educators along with recommendations and solutions. Part 4 is the actual directory of disabled educators which is arranged alphabetically and provides name, address, telephone number (and teletype-writer-TTY number); degrees received; most recent position; disability and age became disabled; and areas in which the educator will act as a consultant or resource. Indexes to the directory provide access by region, specialization (teaching/administration area), and disability. Part 5 consists of an annotated bibliography of print and nonprint items, organizations, and legal resources related to disabled educators. This unique reference tool is an inspiration to handicapped young people and a revelation to all users of the major contributions made to the field of education by handicapped personnel.

The FCLD Learning Disabilities Resource Guide: A State-by-State Directory of Special Programs, Schools, and Services. New York: New York University Press; distr., Columbia University Press, 1985. 408p. $35.00. LC 85-13874. ISBN 0-8147-2579-1.

Special programs, schools, and services for the learning disabled are provided in the directory section of this guide, arranged alphabetically by state in several broad categories. These categories include "Private and Day Schools," "College and University Special Programs and Services," "Organizations Concerned with Learning Disabilities," "State Department of Education Learning Disabilities Personnel," "Hospital Clinics and Other Services," and "Summer Camps and Programs."

Other features of this guide include a section on information sources for parents, guidance counselors, tutors, and the learning disabled, themselves, who are trying to identify specific sources of help. A most interesting and valuable contribution is the material that provides an overview of what is known about learning disabilities including definitions, characteristics, attribution, and the rights of children diagnosed as LD (learning disabled) students. Also useful are the glossary of terms and annotated bibliography. A proper name and subject index conclude this guide, which was formerly known as *The FCLD Guide for Parents of Children with Learning Disabilities* (1984).

Gollay, Elinor, and Alwina Bennett. **The College Guide for Students with Disabilities: A Detailed Directory of Higher Education Services, Programs, and Facilities Accessible to Handicapped Students in the United States**. Cambridge, Mass.: Abt Publications, and Boulder, Colo.: Westview, 1985. 554p. $47.50. ISBN 0-8191-4498-3.

The purpose of this directory is to identify colleges and universities in the United States that have special programs, facilities, and services for handicapped students. Students, parents, guidance counselors, and administrators can find an overview of state and national resources available as options to the disabled. Type of information provided includes the percentage of disabled students enrolled, number of buildings with access ramps, number of restrooms that can accommodate wheelchairs, availability of special counseling programs, notetaker services, specialized audiovisual instructional resources (e.g., captioned filmstrips, braille books), as well as profiles of individual schools, policies and procedures, and resources available in the community.

In addition to the directory, the first section of the book discusses admissions testing programs, sources of financial aid, agencies providing assistance to the handicapped, and a bibliography of related references. Although this directory should be used in conjunction with the major standard college guides, as some major schools are eliminated, it conveniently highlights alternative choices for handicapped students interested in higher education.

Liscio, Mary Ann. **A Guide to Colleges for Learning Disabled Students**. Rev. ed. Orlando, Fla.: Academic Press, 1986. 423p. $26.95pa. LC 85-48291. ISBN 0-12-452244-0.

Colleges that have special facilities and services for the learning disabled are listed in two separate listings in this directory: one for two-year programs, the other for four-year courses of study. Each list is arranged alphabetically by state first and then by college. Information in each entry covers school name, address, telephone number, contact person, school enrollment, application procedures, costs (tuition and room and board), admission requirements, access and other provisions for disabled students, other special services for the handicapped, as well as degree majors available.

Other special education directories edited by Liscio include *A Guide to Colleges for Hearing Impaired Students* (Academic Press, 1986), *A Guide to Colleges for Mobility Impaired Students* (Academic Press, 1986), and *A Guide to Colleges for Visually Impaired Students* (Academic Press, 1986).

Mangrum, Charles T., II, and Stephen S. Strichart, eds. **Peterson's Guides to Colleges with Programs for Learning-Disabled Students**. Princeton, N.J.: Peterson's Guides, 1985. 314p. $13.95pa. LC 85-3497. ISBN 0-87866-327-4.

Students diagnosed as learning disabled will benefit from this guide to colleges with programs for them. Arrangment of the 279 entries is alphabetical by school name. For each school the following information is provided: name of college and location; type of college; degrees conferred; student enrollment; programs and services (remedial, testing, counseling, and tutoring) for the learning disabled, as well as the students using them;

faculty; costs; majors; staff; and admission requirements. Data are summarized in charts and page columns. Articles provide advice and tips on selecting a school and information about organizations that serve the learning disabled.

Pernecke, Raegene B., and Sara M. Schreiner, comps. and eds. **Schooling for the Learning Disabled: A Selective Guide to LD Programs in Elementary and Secondary Schools throughout the United States**. Glenview, Ill.: SMS Publishing, 1983. 173p. $9.95pa. LC 83-050934. ISBN 0-914985-00-0.

Parents, teachers, and counselors working with children diagnosed as LD, or learning disabled, should be interested in this directory to elementary and secondary programs deemed qualitative models. In addition to descriptions of over fifty school programs, chapters in this work provide information on the definitions and characteristics of the learning disabled and about human development and learning in general. Entries for school programs are arranged geographically and contain information on physical facilities and environment, staff, curriculum, and diagnostic and assessment procedures. Although lack of an index limits this guide's usefulness, it does provide a lot of information about LD children and their special needs. A title edited by P. M. Fielding is similar in coverage, *A National Directory of Four Year Colleges, Two Year Colleges, and Post High School Training Programs for Young People with Learning Disabilities* (Partners in Publishing, 1986).

Slovak, Irene, comp. and ed. **BOSC Directory: Facilities for Learning Disabled People**. Congers, N.Y.: BOSC Publishers, 1985. 200p. $28.00pa. LC 84-72701. ISBN 0-9613860-0-2.

Facilities for the learning disabled described here include a wide range of programs, including day and residential schools; learning and diagnostic centers; preschools; primary, middle, secondary, and post-high schools; colleges and universities; hospital care centers and clinics; vocational schools; independent living; and group homes. In addition, the reader will find listed public and private agencies that provide information and/or service to the learning disabled.

Information is based on questionnaires completed by officials at the centers, schools, and agencies, and includes name, address, and telephone number; contact person; number of males and females in the program; ages; fees (registration, tuition, room and board); health (availability of medical, guidance, therapy personnel); courses; faculty; accommodations; activities; student obligations; and publications. Entries are arranged alphabetically by state first, and then city. The author, herself a parent of a "special" child, includes articles of interest to other parents and/or educators about getting help, placement, diagnosis, therapy, and the roles of other professionals concerned with the learning disabled.

This directory has been updated by a ninety-two-page supplement of the same title (*1987 Supplement*, 1987, $5.00pa., LC 84-72701, ISBN 0-9613860-2-9).

Straugn, Charles T., and Marvelle S. Colby. **Lovejoy's College Guide for the Learning Disabled**. New York: Monarch Press, 1985. 119p. $9.95pa. LC 84-62261. ISBN 0-671-52719-3.

Schools that accept learning disabled students and/or provide remedial work in specific courses are listed in this specialized college directory. Brief college profiles, describing approximately 380 schools, are arranged by state. Each entry provides information on school name, address, enrollment, costs, admissions criteria, majors offered, and special support services for the learning disabled.

Introductory material presents, for parents, students, counselors, and teachers, suggestions for choosing the optimum college, testing, course load, assessment of special needs, and coping strategies.

Thomas, Carol H., and James L. Thomas. **Directory of College Facilities and Services for the Disabled**. 2d ed. Phoenix, Ariz.: Oryx Press, 1986. 410p. $99.00. LC 85-43111. ISBN 0-89774-134-X.

This directory provides information on programs and services for the disabled in most of the postsecondary institutions in the United States, Canada, and outlying areas. Entries include name and address of the institution, telephone number of a contact person, background of school, number of students and number of handicapped students enrolled, and disability categories represented with approximate number of students enrolled in each. Also indicated are the number of specially equipped dormitory spaces (if any) available, manageability of the physical terrain for mobility impaired students, and whether 75 percent or more of the academic programs meet building and facility specifications of the American National Standards Institute. Special services for the disabled (e.g., handicapped student organizations and/or resource centers, counseling, tutoring, physical therapy, speech therapy, job placement, text flexibility, registration assistance, homebound service, attendant care, reader service, restrictions for guide dogs), are also indicated.

Arrangement of entries is alphabetical by institution name under geographic location. A selective list of resources (organizations, clearinghouses, etc.) for professionals working with handicapped students, and an index of institution names conclude the work. This directory is a must for guidance counselors, parents, and disabled students, as it helps in determining which institution best meets special needs. Its use would be further amplified if it had an index of handicapping conditions so that a student could identify schools that meet particular requirements.

12

Educational Media and Technology Reference Sources

INSTRUCTIONAL DESIGN AND TECHNOLOGY

Bibliographies

Duane, James E. **The Instructional Media Library**. Englewood Cliffs, N.J.: Educational Technology Publications, 1981. 16v. $22.95/vol. LC 84-2252. ISBN 0-87-7787161-3.

This multivolume set is concerned with practical description and application and also provides extensive bibliographies on various media formats and their uses in education and training. Volumes in the series include *Books and Other Print Materials; Community Resources; Media about Media; Microforms; Motion Pictures; Multi-Image Media; Overhead Projection; Photography; Real Objects and Models; Slides; Still Pictures; Television Production; Video-Discs*. The series complements the *Instructional Design Library* series (Educational Technology Publications, 1980).

Hodges, Gerald G., and Frances Bryant Bradburn, eds. **Research on Adolescence for Youth Service: An Annotated Bibliography on Adolescent Development, Educational Needs, and Media, 1978-1980**. Chicago: American Library Association, 1984. 148p. $15.00. LC 83-25785. ISBN 0-8389-3279-5.

This compilation was intended to make major research findings from the vast literature related to adolescents more available to educators and other professionals who work with youth. It includes selected abstracts of studies published from 1978 through 1980.

Core journals and abstracts searched were those in the broad areas of psychology, sociology, education, reading, and media. Adolescence was defined as youth in grades seven through twelve, or ages twelve through eighteen. Arrangement of entries is alphabetical by author in broad categories with a separate chapter on studies found in theses and dissertations. Author and subject indexes are provided. Annotations are fairly complete, as they consist of the abstracts of the studies. Researchers in educational media and library science should find these abstracts of interest and useful as a hypothesis-generating source for future research.

Indexes and Abstracts

Green, Douglas A. **An Index to Collected Essays on Educational Media and Technology**. Metuchen, N.J.: Scarecrow Press, 1982. 188p. LC 81-18249. ISBN 0-8108-1490-0.

This index can be used as a companion volume to major reference tools in the field of education (e.g., ERIC databases, *Current Index to Journals in Education, Education Index*) as the ninety-six collections analyzed here were previously unindexed. The 1,310 essays are arranged by LC classification numbers assigned to the collection analyzed. Each entry includes full bibliographic information, as well as subject descriptors. Some of the subject descriptors are the author's own; some have been taken from the *ERIC Thesaurus*. All descriptors are alphabetized together in the subject index. The eclectic approaches to defining the field of educational media and technology, with essays ranging from philosophical treatises by Aristotle, St. Augustine, and others to technology, might be part of the reason that its major thrust is hard to pinpoint. For the researcher who wants to tap a large body of literature accumulated in the 1960s and 1970s when educational media research was federally funded, this would provide useful additional access.

Another bibliographic guide to media research is Razik and Ramroth's *Bibliography of Research in Instructional Media* (Educational Technology Publications, 1974).

Dictionaries and Encyclopedias

Anderson, Scarvia B., Samuel Ball, Richard T. Murphy, and associates. **Encyclopedia of Educational Evaluation: Concepts and Techniques for Evaluating Education and Training Programs**. San Francisco: Jossey-Bass, 1975. 515p. $27.95. LC 74-6736. ISBN 0-87589-238-8.

This well-designed work combines the features of a research handbook with those of an encyclopedia in that it describes measurement approaches and provides essential details about program evaluation. It includes approximately 150 well-written brief reference essays (3 to 4 pages each) which contain cross-references and well-selected annotated bibliographes. Many provide supporting examples, graphs, and tables.

A separate classification guide provides an overview of eleven major subject areas by listing pertinent entries under such broad topics as program objectives and standards, and techniques and measurement approaches. These categorized entries, which could almost substitute for brief courses in the topics addressed, are made up of initialed essays, written by authorities in the field. Emphasis is on program objectives and standards, systems techniques and measurement approaches, the social context of evaluation, and types of variables. A twenty-six page bibliography is included along with subject and author indexes.

Although in need of updating, this encyclopedia fills a definite need in the reference literature in the field of educational evaluation. Its emphasis on research in evaluation adds to its overall usefulness.

Educational Technology: Definition and Glossary of Terms, Volume I. AECT Task Force on Definition and Terminology. Washington, D.C.: Association for Educational Communications and Technology, 1979. 371p. $20.50. LC 79-53125. ISBN 0-89240-000702.

This glossary, an expansion of the 1977 edition, attempts to tie together concepts related to educational technology. In doing so, the compilers define educational technology and attempt to show the relationships of many terms and phrases that have either been considered synonymous with it or have had an ambiguous association; for example, *instructional technology, educational media, audiovisual education,* and *educational communications.*

Part A outlines the theoretical bases of the field and the role of learning psychology in a systems approach. Part B contains sets of glossaries arranged in categories: theory, research, design, production, evaluation and selection, materials, devices, and techniques. It also includes a list of available glossaries covering communication, learning, perception, and systems/cybernetic information theory. Part B lacks organization; relationships between terms are not tied together (e.g., the eight learning types defined by Gagne), nor is documentation of definitions always provided. An alphabetical index to terms in the glossary is somewhat helpful in overcoming this deficiency. In spite of some weaknesses, this glossary is a recognized authoritative work for standardization of the language used in the area of educational communications and technology.

Ellington, Henry, and Duncan Harris, comps. **Dictionary and Instructional Technology**. New York: Nichols, 1986. 189p. (AECT Occasional Publishing, No. 6). $32.50. LC 85-28530. ISBN 0-98397-243-6.

Over 2,800 terms related to the field of instructional technology are briefly defined in this illustrated dictionary. Because of some ambiguity among scholars as to what is actually included in this field, and because a current dictionary has not been available, educators should welcome this reference tool. Terms defined are from a wide variety of areas including evaluation and measurement, instructional design, educational media, and audiovisual instruction, among others.

Glossary of Educational Technology Terms. Division of Educational Sciences, UNESCO for the International Bureau of Education. Paris: UNESCO; distr., Lanham, Md.: UNIPUB, 1986. 239p. $14.50pa. LC 87-166729. ISBN 92-3-002517-8.

Terms related to the design, development, production, implementation, and evaluation of instruction through a variety of delivery systems (lecture, film, video, self-instructional module, game, etc.) are covered in this bilingual (English-Russian) glossary. Emphasis is given to terms related to audiovisual software and hardware, but systems models are not adequately covered. Definitions for many general education terms (e.g., *pupil, lecture*) are also included, probably unnecessarily.

Rosenberg, Kenyon C., and Paul T. Feinstein. **Dictionary of Library and Educational Technology**. 2d ed. Littleton, Colo.: Libraries Unlimited, 1983. 197p. $24.50. LC 83-19641. ISBN 0-87287-396-X.

This dictionary was designed to help school media specialists and educators understand the terminology associated with the latest developments in the field of educational technology. Rosenberg indicates that this work "constitutes the second edition of *Media Equipment: A Guide and Dictionary* by Kenyon C. Rosenberg and John S. Doshey (Libraries Unlimited, 1976)" (p. xi) with revisions and additions of terms related to the field of reprography, macrographics, communications, and computers.

Arranged in three sections, the first part of the work describes audiovisual equipment and presents selection criteria for various types. The dictionary of terms constitutes the main body of the work, and a selective bibliography of additional literature concludes the work. Entries are arranged by equipment type also. A work of this nature is especially helpful to teachers and librarians who lack background and/or confidence in hardware aspects of educational technology.

Unwin, Derick, and Ray McAleese. **The Encyclopedia of Educational Media Communications and Technology**. Westport, Conn.: Greenwood, 1978. 800p. $75.00. LC 78-15049. ISBN 0-313-23996-7.

This comprehensive one-volume reference work is a mixture of dictionary-type definition entries of one or two lines to multipage treatments complete with bibliographic references. (Closed circuit television is presented in a fifteen-page discussion, audiovisual media in nineteen pages, educational technology in twenty-six pages, and educational cybernetics in forty-one pages.) It is international in scope, since its editors are from

Australia and Scotland, respectively; the international advisory panel members are from the United States and Canada. British spellings of words are found throughout the work.

Although this reference is supposed to treat topics in the educational media and technology fields, entries reflect a more generic approach, with such terms as *ability grouping, adult literacy project, developing world, curriculum design, curriculum theory* included, as well as the more expected ones such as *computers in education, audiovisual media, aperture, artificial intelligence,* and so on. Some of the more outstanding entries are those giving an overview and history of the field, or special aspects of it.

Handbooks and Yearbooks

Educational Media and Technology Yearbook. Englewood, Colo.: Libraries Unlimited, in cooperation with the Association for Educational Communities and Technology (AECT), 1973- . Annual. $50.00. ISSN 8755-2094.

The first ten volumes (1973-1984) in this series were known as the *Educational Media Yearbook*. The change of title with volume 11 in 1985 reflected the impact of the technological innovations associated with the electronic revolution in education.

The 14th volume (1988), edited by Donald P. Ely, is arranged in the same five sections typical of others in the series. In part 1, articles reflect the latest trends and issues in the field, including CD-ROM, distance education, and instructional television. One article, "The Promises of Educational Technology: A Reassessment," by Donald P. Ely and Tjeerd Plomp, covers a familiar theme. Another presents a summary of research on instructional media from 1978 to 1988. Part 2 is entitled "Leadership Profiles in Educational Media and Technology," and part 3 classifies and alphabetically lists organizations and associations and the periodicals they publish in the United States and Canada. Part 4 describes graduate programs in instructional technology at the doctoral and master's degree levels, and available scholarships, fellowships, and awards. Part 5, "Mediagraphy," covering reference and general information sources, includes a directory of publishers, producers, and distributors.

The yearbook is an excellent way to keep abreast of issues, trends, and innovations related to educational media. The information is current and reliable and reflects the diversity and breadth of the field of educational technology.

International Yearbook of Educational and Instructional Technology. Edited by Chris W. Osborne. New York: Nichols, 1976- . Biennial. $39.50. ISSN 0307-9732.

This yearbook reports on trends and events in educational communications and instructional technology as they occur internationally. Similar in format to *Educational Media and Technology Yearbook* which emphasizes educational technology in the United States, the volume includes readings and discussions about specific technologies in specific countries, latest developments in computer education, interactive video, and other technological advances for instructional purposes.

A major section of each yearbook is devoted to a directory of resources including databases, courses, conferences, consultants, and networks. Professional organizations, centers of activity, and hardware and software producers and distributors comprise some of the varied listings.

This reference guide is helpful in providing an overview of the impact and progress of instructional technology in countries throughout the world. Centers throughout the world involved in research, conferences, and other activities related to instructional technology are listed in a directory section. Entries contain information on the center's services, specific areas of emphasis, and research projects.

Directories

Johnson, Jenny K., ed. **Masters Curricula in Educational Communications and Technology: A Descriptive Directory, March 1985**. Washington, D.C.: Association for Educational Communications and Technology, 1985. 377p. $15.00pa. LC 85-71534. ISBN 0-89240-051-X.

Course offerings and master's degree programs in educational communications and technology are listed in this directory. Questionnaires were sent to colleges and universities in the United States and abroad in order to ascertain the location of such programs and/or courses. Because programs are called by different names in different institutions, the user has difficulty comparing course offerings from one school to another. For example, course titles in educational media, instructional technology, instructional development, educational technology, educational communications, and even audiovisual instruction can all refer to the same type of program or to something entirely different.

Lloyd-Kolkin, Donna, Sharon Taylor, and Guiselle Maffioli-Hesemann. **Directory of Resources for Technology in Education, 1984**. San Francisco: Far West Laboratory, 1984. 243p. $12.95pa. ISBN 0-914409-02-6.

In this directory, resources for technology are defined as those organizations concerned with the use of microcomputers in education, and, to some extent, associations involved with instructional television. Arranged in five sections, the first is devoted to national organizations; the second describes those at the state level. The third section identifies computer camps, conferences, and summer institutes and programs available in 1984. Section 4 covers periodicals, databases, electronic bulletin-board services, and sources of software evaluation. Section 5 is a very brief list of hardware companies and funding sources.

Entries provide complete name and address of organizations, telephone number, purpose, description, publications (if any), services, and fees charged. Since many teachers, school librarians, educators in nonschool settings, as well as individuals are just beginning systematic development of software collections, a guide such as this, updated on a regular basis, could save time and money.

SCHOOL MEDIA CENTERS

Guides

Dyer, Esther R. and Pam Berger, eds. **Public, School and Academic Media Centers: A Guide to Information Sources**. Detroit: Gale, 1980. 350p. (Books, Publishing & Libraries Information Guide Series: Vol. 3). $65.00. LC 74-11554. ISBN 0-8103-1286-7.

Materials in the bibliography emphasize the changes in media centers that are continually developing with new electronic means of communications and sources of information. The attempt is made to balance and combine traditional media center activities and values with the changes brought about by today's "high tech" capabilities of retrieving information. The introductions to each section are helpful in understanding the nature of that segment of the bibliography. A list of abbreviations is provided. Arrangement of entries is topical: general works defining theoretical and philosophical bases of the media center and communication issues, legislation related to emerging technologies and copyright, educational media periodicals, standards and recommended guidelines for development of excellent media programs and certification models, architecture and equipment, networking, and other trends. Entries have complete bibliographic information, but prices are not indicated. Annotations are brief, and, for the most part, descriptive. The appendixes cover media organizations; and a glossary of terms, and author, title, and subject indexes are included.

Emmens, Carol A., ed. **Children's Media Market Place**. 2d ed. New York: Neal-Schuman, 1987. 353p. $29.95. LC 82-82058. ISBN 0-918212-33-2.

This handy, one-volume reference work is a guide for teachers, school media specialists, and others who work with children from preschool through the eighth grade. The major parts of the book are devoted to directories of publishers and audiovisual producers and distributors of audiovisual materials. Entries in these sections provide name and address of publisher, personnel officers (executives, managers, sales managers, editors-in-chief, etc.), publications (trade books, textbooks, etc.), audience, subjects, special interests, discount, and services. Publishers and producers are also classified by publishing format (multimedia kits, paperback originals, learning systems, textbooks, etc.) and by subject.

Other sections devoted to public and school library selection centers cover state school media officials. Additional chapters in this volume provide information on periodicals for children, review sources, wholesalers, juvenile bookstores and book clubs, agents, children's television program stations and distributors, organizations, children's media grants, events, awards, and an annotated bibliography.

The arrangement of information makes this tool easy to use; the subject indexes are particularly useful in identifying specialties of each publisher/producer. Although this information can be found in other sources, it is convenient to have all aspects of media for children in one volume.

Bibliographies

Aids to Media Selection for Students and Teachers. Rev. ed. Compiled by Yvonne B. Carter and Barbara Spriestersbach. McFarland, Wis.: National Association of State Educational Media Professionals, Division of Publications, 1985. 158p. ISBN 0-9614484-0-7.

This selective bibliography of instructional media selection aids was first published in 1971. Updated and expanded, it also includes materials for microcomputers. It is divided into four sections covering book selection sources, periodicals, sources of audiovisual materials, and sources of multiethnic materials.

This title is well organized and has long been recognized as a significant selection tool for children's literature and other titles. It includes a directory of publishers and an author-title index.

AIT Catalog of Educational Materials: Elementary, Secondary, Post-Secondary, In-Service Broadcast Videotape, Videocassette, 16mm Film. Bloomington, Ind.: Agency for Instructional Television, 1981- . Annual. Free. ISSN 0193-5801.

This annual catalog of the Agency for Instructional Television at Indiana University describes approximately 120 educational TV series that can be used in classroom settings. Over 2,000 individual titles are arranged by various areas that comprise the curriculum in elementary, secondary, college, and professional level programs. (Subject categories are subdivided by level.) Each entry provides title of the series and individual titles within it, producer, format (broadcast, film, videocassette, and videokit), extent of program, summary, and indication of availability of instructor's guide, and/or discussion manual. The appendixes provide information about use policies and prices. An individual title index is included.

Bell, Irene Wood, and Jeanne E. Wieckert. **Basic Media Skills through Games, Volume 1**. 2d ed. Littleton, Colo.: Libraries Unlimited, 1985. 415p. $28.50. LC 84-25058. ISBN 0-87287-438-9.

School library media specialists and classroom teachers will find this reference tool a very dependable and comprehensive source of instructional games for teaching skills in language arts, reading, and social studies, as well as in using basic research and reference tools. The authors have shown the same care in selecting games that are motivational and adaptable to a range of learners, and that cover a variety of situations, that was demonstrated in the first edition of this work (1979). Games may be copied by teachers and school librarians for classroom and media center use. Each game includes the following information: purpose (skill taught or reinforced), grade level, time required to play, optimum number of players, method of checking on results (by teacher, specialist, student), materials required, and procedures for playing. *Volume 1* emphasizes games that introduce the student to the media center and teach about the card catalog, the Dewey Decimal system, reference books in general, and operation of AV equipment (including computers). A useful chart in the appendix section provides a progression of media center skills as they should be presented in the curriculum. A companion text is *Basic Classroom Skills through Games* (Libraries Unlimited, 1980).

Bell, Irene Wood, and Jeanne E. Wieckert. **Basic Media Skills through Games, Volume 2**. 2d ed. Littleton, Colo.: Libraries Unlimited, 1985. 413p. $23.50. LC 84-25058. ISBN 0-87287-470-2.

This second volume, devoted to games that teach library media skills, focuses on the following: the alphabet, the dictionary, encyclopedias and single volume reference books, prominent authors, and atlases, maps and globes. As in the first volume, information provided for each game includes: purpose (skill taught or reinforced), grade level, time required to play, optimum number of players, method of checking on results (by teacher, specialist, student), materials required, and procedures for playing. Likewise, both volumes are liberally illustrated, and the games represent an assortment that allows both individual and team competition for students from kindergarten through the sixth grade. Arrangement is by grade level; title indexes are included. These volumes are excellent sources of stimulating and challenging learning activities conveniently organized for teachers and school library media specialists. A related title is *Gaming in the Media Center Made Easy* by Irene Wood Bell and Robert B. Brown (Libraries Unlimited, 1982).

Books for Secondary School Libraries. 6th ed. Compiled by the National Association of Independent Schools Library Committee. New York: Bowker, 1981. 844p. LC 80-26369. ISBN 0-8352-1111-8.

This core collection list is intended as a comprehensive selection aid to provide nonfiction reading materials for gifted students and those who are in college preparatory programs. There are over 9,000 entries which are arranged by Dewey Decimal classification numbers. Emphasis is on titles in the humanities. Full bibliographic description and subject headings are included, but annotations are not provided.

Brown, Lucy G. **Core Media Collection for Secondary Schools**. 2d ed. Bowker, 1979. 263p. $18.95. LC 79-6969. ISBN 0-8352-1162-2.

This reference tool is a qualitative selection guide to some 3,000 nonprint instructional materials representing a basic core media collection at the high school level. Titles selected include a wide range of media formats (filmstrips, film loops, transparencies, 16mm motion pictures, audio recordings, art prints, study prints, kits, specimens, slides, and models) and cover all subjects associated with the curricula of grades 7 through 12. The list includes some materials that are "classics" and award winners, and all have received favorable reviews in reliable reviewing sources. However, this list would have to be supplemented by more current titles, as well as those that support unique curricular requirements of a particular school program.

Entries are arranged by subject headings based on the *Sears List of Subject Headings*. The main entry provides enough information to make selection decisions, and also gives information for ordering. Information includes title, medium, producer/distributor, release date, collation, order number, list price, grade level, recommending sources, and annotation/contents. Provision of the Dewey Decimal number also assists cataloging personnel. The corresponding title at the elementary level is *Core Media Collection for Elementary Schools* (2d ed., Bowker, 1978), edited by Lucy G. Brown and Betty McDavid.

Educational Film/Video Locator of the Consortium of University Film Centers and R. R. Bowker. 3d ed. New York: Bowker, 1986. 2v. $150.00. LC 86-71233. ISBN 0-8352-2179-2 (set). V. 1: LC 86-71233; ISBN 0-8352-2180-6. V. 2: LC 86-71233; ISBN 0-8352-2181-4.

This is the third edition of this union list of film and video titles. Titles represent those owned by fifty-two university film/video libraries with combined holdings of 194,000. Some producers were required to submit all of their titles for listing, including those not yet owned by the consortium members; sources for these titles are also indicated.

This monumental guide has received very positive reviews in a number of professional journals, and, as the first bibliographical tool for educational films in the United States, it has filled a large gap in the reference literature. It is an absolute must for university film librarians and other educators involved with instructional film and video recordings. Arrangement of titles is alphabetical, but access to titles is provided through subject, title, and series approaches. The subject approach has an index section called "Major Subject Groupings," where titles are categorized in twenty-nine major areas. There is also a "Subject Heading and Cross Index to Subjects," and a "Subject, Title and Audience Level Index." The title approach comprises the largest section of the work and includes descriptive annotations for each title. Information in each entry includes title, color (or black-and-white), time, sound or silent, format, producer/distributor, production and/or copyright date, subject, audience level, and consortium member libraries which hold copies. A series index lists 1,780 series titles. In addition, a "Foreign Titles Index" is included. Lists of producers and distributors conclude the work.

Other film guides also of relevance to teachers and media specialists are *The Film File* (4th ed., Media Referral Service, 1984) and *Feature Films: A Directory of Feature Films on 16mm and Videotape Available for Rental, Sales, and Lease* (8th ed., Bowker, 1985) by James L. Limbacher; a directory to companies and personnel in the film and video industry, *Kemp's International Film and Television Year: 1985/86* (Bowker, 1985), and *Landers Film Reviews* (Landers Associates, 1956- , bimonthly, September-June).

Educational Media Catalogs on Microfiche. Edited by Walter J. Carroll. New York: Olympic Media Information, 1975- . Annual. $175.00; annual update, $87.50. LC 86-10713. ISSN 0891-8228.

Over 900 catalogs from media producers and distributors have been filmed and maintained on microfiche format. A card index to products helps users identify materials that are available for free loan, rental, or purchases for all types of media formats. Catalogs include descriptions of materials for elementary, secondary, and college levels. The hardcopy card index also includes cards that have suggestions and recommendations for media utilization. Information for preview and/or acquisition is also included. Approximately 135 microfiche are included with semiannual updates. While materials described reflect the bias of the publisher/distributor, titles can be identified that might not appear in selection and reviewing aids.

Educators Guide to Free Audio and Video Materials. Randolph, Wis.: Educators Progress Service, 1955- . Annual. $22.25pa. LC 55-2784.

Audio and video instructional materials that are available free of charge from private sources in business and industry, or are loaned free of charge from the producer, are described in this bibliographic tool. A total of 1,602 entries are arranged in fifteen broad subject categories and contain a complete bibliographic citation and an annotation that allows teachers and school media specialists to determine the content of the item, as well as its instructional potential in K-12 curriculum.

This thirty-first edition incorporates 588 new items not described in previous editions. Access is available through a series of indexes: title, subject, source, and availability. This title was frequently known as the *Educators Guide to Free Tapes, Scripts, and Transcriptions* (1955-1976).

Educators Guide to Free Films. Randolph, Wis.: Educators Progress Service, 1945- . Annual. $27.00pa. LC 45-412. ISSN 0070-9395.

This comprehensive listing of free filmed materials, covering 690 pages in the forty-fourth edition, describes 4,098 16mm films available on free loan. The films are available from businesses and other agencies that provide this educational service to schools, libraries, and media centers, and other nonschool settings where instruction is provided. This edition includes 515 new titles.

Entries are arranged in broad subject categories and information provided in each includes film title, running time (in minutes), release date, whether sound or silent, black-and-white or color, name of the distributor, and a short summary of the content. Directions for ordering films are also given in each volume. In most cases Educators Progress Service has provided grade levels in their publications, but in the film guide the range of films was considered too broad to assign to a particular grade level (e.g., primary, intermediate). Title and specific subject indexes are also provided.

Educators Guide to Free Filmstrips. Randolph, Wis.: Educators Progress Service, 1949- . Annual. $20.00pa. LC 50-11650. ISSN 0070-9409.

Although the title suggests that this guide only identifies and describes free filmstrips, in actuality it covers filmstrips, transparencies, and slides, with strong emphasis on the latter. Of the 438 titles, 313 are slide sets, 124 are filmstrips, and one set of transparencies is included; 84 titles are new to this edition. As in all guides provided by Educators Progress Service, entries are arranged in broad subject categories with information provided about the extent of the item (or running time) and availability of accompanying sound cassettes, when appropriate. Some of the summary descriptions include suggested grade level usage. Different indexes provide access by title and specific subject. This guide is now in its thirty-sixth edition.

Educators Index of Free Materials. Randolph, Wis.: Educators Progress Service, 1937- .
   Annual. $45.50. LC 44-32700.

This index to materials available free of charge to teachers and school library media specialists was first published in 1937. Since then the Educators Progress Service has developed a whole series of guides that are annotated bibliographies to available instructional materials. Entries are alphabetical by subject with a section also included of titles for the professional collection. Directions for requesting free materials provided by private businesses and educational and other organizations, along with a sample letter, are provided. Annotations are both descriptive and evaluative. One weakness to the titles in this series is that copyright dates of items are usually not included. However, when budgets are inadequate, they can be a very important source for rounding out areas of the media center collection and for developing a solid vertical file.

El-Hi Textbooks and Serials in Print: Subject Index, Author Index, Title Index, Series Index, Serials-Subject Index, Serials-Title Index. New York: Bowker, 1969- .
   Annual. $85.00. LC 70-105104. ISSN 0000-0825.

This guide to approximately 35,000 preschool, elementary, and secondary textbooks, reference books (encyclopedias, dictionaries, atlases, etc.), audiovisual instructional materials, and professional books, was originally published as part of *Publishers Weekly*, then as *American Education Catalog*, and next appeared as *Textbooks in Print*. Although the emphasis is definitely on texts at the K-12 level, some college-level works are included. Six different indexes provide access to titles, but main entries are given in the subject index and include title, author, grade and reading level, publisher and publication date, binding, price, ISBN, and related teaching materials. Entries are alphabetical under twenty-two academic subject categories. Other indexes include author, title, series, serials subject, and serials title.

The Elementary School Library Collection: A Guide to Books and Other Media, Phases 1-2-3. Edited by Lois Winkel. 15th ed. Newark, N.J.: Bro-Dart Foundations, 1986.
   1,067p. $79.95. LC 85-24287. ISBN 0-87272-091-8.

This major selection tool aids school media specialists in developing a well-balanced core collection of over 13,000 reference books, as well as general print and nonprint sources. Titles included are recommended for preschool through the sixth grade.

The main sections of the book, reference and nonfiction titles, are arranged by Dewey Decimal classification system. The fiction section is alphabetical by author. Also included are good-quality periodicals for elementary children and an adult professional collection. Full bibliographic information and grade level are provided for each entry, as well as a critical annotation. Tips for utilization of the media are often included. Author, title, and subject indexes and a directory of publishers and distributors conclude the volume.

A feature that helps make this tool a reliable classic selection aid is its continuous revision policy. New titles are carefully selected for inclusion; all former titles are reevaluated for inclusion or replacement. It also offers general selection and specific collection policies along with evaluation criteria. Another valuable feature is information related to the phase of acquisition or suggestions about what size and type of collection for which an item is appropriate.

Free and Inexpensive Learning Materials. 21st biennial ed. Edited by Norman R. Moore. Nashville, Tenn.: George Peabody College for Teachers; distr., Nashville, Tenn.: Incentive Publications, 1983. 248p. $4.95pa. LC 53-2471. ISBN 0-933436-02-5.

This guide describes over 3,000 various types of instructional materials that may be obtained free of charge or at a minimal cost from organizations, industries, and governmental agencies. Items were chosen because of their usefulness as instructional aids or references, factual content, interest level, and minimal advertising bias. Included are posters, charts, maps, pictures, photos, pamphlets, films, recordings, teaching units, and bibliographies, among other items.

Entries are arranged by subjects related to elementary and secondary curricula and consist of a brief annotation explaining the type of material, size, price, grade level, and name and address of the distributor. School media specialists will find this a useful source when budgets are limited, and especially good for updating and developing a vertical file collection.

Green, Jo Ann, ed. **Televised Higher Education: Catalog of Resources**. Boulder, Colo.: Western Interstate Commission for Higher Education, 1984. 349p.

This catalog to over 1,100 video courses covers television instruction designed for use in a variety of disciplines at the postsecondary level. Courses described were produced by over 200 colleges, universities, businesses, associations, and television stations, and are arranged alphabetically in broad subject categories in the humanities, sciences, and social sciences. Information in each entry includes title, video format, date, content, lease/purchase prices, and use restrictions. Appendix material includes video courses available through training companies and other sources, a list of distributors, and a list of producers. Subject keyword, title keyword, and producer/course title indexes are provided.

Hendershot, Carl H. **Programmed Learning and Individually Paced Instruction: Bibliography**. 5th ed. 4114 Ridgewood Dr., Bay City, Mich.: Hendershot Programmed Learning Consultants, 1985. Suppl. 1-6, 2v. $105.00/set. ISBN 0-911832-16-5; suppl. 6. $35.50. ISBN 0-911832-15-7.

This two-volume set with six supplements is a comprehensive ongoing bibliography of materials on programmed learning and individualized instruction. Entries are arranged alphabetically under 167 subject areas that would be pertinent to elementary and secondary school curricula, and for instruction at higher education levels, in business and other adult nonschool settings. Information provided includes name of program, author, publishers, publication date, length (time to complete and number of frames), price, entry level skills required, content, and availability of teacher's guide or manual.

Other sections list titles by publisher and packages by publisher. Teaching machines and other hardware equipment are presented by producers' names. Although the enthusiasm for programmed learning of the 1960s and 1970s has waned, these materials are still of interest to educators in special education, training and development, and educational technology programs. Hendershot has also published *Individually Paced or Self Teaching Instruction: Sourcebook, Vol. 1* (1985).

Horn, Robert E., and Anne Cleaves, eds. **The Guide to Simulations/Games for Education and Training**. 4th ed. Beverly Hills, Calif.: Sage, 1980. 692p. $49.95. LC 79-19823. ISBN 0-8039-1375-3.

Over 1,400 games and simulation activities designed for educational purposes are described. Entries are organized in thirty-one broad subject categories, most of which (twenty-five) are classified as academic games, and the remaining six categories are related to training for business. Information in each entry includes game/simulation title, producer, copyright date, recommended age level, number of players required, game rules and/or instructions, playing time, and brief annotation describing the game. A series of twenty-four articles evaluates games, as well. Access is available through author, game title, and producer indexes.

Meacham, Mary. **Information Sources in Children's Literature: A Practical Reference Guide for Children's Librarians, Elementary School Teachers, and Students of Children's Literature**. Westport, Conn.: Greenwood, 1978. 256p. $35.00. LC 77-91107. ISBN 0-313-20045-9.

Although this guide is somewhat dated, there is none of its kind to replace it, and the sources and suggestions for locating trade books for children are still valid. Meacham has prepared a series of chapters that provide sound selection criteria for building a core collection, hints on how to maintain an up-to-date knowledge of children's materials, reviewing tools, information on sources of special ethnic literature, or on special topics, and information about books of award-winning authors and illustrators. In addition, she includes chapters addressing using books with children, ordering, and other technical processes procedures. Appendix 1 is a bibliography of titles on library/media center organization and administration. Appendix 2 is entitled "Criteria for Evaluating a Children's Book." An extensive bibliography of reference sources in the field is included in appendix 3. A combined subject and title index concludes the work.

Media and the Young Adult: A Selected Bibliography 1973-1977. Media and Young Adult Subcommittee, Research Committee, Young Adult Services Division, American Library Association. Edited by W. Bernard Lukenbill and Elaine P. Adams. Chicago: American Library Association, 1981. 328p. $10.00pa. LC 81-7977. ISBN 0-8389-3264-9.

This bibliography provides references to almost 600 studies on the young adult. Arranged in two parts, the first part is devoted to research studies on the social, psychological, and developmental needs of people eleven to twenty-two years old. The emphasis is on attitudes they have about themselves and their environment. Some studies examine how multiple environmental influences dictate what youngsters read. Collecting data from such studies can be used to plan media programs and services, and to develop the collection for young adults.

Part 2 of the bibliography is devoted to research on factors that influence and promote access to library media and information sources. Entries in each part are arranged by subject (e.g., sex role identity and family relations). Only an author index is provided.

This title is a continuation of an earlier work, *Media and the Young Adult: A Selected Bibliography, 1950-1972* and, therefore, provides an almost thirty-year look at adolescents and media. School media specialists, particularly, should find this a significant source for professional collections.

Media Resource Catalog, 1986. Capitol Heights, Md.: National Audiovisual Center, 1986. 253p. $10.00pa.

Over 2,700 audiovisuals from the collection of the National Audiovisual Center are described in this catalog. Materials included cover a range of subjects related to K-12 and postsecondary curricula and emphasize film and video productions. Entries are arranged alphabetically by title, but access is also available through a subject index. Information in each entry includes complete bibliographic description, a descriptive annotation, order number, and costs for purchase and/or rental.

National Information Center for Educational Media. **Film & Video Finder**. Albuquerque, N. Mex.: National Information Center for Educational Media, 1987. 3v. $295.00/set; $120.00pa./set. LC 87-644068; 82-60347pa. ISBN 0-89320-110-3; 0-89320-053-0pa. ISSN 0898-1582.

This comprehensive list includes 90,000 film and/or video titles useful in educational settings. Entries are arranged alphabetically by title and include information related to title, producer, distributor, format, running time, date, and recommended audience level. Annotations are extremely brief and only summarize content. Evaluative comments have to be traced through reviewing journals. Access is available through NICEM's own subject headings.

The *Film & Video Finder* is a new NICEM publication, combining in one title the former *NICEM Index to 16mm Educational Films* and the *NICEM Index to Educational Videotapes*, which is more convenient since many film titles are now available in both film and video formats. A directory of some 5,000 distributors and producers is also included in this set.

The National Information Center for Educational Media has the most comprehensive database (over 350,000 titles) of nonprint educational materials. It is available in print or in magnetic tape format either through DIALOG Information Service or on CD-ROM disk from NICEM. Since the database was purchased by Access Innovations, Inc., in 1984, several of the original long-standing index titles have been revamped. Another example would be *Audiocassette Finder: A Subject Guide to Literature Recorded on Audiocassettes* (1986). Other NICEM indexes include *Index to Educational Records; Index to 8mm Motion Cartridges; Index to Educational Overhead Transparencies; Index to 35mm Educational Filmstrips* (3v., 8th ed., 1985); *Index to Educational Slides;* and an *Index to Producers and Distributors* (6th ed., 1985).

Richardson, Selma K., ed. **Magazines for Children: A Guide for Parents, Teachers, and Librarians**. Chicago: American Library Association, 1983. 147p. $12.50pa. LC 83-13518. ISBN 0-8389-0392-4.

This title represents a list of periodicals typically found in the children's collections of school media centers and public libraries. It has been taken from a larger publication, *Periodicals for School Media Programs*, which describes and evaluates over 500 periodical titles. New, longer, and more detailed annotations have been written. They provide useful information for school media specialists and teachers, as they indicate which magazine titles support different subject areas in the curriculum.

Titles included are appropriate for children from preschool through the eighth grade, and represent a wide range of interests and abilities. Each entry includes the magazine title, name and address of the publisher, frequency of publication, subscription price, and a critical annotation. Arrangement is alphabetical by title. Appendix A lists periodicals indexed in *Children's Magazine Guide*; appendix B classifies titles by age and grade level. Other appendixes provide circulation and publishing information. A subject index classifies titles in twenty broad categories, further making this a very helpful selection and acquisition tool. A related title, of broader scope, of interest to school media specialists selecting periodicals for older children and young adults is *Magazines for Libraries*, edited by Bill Katz and Linda Sternberg (5th ed., Bowker, 1986).

Richardson, Selma K., ed. **Magazines for Young Adults: Selections for School and Public Libraries**. Chicago: American Library Association, 1984. 329p. $22.50pa. LC 83-26652. ISBN 0-83890-407-6.

This selection guide provides evaluative annotations for over 600 periodicals appropriate for young adults in school and public libraries. Titles are appropriate for children from all kinds of environments, for slow readers to gifted students, for meeting instructional demands and for recreational reading. Most magazines selected are for student use, but some professional titles are also included. All periodicals indexed in *Readers' Guide to Periodical Literature* are included, as well as major newspaper publications. A few titles are relevant to ethnic and/or minority students.

Entries are arranged by title (including title variations), and include name of publisher, address, grade level, frequency, school subscription rate, and an annotation. Annotations describe the type and flavor of material covered, discuss the quantity and quality of illustrations provided, and comment on the usefulness of the format. A companion volume for younger children by the same author is *Magazines for Children: A Guide for Parents, Teachers and Librarians* (American Library Association, 1983).

Senior High School Library Catalog. 13th ed. New York: H. W. Wilson, 1987. $90.00pa. LC 87-7377. ISBN 0-8242-0755-6.

Fiction and nonfiction titles for students in grades 10 through 12 are analyzed. The catalog is updated by annual supplements. Part 1 is a listing of titles arranged in Dewey Decimal classification number order. Part 2 contains author, title, subject, and analytical indexes; the book concludes with a directory of publishers in the third part. Almost 6,000 titles are included in this core collection for high school library/media centers. Users should remember that these titles represent a recommended basic collection of print materials only, as audiovisual materials are not covered here. *Junior High School Catalog* (5th ed., 1985) covers books for grades 7 through 9.

Sive, Mary Robinson. **Selecting Instructional Media: A Guide to Audiovisual and Other Instructional Media Lists**. 3d ed. Littleton, Colo.: Libraries Unlimited, 1983. 330p. $22.50. LC 82-21675. ISBN 0-87287-342-0.

This guide for educators and school librarians provides descriptions of over 700 multimedia lists on a wide variety of topics. Major reviewing sources are also included, making this work a handy selection tool for media center collection development. Descriptions of published lists of audiovisual and instructional media provide complete bibliographic information and are fully annotated. Most print materials are excluded as media here cover such formats as audio and video recordings, films, filmstrips, slides, transparencies, simulation games, study prints, multimedia kits, and microcomputer programs.

Entries are arranged in three main lists: comprehensive (multimedia and multisubject), subject lists (such as bilingual education or vocational education), and media lists (by media format, such as computer software). Information in each entry includes list title, author/compiler, where published, length in pages, date, price, purpose, grade level, arrangement, subjects covered, number of entries, indexes provided, period covered, revision and updating, media represented, producers, features, and subject terms (descriptors). Indexes provide access by subject, medium, instructional level, author, and title.

In addition, the guide provides information to assist users in locating other media, such as reproductions, photographs, microforms, video programs, and documentaries, on particular topics. *Selecting Instructional Media* is a must for determining the audiovisual instructional materials available on any topic.

Smallwood, Carol. **Exceptional Free Library Resource Materials**. Littleton, Colo.: Libraries Unlimited, 1984. 233p. $18.50. LC 83-22166. ISBN 0-87287-406-0.

Over 850 sources of free materials from government agencies, businesses, and non-profit organizations are described in this guide. Teachers and school media specialists will find it an essential source for acquiring curricular materials and developing the school media center collection, particularly the vertical file. Free materials are often in the form of pamphlets, posters, charts, and maps, but others are represented by hardcover and paperback books, curriculum guides, coloring or activity books, kits, games, and puzzles. Bibliographies on various subjects that are part of K-12 instructional programs are also available.

Entries are arranged alphabetically by subjects, some of which include alcohol, drugs, and tobacco; American history; arts and crafts; business; consumer education; English; geography; government; guidance; health; home economics; and library reference. Grade level indication is identified as primary, intermediate, junior high, high school, or adult (advanced high school and adult education). Appendix information addresses cooperative extension service state offices, state labor information offices, NASA regional film libraries, state travel information bureaus, and U.S. Forest Service regional offices.

Video Source Book. Syosset, N.Y.: National Video Clearinghouse, 1979- . Annual. $199.00. ISSN 0277-3317.

This guide describes 40,000 currently available video programs. It is divided into five major sections: (1) "Videodisc Index," (2) "Program Listings," (3) "Main Category Index," (4) "Subject Category Index," and (5) "Video Program Sources Index."

The program listings section constitutes the main body of the work. Entries are arranged alphabetically by title in eight main categories, one of which is "General Interest/Education." Related categories include "Children/Juvenile," "Health/Science," "How to/Instruction," and "Sports/Recreation." These major categories are further subdivided.

Each entry contains program title, format, color or black-and-white, running time, descriptive summary, use availability, awards, audience ratings, demographic code, purpose of the program, and acquisition availability.

The subject category index is of the most interest to educators. However, titles must be traced through the main program listings section for grade level, annotation, and so on. The work also includes names, addresses, and telephone numbers of companies whose programs are listed. Since many programs are available for free loan and/or duplication, this is an important tool for media specialists to examine.

A similar, but less comprehensive, title is Lewis Raymond's *Meeting Learners' Needs through Telecommunications: A Directory and Guide to Programs* (American Association for Higher Education, 1983).

Wasserman, Paul, and Esther Herman, eds. **Catalog of Museum Publications and Media**. 2d ed. Detroit: Gale, 1980. 1,044p. $265.00. LC 79-22633. ISBN 0-8103-0388-4.

This guide to instructional media productions available through museums, art galleries, historical societies, and other education-related institutions in the United States provides a geographically arranged catalog of materials. Formerly published as *Museum Media* (1974), this catalog is a valuable source of free loan educational programs that support curricula from elementary through the college level. Four indexes provide title, keyword, subject access, geographic access, and a list of available related periodicals. An additional related title is *World Museum Publications 1982: Directory of Art and Cultural Museums, Their Publications and Audio-Visual Materials* (New York: Bowker, 1982).

Wynar, Bohdan S., ed. **Recommended Reference Books for Small and Medium-sized Libraries and Media Centers**. Littleton, Colo.: Libraries Unlimited, 1981- . Annual. $32.50. LC 81-12394. ISSN 0297-5948.

This work is designed to be a selection aid for personnel in smaller libraries. Titles are selected from the latest edition of the *American Reference Book Annual* (*ARBA*), and while all are recommended for purchase, the evaluative descriptions of the *ARBA* reviews are retained. Entries are arranged in subject-category chapters and include descriptions of dictionaries, encyclopedias, indexes, directories, bibliographies, atlases, handbooks, and other reference guides. In addition to critical comments, each entry is coded (C, P, or S) to indicate whether the title is recommended for a small college, public, or school library/media center.

Since its first appearance in 1981, this reference tool has received favorable reviews in major library/media reviewing journals, including *Library Journal, Booklist, Voice of Youth Advocates*, and *Wilson Library Bulletin*. As media center budgets are being stretched to attempt to buy more with less, it is important for administrators to purchase appropriate titles. This annual guide will facilitate systematic development of a basic core reference collection.

Wynar, Christine. **Guide to Reference Books for School Media Centers**. 3d ed. Littleton, Colo.: Libraries Unlimited, 1986. $35.00. LC 86-20156. ISBN 0-87287-545-8.

Reference books appropriate for school media centers at all levels are identified and described in the third edition of this annotated guide. Previous editions appeared in 1973 and 1981. The 2,011 entries are arranged in fifty-six subject categories, most of which reflect areas of the K-12 curriculum. Selection and reviewing sources for print and nonprint materials are included, as are general reference tools (guides, almanacs and digests, database utilities, dictionaries, directories, encyclopedias, and indexes), media sources, and subject-specific tools.

Public librarians would also find useful the extensive coverage of sources of children's literature, and materials on hobbies and games, holidays, sports, pets, music, fine arts, technology, and ethnic minorities. Annotations are evaluative as well as descriptive, and include citations to published reviews from major reviewing journals. An author/title/subject index directs the user to sources listed as numbered entries or to related references included within annotations.

Indexes and Abstracts

Media Review Digest. Ann Arbor, Mich.: Pierian Press, 1970- . Annual. $245.00/yr. LC 73-172772. ISSN 0363-7778.

Subtitled *The Only Complete Guide to Reviews of Non-Book Media*, this annual index to reviews of nonprint materials was first published in 1970 as *Multimedia Reviews Index* (1970-1972). It covers films and filmstrips, education records and tapes, slides, transparencies, illustrations, globes, charts, media kits, games, and other miscellaneous media forms. Entries are arranged by media format, then alphabetically by main entry—in most cases, the title. Over 40,000 citations to reviews appearing in approximately 150 reviewing journals are included. Some entertainment media are covered, but the emphasis is definitely on nonprint materials with educational application. Entries provide the following data: producer and/or distributor, date, technical features (sound or silent, color or black-and-white, etc.), length, price, citations to reviews in American, British, Australian, Italian and Canadian sources. A mediagraphy is also included.

Handbooks and Yearbooks

Aaron, Shirley L., and Pat R. Scales, eds. **School Library Media Annual**. Littleton,
Colo.: Libraries Unlimited, 1983- . Annual. $40.00. ISSN 0739-7712.

This annual publication was designed to cover important events, issues, concepts, and
trends that are of relevance to school media specialists. It is concerned with media program
policies and policymaking, program and collection development. Chapters are typically
arranged in sections that cover these topics and might include recent legislation at state or
federal levels, changes in certification standards, conferences and other activities
sponsored by professional associations, and writings on policies and services. Outstanding
books and audiovisual materials published and/or produced in the recent year are also
listed by reading level.

School Library Media Annual also covers research in the field and examines how the
latest technological developments affect school media programs. The work is indexed.
Another title concerned with school media center programs is the *Elementary School
Librarian's Almanac* by Hilda K. Weisburg (Center for Applied Research in Education,
1979).

Adams, Helen R. **School Media Policy Development: A Practical Process for Small
Districts**. Littleton, Colo.: Libraries Unlimited, 1986. 174p. $23.50. LC 86-18587.
ISBN 0-87287-450-8.

School media specialists, and/or students preparing for this field, will find this guide a
very useful tool. Developing policies for media selection and evaluation, use of materials,
sharing of resources, equipment, and personnel constitute some of the professional's most
difficult assignments, and the samples, case studies, and step-by-step procedures in the
processes provided here greatly facilitate the task. A combination of philosophical issues
and pragmatic processes are included in this discussion of policy formulation,
development, and implementation. Another title directed at helping effect media goals and
objectives is *Evaluating Media Programs: District and School, a Method and an
Instrument* (Association for Educational Communications and Technology, 1980).

Information Power: Guidelines for School Library Media Programs. Prepared by the
American Association of School Librarians and Association for Educational Commu-
nications and Technology. Chicago: American Library Association; Washington,
D.C.: Association for Educational Communications and Technology, 1988. 171p.
$10.00. LC 88-3480. ISBN 0-8389-3352-1.

Two professional organizations concerned with school media centers, AASL
(American Association of School Librarians) and AECT (Association for Educational
Communications and Technology) collaborated to develop new guidelines for school
library media programs. The previous standards, *Media Programs: District and School*
(1975) were the first to emphasize media programs at the district and building levels and the
role of the media center as one central to instruction, rather than as an equipment and
materials support service. *Information Power* further develops this concept in eight
chapters covering the mission of the school library program; responsibilities of the media
specialist; management; personnel; resources; and facilities; and a chapter entitled,
"District, Regional, and State Leadership." The appendix section contains the findings of a
federal survey of facilities, staff, collections, and expenditures of media programs in

American schools, as well as formulas for calculating materials and equipment budgets; facilities guidelines; access policies and statements (including the Library Bill of Rights); bibliographies; and contributors to the new AASL/AECT Standards Writing Committee.

Jones, Milbrey L. **Survey of School Media Standards**. Washington, D.C.: U.S. Department of Health, Education, and Welfare, Office of Education; distr., Government Printing Office, 1977. 259p. LC 77-603527. S/N 017-080-01565-0.

This publication attempts to examine the influence of Title II of the Elementary and Secondary Act on the standards for media programs at national, state, and regional levels. The opening chapter provides a survey and the historical background of school media standards. Subsequent chapters describe the contribution of Title II, and standards from the building level up that were in effect at the time of publication. It also covers changes in standards from 1964 to 1975, the influences of major school media professional organizations, and future trends. The bulk of the volume is devoted to the four appendixes which present a "Bibliography of Documents Containing Regional and State School Media Standards"; "Summaries of National, Regional, and State Standards for School Media Programs"; the "School Library Bill of Rights"; and numerous tables.

Although newer standards than this third compilation prepared by the U.S. Office of Education are to be adopted, this source provides citations and documents that help trace the development and evolution of school media standards. It should be an important reference for researchers studying school media standards, particularly from a historical perspective.

Loertscher, David V. **Taxonomies of the School Library Media Program**. Littleton, Colo.: Libraries Unlimited, 1988. 336p. $23.50. LC 87-3567. ISBN 0-87287-662-4.

While Loertscher's book could easily serve as a valuable text for courses in school media center administration, it could also serve as a useful handbook for school media specialists, particularly in light of its emphases and recommendations on evaluation. The work represents a unique integration of the theoretical concepts of instructional design and technology and the practical and personal qualifications of a media specialist. Taxonomies provided include roles at different levels of functioning for media centers, and evaluation is concerned with roles of the media specialist, teacher, student, and school administrator. Numerous sample evaluative instruments for media programs are included. Loertscher has not only amassed a lot of information about what constitutes an effective media program that is actively contributing to curriculum and instruction, but presents it in a clear and highly readable style.

Martin, Betty. **A Survival Handbook for the School Library Media Specialist**. Hamden, Conn.: Shoe String Press, 1983. 146p. $19.50; $13.50pa. LC 83-14851. ISBN 0-208-01997-9; 0-208-01998-7pa.

Since public schools have exploited the new technologies of the past two decades, school media specialists are called on to increasingly expand their knowledge of new hardware and the nonprint collections they support. They are also expected to help classroom teachers in the design of instructional materials in addition to their more traditional roles of selection, acquisition, and organization of print and nonprint items.

Martin opens her book with a discussion of stress and coping with the pressures placed on school media programs. In subsequent chapters she identifies internal and external survival strategies, stress reduction programs, and discusses relations with school administrators and teachers. The role of change in various aspects of education is also covered. Appendixes provide the following information: A, two general approaches to therapeutic relaxation; B, a "Test on Principal/Library Media Specialist Relationships"; C, a chart of child needs; D, an outline for a volunteer program; E, a materials selection policy; F, evaluation of computer software; G, "Information for the Mentally and Physically Handicapped and the Culturally and Ethnically Different"; H, "Planning Curriculum Units"; and I, "Guidelines for Group Leadership." A bibliography of 163 non-annotated entries and an index conclude the work.

Martin, Betty, and Ben Carson. **The Principal's Handbook on the School Media Center**. Hamden, Conn.: Shoe String Press, 1981. 212p. $16.50. LC 81-801. ISBN 0-208-01912-X.

This reference tool is one that principals (and other educators) may consult either to develop an exemplary school library media program or to understand the role and function of the media program as an integral component of the school program. The major sections of the work discuss philosophical bases of school media centers, roles of school personnel in relation to the media program, and all the skills and tasks involved in media center organization, administration, and evaluation.

This volume provides a good overview of school media center philosophy and operation not only for building principals, but for prospective school library media specialists and students in teacher education programs.

A similar title addressed to the classroom teacher is Betty Martin and Linda Sargent's *The Teacher's Handbook on the School Library Media Center* (Shoe String Press, 1980).

Martin, Betty, and Frances Hatfield. **The School District Library Media Director's Handbook**. Hamden, Conn.: Shoe String Press, 1982. 239p. $23.00; $16.50pa. LC 81-14292. ISBN 2-208-01889-1; 0-208-01890-5pa.

This handbook outlines the range of responsibilities associated with the position of director of local school district library media programs. It is arranged in five sections as follows: (1) "Initial Assessment," (2) "Organizing the District Program," (3) "Communication and Working Relationships," (4) "Instructional Media," and (5) "Strategies for Improving the Media Program."

This volume is particularly useful to the newly appointed director who needs an overview of all aspects of the director's role and the roles of other subordinate personnel, as well as an overview of the components of a school media program. The final chapter discusses trends in changes in education and school library media services. The appendixes are valuable sources of information, including a self-test to determine one's administrative style, a sample inventory form for school library media centers, a sample media specialists's weekly report form, sample library book bid specifications, sample book ordering instructions, sample interview sheet for educational media applicants, and a 170-item bibliography of literature related to media specialists at the supervisory level.

Media Programs: District and School. Prepared by the American Association of School Librarians, American Library Association and Association for Educational Communications and Technology. Chicago: American Library Association, 1975. 128p. $8.50pa. LC 74-32316. ISBN 0-8389-3159-6.

This joint publication of ALA and AECT recommends standards for school media programs. Both qualitative and quantitative criteria for maintaining programs at both districtwide and building levels are included. These guidelines are dated, but as of yet have not been replaced by a more recent publication, although one is expected to be forthcoming in 1988. This is a useful guide for school library/media specialists and school administrators who are attempting to evaluate their school media programs in light of the recommendations set forth by professional associations, as well as state standards.

Nickel, Mildred L. **Steps to Service: A Handbook of Procedures for the School Library Media Center.** Rev. ed. Chicago: American Library Association, 1984. 129p. $9.95pa. LC 84-9368. ISBN 0-8389-0387-8.

This handbook provides a "how-to-do-it" approach to organizing and administering a school library media program. Beginning media center directors or staff members can follow the procedures outlined to provide good service; experienced personnel can expand their programs. Arrangement of the volume is in five sections covering school library media center functions, standards, administration, activities, and facilities. The section on administration covers such topics as budget, automation, evaluation and selection of materials, acquisition, processing, organization and use, repair, weeding and inventory of materials, and reports and supplies. The section on activities emphasizes services, instruction in school library skills, staff, participation in curriculum planning, professional growth, and public relations. A glossary of terms, a directory of publishers, producers, and suppliers, and an index conclude the work.

Seaver, Alice R. **Library Media Skills: Strategies for Instructing Primary Students.** Littleton, Colo.: Libraries Unlimited, 1984. 147p. (Teaching Library, Media, Research and Information Skills Series). $18.50pa. LC 84-965. ISBN 0-87287-409-5.

Teaching library media skills is a major function of the professional, and this reference work provides educators and media specialists with practical strategies and activities as well as a discussion of the considerations to be made in systematic implementation of a library media skills program for primary students. The first half of the book, part 1, focuses on planning and implementing a program, establishing objectives, strategies and materials, providing literary experiences, evaluation of learning, and record keeping. Part 2 focuses on creating and storing learning materials and the actual learning activities which serve as models for programs at different age/grade levels. Library media skills covered include card catalog use, authors of children's literature, dictionary use, encyclopedia use, analyzing the novel (identifying plot, major characters, etc.), and locating materials in the collection.

School media specialists will find this a helpful resource for enhancing their instructional role. A similar title for middle school educators and media specialists is Lucille W. Van Vliet's *Media Skills for Middle Schools: Strategies for Library Media Specialists and Teachers* (Libraries Unlimited, 1984). Another highly recommended title for elementary and middle school students is by H. Thomas Walker and Paula Kay Montgomery, *Teaching Library Media Skills: An Instructional Program for Elementary and Middle School Students* (2d ed., Libraries Unlimited, 1983).

Sive, Mary Robinson. **Media Selection Handbook.** Littleton, Colo.: Libraries Unlimited, 1983. 171p. $22.50. LC 83-932. ISBN 0-87287-350-1.

This handbook has been compiled to provide a shortcut for media specialists, as information managers. It lists a core collection of the most basic selection tools so that media personnel can develop optimum programs, and enhance media center use by both faculty and students. Arrangement of the volume is in three parts. Part 1 is devoted to the media selection process, including media and systematic design of instruction, decisions about media formats, individualized instruction, and selection criteria with a brief list of references for each different topic, needs assessment, and previewing and reviews. A brief list of references accompanies each topic.

Part 2 is devoted to fifteen selection tools and sources with descriptions of their special features and uses. It outlines the most efficient search strategies for identifying potential media purchases. Hypothetical situations or cases are used as examples to illustrate the steps in media selection.

This handbook could be used as a text in a selection course, as it summarizes some of the most commonly used bibliographic guides. By inclusion of sample pages the reader is provided with simulated selection exercises, further enhancing its usefulness.

Taylor, Mary M., ed. **School Library and Media Center Acquisitions Policies and Procedures**. Phoenix, Ariz.: Oryx Press, 1986. 274p. $44.50. LC 86-42752. ISBN 0-897741-60-9.

Some of the school librarian's most important tasks are to develop and evaluate selection and acquisition policies. In this volume, Taylor provides suggestions for policy development gleaned from survey questionnaire responses. Sample policies, including fifteen complete and thirty-three partial policies, are provided. A reprint of the AASL's Statement on the Library Bill of Rights, and a list of state education agencies are also included in the appendix. Topics discussed include philosophical considerations, objectives, responsibility for selection, recommendations, selection criteria, interlibrary loan, ordering, weeding, and challenged materials. It will provide models and insights necessary for school media specialists who find themselves with the responsibility for policy development and implementation. Instructors in library science and educational media programs will also find this to be a very valuable instructional tool.

Turner, Phillip M. **Handbook for School Media Personnel**. 2d ed. Littleton, Colo.: Libraries Unlimited, 1980. 132p. $13.50pa. LC 80-21152. ISBN 0-87287-225-4.

Practical information for media center administrators in charge of nonprint materials at the building level is provided in this handbook. Chapters include samples of various forms, checklists, memos, and charts that can be implemented in the development and maintenance of an audiovisual collection. Chapter topics include those of communications (from program visibility, meeting staff needs, to media fairs); equipment distribution and selection; materials production; audiovisual projection concerns; selecting, organizing, and training student helpers; cataloging; and inservice programs.

The information included provides an overview of the services, functions, and personnel roles required for successful media center programs. Other titles related to this handbook include one where media personnel can find an overview of the collective bargaining process, and negotiations relevant to library/media professionals and programs, *Professional Negotiations for Media/Library Professionals District and School* by Rolland G. Billings and Errol Goldman (Association for Educational Communications and Technology, 1980); and another which provides examples of fair use of media materials in schools, *Copyright and Educational Media: A Guide to Fair Use and Permissions Procedures* (Association for Educational Communications and Technology, 1977). A manual limited to secondary personnel is *Secondary School Library Management Manual* by LaVerne H. Ireland (Petervin Press, 1984).

Van Orden, Phyllis J. **The Collection Program in High Schools: Concepts, Practices, & Information Sources**. Littleton, Colo.: Libraries Unlimited, 1985. 289p. $23.50. LC 84-28872. ISBN 0-87287-483-4.

School media specialists would find this a useful overview of the processes and procedures concerned with developing, maintaining, and evaluating high school media collections. Each chapter is concluded with a bibliography and/or additional readings for a total of over 600 reference sources. Chapters are devoted to effective media programs, the collection and issues about the collection program (censorship and intellectual freedom for children, etc.); developing policy statements and sample policy statements; selection criteria; selecting materials for the curriculum and special education; and acquiring, maintaining, and evaluating a collection.

Appendix 1 lists associations and agencies; appendix 2 covers bibliographic and selection tools. A companion volume is *The Collection Program in Elementary and Middle Schools: Concepts, Practices, & Information Sources* (Libraries Unlimited, 1982) which is still available for $18.50.

Zlotnick, Barbara Bradley. **Ready for Reference: Media Skills for Intermediate Students**. Edited by Paula Kay Montgomery. Littleton, Colo.: Libraries Unlimited, 1984. 289p. $19.50pa. LC 84-11222. ISBN 0-87287-411-7.

The author, a classroom teacher for sixteen years at the time she wrote this book, addresses the cooperative efforts required of both teachers and school media specialists in planning and implementing a library media skills program for the upper elementary grades. She includes many practical suggestions and sample activities for use in instruction in all subjects for grades 3 through 6.

The first three chapters cover library media research and study skills (including an extensive checklist in chart form), a nonintegrated model for instruction, and instructional strategies. Although other chapters have activities, chapter 4 focuses entirely on specific lesson plans and includes many worksheets for actual classroom use.

The school media specialist would find valuable tips and ideas not only for teaching library skills, but for helping teachers compile instructional materials that promote research and study skills in all areas of the curriculum.

Directories

Equipment Directory of Audio-Visual Computer and Video Products. Edited by Mary Stevens. Fairfax, Va.: The International Communications Industries Association, 1953- . Annual. $37.00. LC 53-35264. ISSN 0571-8759.

This annual directory describes over 2,000 pieces of audiovisual equipment and other products, including audiovisual furniture, learning systems, and many accessories. Products are photographed and listed by categories, with specifications and prices included so that prospective buyers can compare various manufacturer's models. Arrangement is by media format; for example, motion picture projectors, filmstrip projectors, slide projectors, and overhead and opaque projectors. A glossary of terms pertinent to audiovisual equipment and use is another feature of this work. An index to contributors concludes the volume.

This annual is a must for all libraries and media centers, especially those linked with audiovisual services and/or instructional resources centers. Until 1984, this directory was known as *Audio-Visual Equipment Directory* (1953-1983). Its publisher, ICIA, was formerly the National Audio-Visual Association.

EDUCATIONAL COMPUTING

Bibliographies

Braun, Joseph A., Jr. **Microcomputers and the Social Studies: A Resource Guide for the Middle and Secondary Grades**. New York: Garland, 1986. 231p. (Garland Reference Library of Social Science, Vol. 341). LC 86-25617. ISBN 0-8240-8579-5.

Computer software packages designed for instruction in the social sciences for grades 4 through 12 are described in this guide. Entries are arranged in subject chapters and include listings of materials that have proven very popular with students, or by type of intended function of a program (e.g., utility, computer-managed instruction, tutorial, simulation).

Criteria for evaluating the software programs are included in the appendix. Not all citations include an annotation. The work is an offset publication and suffers from inadequate technical editing.

Burke, Walter. **Computers in the Classroom ... What Shall I Do? A Guide.** New York: Garland, 1986. 325p. (Garland Reference Library of Social Science, Vol. 359). $34.00. LC 86-4653. ISBN 0-8240-8921-9.

This guide to educational computing is arranged in subject chapters, each of which includes an annotated bibliography. Each chapter covers a specific aspect of using computers in the elementary classroom, including a history of computers and their educational applications. One chapter discusses hardware selection; others cover selection of different types of software and computer packages for special education students, as well as print sources. Evaluations of programs are descriptive and critical. A glossary of computer terms is also included. Although already somewhat dated, this guide can be used as a basis for developing a core elementary school software collection.

Guide to Free Computer Materials. Edited by Kathleen Suttles Nehmer. Randolph, Wis.: Educators Progress Service, 1983- . Annual. $30.25. ISSN 0748-6235.

Instructional resources related to computers, that are available free of charge or for free loan, are described in the sixth edition of this annual guide. Types of materials include books, pamphlets, magazines, films, videotapes, disks, and posters. A listing of 174 entries in the main body is arranged alphabetically in the following categories: "Business," "Communications," "Education," "Electrical Engineering," "Graphics," "Hardware," "Magazines," "Maintenance," "Micro- and Mini-Computers," "Peripherals," "Software," and "Systems." The subject index presents a more detailed breakdown with entries listed under 206 subject headings. The source index lists the names and addresses of the organizations providing free loan materials, along with instructions for obtaining them. The "Programs" section includes programs ready to be typed in on a microcomputer and run or obtained by sending a blank disk to the publisher. User groups are listed alphabetically first by type of computer, and then by state for the possibility of sharing ideas and increasing public domain software collections. A glossary contains over 1,000 definitions of computer terms.

Although this guide provides some very useful information about computer materials, it should be noted that most of the free materials are pamphlets and brochures with fewer computer demonstration disks and free loan films and videotapes. Also, while the new "Programs" and "Users' Groups" sections sound very attractive, they are, in fact, still very limited in this edition. Another source of identifying free computer programs is Alfred Glossbrenner's *How to Get Free Software: The Master Guide to Free Programs for Every Brand of Personal or Home Computer* (New York: St. Martin's Press, 1984, 432p., $14.95, LC 84-13284, ISBN 0-312-39563-9).

Hall, Keith A. **Computer-based Education: The Best of ERIC, June 1976-August, 1982.** Syracuse, N.Y.: Syracuse University, ERIC Clearinghouse on Information Resources, 1982. 147p. $6.50.

This bibliography culls all ERIC citations concerned with computer-based education from 1976 through 1982. Entries reflect titles of computer-managed instruction, interactive instruction, and instructional simulations. Entries are arranged by subject, and the following information is provided: author, title, descriptive annotation, cost of reprint, and ERIC number for ordering convenience. The table of contents can be used to provide subject access; an author index is also included. This listing will be of interest to designers of individualized instruction, distance education modules, and other learning packages.

Neill, Shirley B., and George W. Neill. **Only the Best: The Discriminating Software Guide for Preschool-Grade 12: 1987-1988**. Carmichael, Calif.: Education News Service, 1986. 128p. $23.95pa. ISBN 0-936423-00-5. Check previous eds.

The computer software programs included in this compilation are supposedly those that have received the highest ratings from review sources and other professional organizations. Most of the programs were produced in the early 1980s (through 1984) and cover various areas of the curriculum.

Entries are arranged in four major lists including the 168 titles that met all criteria to be rated as the "best," another 54 that did not quite satisfy all requirements, 28 top-rated computer programs designed for special education students, and 113 highly rated programs which appeared in the previous year's edition of this guide.

Neumann, Stella Lynn. **The Educational Software PC Compatibility Guide: Reference Guide for Compatibility of Educational and Entertainment Software for IBM PC Compatibles**. V. 1, No. 1. Tacoma, Wash.: PC Compatibility Guide, 1987. 66p. $49.95. looseleaf. ISSN 0892-2527.

Over 1,000 IBM educational and entertainment software programs are listed alphabetically in this guide. System requirements for each program are included based on information provided by the program developers. It is essential that school media specialists and faculty members involved in computer literacy, computer programming, or any kind of computer instruction or evaluation of software programs be aware of the hardware required to use them, or of their compatibility with hardware they have available.

The Educational Software PC Compatibility Guide lists, for each software package included, the numbers of thirty-eight different makes and models of microcomputers. If the program in question is compatible with a particular computer, the computer number associated with it is marked with a plus sign(+), indicating that it is compatible; if it is marked with a minus sign (-), the program will not run on that computer. Absence of either sign indicates that information about compatibility is unknown. There is no subject access provided, and the price is high for a sixty-six page publication.

Parent-Teacher's Microcomputer Sourcebook for Children 1985. New York: Bowker, 1985. 846p. $19.95pa. LC 84-20517. ISBN 0-8352-1959-3.

This specialized guide from the Bowker family lists programs suitable for use by children either at home or in curricular programs in the school setting. It is divided into two major sections, and the first part is devoted to microcomputers, peripherals, and over 5,000 software titles, including a variety of games, drill and practice programs, tutorials, stories, and so on. The second part of the volume includes a briefly annotated bibliography of approximately 5,800 titles related to all aspects of microcomputer use. Major reference titles include guides to periodicals (both for instructors and for children to use). Computer clubs and user groups, computer associations, courses of study, workshops, and databases available are also indicated. Entries include full bibliographic information including title, producer and/or distributor, price, age level, and hardware requirements.

Parents who want to provide enrichment or remediation as extracurricular learning activities will find this guide useful, as will teachers and school media specialists.

The Software Encyclopedia 1987/88. New York: Bowker, 1987. 2v. $149.95/set. LC 85-64347. ISBN 0-8352-2410-X.

Over 22,000 software programs from 3,000 producers and publishers are described in this major software guide. Bowker catalogs are typically comprehensive and reliable, and in this collection they are particularly so, because the company purchased rights to various databases including Dekatek (publishers of Microcomputer Market Place). The first volume begins with a "Guide to Applications," a list of the 830 subject headings arranged under four major categories: (1) business/professional applications, (2) consumer applications, (3) educational applications, and (4) utility applications. The main body of volume 1 is the "Title Index," where programs are arranged alphabetically by title with full descriptive information. The latter includes title, compatible hardware, memory required, operation systems, and so on, and price or price information in every case; a brief annotation in almost every case; and grade levels and program writers are provided in many, but not all, entries. The production date is not consistently provided, which makes selecting software programs difficult. This is particularly critical when looking at social sciences (geography, current affairs, social issues, civics, and government topics) where currency of information is important. The second volume is devoted to the "Expanded Applications Index" (software products organized by application) and a "Publishers Index" providing name, address, and telephone numbers of producers/publishers.

The scope and comprehensiveness of this work make it, along with *TESS: The Educational Software Selector* (Teachers College Press, 1986), two of the most widely consulted guides for microcomputer software.

TESS: The Educational Software Selector. Edited by the EPIE Institute. New York: Teachers College Press, 1984- . Annual. $65.00. LC 87-644340. ISSN 8755-5107.

This comprehensive software selection aid contains over 6,700 product descriptions from 560 suppliers. It covers software for all of the different types of microcomputer hardware found in schools. Software included aims at covering a major portion of curricula from preschool to graduate school level with programs addressing over 100 subjects, as well as aids to classroom management. Entries can be accessed by subject, specific topic, grade level, and program title. Each contains bibliographic information and a fairly complete summary of the product (average length of annotations is 190 words). Annotations also provide information about the function of the program (e.g., tutorial, drill and practice, simulation) and citations to reviews and ratings. Forms for courseware evaluation are included in the appendix. Subject and product name indexes conclude the volume. TESS has proved to be a reliable, convenient, and extensive selection list for educators; it is also available online.

Truett, Carol, and Lori Gillespie. **Choosing Educational Software: A Buyer's Guide.** Littleton, Colo.: Libraries Unlimited, 1984. 202p. $18.50. LC 83-24906. ISBN 0-87287-388-9.

This guide is intended to introduce the media specialist and other educators to software evaluation sources and selection aids. The first part discusses problems unique to software selection; it includes sample evaluation forms and lists of selection criteria. The second part lists sources of microcomputer software including commercially produced programs, ways to obtain free and inexpensive materials, and software for preview and/or ordering. Other chapters describe computer journals that are selection tools, as well as microcomputer consortia, user groups, and regional educational organizations.

An annotated bibliography of approximately 120 books, articles, and ERIC reports on selection, evaluation, and design of microcomputer software is included. An index concludes this work. *Choosing Educational Software* is a very useful guide for educators who are developing basic microcomputer software collections. A related title is *Educational Software Directory*, compiled by Marilyn J. Chartrand and Constance D. Williams (Libraries Unlimited, 1982).

Handbooks and Yearbooks

Tashner, John N., ed. **Educational Microcomputing Annual**. Phoenix, Ariz.: Oryx Press, 1985- . Annual. $31.00. ISSN 8755-836X.

This annual publication is comprised of detailed articles by experts on aspects of educational microcomputing. These include (1) general trends, (2) hardware trends, (3) computer languages and software development, (4) software curriculum, and (5) instructional management and personnel training. Each topical section is preceded by an introductory overview essay delineating the issues addressed by individual articles in the section. An annotated bibliography of additional references is also included for each of the five topics. Periodical titles related to microcomputing in education, and national associations and materials they publish are also listed. A glossary of terms and an index conclude the work.

Directories

Kelman, Peter, ed. **Classroom Computer News Directory of Educational Computing Resources, 1983**. Watertown, Mass.: Intentional Educations, 1982. 199p. $14.95pa. ISBN 0-9607-9700-9.

This directory of resources for educators using computers emphasizes resource publications, user groups and contact people, ongoing computer projects, and available conferences and workshops. The section of published sources and information includes anthologies and bibliographies, as well as lists of databases, computer resource centers, and organizations involved in research and development. This tool identifies computer software directories, reviewing periodicals, and clearinghouses; it lists associations that have a link to instructional computing and educational technology, as well as periodicals that specialize in computers in education. While this type of information requires constant updating in the rapidly changing computer field, the fact that this directory also covers funding sources makes it of interest to the educational researcher.

13

Career and Vocational Education Reference Sources

BIBLIOGRAPHIES

Bienstock, June Klein, and Ruth Bienstock Anolik, comps. **Careers in Fact and Fiction: A Selective, Annotated List of Books for Career Backgrounds**. Chicago: American Library Association, 1985. 178p. $18.95pa. LC 84-21551. ISBN 0-8389-04240-6.

School media specialists and teachers in vocational guidance programs would find this bibliography useful in helping students learn more about particular careers and occupations through the books described in this annotated bibliography. Biographies, fiction books, and dramas paint a very realistic picture of what working in a particular field is like. Entries are arranged within broad career subject categories; science, business and industry, and so on. Each section begins with an introductory overview which, along with the annotations, is addressed to a secondary and two-year college level audience.

Buros, Oscar Krisen, ed. **Vocational Tests and Reviews: A Monograph Consisting of the Vocational Sections of the Seven Mental Measurements Yearbooks (1938-72) and Tests in Print II (1974)**. Lincoln: University of Nebraska Press, 1975. xxvi, 1,087p. $65.00. LC 75-8116. ISBN 0-8032-4650-1.

This comprehensive guide to diagnostic instruments in the area of vocational education and counseling has been compiled and edited by an outstanding authority in the field of testing and evaluation. As the subtitle indicates, the contents of this volume are reprinted from the *Mental Measurements Yearbooks* and *Tests in Print II* series.

Information about each vocational test includes name, publisher and publication date, test content description (including extent of the test and manual in terms of pages, etc.), means and standard deviations, evaluative comment, and grade level range for which test is suitable. Buros states that his purpose is threefold: (a) to provide information about tests published in the English language on an international basis, (b) to provide critical reviews by subject and testing specialists, and (c) to provide bibliographies of verified references on test construction, use, and validity. Although all of this information can be duplicated in the sources mentioned, it is convenient to have it in a less expensive, and more specific, compilation.

Chronicle Career Index. Edited by Paul Downes. Moravia, N.Y.: Chronicle Guidance Publications, 1981- . Annual. $14.95pa. LC 79-640396. ISSN 0276-0355.

This compilation covers 842 sources of publications and audiovisual materials for students and vocational and educational guidance counselors. Materials are cross-referenced in two sections. In the occupational information section they are arranged alphabetically by source and cross-referenced by occupational, professional, or educational subjects. Most entries are briefly annotated and include code numbers from the *Dictionary of Occupational Titles*. This list can be used as a selection aid in developing a solid career guidance school media center collection. From 1978 to 1980 this publication was known as *Chronicle Career Index Annual*.

Educators Guide to Free Guidance Materials. Randolph, Wis.: Educators Progress Service, 1962- . Annual. $24.95pa. LC 62-18761. ISSN 0070-9417.

The twenty-third edition (1984), compiled and edited by Mary H. Saterstrom, describes 2,915 current multimedia materials related to guidance and counseling and available free of charge from 582 sources. These materials include films, filmstrips, transparencies, audio recordings, video recordings, and print materials. The descriptions of free materials are arranged by subject in four major categories: "Career Planning," "Social-Personal Material," "Responsibility to Self and Others," and "Use of Leisure Time." Each entry includes bibliographic information, including producer, date of release, and extent of item (or running time); whether the medium is black-and-white or color; sound or silent; and so on. Various indexes provide access by title, subject, and source. Instructions for obtaining materials are clearly delineated.

Egelston, Roberta Riethmiller. **Career Planning Materials: A Guide to Sources and Their Use**. Chicago: American Library Association, 1981. 177p. $20.00. LC 81-12801. ISBN 0-8389-0343-6.

This outstanding guide to resources available in the field of career planning and placement is very useful to guidance counselors and school media specialists, as well as librarians who are providing reference service in school and public libraries. In the first section, "Occupations and Careers," complete information is provided in describing possible vocational choices. The subsequent chapters or sections are "Education and Training," "Where Jobs Exist," and "Job Search Skills." Special attention (tagging) is given to career options for women, minorities, and special education students. Librarians are further helped by a chapter describing how to acquire, catalog, organize, circulate, and maintain career planning materials.

This reference tool is convenient to use because it has title, subject, and author indexes, as well as the following appendixes: A, "Occupational Title List"; B, "Sources for Ordering Materials"; and C, "State Employment Security Agencies." Other well-prepared guides include *Key Resources in Career Education: An Annotated Guide* prepared by David V. Tiedeman, Marilyn Schreiber, and Tyrus R. Wessell, Jr. (Government Printing Office, 1976), and *A Bibliography of Vocational Education: An Annotated Guide* edited by Francesco Cordasco (AMS Press, 1977).

Gersoni-Edelman, Diane. **Work-Wise: Learning about the World of Work from Books—A Critical Guide to Book Selection and Usage**. New York: Neal-Schuman, 1980. 258p. (Selection Guide Series, No. 3). $27.95. LC 79-11920. ISBN 0-87436-264-4.

This selection tool for educators and school media specialists contains critical annotations of 500 books for children from preschool through high school on topics related to career education. Books included were published between 1957 and 1979 and include fiction as well as nonfiction titles on career planning, job hunting, individual occupations, and self-help types of information. A section on materials for minority groups, including the handicapped, is particularly useful. The work is well organized, and bibliographic information, including a reading/grade level, is complete.

Goodman, Leonard H. **Current Career and Occupational Literature: 1984**. New York: H. W. Wilson, 1984. 198p. (Current Career & Occupational Literature Series). $35.00. LC 80-646591. ISBN 0-8242-0703-3. ISSN 0161-0562.

Career-education pamphlets and books published between 1981 and 1983 are annotated in this fourth volume in a series that was first published in 1978 covering the years 1973 to 1977. In part 1, the bibliography entries are arranged alphabetically by 699 occupations and include title, publisher, date, pages, price, grade level; items preceded by an asterisk are those most highly recommended. Items in part 2, "Career Planning and Education," include guides and directories to educational programs, financial aid, test materials, apprenticeships, internships, career planning, and job searching. Bibliographies and other reference sources, journals, professional counseling materials, and materials related to minorities, handicapped, the aging, and opportunities for foreign or international study and self-employment are also covered. The fourth volume also incorporates a new section, "Training and Development for the Professional," which also includes evaluation of recent texts. A "Directory of Publishers and Distributors" and an index conclude the work.

Hall, Jack, and Victoria Cheponis Lessard. **The Vocational-Technical Core Collection**. New York: Neal-Schuman, Vol. 1: *Books*, 1981. 394p. $39.95. LC 81-11048. ISBN 0-918212-46-1; Vol. 2: *Films and Video*, 1984. 250p. $39.95. LC 81-11048. ISBN 0-918212-47-2.

This selection guide describes materials recommended by specialists in vocational-technical programs or reviewed in a reputable reviewing journal in the field (e.g., *Industrial Education, School Shop, Vocational Education*). Approximately 2,500 titles are arranged in broad subject categories (general, business, communications, building trades, graphics, health, personal services, manufacturing, and transportation) and each entry gives full bibliographic information plus Library of Congress subject headings and tracings, LC card number, Dewey and LC classification number.

In 1984, volume 2, *Films and Video* was published as an annotated listing of 16mm films and ¾-inch videotapes covering the same subject categories (but Dewey and LC numbers are not provided). Both volumes have title and subject indexes; there is access to Volume 1, *Books* via an author index as well. These two volumes represent a major bibliography of print and nonprint materials that should be considered part of a basic core collection in vocational-technical programs in secondary and trade schools.

Schuman, Patricia Glass, ed., with Sue A. Rodriguez and Denise M. Jacobs. **Materials for Occupational Education: An Annotated Source Guide**. 2d ed. New York: Neal-Schuman, 1983. 384p. (Neal-Schuman Sourcebook Series). $39.95. LC 83-8195. ISBN 0-918212-17-0.

Schuman contends that since more than 50 percent of college freshmen and sophomores attend community and junior colleges where they are in a specific career training program, this guide was prepared to help identify instructional materials for occupational education.

Arrangement of sources is alphabetical by subject field except for the first section devoted to general sources, including agencies and publishers, and the second devoted to background materials on vocational education in general, as well as curriculum guides to specific programs. Entries include agency name, address and telephone number, description of types of materials produced and specific titles with publication/production date; length of item (pages, minutes, etc.); and price. An alphabetical "List of Sources" and an "Index of Occupational Categories" conclude the work.

As compared to the first edition (Bowker, 1971), which covered about 500 sources, the second edition of this bibliography covers over 800 sources, indicating a rapid expansion of materials related to occupational education.

Where to Start Career Planning: Essential Resource Guide for Career Planning and Job Hunting, 1987-1989. 6th ed. Edited by Carolyn Lloyd Lindquist. Ithaca, N.Y.: Cornell University Career Center, 1987. 288p. $14.95. ISBN 0-87866-384-3.

The latest titles in career planning and education, as well as basic titles that should be in a core collection, are included in this sixth edition of this annotated bibliography. Entries are arranged in subject categories, some of which are self-explanatory (e.g., "Financial Aids") and others too broad for convenient use (e.g., "Humanities and Social Sciences"). Appendix materials include lists of relevant periodicals, publishers, and other sources of information.

INDEXES AND ABSTRACTS

Business Education Index. St. Peter, Minn.: Delta Pi Epsilon Graduate Business Education Fraternity, Gustavus Adolphus College, 1940- . Annual. Subscription service. $12.00. ISSN 0068-4414.

Subtitled *Index of Business Educational Articles, Research Studies, and Textbooks Compiled from a Selected List of Periodicals, Publishers, and Yearbooks Published during the Year*, this index has had various publishers and sponsors over the years. It is currently published by Delta Pi Epsilon, National Honorary Professional Graduate Society in Business Education. It indexes approximately sixty general and business education periodicals. Subject headings cover particular topics related to business education, business English, business organization and management, and business law.

DICTIONARIES AND ENCYCLOPEDIAS

The Encyclopedia of Career and Vocational Guidance. 7th ed. Edited by William E. Hopke. Chicago: J. G. Ferguson Publishing, 1987. 3v. $89.95. LC 87-19084. ISBN 0-89434-083-2.

General information about some 900 job opportunities available, the labor market, and how to match skills and abilities to a potential career are part of the first volume of this encyclopedia. Signed articles are arranged in alphabetical order by broad career field from "Advertising Business" to "Truck Transportation." Alphabetical descriptions of specific professional, managerial, and technical occupations are also included. Each entry includes information in the following categories: definition, history, nature of the work, requirements, opportunities for experience and exploration, methods of entering, advancement, employment outlook, earnings, conditions of work, social and psychological factors, and sources of additional information.

Vocational Training: Glossary of Selected Terms. Washington, D.C.: International Labor Office, 1986. 132p. $10.50pa. ISBN 92-2-105457-8.

Updated and expanded from its first appearance in 1975, this glossary will serve the needs of vocational educational students in countries where English, French, or Spanish is spoken. The 300 most commonly used terms in the field are defined according to interpretations in usage by the International Labour Organisation, and definitions incorporate concepts, policies, practices, legislation, and regulations emphasized by international experts in vocational training. Terms are in English with French and Spanish translations provided.

HANDBOOKS AND YEARBOOKS

AVA Yearbooks. American Vocational Association. Washington, D.C.: American Vocational Association, 1971-1978. Annual. 8v. $65.00/set. ISBN 0-89514-032-2.

Various editors and themes are represented in this series of yearbooks which reflect the vanguard of thought and practice in vocational education during the years of their publication. Each yearbook is a compilation of independently written articles representing a wide spectrum of views and positions on contemporary aspects and issues in the field. Titles in the series include *Contemporary Concepts in Vocational Education*, 1971; *The Individual and His Education*, 1972; *Career Education*, 1973; *Philosophy for Quality Vocational Education Programs*, 1974; *Developing the Nation's Work Force*, 1975; *Vocational Education for Special Groups*, 1976; *Vocational Education and the Nation's Economy*, 1977; and *Comprehensive Planning for Vocational Education: A Guide for Administrators*, 1978.

The Handbook. A Vocational Education Legislative Reference: Federal Laws and Regulations Affecting Vocational Education. Edited by Mariscal and Company for the Bureau of Occupational and Adult Education. Washington, D.C.: Government Printing Office, 1978. xxix, 582p. HE 29.208:V85/3.

The purpose of this reference tool is to assist school administrators, curriculum specialists, and other educators in interpreting and implementing the Vocational Education Act (1963) amended by Public Law 94-482 and other related legislation. Contents include in-depth coverage of the provisions of the act, rules and regulations, provisions of related legislation, statements based on public hearings, and citations.

Arrangement is in three major sections: "Vocational Education Act of 1963," "Legislation/Rules and Regulations Relating to Vocational Education," and appendixes covering critical issues, questions, and answers.

Although no longer a current publication, this handbook provides comprehensive and convenient access to laws related to vocational education and is useful to the practitioner and historical researcher alike.

DIRECTORIES

The College Blue Book of Occupational Information. 6th ed. New York: Macmillan, 1983. 1,006p. $40.00. LC 79-66191. ISBN 0-02-69550-4.

This comprehensive directory to occupational schools in the United States is a geographical arrangement of postsecondary institutions that offer vocational training programs. Courses of study prepare students for technical and semiprofessional jobs in engineering, health services, fire and police protection, retailing, and secretarial and business-related work. Many of the entries describe two-year programs in junior or community colleges, as well as business, trade, and technical schools.

Entries are arranged alphabetically by state, city, and then name of the institution. Information provided includes name and address, occupational program classification, date founded, accreditation, contact official, telephone number, tuition, enrollment, term, housing availability, financial aid, degrees awarded, and curricula. Schools are also identified by curricula and programs of instruction. Lists of vocational and occupational programs are "Accredited Business Schools," "Two-Year Institutions," "Library Technology Programs," "Accredited Medical and Dental Programs," "Nursing Schools," and others. A section entitled "Occupational Descriptions" gives an overview of the nature of each job, eligibility requirements, training required, and employment outlook. Sources of financial aid and additional information are also included in this comprehensive vocational education guide.

Downes, Paul, ed. **Chronicle Vocational School Manual: 1987**. Moravia, N.Y.: Chronicle Guidance Publications, 1987. 379p. $16.50pa. LC 79-642591. ISBN 1-55631-009-9.

This comprehensive directory lists vocational and occupational programs in postsecondary schools in the United States and its territories: Canal Zone, Puerto Rico, and the Virgin Islands. A wide variety of vocations and occupations is included in engineering, health sciences, and various technologies. Courses related to hobbies and recreation are not included, nor are those vocational programs sponsored by educational agencies at the local or state level. Schools that offer programs are briefly described, with information given related to tuition and costs, requirements for admission, federal and other financial aid, enrollment, student services, and other characteristics of the schools. Programs are not evaluated or recommended.

Johnston, Marliss, chief ed. **A Directory of Public Vocational-Technical Schools and Institutes in the U.S.A.** 3d ed. Mankato, Minn.: Minnesota Scholarly Press, 1986. 350p. $65.00. LC 79-888903. ISBN 0-933474-40-7.

Over 1,000 nondegree vocational technical school programs offered in postsecondary public schools and institutes are described in this geographically arranged directory. Entries are arranged alphabetically first by state and then by school name. Information included covers school name, address, telephone number, and director's name followed by a list of specific courses offered. Listings for each state are preceded by a very brief introductory overview and the names and addresses of officials who may be contacted for further information about occupational education in the state.

This directory will be particularly useful to parents, educators, and guidance counselors who are helping students who are not college bound to identify courses of training in specific occupations. A school index and a comprehensive program that classifies individual occupational programs by state conclude the work.

Lovejoy's Career and Vocational School Guide: A Source Book, Clue Book and Directory of Institutions Training for Job Opportunities. Edited by Clarence Earle Lovejoy. New York: Simon & Schuster, 1982. 119p. $16.50. LC 82-142228. ISBN 0-67143-521-3.

This guide emphasizes jobs that require technical training rather than academic degrees. The first chapter discusses federal legislation appropriating funds for vocational education, followed in chapter 2 by a list of 35,550 recognized career titles. Chapters 3 through 5 describe the training and employment resources of the armed services, professional and trade organizations, and institutions that offer courses in particular vocations. Capsule descriptions of the schools presented in chapter 6 comprise the major part of the work. Listed alphabetically by state, information in each entry might include school name and address; type of programs offered (e.g., business, business and secretarial, technical, cosmetology, nursing); tuition; length of course; admission requirements; and certificate, diploma, or degree awarded. The index is an alphabetical list of the schools offering training programs.

Nassif, Janet Zhun. **Handbook of Health Careers: A Guide to Employment Opportunities**. New York: Human Sciences Press, 1980. 354p. $39.95; $19.95pa. LC 79-23027. ISBN 0-87705-489-4; 0-87705-413-4pa.

Nassif has successfully compiled a career information handbook of over 200 job opportunities available in the complex and growing health industry, including health education. It provides practical advice on planning for, and seeking admission to, educational programs. Within this framework, a number of classifications of educational programs are defined and caution is stressed concerning the quality of certain types of programs. Several appendixes include a listing of national health organizations, salaries of various careers, job opportunities with the federal government, and an annotated bibliography.

Nassif writes in a concise and objective manner and provides the reader with a basic knowledge and understanding of the expectations, opportunities, and tasks in health careers. Brief explanations of traditional and nontraditional careers and the growth of professional credentialism, which has become paramount to the health field, are also given. This work may be very helpful to high school and lower division undergraduate students interested in exploring a career in the health field. High school counselors and student advisors in undergraduate health care education programs will also find it useful.

Technician Education Directory. Edited by Lawrence W. Prakken. Ann Arbor, Mich.: Prakken Publications, 1963- . Biennial. $45.00. LC 63-22652. ISSN 0082-2353.

Over 20,000 institutions in the United States that offer technical education programs are included. Most programs are offered in postsecondary schools and each entry provides information on institutional name and location, faculty, staff and other personnel, enrollment, admission requirements, accreditation, and costs. Other sections in the yearbook cover government officials and professional organizations related to technician education, information about occupations in the technologies, case studies of exemplary programs, and an annotated bibliography. This directory was known as *Technical Education Yearbook* until 1986.

14

Adult and Nontraditional Education Reference Sources

GUIDES

French, Joyce. **Adult Literacy: A Source Book and Guide**. New York: Garland, 1987. 435p. (Source Books on Education, Vol. 14; Garland Reference Library of Social Science, Vol. 346). $58.00. LC 87-21075. ISBN 0-8240-8574-4.

In addition to bibliographical sources on adult literacy, this guide covers definitions of literacy and illiteracy, literacy instruction theories, and models and programs of adult learning. Also covered is instruction addressed to various adult groups: the elderly, members of the military, college students, and immigrants or other non-natives who are learning English as a second language.

Entries in the book consist of books, monographs, journal articles, speeches, and reports from 1980 on. Access is available through author and subject indexes.

Smith, Robert M., and Phyllis M. Cunningham. **The Independent Learners' Sourcebook: Resources & Materials for Selected Topics**. Chicago: American Library Association, 1987. 306p. $30.00. LC 87-1018. ISBN 0-8389-0459-9.

Students who wish to pursue paths of independent study, and librarians and other professionals who help them would find this guide useful. It has been compiled by two specialists in adult education who selected what they felt were the most commonly selected subjects for independent study, based on research findings, course offerings chosen in adult education programs, and interviews with librarians. Under these thirty-four subject categories the authors have compiled critical reference works, general overviews, indexes, books, periodicals, government documents, online databases, key organizations, and agencies associated with the subject. Annotations are both descriptive and evaluative; access to entries is available through author/title and organization indexes.

BIBLIOGRAPHIES

Kulich, Jindra, ed. **Adult Education in Continental Europe: An Annotated Bibliography of English-Language Materials 1983-1985**. Vancouver, B.C.: Centre for Continuing Education, University of British Columbia, 1987. 145p. (Monographs on Comparative and Area Studies in Adult Education). $18.00pa. LC 87-91194. ISBN 0-88843-135-X.

The original bibliography of materials on adult education in continental Europe published in 1971 covered the years 1945 to 1969. This fourth volume brings the coverage up to a forty-year period through 1985. The definition of adult education is given a broad range in this reference source with materials covering vocational education, postsecondary education, in general, as well as specific programs provided by education-related institutions such as museums and libraries. Kulich explains that adequate bibliographic coverage has already been given to countries of Great Britain and they have been excluded in this work.

Entries are arranged geographically first by country, and then by methods and techniques, subjects, publication format, and other subdivisions. Books, articles, dissertations (if listed in *Dissertation Abstracts International*), and theses are included. Author and subject indexes are provided.

Russ-Eft, Darlene F., David P. Rubin, and Rachel E. Holmen. **Issues in Adult Basic Education and Other Adult Education: An Annotated Bibliography and Guide to Research**. New York: Garland, 1981. 180p. (Garland Bibliographies in Contemporary Education, Vol. 1, Garland Reference Library of Social Science, Vol. 67). $31.00. LC 80-16926. ISBN 0-8240-9551-0.

Adult competency and education have been critical issues related to social and economic issues in America. Legislation on adult education in the decades of the 1960s and 1970s has resulted in federally funded programs for functionally illiterate and otherwise undereducated adults. The first section of this guide addresses the major issues involved in ABE (Adult Basic Education) and the second part is an annotated bibliography of 362 entries describing selected works that provide an overview of background information. Materials described include reference works, reviews of research studies, and general discussions of the field in general. Items are arranged in subject categories under administration, APL (Adult Performance Level), characteristics, learning disabilities, government, instruction, international concerns, program planning, women and minorities, and other topics.

Schmelter, Harvey, B., and Carol B. Aslanian. **Adult Access to Education and New Careers: A Handbook for Action**. New York: College Entrance Examination Board, 1980. 141p. ISBN 0-87447-125-7.

Educators in postsecondary institutions or community administrators interested in establishing an adult career center would find the guidelines in this handbook helpful. It is the major product of a grant project developed by the College Board and funded by the Exxon Education Foundation called the FDLS (Future Directions for a Learning Society) program. The focus of the program is on "improving access and transition" to new careers for current and potential adult learners in college and university continuing education programs and college communities.

Suggestions and advice from those who have established adult career centers are included in eight chapters, covering program objectives, services offered, developing a career materials collection, facilities, staff, finances, marketing and public relations goals, and evaluation of the center.

HANDBOOKS AND YEARBOOKS

Merriam, Sharan B., and Edwin L. Simpson. **A Guide to Research for Educators and Trainers of Adults**. Malabar, Fla.: Robert E. Krieger Publishing, 1984. 200p. $14.95. LC 83-11978. ISBN 0-89874-655-8.

Methodologies for doing educational research on and with adults in adult settings are described from the traditional, experimental, descriptive, and historical methods to more contemporary models, including ethnography, case study, grounded theory, philosophical inquiry, interactive, ecological, and futures research. Information in each covers types of research problems, assumptions underlying methodology, ways the research phenomenon is delineated, and use of data gathering procedures and techniques. A glossary of research terms is also included. The work is indexed.

Although the authors claim that those involved in the education and training of adults must know something about research (p.iii), this book, in spite of its title, is really concerned with research design and procedures and, to a lesser extent, educational research in particular.

DIRECTORIES

Egelston, Roberta Riethmiller. **Credits and Careers for Adult Learners**. Jefferson, N.C.: McFarland, 1985. 174p. $19.95pa. LC 85-42834. ISBN 0-89950-188-5.

Students who want to continue their education beyond the high school diploma (or General Educational Development certificate) can identify options available to them in innovative, nontraditional programs, as well as career opportunities.

The appendixes are particularly important as they list colleges and universities that grant academic credit based on examination scores: the College Level Examination Program (CLEP), Proficiency Examination Program (PEP), Advanced Placement Program (AP), Graduate Record Examination (GRE), and others. Schools that offer Cooperative Education Programs are also identified.

Although information is selective and much is found in standard college directories, the advantage of this inexpensive reference tool is that it not only describes the different routes to earning academic credit, but thoroughly explains the difference between nonformal educational programs, different degree requirements, and prerequisites for the various educational options. The user who is unsophisticated in the area of academic terminology will find this volume very useful.

A related title for adult learners who need help financing their further education is *Finding Financial Resources for Adult Learners: Profiles for Practice* (College Entrance Examination Board/College Board, 1985).

Halterman, William J. **The Complete Guide to Nontraditional Education**. New York: Facts on File, 1983. 172p. $19.95. $7.95pa. LC 82-12105. ISBN 0-87196-798-7; 0-87196-796-0pa.

Courses and programs that may be taken via correspondence or in other self-paced, individualized formats and that lead to college degrees are the focal point of this guide. In the beginning chapters, Halterman defines nontraditional education and discusses rules for assessing the credibility of a program. Other chapters cover programs sponsored by the Department of Defense and Veterans Administration, testing, and financial aid. The major portion of the guide constitutes the descriptions of nontraditional schools, arranged alphabetically by state.

While this guide is not as complete a listing as *The Independent Study Catalog: NUCEA's Guide to Independent Study Through Correspondence Instruction 1986-1988* (Peterson's Guides, 1986), which covers approximately 300 titles as compared to about 125, it does provide more detailed information about the schools and advice to potential external degree students. Entries are arranged by state, and information in each covers school name, address and telephone, background of school, admission, degrees awarded, tuition, study program, credit for life experience, and time required. An index of institutions is given.

The Independent Study Catalog: NUCEA's Guide to Independent Study through Correspondence Instruction 1986-1988. Edited by Barbara C. Ready and Raymond D. Sacchetti. Princeton, N.J.: Peterson's Guides, 1977- . Biennial. $8.95pa. ISSN 0733-6020.

Published by Peterson's Guides for the National University Continuing Education Association (NUCEA), this catalog covers over 12,000 independent study courses from high school to graduate level work. Programs range from noncredit ones to full credit courses and are available through seventy-one institutions that belong to the NUCEA. Schools and the courses they offer are arranged alphabetically by institution name. Additional information includes school official to contact (e.g., Dean of Continuing Education, Director of Independent Study); address and telephone number; brief statement on policies for enrollment; charges; credit; and other requirements. The course listings follow and are arranged in categories as follows: high school, college, graduate, and noncredit courses.

This guide was previously published under the title *Guide to Independent Study through Correspondence Instruction* (Peterson's Guides, 1980, 1977).

Jones, John Harding. **The Correspondence Educational Directory and Alternative Educational Opportunities**. 3d ed. Oxnard, Calif.: Racz Publishing, 1984. 581p. $46.50. LC 84-060549. ISBN 0-916546-08-X.

Programs that allow students to obtain college credits and degrees by instruction offered via extension evening class or correspondence in the United States and parts of the United Kingdom are described in this directory. Arrangement is in twenty-three sections, the first being a listing of institutions (with address, telephone number, and contact officers) participating in the University without Walls (UWW) alternative undergraduate education plan.

The third, greatly expanded edition of this directory provides a listing of accredited correspondence programs in the United States arranged alphabetically by state, plus listings of external degree programs; accepted trade, technical, and international degree programs; religious and spiritual schools and philosophical societies; unlisted correspondence universities and colleges; and nationally recognized accrediting agencies and associations. Other listings cover schools with one-year residency requirements; examination locations; proficiency examinations; specialized professional schools (e.g., medicine, dentistry, law); educational translators; vocational guidance and educational consultants; and headquarters of denominations; among other aspects related to external degree programs.

The Macmillan Guide to Correspondence Study. 3d ed. Compiled and edited by Modoc Press. New York: Macmillan, 1988. 617p. $65.00. LC 88-8603. ISBN 0-02-921641-9.

Courses that range from noncredit ones to those accepted for graduate credit are described in this directory to schools offering educational programs through the mail. The coverage is broader than Halterman's *The Complete Guide to Nontraditional Education* (New York: Facts on File, 1983) which emphasizes courses leading to an academic degree. It covers correspondence or home study curricula of 174 proprietary schools, colleges, and universities with each entry giving school name, address, background information, and details about admission, fees, credit, degrees/certificates awarded, and time requirements.

A related title is John Bear's *Guide to Non-Traditional College Degrees* (9th ed., Berkeley, Calif.: Ten Speed Press, 1982).

Wasserman, Steven, Jacqueline Wasserman O'Brien, and Edmond L. Applebaum, eds. **Learning Independently: A Directory of Self-Instruction Resources, Including Correspondence Courses, Programmed Learning Products, Audio Cassettes, Multi-Media Kits & Conversational Learning Materials, Such As Books Intended for Non-Formal Education.** 3d ed. Detroit: Gale, 1987. 437p. $21.00. LC 82-3006. ISBN 0-8103-0362-0.

The recent attention to distance education has put a new emphasis on packages designed for programs of independent learning. As a result of inquiries sent to producers and distributors of learning materials, training organizations, institutions of higher education, and trade associations, this directory describes approximately 2,500 items in a variety of formats that can be used as self-instructional resources by adults.

Entries are arrranged by format in subject categories, and information in each entry includes title, producer and address, format, price, and data (when provided). Formats include correspondence courses, audio cassettes, programmed learning, filmstrips, games, and simulations. Over 500 specific subject categories are used and range from health and medical care to art; from credit management and financial analysis to relaxation. Materials can also be accessed through author and keyword indexes. A list of producers and distributors is also included. The price of this directory is quite high, but it is does provide a unique compilation that fills a gap in the literature providing bibliographic control of this field.

15
Bilingual and Multicultural Education Reference Sources

GUIDES

Thomas, Carol H., and James L. Thomas, eds. **Bilingual Special Education Resource Guide**. Phoenix, Ariz.: Oryx Press, 1982. 189p. $36.00. LC 82-8149. ISBN 0-89774-008-4.

This guide, aimed at special education teachers and administrators, is divided into two major sections. Part 1 covers diagnosis and assessment of special needs among bilingual children: curricular content, teaching methodologies, and preservice programs of teacher education. Part 2 contains useful lists of centers (e.g., curriculum centers, resource centers) and special agencies whose objectives are to provide assistance (including funding) and/or materials to facilitate bilingual special education. Networks, training projects and programs, periodicals, databases, and resource producers are among the many types of information provided. A bibliography is also included which, when combined with the citations provided at the conclusion of each essay in part 1, provides a substantial number of references on the subject. An index concludes the work. A wide variety of resources available to special educators dealing with bilingual children are identified and pulled together in this convenient one-volume resource guide.

BIBLIOGRAPHIES

Ambert, Alba N., and Sarah E. Melendez. **Bilingual Education: A Sourcebook**. New York: Garland, 1986. 340p. (Garland Reference Library of Social Science, Vol. 197). $17.95. LC 83-48211. ISBN 0-8077-2853-5.

This sourcebook consists of bibliographic references centered around eleven thematic overviews on different issues related to bilingual education, such as antibilingualism (English-only slogans and other criticisms of bilingual education), monolingual versus bilingual education approaches to teaching the non-English speaking student, assimilation versus pluralism as desirable characteristics of American society, English as a second language, language assessment, reading, and other topics. The entries contain complete bibliographic description and well-written annotations.

Austin, Mary C., and Esther C. Jenkins. **Promoting World Understanding through Literature, K-8**. Littleton, Colo.: Libraries Unlimited, 1983. 266p. $22.50. LC 83-22229. ISBN 0-87287-356-0.

This annotated bibliography will be useful to classroom teachers at the K-8 level, librarians and school media specialists, teacher-educators, students, and researchers in the field of children's literature. Materials about the following ethnic groups are described: blacks, native Americans, and Mexicans. Titles included were published since 1965 and were selected for their story value, how well they express the values of a culture, and how much information they provide about the group's history, customs, and experience. Arrangement of materials is by ethnic group, and each section is introduced with background information about the geographic and cultural features of the country and peoples, each group's folk literature, special themes predominant in the literature for children, storytelling devices used, and the various forms of literature (e.g., poetry, picture books, historical fiction, nonfiction, biography). Entries in each section are then arranged in these form categories.

Other important sections of the book cover topics critical to planning and implementing a multiethnic literature program, and encouraging children to respond to and appreciate stories about culturally different characters. Although annotations are mainly descriptive (only titles evaluated positively in relation to the criteria were selected for inclusion), they do provide the flavor of the work. Supplementary bibliographies which list books for children and adults follow each section, but do not provide annotations. Name (author), title, and subject indexes conclude the work.

Ballesteros, Octavio A. **Bilingual-Bicultural Education: An Annotated Bibliography 1936-1982**. Jefferson, N.C., and London: McFarland, 1983. 96p. $15.95pa. LC 83-42884. ISBN 0-89950-077-3.

Ballesteros defines bilingual-bicultural education as a comprehensive educational program which produces students "who can communicate in two languages and who function in, and are knowledgable about, the customs of two cultures." This annotated bibliography focuses on all aspects of the bilingual-bicultural education of Hispanic-American students. The 556 sources include books, periodical articles, and ERIC reports, and are organized into eleven chapters covering such topics as bilingualism, biculturalism and bilingual-bicultural education, language and linguistics, bilingual students, and socio-cultural and psychological perspectives. The concluding chapter is a list of references, textbooks, and bibliographies. Each chapter is introduced with a brief overview of the focus of the references included there, and to whom they would be most useful.

The arrangement of materials makes this work convenient for educators to use whether they are classroom teachers, administrators, program and curriculum development personnel, or researchers. Titles are alphabetical by author in each chapter; complete bibliographic information and a brief annotation are provided. However, because the annotations are so brief and so general, their usefulness is somewhat limited. While a similar bibliography, *Guide to Material for English as a Second Language*, compiled by William P. Reich and Jennifer C. Gage (National Clearinghouse for Bilingual Education, 1981) includes more titles, they do not have annotations. Both titles are already dated, but they should be of utmost historical interest to researchers in this field where reference guides are still limited. Doctoral research about bilingual education can be located in *Outstanding Dissertations in Bilingual Education* (National Clearinghouse for Bilingual Education, 1983).

Benitez, Mario A., and Lupita G. Villarreal. **The Education of the Mexican American: A Selected Bibliography**. Rosslyn, Va.: National Clearinghouse for Bilingual Education; Austin, Tex.: Dissemination and Assessment Center for Bilingual Education, 1979. 270p. o.p. LC 79-120074. ISBN 0-89417-353-7.

Items contained in this bibliography cover the period from 1896 to 1976 and include books, monographs, journal articles, theses, dissertations, ERIC documents, laws, court decisions, and government documents. Entries are arranged first in broad subject categories and then chronologically within them. Subject categories include "General,"

"Mexican American Students," "Schools," "Curriculum," "Migrant Education," "Bilingual Education," "Higher Education," "Adult Education," and "Community." Author and chronological indexes are provided.

Bibliographic Guide to Black Studies, 1984. Schomberg Center for Research in Black Culture. Boston: G. K. Hall, 1975- . Annual. $95.00. LC 76-64432. ISSN 0360-2710.

This bibliography supplements the major compilation of black history and experience published by the Schomberg Center for Research in Black Culture of the New York Public Library, *Dictionary Catalog of the Schomberg Collection of Negro Literature and History* (G. K. Hall, 1962). As one of the major international centers for the study of peoples of African descent, these guides, of course, only list materials owned by the New York Public Library, but the center attempts to collect all significant books and other materials by and about blacks. Arrangement of materials is alphabetical by author, subject, and title, using a combination of Library of Congress subject headings interspersed with those developed for the Schomberg collection, as they would appear in the library's dictionary catalog. Each entry includes catalog card information: author; title; subjects; physical description; LC, ISBN, and ISSN numbers; Library of Congress classification number; and location in the New York Public Library collection.

Bibliography of Resources in Bilingual Education: Curricular Materials. Rosslyn, Va.: National Clearinghouse for Bilingual Education, 1980. 322p. index. $4.00pa. LC 81-106818. ISBN 0-89763-016-5.

This collection of 400 entries describing curricular materials for use in bilingual education programs is derived from the computerized database of the National Clearinghouse for Bilingual Education. Each entry contains accession number, complete author, title, series, date, originating institution, sponsoring agency, language, availability, ERIC Thesaurus subject descriptors, subject identifiers, and an abstract. Information in the abstract indicates level of material and/or grades at which it is appropriate for use. Types of curriculum materials include readers, books of tests on English grammar and idioms, information on history and heritage of various cultures, lesson plans for teaching language usage, and so on. Many of the titles included also have extensive bibliographies to lead the educator to additional sources. Materials can be accessed through five indexes: author, language, subject, series title, or title, making this a very useful compilation.

Another guide devoted to bilingual curricular materials is one by Joan E. Friedenberg, *Instructional Materials for Bilingual Vocational Education: Evaluation, Modification, and Development* (Harcourt Brace Jovanovich, 1984), which is limited to programs in vocational education.

Bilingual Educational Publications in Print 1983: Including Audio-Visual Materials. New York: Bowker, 1983. 539p. index. $49.50. LC 84-40345. ISBN 0-8352-1605-5. ISSN 0000-0744.

This tool can lead educators, librarians, and researchers to over 30,000 print and nonprint sources related to bilingual education, ESL (English as a Second Language) programs at the K-12 level, and testing and teaching in such programs. Since materials included are published and/or produced by companies in over 100 countries, they are written in over forty languages, and many emphasize foreign language teaching and various topics related to ethnic studies. This is a computer-produced bibliography with about 50 percent of the entries being U.S. publications; an overwhelming number of entries are Spanish-language titles. Arrangement is in a series of indexes where entries are either alphabetical or, as in the subject index, by language first and then topical headings. Other indexes include the young peoples reading, author, title, and series. The complete entry is provided in the subject index.

This a very useful selection source for identifying what is available, particularly for Spanish-speaking youngsters, when developing bilingual collections. However, it is limited in that annotations, when provided, are quite brief and noncritical in nature. A similar, but less extensive listing limited to nonannotated entries related to the Spanish-speaking is *Bilingual Bicultural Education for the Spanish Speaking in the United States: A Preliminary Bibliography*, compiled by Henry T. Trueba, Joan Moran, and others (Stipes, 1977).

Chambers, Frederick, comp. **Black Higher Education in the United States: A Selected Bibliography of Negro Higher Education and Historically Black Colleges and Universities**. Westport, Conn.: Greenwood, 1978. 268p. index. $35.00. LC 77-91100. ISBN 0-313-20037-8.

Negro colleges and universities have definitely been a major contributing factor to the black American experience in American society. This bibliographical guide attempts to bring together the literature and research on black higher education and historically black colleges and universities. A detailed twelve-page introduction by James Louis provides an informative overview of the history of black institutions of higher education, their impact on black life and culture overall, and their future role in American society. Louis points out the need for research and scholarship devoted to these institutions with respect to studying black education.

Arrangement of entries is in six chapters. Chapter 1 is an extensive list of approximately 500 doctoral dissertations written from 1918 to 1976. Chapter 2 lists citations to approximately seventy institutional histories, and also serves somewhat as a directory to black schools. Chapter 3, the largest section, is entitled "Periodical Literature, 1857-1976," and includes over 1,500 references to black higher education. Master's theses (1922-1974) are covered in chapter 4; works emphasizing black colleges in chapter 5, "Selected Books and General References." Chapter 6 is a miscellaneous selection of autobiographical and biographical materials (books and articles), proceedings and reports of various associations, organizations and institutions related to black education, and selected U.S. government periodicals. Entries are alphabetical by author in each chapter, with the exception of chapter 2 where they are organized geographically. A subject index concludes the work.

Chambers's work is useful to librarians, educators, and researchers in education, ethnic studies, history, and the social sciences.

Dale, Doris Cruger. **Bilingual Books in Spanish and English for Children**. Littleton, Colo.: Libraries Unlimited, 1985. 163p. $23.50. LC 84-28916. ISBN 0-87287-477-X.

Hispanics are the second largest and fastest-growing minority in the United States, and Spanish is the most popular language spoken in the United States, after English. This bibliography identifies all bilingual Spanish/English titles (approximately 450) for children published in the United States from 1949 through 1982. Arrangement is in two major sections. Part 1 explains how titles were identified from catalogs of book dealers and publishers, bibliographies, and library catalogs (including those issued by state education offices, school districts, universities, trade publishers, and periodical publications), reviewing journals, and personal inspection by the author of major children's literature collections.

Part 2, the bibliography itself, is arranged alphabetically by title in five chronological sections each covering a decade from the 1940s through the early 1980s. Each period division is preceded by a brief introductory essay providing an overview of the nature and number of bilingual titles published in that decade. Each entry provides complete bibliographic information, as well as sources of reviews and an annotation that is descriptive and critical in nature. Inasmuch as most library catalogs do not access titles by language, this is a unique and useful compilation for elementary teachers and school librarians. It should also be of interest to library science faculty who wish to include bilingual sources in a unit on selection and evaluation of library materials.

Children's books in the Spanish language only can be identified in Isabel Schon's three-volume series, *Books in Spanish for Children and Young Adults: An Annotated Guide, Series III* (Scarecrow Press, 1985). Previous editions were *Series I* (1978) and *Series II* (1983).

Davis, Lenwood G., and George Hill, comps. **Bibliographical Guide to Black Studies Programs in the United States: An Annotated Bibliography**. Westport, Conn.: Greenwood, 1985. 120p. (Bibliographies and Indexes in Afro-American and African Studies, No. 6). $29.95. LC 85-12722. ISBN 0-313-23328-4. ISSN 0742-6925.

Davis and Hill, compilers of this bibliography, are historian and journalist, respectively. They have produced an extensive listing (over 700 entries) of black studies programs in academic institutions in the United States. Programs range from those of elementary school level to those of higher education, as well as continuing adult education courses, and include those available in both traditionally black and white schools.

The emphasis is on periodical literature but books, pamphlets, and dissertations are also included. Most of the items are not annotated, as only books and dissertations are summarized, leaving over 500 items without descriptions. Coverage ranges from the late 1800s to the 1970s, but emphasis is on the decade (approximately 1965 to 1975) when black studies programs became popular in light of the civil rights activities of the period and the years just preceding. Students and scholars should also be aware of *The Directory of Special Black Libraries, Museums, Halls of Fame, Colleges, Art Galleries, Etc.* (Biblioteca Press, 1983) and *Guide to Scholarly Journals in Black Studies*, with introduction by Gerald A. McWorter (Chicago: Center for Afro-American Studies and Research, 1981).

Goldstein, Wallace L. **Teaching English as a Second Language: An Annotated Bibliography**. 2d ed. New York: Garland, 1984. 323p. index. (Garland Reference Library of Social Science, Vol. 181). $41.00. LC 83-48197. ISBN 0-8240-9097-7.

This volume updates the 1975 publication by the same title and is an annotated bibliography of materials that would help educators understand the issues and enhance their skills in teaching English as a second language. A total of 935 entries, arranged alphabetically, are divided into the following subjects: audiovisual, bilingual, curriculum, general instruction, grammar, language, reading, reference, sociocultural, special purposes, spoken English and listening, teacher training, teaching aids, testing and evaluation, vocabulary, and writing. Annotations are concise and are both descriptive and evaluative in nature. ERIC document numbers are provided for materials not available through a publisher. Although this is a multidisciplinary listing, only author and keyword indexes are provided.

Because teachers are increasingly faced with students who do not speak English as their native tongue, ESL continues to be an important issue for educators, and *Teaching English as a Second Language* should find a useful place among library reference sources.

A more limited title, but one that also annotates sources on the rationale for bilingual education, historical background, sociological and psychological aspects of it, as well as teaching strategies and instructional models, is one prepared by Juan Juarez, *Language Acquisition: An Annotated Bibliography on Bilingual Education* (Office of Bilingual Education and Minority Language Affairs, 1984).

Another title related to language arts instruction of children of migrant laborers, many of whom are of Hispanic descent, is one compiled by Barbara C. Palmer for IRA Migratory Children and Reading Committee, *Migrant Education: An Annotated Bibliography* (International Reading Association, 1982).

Gollnick, Donna M., Frank H. Klassen, and Joost Yff. **Multicultural Education and Ethnic Studies in the United States: An Analysis and Annotated Bibliography of Selected ERIC Documents**. Washington, D.C.: American Association of Colleges for Teacher Education and ERIC Clearinghouse on Teacher Education, 1976. 164p. LC 76-10056. ISBN 0-910052-96-4. SP 009 854.

Over 200 ERIC documents related to multicultural education, most of which are unpublished, are described in this bibliography. Documents related to bilingual education are excluded from this listing. The book is arranged in three chapters. The first defines multicultural education, discusses its historical background, related concepts, and the need for preparing teachers. Chapter 2 presents a matrix for classifying and analyzing materials (by use, document type, and ethnic group) included in the bibliography. Matrix categories for the latter include multicultural, Afro-American, Mexican American, native American, and other ethnic groups.

Entries are arranged in use categories given an ethnic group coverage code, and contain author, title, institution or publisher, date of publication, number of pages, ED (ERIC index) number, and document format availability (microfiche, hard copy, etc.). Addresses are provided where the documents can be obtained. Annotations average about 160 words in length and are fairly comprehensive abstracts. In chapter 3, the ERIC system of indexing is explained, including descriptor terms used and the search strategy for compiling this bibliography. Appendix A is a geographical listing of ERIC Microfiche Collections by state; appendix B is a glossary of ERIC terminology.

Jones, Leon. **From Brown to Boston: Desegregation in Education, 1954-1974**. Metuchen, N.J.: Scarecrow Press, 1979. 2v. 2,189p. $85.00/set. LC 78-8312. ISBN 0-8108-1147-2.

This major bibliography lists books and articles written in the aftermath of the 1954 landmark civil rights case of *Brown v. the Topeka, Kansas, Board of Education* and the unprecedented Supreme Court decision that racial segregation in education was unlawful. Jones's purpose is to help educators, researchers, and other professionals examine social movements related to desegregation in education by highlighting and making accessible critical studies, legal and other issues that developed between 1954 and 1974.

Volume 1, *Articles and Books*, includes a four-part introductory essay by Jones: overview, Brown revisited, the desegregation struggle, and references. The major part of the volume is devoted to 2,839 references to articles, followed by 441 references to books. Titles are alphabetical by year. In volume 2, *Legal Cases and Indexes*, arrangement is also first chronological and then alphabetical, covering 1,766 citations to legal cases. Annotations range from two to three paragraphs in length. The appendixes and indexes are all in volume 2. Appendix A contains material from the opinion of the court delivered by Chief Justice Warren in the the U.S. Supreme Court's 1954 decision; appendix B includes Chief Justice Burger's delivery in *Miliken v. Bradley* (1975). Three indexes conclude volume 2: author/title, cases/legal issues, and subject.

Jones's work is an extensive effort at organizing the voluminous literature on a major issue in American education for a twenty-year period, and is a must for researchers in the history of American education, school law, ethnicity, and related topics.

Lange, Dale L., and Ray J. Clifford, comps. **Testing in Foreign Languages, ESL, and Bilingual Education, 1966-1979: A Select, Annotated ERIC Bibliography.** With assistance of Sophia Behrens, and others. Washington, D.C.: Center for Applied Linguistics, ERIC Clearinghouse on Languages and Linguistics, 1980. 340p. (Language in Education: Theory and Practice, Vol. 3, No. 24). LC 80-114791. ISBN 0-87281-112-3.

Language testing plays a major role in bilingual education, particularly in ESL (English as a Second Language) teaching. This is a computer-produced bibliography of titles in the entire ERIC database related to language testing from 1966 to 1979. Native as well as foreign language references are included, as all "language" and "test" descriptors were analyzed, but the emphasis is on second language testing and bilingual education. Each entry contains complete bibliographic information and the ERIC annotations. Entries are arranged in two sections: ERIC document resumes and journal article resumes. The computer-generated indexes are also similar to the ERIC indexes in style and include subject and author indexes. Although this bibliography is already somewhat dated, it is still useful to the researcher and of interest and import to teachers of language and linguistics.

Mallea, John R., and Edward C. Shea. **Multiculturalism and Education: A Select Bibliography.** Toronto: Ontario Institute for Studies in Education, Ontario Ministry of Culture and Recreation, 1979. 292p. (Informal Series-Ontario Institute for Studies in Education, Vol. 9). LC 80-481969. ISBN 0-7744-5019-3.

Although this bibliography began as an attempt to compile sources on ethnicity and education in Canada, it was expanded to provide international coverage of multicultural education in many pluralistic communities throughout the world. Print materials are arranged in nine subject chapters covering plural societies, culture, language, minorities, race, ethnicity, immigration, attitudes, and multicultural education. Chapter subdivisions include sources on human and legal rights, social and political integration, assimilation and acculturation, bilingualism, prejudice and discrimination, textbooks, adult education, and others. The tenth chapter is devoted to audiovisual materials. The appendix includes a list of bibliographies, and an author index concludes the work. Sources are not annotated, but the international flavor of this work makes it a unique reference tool.

Malval, Fritz J., comp. **A Guide to the Archives of Hampton Institute.** Westport, Conn.: Greenwood, 1985. 599p. (Bibliographies and Indexes in Afro-American and African Studies, No. 5). $85.00. LC 85-5599. ISBN 0-313-24968-7.

This comprehensive catalog describes the holdings of the Hampton Institute's archival collection. Materials are arranged in record groups such as documents related to the positions held by various university administrators, the history and development of Hampton Institute, or special offices within it. Some entries cover biographical portraits of individuals. Information in each entry describes the type of materials held, collection size, and sources of documents. An index is also provided.

McCarty, T. L. and associates, comps. **A Bibliography of Navajo and Native American Teaching Materials.** Rev. ed. Rough Rock, Ariz.: Navajo Curriculum Center, 1983. 104p. LC 83-061730. ISBN 0-936008-15-6.

This bibliographic guide emphasizes curricular materials related to the Navajo Indians, although other native American tribal groups are included as well. Materials are useful for teaching native Americans, as well as for teaching about them. This edition has been revised based on feedback from teachers and other professionals involved in ethnic studies and multicultural education. It is arranged in six major sections, the first two of which include the instructional materials divided into grade levels K-12.

Each entry includes complete bibliographic information, as well as an evaluative description commenting on readability and usefulness of the book for children and/or teachers and school library media specialists. Section 3 consists of a directory of major audiovisual resources; section 4 lists periodicals (newspapers, magazines, and professional journals) concerned with the Navajos. Section 5 is devoted to a selected overview of literature on the Navajo, and section 6 lists relevant teacher resource institutions such as curriculum development centers, libraries, and museums.

McGee, Leo, and Harvey G. Neufeldt, comps. **Education of the Black Adult in the United States: An Annotated Bibliography**. Westport, Conn.: Greenwood, 1985. 108p. (Bibliographies and Indexes in Afro-American and African Studies, No. 4). $35.00. LC 84-19785. ISBN 0-0313-23473-6.

Education of the black Americans from the 1600s to the 1980s is covered by the 367 articles, books, dissertations, and bibliographic references described in this annotated bibliography. Titles are arranged chronologically in five sections. The first covers the period prior to the Civil War (1619-1860), and focuses on education for plantation slaves, special schools, and the role of particular groups, such as the Quakers, in promoting education for blacks. The second period covered is that of the Civil War and Reconstruction years (1860-1880) and involvement and protection of the government. The next section is entitled "Separate But Equal" (1880-1930) emphasizing segregated education practices, followed by a section from 1930 on covering desegregation. The last section consists of general sources that are generic to all periods. Although criteria for inclusion are not included in this selective listing, it is, however, a unique compilation which should be of use to educational historians, sociologists, and scholars of black studies.

Newby, James Edward. **Black Authors and Education: An Annotated Bibliography of Books**. Washington, D.C.: University Press of America, 1980. 103p. $22.25; $9.50pa. LC 79-9677. ISBN 0-8191-0974-6; 0-8191-0975-4pa.

A major objective of this reference guide is to identify books on education and educational policy by black authors. Individuals, organizations, publishers, and colleges and universities were sent questionnaires to identify over 200 black authors who had at least one book published in the field of education. The 237 titles are arranged alphabetically by author. Each entry provides bibliographic information (page numbers are excluded) and an annotation describing the major content of the work. An author index and a title index are included; access by subject is not available. Most of the titles were published in the 1970s, but coverage goes back to the 1800s. This bibliography would be of particular interest to scholars in the area of ethnic studies and black contributions to American life in particular.

Newman, Richard. **Afro-American Education, 1907-1932: A Bibliographic Index**. New York: Lambeth Press, 1984. 178p. $40.00. LC 83-24869. ISBN 0-931186-05-6.

Newman combed the indexes to the literature of the vast library of the U.S. Office of Education (the Bureau of Education prior to 1929) published before the H. W. Wilson company began putting out *Education Index* in 1932. From 45,000 citations in *Education Literature*, 1907-1932, published in twelve volumes by Garland Publishing, he culled 461 entries dealing with Afro-American education for that period, and to a minor extent about blacks in the Caribbean and Africa. These titles are arranged alphabetically by author in the present volume. Newman feels that these sources provide information about black education during a period that has been neglected in American history as it falls halfway between the Civil War and the civil rights movement of the 1950s and 1960s.

Annotations for each entry vary in length from extremely brief ones to those of average or medium length (100 words), with more being quite short and none long. A list of the 814 journals indexed and an index providing access by subject follow the bibliography. The careful and thorough scrutiny of the Bureau of Education's voluminous library of materials make this a very useful guide for the researchers in education, ethnic studies, and the social sciences.

Sauve, Deborah, comp. **Guide to Microcomputer Courseware for Bilingual Education**. Rev. and exp. ed. Rosslyn, Va.: National Clearinghouse for Bilingual Education, 1985. 296p. $11.00pa. LC 84-63153. ISBN 0-89763-106-4.

Software programs suitable for CAI (computer-assisted instruction) and CMI (computer-managed instruction) in programs of bilingual education and second language acquisition are described in this bibliography which updates and expands the 1983 edition. Included are 230 new program titles, for a total of 466 software programs. Entries have been retrieved from the database of the National Clearinghouse for Bilingual Education and are arranged sequentially by MICRO or MC number. Information provided was extracted from courseware catalogs and includes program name/title; producer's name, address, and telephone number; required hardware peripherals, and so on; language; type of program/instructional technique (authoring, drill and practice, games, problem solving, record keeping, simulation, tutorial); content area; grade/proficiency level; and brief nonevaluative abstract. Following the abstract, in some cases, are references to identified reviews in the literature or evaluations by courseware evaluation services.

A series of indexes provides access by title, producer, subject, language, and grade level. A quick perusal of the latter index reveals that most programs are available for some kind of Apple II computer. Finding programs appropriate for particular language instruction and grade level can be done through the "Language, Grade Level Index," which concludes the work.

As would be expected, there are many programs suitable for English and Spanish speaking students, but there are also a good number for Dutch, French, German, Italian, Norwegian, Portuguese, Swedish, Turkish, and Vietnamese. A total of forty-two different languages are represented in the different courseware programs covering a wide variety of subjects at different grade levels.

Weinberg, Meyer, comp. **The Education of Poor and Minority Children: A World Bibliography, Supplement 1979-1985**. Westport, Conn.: Greenwood, 1986. 849p. LC 86-12161. ISBN 0-313-24880-X.

This international bibliography includes over 60,000 references in English, Spanish, French, German, and Italian. Entries for books, articles, government documents, newspaper items, and legal proceedings are arranged by broad subject categories related to the education of minority children. Some of the subjects are specific minority groups, such as native Americans, Spanish-speaking peoples, Asian Americans, and black women. Others cover the topic from a special aspect, such as history or higher education. Materials of both a popular and a scholarly nature are included, with emphasis in coverage being definitely on the United States.

Weinberg attempted to uncover all publications by minority authors or minority groups. Although the work is broad in scope and comprehensive, the entries are not annotated. Its subject arrangement, which is not alphabetical, forces the user to rely very heavily on the table of contents. One useful feature is the inclusion of useful bibliographies at the end of each subject section. An author index concludes the work. This publication adds 20,000 citations to the 40,000 included in Weinberg's original 1981 two-volume compilation, *The Education of Poor and Minority Children: A World Bibliography.*

HANDBOOKS AND YEARBOOKS

Cordasco, Francesco. **Bilingual Schooling in the United States: A Sourcebook for Educational Personnel**. New York: McGraw-Hill, 1976. 387p. $33.12. LC 76-29056. ISBN 0-07-013127-9.

This comprehensive sourcebook could be used as a textbook for education students and as a reference tool for librarians, educational administrators, teachers, students, and researchers. It is arranged in four main sections. Part 1, "Historical Backgrounds," provides information in six brief articles on early instances of bilingual education and language maintenance by immigrant members of ethnic groups. Articles in part 2 focus on defining and characterizing bilingual education; part 3 includes materials discussing the subject from the perspective of linguistics. Part 4 surveys programs, practices, and administrative problems of bilingual education.

Appendix A is an overview of court decisions and legislation affecting bilingual education. Appendix B is a geographical arrangement (by state) of selected program and project descriptions. A "Bibliography of Selected References" provides complete bibliographic information on over 500 books and journal articles on all aspects of bilingual schooling, including learning language as mother tongue and second language; teaching language to native Americans, Mexican Americans, Puerto Ricans, and other groups; and a rationale for bilingual education. An author/title/subject index concludes this comprehensive guide by a well-published scholar in the field of ethnic studies and ethnic bibliography.

Cordasco has also coauthored (with George Bernstein) *Bilingual Education in American Schools: A Guide to Information Sources* (Gale, 1979), and has edited *Materials and Human Resources for Teaching Ethnic Studies* (Arno Press, 1978, reprint of 1975 ed.), and compiled *Immigrant Children in American Schools: A Classified and Annotated Bibliography with Selected Source Documents* (A. M. Kelly, 1976).

Council on Interracial Books for Children. **Guidelines for Selecting Bias-Free Textbooks and Storybooks**. New York: Council on Interracial Books for Children, 1980. 105p. $7.95pa. LC 80-16903. ISBN 0-930040-33-3.

Programs of the Council on Interracial Books for Children aim to promote learning materials that are free of biases associated with sex, age, race, or handicaps. These guidelines emphasize positive human values within culturally plural settings and consist, for the most part, of a series of checklists and rating instruments covering bias in children's storybooks and textbooks (including readers, literature anthologies, biographies, and books in math and other subjects). One section deals entirely with examples of history text bias. Evidences of stereotyping and biased treatment of Afro-Americans, Asian Americans, Latinos, and native Americans, in particular, are pointed out in the thought-provoking narrative discussions. A section entitled "Terminology and Definitions" precedes the main body of the work. Teachers and school media specialists should be able to make practical applications of these guidelines.

Friedman, Delores Lowe. **Education Handbook for Black Families**. Garden City, N.Y.: Anchor Press/Doubleday, 1980. 428p. LC 79-6537. ISBN 0-385-14881-X.

This handbook is aimed primarily at black students and parents who want to help their children get the best education possible. It helps parents develop skills at home that will help preschool children prepare for learning at school, suggests developmental activities and multimedia materials for children of all ages, describes academic programs and courses in preparation for college, lists black colleges and universities, and provides information that will help high school dropouts resume their education. The variety and range of information presented here, including useful bibliographies, make this a comprehensive reference tool that would be very useful in high schools and undergraduate colleges serving large black populations.

Parker, Dennis R. **Individual Learning Programs for Limited-English-Proficient Students: A Handbook for School Personnel**. Sacramento, Calif.: California State Department of Education, 1984. 86p. $3.50. ED 253 116. FL 014 870.

This handbook is designed to help California educators design a comprehensive program for LEP (limited-English-proficient) students. Arranged in four sections, it covers (1) legal requirements related to assessment, diagnosis, placement, program content, and funding; (2) theoretical background of primary and secondary language instruction; (3) the ILP (Individual Learning Program); and (4) step-by-step instructions on implementing an ILP. Similar reference tools for school administrators in other states include *Effective Practices for Successful Bilingual Parent Involvement Programs: An Administrator's Handbook* (New Jersey State Department of Education, Division of Compensatory/ Bilingual Education, 1984); *Guidelines for the Establishment and Implementation of Exit and Entry Criteria for Bilingual Problems* (Ohio State Department of Education, 1983); and Elizabeth R. Reisner's publication, *Building Capacity and Commitment in Bilingual Education: A Practical Guide for Educators* (NTS Research Corp., Educational Policy Development Center, 1983).

Pasternak, Michael G. **Helping Kids Learn Multi-Cultural Concepts: A Handbook of Strategies**. Champaign, Ill.: Research Press, 1979. 249p. $13.95pa. LC 79-63052. ISBN 0-87822-194-8.

Teaching strategies, activities, and an extensive list of resources of multicultural education are included in this handbook. Pasternak's goal is to help educators provide children with opportunities to increase crosscultural understanding through learning centers, simulation games, literature, arts and crafts, and music. Having established multicultural programs in schools in Nashville, Tennessee, Pasternak brings a realistic attitude and many plausible suggestions and activities that can be integrated into the curriculum allowing children to build multicultural relationships, as well as healthy self-images of their own. Unfortunately, Pasternak does not credit the originators of many of these activities. One of the most useful chapters is a guide to development of inservice training programs for teachers. A related title in the same vein is one by Fred Rodriguez, *Mainstreaming a Multicultural Concept into Teacher Education Guidelines for Teacher Trainers* (R & E Publishers, 1983) which is devoted entirely to preservice teachers and teacher trainers.

Provenzano, Johanna Z., comp. **Promising Practices: A Teacher Resource (Grades K-3).** Rosslyn, Va.: National Clearinghouse for Bilingual Education, 1985. 96p. $6.00. LC 85-61124. ISBN 0-89763-108-0.

This small but unique guide contains learning activities identified by a panel of master teachers for instructing limited-English-proficient (LEP) students. These teaching practices and their implementation are covered in four chapters: "Planning," "Classroom Management," "Teaching Procedures," and "Evaluation." Each chapter includes an introduction to the topic, suggestions, and reminders with respect to educating LEP students, as well as relevant learning activities.

Teachers who find themselves with primary pupils from different cultures and language groups will find these lesson plans extremely helpful, as they include the subject area, specific grade level, English proficiency level (bilingual, mainstream, English as a Second Language), time allotment required, instructional objectives, prerequisite skills, materials, procedures, sample questions, and name of teacher who submitted the activity. A lesson evaluation checklist is included to assist in implementation of the practices into instruction; a brief, but relevant, bibliography concludes the volume. A publication by the same title is also published for grades 4 through 6 (1985).

Young, John, and John Lum. **Asian Bilingual Education Teacher Handbook.** Cambridge, Mass.: Evaluation, Dissemination and Assessment Center for Bilingual Education, Lesley College, 1982. 246p. ED 258 466. FL 015 094.

Developed through the Asian Bilingual Curriculum Center of Seton Hall University, this handbook emphasizes the development of Asian bilingual education, as well as issues and materials related to it. Particular language and culture groups included are Chinese, Filipino, Korean, Japanese, and Asians, in general. Chapters cover such subjects as bilingual teacher training and state certification requirements, problems in bilingual-bicultural education, an example of a multicultural alternative curriculum and bilingual curriculum resources, and others. A briefer handbook for designing instruction specifically for the large community of Korean-American students of California is *A Handbook for Teaching Korean-Speaking Students* by Chong K. Park (California State Department of Education, Office of Bilingual Bicultural Education and Los Angeles: California State University, Evaluation, Dissemination and Assessment Center, 1983).

DIRECTORIES

Beckham, Barry, ed. **The Black Student's Guide to Colleges.** 2d ed. Providence, R.I.: Beckham House, 1984. 495p. $11.95pa. LC 84-072190. ISBN 0-931761-00-X.

The purpose of this directory is to help black students select and apply to a college. The emphasis is on selective residential, predominantly white, colleges, but profiles of some historically black institutions are also included. Others included are popular schools with high black student enrollment and those with geographic diversity. Some essays written by college students describe various aspects of the application process and college life; a glossary defines some college-related terms. Reference sources and organizations to help in identifying scholarships are listed, as are some general college handbooks.

A total of 158 school profiles are listed alphabetically and provide information related to college address, statistics about black and white student enrollment and graduation, black and white faculty, percentage of blacks receiving aid and total aid received by blacks, and average scholarship or award (with the intent being that the prospective black student can have an idea of the attrition rate for blacks at that school). Narrative descriptions provide black students' comments on interaction between blacks and whites, race relations, and the atmosphere in general. They also discuss types of resources and support services available for blacks and other minorities; for example, career and other counseling, tutoring, extracurricular activities, athletics, black organizations, and the overall academic status. A geographic index lists schools by state.

Since this directory provides information of a subjective nature that black students might not find elsewhere, they should use it in conjunction with other standard comprehensive guides, (*The College Blue Book*, titles in the *Barron's Educational Series*, etc.) where many major private schools and large state universities more affordable to students, both black and white, may be considered and which are not listed in this limited, highly selected listing.

Directory of Financial Aids for Minorities. Edited by Gail Ann Schlachter. Santa Barbara, Calif.: ABC-Clio, 1984- . Annual. $42.50. LC 85-25068.

This important guide for minority students, counselors, and librarians serving them is a comprehensive directory to programs providing financial aid solely or primarily for students of Asian, black, Hispanic, or native American heritage. The directory includes a major section of program descriptions which is arrangd by type of aid (scholarships, fellowships, loans, grants, awards, and internships); a list of state agencies providing financial aid; and a bibliography of additional financial aid sources. Indexes access aid programs by title, sponsor, geographic area, subject, and date for application. Program descriptions contain entry number, title, sponsoring organization's name, address and telephone number, purpose, eligibility requirements, financial details, support duration, special benefits, limitations and restrictions, number of recipients, and application deadline.

The format of the directory is convenient to use because it lists programs available to all minorities, as well as by specific ethnic group. Although this information is also included, to a lesser extent, in *Directory of Special Programs for Minority Group Members* edited by Willis L. Johnson (Garrett Park Press, 1986), the latter title emphasizes career information and opportunities.

Johnson, Willis L., ed. Directory of Special Programs for Minority Group Members: Career Information Services, Employment Skills Banks, Financial Aid Sources. 4th ed.Garrett Park, Md.: Garrett Park Press, 1986. 348p. $25.00. LC 73-93533. ISBN 0-317-46324-1.

The focus of this directory is on special programs and career opportunities for minority group members and disadvantaged persons. The organizations included have been arranged in three major sections. The first and largest section covers scholarship programs, career orientation activities, and employment services. The entries are consecutive by a specially assigned serial number. The second section lists economic assistance, job retraining, and student financial aid available via federal programs. Entries here are arranged first alphabetically by name of federal agency or office involved and then numerically. The third section covers activities developed at individual colleges and universities to support minorities (remedial programs, financial aid, etc.).

A list of sources and methodology used to compile the directory, an alphabetical list of organizations, a glossary, a bibliography, a program index, and an alphabetical listing by minority group and type of program are included.

Minority groups, in this directory, refer to blacks, Hispanics, native Americans, and Asian Americans. Most programs are for American citizens, excluding foreign students in this country on a temporary basis. Although annotations are brief, this is a very comprehensive directory to this type of information. William C. Young includes women in *Higher Education Opportunities for Minorities and Women—Annotated Selections* (U.S. Department of Education, 1985). Another directory aimed at minority group members providing information about scholarships, fellowships, and other grants is *Grants for Minorities* (Foundation Center, 1986).

Minority Organizations: A National Directory. 3d ed. Garrett Park, Md.: Garrett Park Press, 1987. 600p. $40.00pa. LC 79-640122. ISBN 0-812048-30-1. ISSN 0162-9034.

This is a comprehensive listing of 7,186 entries on organizations that are either established by minorities or that operate programs to benefit them. Minority groups are defined here to include native Americans, blacks, Hispanics, and Asian Americans. The directory begins with an alphabetical index of organizations and the entry numbers where they are described. The entries follow, also arranged alphabetically by organization name, and include address, telephone number, and a brief annotation describing the major purpose. Some annotations merely state that information on the organization's current status is not available. Journals, newsletters, and other publications of the organization are also listed. Types of organizations range from bowling teams to government programs and academic associations that are part of major universities.

Appended materials include a glossary which defines some of the terms used in the directory, many of which are English translations of Spanish words; a list of major minority periodicals; and cities of large minority populations where telephone directories were consulted under group descriptors. Selected bibliographic references are provided; a geographical index (by state) concludes the work.

The directory is interspersed with sketches, symbols, charts, illustrations, and photographs that document each ethnic group's history, art, and culture. The user interested in organizations related to only one group in particular must peruse the entire alphabetical list as a subject index is not available, seriously limiting the usefulness of this directory. Coverage is about equal for Hispanic and native American groups, followed by that for black and Asian American organizations respectively.

Minority Student Enrollment in Higher Education: A Guide to Institutions with Highest Percent of Asian, Black, Hispanic, and Native American Students. Garrett Park, Md.: Garrett Park Press, 1987. 1v. (unpaged). $15.00pa. LC 87-080852. ISBN 0-912048-49-2.

Students who want to identify schools that have high enrollments of a particular ethnic minority group can consult this directory for general information about these colleges and universities. Guidance counselors and school media specialists, particularly those working in multicultural or minority settings would also find this a handy reference tool. Schools listed in this directory all have at least 20 percent of their total enrollment made up of students from Asian, black, Hispanic, or native American minority groups.

Institutional descriptions are arranged alphabetically by state, and each entry provides school name, address, telephone number, majors offered, enrollment, and minority percentages. Percentages of a particular minority enrollment in business programs or engineering, for example, may be determined by consulting the index of major programs.

Reilly, Marta Torres, Michael Libby, and Deborah Sauve, comps. **Guide to Resource Organizations for Minority Language Groups.** Rosslyn, Va.: National Clearinghouse for Bilingual Education, 1981. 186p. (Resources in Bilingual Education). $12.32 through ERIC: ED 203693. LC 81-149654. ISBN 0-89763-053-Xpa.

This directory describes 242 local and national resource organizations that in some way provide special assistance or benefits to American minority language group members. Organizations are listed alphabetically and by accession number. Each entry provides the following information: full name of organization/association, address, name of director or other officials, sponsoring agencies, date of origin, publications, target minority-language or culture group, and objectives of the resource organization. The user can access information by consulting any of several indexes (e.g., by language, culture group, specific subject, or geographic location). School administrators, teachers, librarians, and social workers who serve minorities would find this directory helpful.

Another directory in this series, *Guide to Publishers and Distributors Serving Minority Languages* (2d ed., 1980) compiled by Harpreet K. Sandhu and Laura A. Bukkila, is useful in identifying publishing companies and centers that develop and disseminate minority language materials.

STATISTICS SOURCES

Deskins, Donald R., Jr. **Minority Recruitment Data: An Analysis of Baccalaureate Degree Production in the United States**. Totowa, N.J.: Rowman & Allanheld, 1983. 819p. $57.50. LC 83-19159. ISBN 0-86598-145-0.

Tabular data obtained from the 1978-79 HEGIS (Higher Education General Information Survey) are organized to determine the undergraduate schools in the United States from which significantly large numbers of minority students graduate with a baccalaureate degree. The major part of the volume is comprised of tables reporting data arranged first by subject discipline, and then by state, and then alphabetically by institution name.

Although the data here are dated, the information has value for historical research and provides recruiters of minority group members for graduate schools, business, or industry, an idea of where potential candidates may be identified.

16

International and Comparative Education Reference Sources

BIBLIOGRAPHIES

Altbach, Philip G. **Comparative Higher Education: Research Trends and Bibliography**. London: Mansell; distr., Salem, N.H.: Mansell, 1979. 206p. $31.00. LC 79-315223. ISBN 0-7201-0825-X.

The titles listed in this bibliography are dated, and while the book is still available, its major value is one of historical interest. Author of earlier compilations on the topic, editor of the *Comparative Education Review* and director of SUNY's (Buffalo) Comparative Education Center, Altbach is well qualified to select the 1,116 books and articles listed here and to write a lengthy, informative essay on the origin, development, and trends and issues in the field of comparative education.

Bibliography items cover all aspects of the field and are arranged geographically. Titles can be accessed by author, country or region, and topic. European coverage is greater than that of the United States; the coverage is fairly comprehensive with respect to geographic representation, although third world countries are underrepresented. There is quite a bit of overlap in this title with a previous one by the same author, *Comparative Higher Education Abroad: Bibliography and Analysis* (Praeger, 1976). The latter title is more extensive (1,732 titles) and, in addition, included a section presenting bibliographical essays on selected topics. According to Altbach, the best or most important materials are included in the 1979 title, with a much larger percentage of them being in the English language than in the 1976 work. Another title by Altbach and David H. Kelly provides five years of bibliographic coverage to third world and developing countries, *Higher Education in Developing Nations: A Selected Bibliography, 1969-1974* (Praeger, 1975).

Altbach, Philip G., and David H. Kelly, with an essay by Jan Kluczynski. **Higher Education in International Perspective: A Survey and Bibliography**. London and New York: Mansell, 1985. 583p. $66.00. LC 84-27311. ISBN 0-7201-1707-0.

This work is composed of two major parts: two essays and a comprehensive bibliography. The essays are "Perspectives on Comparative Higher Education: A Survey of Research and Literature," by Philip G. Altbach, and "Research on Higher Education in European Socialist Countries," by Jan Kluczynski. The aim of the work as a whole is to survey the literature on higher education in an international context, providing an overview of the field. The emphasis is on research in not only the American and European industrialized nations, but on the third world countries as well. The purpose is to discover "how such research can be more efficiently developed and used in light of the needs of society and of the higher education institutions" (p. xiii).

This selective, but extensive, bibliography includes 6,901 entries arranged in twenty-three topical categories. Some of the topics represented are related to history, economics, statistical and descriptive works, policy and planning, student adjustment (socialization

197

and psychological problems), education for the professions, teaching, intercultural relations, theory, education, and technology. A final section lists bibliographies, by country. Materials selected reflect the state of the art for the period between 1970 and 1983. Entries are not annotated; the work is not indexed.

Altbach, Philip G., David H. Kelly, and Y. G.-M. Lulat. **Research on Foreign Students and International Study: An Overview and Bibliography**. New York: Praeger, 1985. 403p. (Praeger Special Studies Series in Comparative Education). $39.95pa. LC 85-3372. ISBN 0-03-071922-4.

As director of the Comparative Education Center at SUNY-Buffalo and editor of the *Comparative Education Review*, Altbach is well versed in the international literature in this field. According to Altbach and Lulat, international students constitute a major growth industry in American higher education, representing 3 percent of the undergraduate enrollment, 15 percent of the total graduate students, and close to 50 percent in fields such as engineering and computer science.

This reference tool is divided into two major sections: an overview essay and a partially annotated bibliography of 2,811 books, articles, theses and dissertations, reports, and government documents. Arrangement of entries is alphabetical in thirty-seven topical subdivisions including a beginning section on reference and bibliographical materials. Some selected topics include the policies of both the sending and host countries, economic aspects, legal issues, recruitment procedures, adaption problems, academic performance, language problems, and return and re-entry issues and concerns about the "brain drain."

Altbach, Philip G., and Denzil Saldhana, and Jeanne Weiler. **Education in South Asia: A Select Annotated Bibliography**. New York: Garland, 1987. 360p. (Reference Books in International Education, Vol. 3; Garland Reference Library of Social Science, Vol. 390). $56.00. LC 86-29548. ISBN 0-8240-8453-5.

Education in the countries of Bangladesh, India, Nepal, Pakistan, and Sri Lanka are covered in this bibliography of 1,419 English-language publications. Materials were published between 1960 and 1985. Arrangement of entries is by subject in thirty-five categories related to educational history, sociology, economics and reform, and education for all groups and levels, and then further subdivided by country. Emphasis is on books and periodicals and reports have been included on a highly selective basis; dissertations are excluded.

Altbach provides an introductory summary of the historical background of education in these South Asian countries, as well as a discussion of some of the trends and issues in educational research.

Altbach, Philip G., Gail Kelly, and David H. Kelly. **International Bibliography of Comparative Education**. New York: Praeger, 1981. 300p. $52.95. LC 81-962. ISBN 0-03-056881-1.

The development of comparative education as a distinct and legitimate academic area of inquiry is traced in a twenty-seven page essay which precedes a 3,080-entry bibliography on the subject. The bibliography is divided into two major sections: "Comparative Education as a Field of Inquiry" and "Selective Bibliography on Regions and Countries." The former is arranged alphabetically by author under subject categories; for example, definitions of the field, overviews, methodology, academic disciplines, and other topical studies. Entries in the latter section are arranged alphabetically by country. Entries include books and articles; annotations are not provided. A "Cross-Reference Index" provides entry numbers under various topics.

Specific country bibliographies are two compilations by Nellie M. Apanasewicz, *Education in the USSR: An Annotated Bibliography of English-Language Materials, 1965-1973* (GPO, 1975); *Education in Eastern Europe: An Annotated Bibliography of English-Language Materials, 1965-1976* (GPO, 1980), and *Soviet Education: An Annotated Bibliography and Readers' Guide to Works in English, 1893-1978* by Yushin Yoo (Greenwood, 1980).

Fomerand, Jacques, John H. Van de Graaff, and Henry Wasser. **Higher Education in Western Europe and North America: A Selected and Annotated Bibliography**. New York: Council for European Studies, 1979. 229p. o.p. LC 79-114093.

Books, articles, dissertations, government documents, and interagency publications dealing with postsecondary education systems in Western Europe and North America are included in this selected listing. The emphasis is on research studies in the United States. Materials are alphabeticaly arranged in four subject chapters: "Mission and Function of the University," "The University and the Modernization of Society," "The Government of Higher Education," and "The Economics of Higher Education." Each chapter is introduced by a thematic essay providing a brief overview of the topic.

Each entry provides complete bibliographic information and an annotation averaging about 75 to 100 words. Annotations for foreign language titles are always in English. Appendixes A and B list selected reference materials and periodicals, respectively. Author and subject indexes are provided.

Fraser, Stewart E., and Barbara J. Fraser. **Scandanavian Education: A Bibliography of English-Language Materials**. White Plains, N.Y.: International Arts and Sciences Press, 1973. 271p. LC 73-85481. ISBN 0-87332-45-X.

Books and articles in the English language on education in Scandinavia during the years 1960 to 1973 are described in this bibliography. Emphasis is on education in Sweden, Denmark, and Norway, but a broader section on Scandinavia, in general, includes materials about education in Finland and Iceland.

The bibliography is arranged in four major geographical sections and then by subject categories within the country subdivisions. Major subjects covered include general education; research; preschool, primary, lower and upper secondary, and higher education; special education; sex education; international studies; educational experimentation; guidance and counseling; vocational and technical education; administration; educational media; physical education; minorities education; teacher education; folk high schools; and bibliography. The work is briefly annotated, but since an index is not provided, the table of contents must serve this purpose. Fraser has also compiled, with Kuang-Liang Hus, *Chinese Education & Society: A Bibliographic Guide, the Cultural Revolution and Its Aftermath* (Bks Demand, UMI, 1981).

Harris, Robin S., and Arthur Tremblay. **A Bibliography of Higher Education in Canada: Supplement 1981**. Toronto: University of Toronto Press, 1981. 212p. (Studies in Higher Education in Canada, No. 3, 5; Studies in the History of Higher Education in Canada, No. 8). $20.00. LC 83-130731. ISBN 0-8020-24440-8.

This supplementary compilation extends bibliographic control of the literature related to higher education in Canada. The original bibliography was published in 1960 (thirteen volumes) and covered items published up to December 31, 1958. A 1965 supplement extended coverage to 1963, the 1971 supplement brought it up to 1969, and this 1981 supplement extends coverage up to the 1980s. Books, articles, reports, theses, and disserta-tions are included. The entries are arranged chronologically by subject, and lists of sources, bibliographies, and periodicals searched are provided. An author index concludes the work.

Inglis, Christine, and Rita Nash. **Education in Southeast Asia: A Select Bibliography of English Language Materials on Education in Indonesia, Malaysia, Philippines, Singapore and Thailand (1945-1983)**. Brookfield, Vt.: Gower Publishing, 1985. 554p. $74.95. LC 85-17731. ISBN 0-566-03521-9.

Inglis and Nash compiled this bibliography with assistance from colleagues from Australian universities, Frances Wong and Margaret Carron. A major focus of materials is on the historical development of education during the colonial period of dependence and on events since independence. Works selected for inclusion were concerned with the social processes involved in education and teaching and include books, articles, doctoral theses, conference papers, reports, and government documents. Entries are organized geographically by country and region, and then by categories as follows: "General"; "Primary and Pre-Primary Education"; "Secondary Education"; "Post-Secondary Education"; "Adult and Community Education"; "Education for Special Groups"; "Educators, Students, Parents, and Communities"; "Guidance and Counseling"; and "Theories and Philosophies of Education." A list of acronyms and abbreviations of organizations related to education in Southeast Asia precedes the bibliography. Two serious limitations—the absence of annotations and lack of any type of indexing—affect the usefulness of this comprehensive listing.

International Bulletin of Bibliography on Education. Boletin internacional de bibliografia sobre educacion. No. 0; V. 1, 1971/80- . Madrid. Bibliografics Internationales Badesco, 1981- . Quarterly with annual summary. $263.00. ISSN 0211-8335.

This international bibliography has at the head of its title, *B.I.B.E. Project*, and is published in English, French, German, Italian, Portuguese, and Spanish. Entries are arranged according to Universal Decimal classification number. In the annual summary, a number indicates the quarterly issue where a particular title was published, and where the complete bibliographic information can be located.

Lakhanpal, S. K., comp. **American Dissertations on Education in India: A Bibliography**. Saskatoon, Sask.: University of Saskatchewan, 1987. 48p. $6.00pa. ISBN 0-88880-181-5.

Doctoral research on various aspects of education in India that has been completed in American universities is documented for a seventy-nine-year period (1907-1985) in this unique bibliography. A total of 322 titles are included. Entries are arranged alphabetically by author's name; information in each includes complete dissertation title, name of the institution at which the doctoral degree was granted, date, and source of information. The research on Indian education was conducted at eighty different institutions, and a list of these schools with complete mailing addresses is provided. The bibliography concludes with a subject and keyword index.

Lauerhass, Ludwig, Jr., and Vera Oliveira de Araujo Haugse, comps. **Education in Latin America: A Bibliography**. Boston: G. K. Hall, 1980. 431p. (University of California Latin American Center Publications, Reference Series, Vol. 9). $57.50. LC 80-18702. ISBN 0-8161-8516-6.

Research on all aspects of education in countries of Latin America and the Caribbean would be facilitated by this extensive bibliography of 9,866 books, monographs, and pamphlets. Materials cover pre-Columbian history to the middle 1970s and were published over a 135-year period from 1839 to 1975. Emphasis is on the history, philosophy, and sociology of education in Brazil, Mexico, and Cuba, and on materials published in the last half of the twentieth century. Materials were identified from library catalogs (including Library of Congress subject catalogs), general and specialized bibliographies, national bibliographies, and specialized sources on Latin America. Each geographic subdivision (Latin America: General, Middle America and the Caribbean, Spanish South America, Brazil) begins with major serials and reference sources, followed by education in general, in-school and out-of-school programs, and educational planning and administration. Entries are not annotated; a name and title index concludes the work.

Mellor, Warren L., ed. **An Inventory of Documents on Educational Planning and Management in Asia and the Pacific. Volume 2**. Bangkok, Thailand: UNESCO Regional Office of Education in Asia and the Pacific; distr., Lanham, Md.: UNIPUB, 1987. 142p. $20.00pa. UB 176, UNESCO.

A total of 412 countries on educational planning and management in eighteen member countries of UNESCO located in Asia and the Pacific are contained in this compilation. It updates and expands the coverage of the first volume of 714 entries published in 1984. Entries are arranged geographically by country, with the exception of one major section which covers documents related to all countries in the region. The countries covered include Australia, Bangladesh, Burma, China, India, Indonesia, Iran, Japan, Republic of Korea, Malaysia, Nepal, New Zealand, Pakistan, Papua New Guinea, the Philippines, Sri Lanka, Thailand, and Vietnam. Entries within each section are arranged by a code number and provide information about author, title, publishers, and date of the document, number of pages, and indexing descriptors from the *UNESCO IBE Education Thesaurus*. Some brief annotations and subject and author indexes are provided.

Pantelidis, Veronica S. **Arab Education, 1956-1978: A Bibliography**. London: Mansell; distr., New York: H. W. Wilson, 1982. 552p. $96.00. ISBN 0-7201-1588-4.

Sources of information on education in twenty-one Arab countries (members of the Arab League) are included in this bibliography of books, journal articles, dissertations, papers, government documents, pamphlets, abstracts, and ERIC documents. All titles, with the exception of a few directories, are in English, and the purpose was to provide a comprehensive, as opposed to selective, compilation.

Information provided is not always consistent, as only items personally examined by the author have been annotated. In spite of this, this volume is an attractive, well-organized, and much needed work. Under each country division, subtopics are "Administration and Supervision," "Adult Education," "Associations," "Bibliographies," "Educational Technology," "Higher Education," "Human Resources Development," "Instructional Media," "Instructional Techniques," "Libraries," "Literacy," "Periodicals," "Religious Education," "Teacher Education," and many others. Under each subdivision entries are arranged in chronological order. A total of 5,653 titles are included in the work covering 1956 to 1978. A second volume extends the coverage another six years, *Arab Education, 1970-1984* (1982) by the same author and publisher.

Parker, Franklin, and Betty June Parker, eds. **American Dissertations on Foreign Education: A Bibliography with Abstracts**. Troy, N.Y.: Whitston, 1971-1987. 19v to date.

The volumes in this series provide bibliographical references to dissertations on public and private education in foreign countries. The entires are arranged alphabetically by author; most of the annotations consist of word-for-word summaries that appear in *Dissertation Abstracts International.* Other information includes dissertation title, university, date, number of pages, and type of doctorate (Ph.D., Ed.D., M.D.). Because the dissertations in each volume treat a variety of related subject areas, a thematic arrangement would facilitate use of these sources. The indexes provide access by subject, personal names, and geographic area. Although this information can be obtained in comprehensive dissertation indexes, these bibliographies provide convenient compilations for scholars in the fields of international or comparative education. Foreign education is treated in the following volumes: 1, *Canada* (1971, 175p., $9.50, ISBN 0-87875-013-4); 2, *India* (1972, 241p., $11.00, ISBN 0-87875-018-5); 3, *Japan* (1972, 173p. $9.50, ISBN 0-877875-035-5); 4, *Africa* (1973, 508p., $18.00, ISBN 0-87875-043-6); 5, *Scandinavia* (1974, 249p. $12.50, ISBN 0-87875-051-7); 6, *China, Peoples Republic of China (Mainland), Republic of China (Taiwan), Hong Kong, Far East* (1974, 969p. 2v., $40.00/set, ISBN 0-87875-052-5); 7, *Korea* (1974, 250p., $12.00, ISBN 0-87875-082-7); 8, *Mexico* (1976, 456p., $16.00, ISBN 0-87875-086-X); 9, *South America* (1977, 710p., $30.00, ISBN 0-87875-101-7); 10, *Central America* (1979, 3v., $38.50, ISBN 0-87875-133-5); 11, *Pakistan and Bangladesh* (1979, 372p., $24.00, ISBN 0-87875-150-5); 12, *Iran and Iraq* (1980, 425p., $28.50, ISBN 0-87-875-151-3); 13, *Israel* (1986, 464p., $32.00, ISBN 0-897875-152-1); 14, *Middle East: Arab Education, Bahrain, Jordan, Kuwait, Lebanon, Saudi Arabia, Syria* (1981, 496p., $35.00, ISBN 0-897875-239-0); 15, *Thailand* (1983, 929p., $58.00, ISBN 0-87875-264-1); 16, *Asia* (1986, 877p., $58.00, ISBN 0-87875-284-6); 17, *Pacific* (1986, 208p., $25.00, ISBN 0-87875-327-3); 18, *Philippines* (1986, 1,062p., 2v., $80.00, ISBN 0-87875-333-8); and 19, *Australia-New Zealand* (1987, 300p., $30.00, ISBN 0-87875-341-9).

Parker, Franklin, and Betty June Parker. **Education in the People's Republic of China, Past and Present: An Annotated Bibliography**. New York: Garland, 1986. 845p. (Reference Books in International Education, Vol. 2; Garland Reference Library in International Education, Vol. 281). $90.00. LC 84-48394. ISBN 0-8240-8797-6.

All aspects of education, public and private, formal and informal, in the People's Republic of China are covered in the 3,053 books, monographs, pamphlets, serials, published papers, and major newspaper accounts annotated in this bibliography. The work begins with an introduction to China and Chinese schools and education. Research libraries that have developed noteworthy collections on the topic are also listed.

Bibliography entries are arranged primarily by subject, with some chronological subdivisions. Entries include biographies of prominent Chinese educators. Materials on the cultural revolution, as well as those covering elementary to higher education, and education in the various disciplines are covered. Access is available through author and subject indexes.

Rust, Val D. **Education in East and West Germany: A Bibliography**. New York: Garland, 1984. 227p. (Reference Books in International Education, Vol. 1; Garland Reference Library of Social Science, Vol. 202). $35.00. LC 83-48216. ISBN 0-8240-9050-0.

Books, articles, published reports, and dissertations covering education in East and West Germany are described in this annotated bibliography. All materials included here are in the English language, but the emphasis is definitely on materials on the Federal Republic of Germany rather than the Germany behind the iron curtain, the German Democratic Republic.

Entries are listed in a topical organization. Annotations are based on personal reviews by the author. Coverage is provided for a period of slightly more than 100 years, from the 1880s to the 1980s. This bibliography is preceded by an introductory essay that provides historical, social, and economic settings for the items which cover these concerns, to some extent, but emphasize attitudes and practices related to education and schooling since World War II and the partitioning of Germany.

Tysse, Agnes, N., comp. **International Education: The American Experience. A Bibliography**. Metuchen, N.J.: Scarecrow Press, 1974-1977. 3v. in 2. 169p. LC 73-16429. ISBN 0-8108-0686-X.

This bibliography is arranged in three parts. The first covers theses and dissertations on all aspects of foreign study in the United States and Americans overseas as technicians, educators, and businessmen, as well as students. It provides information about 552 doctoral dissertations and 139 master's theses, including author's name, title, institution granting degree, date, Xerox University Microfilms order number, and an annotation consisting of excerpts from abstracts.

The second volume covers periodical literature as follows: *Part 1, General; Part 2, Area Studies and Indexes.*

Waggoner, Barbara Ashton, and George R. Waggoner. **Universities of the Caribbean Region—Struggles to Democratize: An Annotated Bibliography**. Boston: G. K. Hall, 1986. 310p. (A Reference Publication in Latin American Studies). $55.00. LC 85-21864. ISBN 0-81611-8159-4.

Education in the universities in Caribbean countries is the subject of this annotated bibliography. Entries are arranged geographically by country first, and then alphabetically by author. They include references to both published and unpublished items. Codes for locating materials in the library are indicated, and acronyms used are listed. An author index concludes the work.

HANDBOOKS AND YEARBOOKS

Althen, Gary. **The Handbook of Foreign Student Advising**. Yarmouth, Maine: Intercultural Press, 1984. 208p. $21.95. $16.95pa. LC 83-82532. ISBN 0-933662-53-X; 0-933662-55-6pa.

This handbook is aimed at academic counselors and faculty who advise foreign students studying at colleges and universities in the United States. Althen has had many years of involvement working with foreign students and intercultural programs. He outlines the pros and cons of international exchange programs and gives specific information on problems foreign students encounter and how to operate advising programs and services for them. Coverage is given to foreign students at both graduate and undergraduate levels.

Cameron, J., ed. **International Handbook of Education Systems.** Chicester, England, and New York: Wiley, 1983-84. 3v. $81.95(v.1); $81.95(v.2); $85.00(v.3). LC 82-17375. ISBN 0-471-90078-8(v.1); 0-471-90078-8(v.2); 0-471-90214-4(v.3).

These volumes describe educational systems in various countries of the world as follows: Volume 1, *Europe and Canada*; 2, *Africa and the Middle East*; and 3, *Asia, Australasia and Latin America*. Schools that follow a European system, such as Israel, are also included in the first volume. Information covers geographic and demographic information related to population, history, economy, politics, curricula, structure of education, and financial conditions. The United States, Great Britain, and the Soviet Union are not included since, according to the editor, they are covered in other publications.

Commonwealth Universities Yearbook: A Directory to the Universities of the Commonwealth and the Handbook of their Association. London: Association of Commonwealth Universities; distr., Detroit: Gale, 1914- . Annual. 4v. $185.00/set. LC 59-24175. ISSN 0069-7745.

This annual directory is now in its sixty-third year of publication. The 1987 edition includes almost 3,000 pages in four volumes. Arrangement is alphabetical by country sections (Australia, Bangladesh, Botswana, Britain, Brunei Darussalam, Canada, Ghana, Guyana, Hong Kong, India, Kenya, Lesotho, Malawi, Malaysia, Malta, Mauritius, New Zealand, Nigeria, Papua New Guinea, Sierra Leone, Singapore, South Pacific, Sri Lanka, Swaziland, Tanzania, Uganda, West Indies, Zambia, and Zimbabwe), with a chapter for each university. Most sections begin with an introductory article which provides an overview of the university system including such aspects as origins and development, structure, relationship to government, staff, and students. Six appendixes cover "The Association of Commonwealth Universities," "The Commonwealth Scholarship and Fellowship Plan," "National and Regional Inter-University Bodies," "Admission to Universities in Eight Commonwealth Countries," and "Students from Abroad in Certain Commonwealth Countries." A comprehensive index to all faculty and administrators listed, lists of abbreviations, and a twenty-eight page bibliography are also provided.

Goldstein, Amy J., and Andrew T. Rowan, eds. **Applying to Colleges and Universities in the United States 1988: A Handbook for International Students.** 3d ed. Princeton, N.J.: Peterson's Guides, 1987. 450p. $12.95pa. LC 85-3496. ISBN 0-87866-572-2.

International students who wish to study in the United States can consult this handbook. It opens with a detailed essay covering all steps in the admissions process, including legal procedures for obtaining a student visa and entry into the United States. A glossary of terms is also included. The directory section provides brief profiles of 3,300 colleges and universities with information on location; type of school; costs for room, board and tuition; entrance requirements; number and composition of current international student enrollment; and an official person to contact for application to admission. A directory of majors identifies which schools offer degrees in particular majors. Appendix material lists schools with programs in English as a second language and data on two-year associate degree or community colleges.

Higher Education in the United Kingdom 1987-89: A Handbook for Students and their Advisors. 21st ed. New York: Longman, for Association of Commonwealth Universities; distr., Phoenix, Ariz.: Oryx Press, 1987. 271p. $30.00pa. ISBN 0-582-90157-X. ISSN 0306-1744.

This handbook was designed for students outside of Great Britain who wish to identify programs of advanced study offered in the United Kingdom. The book begins with an index of main subject headings, some information about the British university system, courses available, the admission of overseas students and student life. The actual directory is arranged alphabetically by subject identifying schools that award degrees in various aspects of the subject, the types of courses, program length, research facilities, entrance requirements, fees, and so on. Although much of this information can be found in the *Commonwealth Universities Yearbook*, some descriptions are expanded upon in this guide to students considering education abroad.

Additional information includes British Council Offices in Britain, overseas student offices, and a bibliography of additional information. The index provides subject access.

International Handbook of Universities: And Other Institutions of Higher Education. 10th ed. Edited by D. J. Aitken and Ann C. M. Taylor. London: Macmillan for the International Association of Universities; New York: Stockton Press, 1986. 1,300p. $140.00. LC 86-5027. ISBN 0-935859-04-7.

International Handbook of Universities describes over 7,000 institutions in 115 countries and territories with entries arranged first alphabetically by country and then in two main groups: universities (including technical universities) and other institutions of higher education. Institution name, address, faculty, departments, institutes, schools and colleges, history and structure of the institution, admission, degree and diploma requirements, duration of studies, language of instruction, library collection size, enrollment, and so on, are provided. (Information relates to the previous academic year.)

The language of the country is used to describe the names of degrees, diplomas, and professional qualifications, and also when indicating respective titles of academic staff members. When university names are given in the native tongue, English translations are provided. Two additional universities, United Nations University (Tokyo) and The European University Institute (Florence, Italy), are described at the conclusion of the list by countries.

The appendix contains information on the International Association of Universities. Institution names are arranged alphabetically in the index with geographic location also indicated.

This reference work was not designed to be a comprehensive universal worldwide listing, but was first published in 1959 as a companion volume to *The Commonwealth Universities Yearbook* (Association of Commonwealth Universities) and *American Universities and Colleges* (Washington, D.C.: American Council on Education). It is, however, a very important and authoritative source of information about the ever-continuing expansion and restructuring of systems of higher education in all parts of the world which are not covered in other sources. The tenth edition provides greatly expanded coverage to schools in many countries, particularly, for example, in the People's Republic of China.

International Yearbook of Education, 1986: Primary Education on the Threshold of the Twenty-First Century. V.38. Edited by Jose R. Ganew Barrido. Paris: United Nations Educational, Scientific, and Cultural Organization (UNESCO); distr., New York: Bernan-UNIPUB, 1987. 276p. $13.50pa. LC 49-48323. ISBN 92-3-102-448-5.

This yearbook assumed the volume number of its predecessor, *Annuaire international de l'education et de l'enseignement*, published for ten years from 1933 to 1940 and 1945 to 1947. It was then issued jointly by UNESCO and the International Bureau of Education from 1948 to 1969. After the IBE became a part of UNESCO in 1969, the publication was suspended (with volume 31) until it resumed with volume 32 in 1980.

The yearbook represents a compilation of member nation reports and profiles arranged alphabetically by countries. They provide information on current educational trends, conditions and recent developments in UN member states. Statistical tables give demographic and other data related to names and addresses of ministers of education, curricula, finances, administration, and teacher education. The thirty-eighth volume is devoted to primary education.

Regional Education Profile: Central America. New York: Institute of International Education, 1986. 169p. free. pa.

Education in Central America, including an essay summarizing trends and developments in higher education in the 1985-1986 academic year, is profiled in this handbook. Information is organized geographically with a chapter devoted to each individual country of Central America. Countries covered include Belize, Costa Rica, El Salvador, Guatemala, Honduras, Nicaragua, and Panama.

The educational systems of each country are described, covering education from preschool through higher education, including descriptions of the major colleges and universities. A graph in each country section illustrates the educational organizational structure. Another feature is a glossary of terms related to Central American education.

World Yearbook of Education. London: Kogan Page; New York: Nichols, 1932- . Annual. $35.00. LC 32-18413. ISSN 0084-2508.

This yearbook is international in scope, summarizing perspectives and practices on a range of issues in education. Each year the volume is devoted to a particular theme of international interest. The 1987 volume is *Vocational Education*, edited by John Twining; the focus of the 1986 volume, subtitled *The Management of Schools*, edited by Eric Hoyle and Agnes McMahon, is on describing developments in collaboration of practitioners (teachers and principals) with their more theoretically oriented colleagues and professional peers in the management of change in schools, as well as the interaction of organizational theories and management theories as it affects practice. Other recent titles in the series include *Research, Policy, and Practice* (1985), a summary of educational research in fifteen countries (or people groups); *Women and Education* (1984); *Computers in Education* (1982/83); and *Education of Minorities* (1981). This annual was first published in 1931 and was known as *The Year Book of Education*. (Publication was suspended from 1941 to 1947 during the World War II years.) Editors and publishers varied prior to 1979 when the present companies resumed publication on an annual basis.

The articles are well written and concise. Most of them are signed, and have been prepared by experts in the field of study. Case studies are often included when appropriate. The series provides the researcher with a documented record of major areas of concern to educators on a worldwide basis.

DIRECTORIES

Academic Year Abroad. Edited by Edrice Howard. New York: Institute of International Education, 1964- . Annual (The Learning Traveler, Vol. 1). $19.95. ISSN 0196-6251.

This directory to undergraduate study abroad in U.S. college-sponsored programs was first issued in 1964 as a report of the Consultative Service on U.S. Undergraduate Study Abroad. Early editions were published under the titles *Undergraduate Study Abroad* and *The Learning Traveler: U.S. College-Sponsored Programs Abroad: Academic Year*. The latter was continued in 1987 by the present title.

The intent of this directory is to make students aware of programs sponsored by recognized colleges and universities in the United States. All programs offer academic credit that can be transferred to U.S. schools, at their individual discretion. Programs not sponsored by degree-granting institutions are not included, nor are interim session programs. (The latter are usually taught by faculty members from U.S. institutions who are travelling with a group of students.) Programs included fall into one of three categories: (1) A program combines study in a foreign institution with courses arranged for a specific group, (2) a program is fully integrated into a foreign academic institution, and (3) an "island" program offers courses taught by faculty members from the sponsoring U.S. school and the foreign country.

Bajkai, Louis A., comp. and ed., and Connie L. Bonne, asst. ed. **Teachers' Guide to Overseas Teaching: A Complete and Comprehensive Guide of English-Language Schools and Colleges Overseas**. 3d rev. ed. San Diego, Calif.: Friends of World Teaching, 1983. 192p. $19.95. ISBN 0-9601550-2-3.

This directory to English-language schools and colleges around the world is intended to help teachers, administrators, and other personnel who are interested in working in an overseas position. It also provides information about agencies and organizations that might be of assistance in obtaining a job: directors of international teacher recruitment, offices of international programs, placement specialists, and international corporations, among many others. In addition, foreign diplomatic representatives and their embassy office addresses are also provided. This ov • rseas directory was first published in 1977 and revised for the second time in 1979. The third edition is a major update and revision of previous volumes.

British Qualifications: A Comprehensive Guide to Educational, Technical, Professional and Academic Qualifications in Britain. London: Kogan Page; New York: Nichols, 1966- . Annual. $52.50. ISSN 0141-5972.

This guide attempts to help the user understand the structure of education in England, Scotland, Wales, and Ireland and the qualifications for study at various levels in the British system. Part 1 provides basic information about the organization of education; part 2 covers nonvocational secondary school examinations, and part 3 covers technical, business, and management examinations. Part 4 lists all British universities and polytechnics and the certificates, degrees, or diplomas they award. Part 5 lists professional associations and qualifications for membership, part 6 covers the qualifications for individual trades or professions, and part 7 lists accrediting agencies and accredited institutions. An index concludes the work.

Directory of National Centres Associated with APEID. Bangkok, Thailand: UNESCO; distr., New York: UNIPUB, 1984. 260p. $10.50.

This directory covers approximately 125 institutions associated with APEID (The Asian Programme of Educational Innovation for Development). As a UNESCO program with twenty-two member states represented, the purpose of APEID is to promote the ability of individual member nations to develop their countries through educational innovation and exchange of expert personnel among member states. Activities proposed by APEID are typically organized and carried out through these associate institutions or centers, and this directory identifies the goals and functions, projects, major departments, research investigations (past, present, and future), staff members, publications, affiliations, and innovative educational programs of each center. The work is not indexed, but the detailed table of contents is in alphabetical order by country and, if consulted carefully, can lead the user to appropriate information.

Directory of National Institutions of Educational Planning and Administration in Asia and the Pacific. Bangkok, Thailand: UNESCO Regional Office for Education in Asia and the Pacific; distr., New York: UNIPUB, 1987. 72p. $7.50pa. UB 175 5111, UNESCO.

The institutions listed in this directory have programs of inservice training in educational planning and administration. These twenty-three colleges and other national institutions are located in Australia, Bangladesh, India, Malaysia, Nepal, New Zealand, Pakistan, the Philippines, the Republic of Korea, Sri Lanka, and Thailand. Information provided for each institution includes name, address, telephone number or cable code, chief administrator, date of establishment, parent organization, staff, facilities (including libraries), language of instruction and other languages used, historical background, objectives or purposes, training programs, and research in progress, projected or already completed.

Directory of the European Council of International Schools. Petersfield, England: European Council of International Schools; distr., Princeton, N.J. Peterson's Guides, 1987. 467p. $12.95pa. ISBN 0-905115-20-1. ISSN 0307-9430.

Over 750 international schools are listed in this directory to independent primary and secondary schools in Europe and other parts of the world that are members of ECIS (European Council of International Schools). A total of sixty-seven countries are represented. In the first section 146 lengthy (one-page) entries describe European schools arranged first by country, then by city. Information in each entry includes name of school, address, telephone and telex numbers, type of ECIS membership, headmaster/principal, information about composition of faculty, age range of students, grades available, enrollment, student body, school year calendar, physical facilities, admission requirements, accreditation, and other extracurricular activities. The second section lists ninety-six non-European schools, followed by 212 associate member colleges. Almost all (about 90 percent) of the postsecondary institutions are located in the United States. Other sections cover affiliate members and institutions that provide specialized instruction and services (business education, reading, etc.). There is a geographical index to all international schools listing schools alphabetically by country.

Fellowships, Scholarships, and Related Opportunities in International Education. Compiled by the University of Tennessee. Knoxville: Center for International Education, University of Tennessee, 1977- . Annual. $8.00pa. ISSN 0735-8830.

Scholars who are interested in studying abroad will find 151 opportunities for furthering their education in an international setting. Scholarships and fellowships are available in a wide variety of curricular areas, and information about them is arranged alphabetically by sponsoring organization, foundations, and so on. Each entry provides information about the subject field, country where study opportunities are available, eligibility requirements, amount of stipend, application deadlines and procedures, and address. An "Area of Study Index" provides access by fields of study (with a number that indicates the number of scholarship opportunities available). Geographical access would also be helpful.

Hoopes, David S., ed., and Kathleen R. Hoopes, asst. ed. **Global Guide to International Education**. New York: Facts on File, 1984. 704p. $95.00. LC 82-1545. ISBN 0-87196-437-6.

Organizations, academic programs, publications, and other sources of information related to international education are found in this directory-type sourcebook. Contents are arranged in eighteen chapters, and cover a wide range of international studies and programs, including those on peace and conflict resolution; professional education (agriculture, health, business, education, journalism, law, library science, public administration); world areas (Africa, Asia and Pacific, Eastern Europe, Western Europe, Latin America, Middle East); and approximately 185 individual countries.

Coverage is also given to international affairs; cultural relations and world issues; elementary, secondary, and undergraduate international/intercultural studies and global education; educational exchange organizations; international studies programs and research centers; grants, awards, and fellowships for international studies and programs; foreign language learning; English as a second language; and publishers and distributors of books on world area studies. Jewish studies programs were considered as religious or ethnic studies, and receive only limited attention.

Howard, Edrice, ed. **Specialized Study Options U.S.A., 1986-1988: A Guide to Short-term Educational Programs in the United States for Foreign Nationals**. 2d ed. New York: Institute of International Education, 1986. 2v. $19.95pa. ISBN 0-87206-140-X(v.1); 0-87206-141-8(v.2).

Short-term programs of study in U.S. institutions of higher education open to international students, or those who are not U.S. citizens, are described in this directory. Programs covered run from two weeks in length to a year, with emphasis on professional courses of study or technical training and are arranged in two volumes. Volume 1 lists programs that have a high school diploma as a prerequisite. Programs in volume 2 require at least a two-year associate's degree or a baccalaureate. The emphasis is on business and technical programs, including courses in technical English, but all subjects and disciplines are represented. Entries are organized alphabetically within field of study and include information about program specialization, dates, eligibility, and instructional methodologies, costs, application, and contact person's name, address, and telephone number.

Howard, Edrice, ed. **Study in the United Kingdom and Ireland, 1988/89: an IIE Guide to Study Abroad**. New York: Institute of International Education, 1988. $14.95pa. ISBN 0-87206-157-4.

Programs of study in Britain and Ireland are identified for students who want to study in these countries as exchange students. A total of 557 programs are described, and individual entries describe the type of program offered, costs for education and living expenses, and contacts to make and steps to take in applying for study in the United Kingdom and Ireland. The majority of programs described are in England.

International Guide to Qualifications in Education. National Equivalence Information Centre of the British Council. London: Mansell; distr., New York: H. W. Wilson, 1984. 675p. $90.00. LC 84-17083. ISBN 0-07201-1716-X.

The educational systems of 141 countries are covered in this reference source which is arranged alphabetically by country. Coverage is given to all levels of education from primary to postgraduate, and to the education and training of prospective teachers for all types of education, including teachers and instruction in technical and vocational programs. Various educational certificates are defined and qualifications required for various steps in the British educational system are described, as well as means of evaluating educational progress in European and other countries, allowing equivalency comparisons to be made. Even though this is a very comprehensive work, the price might keep many libraries from buying it.

The ISS Directory of Overseas Schools. Edited by Elisabeth Hagen. Princeton, N.J.: International Schools Services, 1981- . Annual. $25.00.

International Schools Services gathers information via questionnaire from approximately sixty overseas schools ranging from the prekindergarten to the baccalaureate level. The seventh (1987-1988) edition maintains the same format as previous editions, but has expanded its coverage with a number of new schools added. All schools included offer instruction in the English language. Arrangement is alphabetical, first by country, then city, and then by school name. Entries are one-half to one page in length and provide school name, address, phone, date founded, academic head, grade levels, staff and faculty, enrollment, tuition, school year calendar, curriculum, and physical features. The directory also includes a series of maps for identifying the locations of the overseas schools, lists of schools offering the International Baccalaureate program, boarding schools, accrediting associations, and special examinations. The work is indexed. This title continues *Directory of Overseas Schools*.

Learning Vacations. 5th ed. Edited by Gerson G. Eisenberg. Princeton, N.J.: Peterson's Guides, 1986. 249p. $9.95pa. LC 85-25444. ISBN 0-87866-535-6.

A wide variety of educational experiences that can be perused on vacation periods include college seminars, conference centers, educational travel tours, folk festivals, wilderness workshops, and archaeological excavations. The objectives range from those that are strictly academic to those that are primarily social and recreational.

Entries are arranged topically and geographically first, and then alphabetically. Information included covers name, address, contact person, program costs, housing accommodations, restrictions, recreational facilities, and other pertinent information. Over 500 learning vacation opportunities are covered in this edition. Sponsor and geographical indexes are provided.

O'Driscoll, James E., with James I. Bauer. **English Language and Orientation Programs in the United States**. New York: Institute of International Education, 1984. 160p. $8.95pa. LC 78-101308. ISBN 0-87206-126-4.

This directory is aimed at international or exchange students studying in the United States, as well as their academic advisers and librarians. It lists academic programs in junior colleges, colleges, universities, and other institutions in English-language training, and other orientation courses and activities. Programs and courses can be accessed by program title or by state. The objective of the Institute of International Education is to provide detailed information about the services and opportunities offered to help foreign students overcome language handicaps and problems related to cultural differences. Each program/course description includes name and address of the institution, program content, level, admission requirements, costs, available housing, and dates of program. This compilation is not only very useful to international students and their families, but also to new immigrants, U.S. embassy offices, and agencies serving individuals involved in cultural exchange.

Overseas Employment Opportunities for Educators: Department of Defense Dependents Schools. Alexandria, Va.: Department of Defense, Overseas Dependents Schools, 1967- . Annual. $5.00. LC 83-7923.

The 1986-1987 school year edition of this annual government publication provides information about teaching and other positions available in approximately 270 elementary and secondary schools on U.S. military bases overseas. These schools, for the children of military and civilian personnel with overseas assignments, are situated in twenty different countries and require about 11,000 employees. Recruitment procedures, qualification requirements, and application procedures for prospective employment in the overseas school system are detailed in this publication.

Packwood, Virginia M., and William T. Packwood. **Admission Requirements for International Students at Colleges and Universities in the United States**. Fargo, N. Dak.: Two Trees Press, 1986. 292p. $22.95pa. LC 85-20852. ISBN 0-935725-67-9.

International students who are interested in enrolling in a U.S. institution of higher education would find this an important college guide. The Packwoods surveyed approximately 2,000 colleges and universities with items on the questionnaire requesting information of particular relevance to foreign students. For example, entries in the directory indicate minimum TOEFL and grade point average requirements, number of international students typically accepted, graduate and undergraduate study opportunities available, and detailed admission requirements and procedures.

Since the authors indicate that some schools did not return the questionnaires, it is obvious that there are schools that have high international student enrollments that are not included in this directory.

Ruble, Blair A., and Mark H. Teeter, eds. **A Scholar's Guide to Humanities and Social Sciences in the Soviet Union: The Academy of Sciences of the USSR and the Academies of Sciences of the Union Republics**. Armonk, N.Y.: M. E. Sharpe, 1985. 310p. $75.00. LC 85-12002. ISBN 0-87332-335-1.

This directory describes 217 institutions in the USSR, including the Academy of Sciences of the USSR, the Academies of Sciences of the Union Republics, and scientific councils and interinstitutional agencies. Information in each entry includes the name, address, and telephone number of the institution; date of establishment; background of the institution; staff; objectives; type of research conducted; facilities; areas of cooperation; and publications. Compilation of the directory was undertaken by the Institute of Scientific Information in the Social Sciences of the USSR Academy of Sciences, and is a unique work of this type available in the English language.

Scholarships for International Students: A Complete Guide to United States Colleges and Universities, 1986-1988. Edited by Anna J. Leider. Alexandria, Va.: Octameron Press, 1986. 271p. $14.95pa. ISBN 0-917760-84-0.

This college guide is aimed at international students who are interested in obtaining financial scholarships to study at an American college or university. Information provided takes the reader from the school selection process, through the application and admission process, to determining the most appropriate course of study. A glossary of terms associated with higher education is also helpful to the foreign student.

One section discusses opportunities for financial aid; others contain information about visas and immigration-related issues, studying English as a second language, helpful explanations of American customs and culture, physical geography and climate ranges, housing, and other aspects of campus life. Schools are listed alphabetically by state and entries include brief standard demographic information.

Schools Abroad of Interest to Americans. 6th ed. Boston: Porter Sargent, 1985. 539p. $29.00. LC 67-18844. ISBN 0-87558-111-0.

Over 1,100 private elementary and secondary schools outside of the United States are described. The emphasis is on schools that provide English-language instruction and on those that are interested in, or have a history of, enrolling American students. School profiles are arranged alphabetically by country in major geographic subdivisions of the world. Entries contain school name, address, telephone number, grade levels, director or other head, curriculum, languages of instruction, enrollment, faculty, tuition, summer sessions, and date established. A brief narrative provides information about other features available at the school or in the surrounding community.

Other information includes lists of postsecondary schools abroad, international education associations and consultants, and a school advertising section of announcements. Although the publishers only describe, rather than comparatively evaluate schools, this is still a valuable introduction to K-12 educational programs available overseas.

The Students' Guide to Graduate Studies in the UK. Cambridge, England: Hobsons Cambridge, 1983- . Annual. $75.00pa. LC 86-16689.

The 1988 edition of this guide covers 559 pages of graduate study opportunities available throughout the United Kingdom. The major part of the work is the section entitled "Research Facilities and Courses," which is subdivided by curricular areas: "Humanities and Social Sciences"; "Biological, Health and Agricultural Sciences"; "Physical Sciences and Engineering"; and "Applied Sciences." Individual subjects can be located under these broad categories.

Prefatory material is aimed at graduate students in the United Kingdom who are from overseas and it attempts to explain the structure, quality, and diversity of education from one department and/or one institution to the next; prospects for admission; degrees awarded; and costs and scholarships. It continues *Students' Graduate Studies Guide: The Guide to Postgraduate Study in the UK* with the 1985 edition.

Study Abroad. Paris: UNESCO; New York: UNIPUB, 1948- . Biennial. $9.95pa. ISSN 0081-895X.

The purpose of this biennial directory is to promote crosscultural interchanges through international educational exchange opportunities. It lists approximately 3,700 international study programs available in all disciplines and professional fields in institutions in more than 125 countries throughout the world. Many of the scholarships offered by these international study programs are cosponsored by UNESCO and information is applicable for academic years 1986 to 1988.

Information describing the scholarships and courses of study is included in English, Spanish, and French, depending on the official language of the correspondence in use by UNESCO with each country. Arrangement is in two major parts. In part 1, scholarships are grouped by discipline first, and then alphabetically by organization. Courses of study are alphabetical by name of organization. Part 2 lists national scholarships and courses in alphabetical order with a chapter for each country. Each chapter has an introductory section for prospective international student visitors, followed by the scholarships and courses in alphabetical order.

Each entry provides information related to name and address of sponsoring institution, degree programs offered, eligibility, duration, scholarships or financial aid, fees, application procedure, and language of instruction. This conveniently arranged and easy-to-use guide was an annual publication for the first fourteen volumes, but became a biennial publication with the fifteenth volume.

Tanlak, Acar, and Ahmed Lajimi. **International Directory of Islamic Cultural Institutions**. Istanbul, Turkey: Research Centre for Islamic History, Art and Culture: distr., New York: Routledge & Kegan Paul/Methuen, 1987, c1984. 337p. LC 85-180373. ISBN 0-7103-0201-0.

Universities and other educational institutions, as well as research centers, libraries, archives, and museums in 106 countries that belong to the Islamic Conference, are listed in this directory. A total of 3,579 cultural institutions are included with entries arranged in categories related to institution type (e.g., academy, research center, university) and by country. Information in each entry includes name of the Islamic cultural institution, location, with translations and/or transliterations provided. Scholars interested in any aspect of Islamic studies or Middle Eastern history and culture would be able to identify formal courses of study in such university departments (or in humanities departments) and would find this a very useful source of information.

Teaching Abroad. Edited by Barbara Cahn Connotillo. New York: Institute of International Education, 1973- . Annual (The Learning Traveler, Vol. 3). $11.95. LC 73-84970. ISSN 0903-049X.

Programs of government agencies and international organizations that make possible opportunities for teachers, administrators, and other educational personnel to teach abroad are described in this directory. Programs are listed in geographical sections and, for each program, a short overview is given with information related to the nature and number of positions available, locations of institutions soliciting teachers from the United States, educational requirements and eligibility, salaries and benefits, language of instruction, availability of housing, and period of assignment. Some coverage is given to international teacher exchange programs. A bibliography of employment directories and source materials is included. U.S. embassies are listed in the appendix.

Vacation Study Abroad. New York: Institute of International Education, 1948- . Annual (The Learning Traveler, Vol. 2). $9.95. LC 80-647933. ISSN 0271-1702.

Over 800 programs offering summer or short-term vacation study sponsored by organizations and accredited institutions of higher education in the United States, as well as foreign countries abroad, are described in this second volume in *The Learning Traveler*

Series. Formerly published as *Summer Study Abroad*, the purpose of this volume is to identify, for prospective college students, undergraduate students, graduate students, and professionals who wish to study abroad, course offerings made available between late spring and early fall. Entries are arranged geographically by region, country and city, but indexes provide access by sponsoring institution and by field of study.

Webster, Steve. **Teach Overseas: The Educator's World-wide Handbook and Directory to International Teaching in Overseas Schools, Colleges, and Universities**. New York: Maple Tree Publishing, 1984. 420p. $12.95pa. LC 83-23866. ISBN 0-915387-01-8.

Teachers and administrators who wish to work abroad can consult this directory to international teaching opportunities in overseas academic settings. Schools from elementary to postgraduate levels are described, with emphasis on programs for English-speaking professionals. Schools are arranged geographically by country and each entry provides information about the country, major cities, population, historical background, language spoken, and addresses of individual schools, colleges, and universities. Major government and professional associations helpful in locating positions (e.g., embassies, ministries of education) are also listed. Introductory material provides an overview of expectations related to teaching abroad, discussing types of educational settings, living conditions, and other relevant considerations.

Wiprud, Helen R., comp. **International Education Programs of the U.S. Government: An Inventory**. Washington, D.C.: U.S. Department of Education, Federal Inter-agency Committee on Education, 1981. xii, 401p. $8.50. LC 81-601981. S/N 052-003-00795-9.

A total of 181 international educational programs sponsored by federal government departments or agencies are briefly described. Information for the directory was compiled from a survey conducted by USOE (U.S. Office of Education) through a special FICE (Federal Interagency Committee on Education) Task Force on International Education. In their inventory, a program was considered an "international education" program if "it fosters understanding and/or cooperation between the United States and another country or other countries through education" (p. 1).

Programs are arranged numerically by agencies which are listed alphabetically, and each program description includes program number, title, explanation of how it furthers international cooperation or understanding; basic information (name, address, and telephone number of the unit administering the program, and its location or place within the agency as a whole); type of program; legislation (authorizing act and date); funding source and amount; statistics; and descriptive publications available from the agency.

World List of Universities, Other Institutions of Higher Education and University Organizations. Edited by H. M. R. Keyes and D. J. Aitken. New York: Stockton Press, 1952- . Biennial. $70.00. LC 79-645502. ISSN 0084-1889.

This worldwide directory to schools of selected countries is a bilingual work published in English and French. Schools are arranged by country and by type of institution (e.g., university or technical school). Information in each entry includes the name of the institution, address, date of establishment, university college or school divisions, and contact officials. Whether or not an institution is a member of the International Association of Universities is also indicated. Organizations related to higher education, including UNESCO, are listed by country.

World of Learning. London: Europa Publications, 1947- . Annual. $190.00. LC 47-30172. ISSN 0084-2117.

Academic institutions including academies, learned societies, research institutes, libraries and archives, museums and art galleries, and colleges and universities are described in this international directory. The thirty-seventh (1987) edition includes about seventy new universities and other institutions of higher education that did not appear in earlier volumes. Added coverage was also given to developing countries with new chapters on Republic of The Gambia, Maldives, and Tonga. An international section covers international educational, scientific, and cultural organizations (including UNESCO, its functions and member states). The main body of the directory follows with entries arranged alphabetically by country (subdivided by states). Information in each entry includes name of institution/organization, telephone number, founding date, objectives or purpose, languages of instruction, academic year, names of officials, faculty, students, departments, selected affiliates, publications, and other pertinent information. The work concludes with a 105-page "Index of Institutions" that lists close to 25,000 names.

STATISTICS SOURCES

Open Doors: Report on International Education Exchange. New York: Institute of International Education, 1949- . Annual. $29.95pa. ISSN 0078-5172.

The Institute of International Education has a census division which compiles and reports data on foreign students and educational exchange between the United States and other countries. The type of information covered in *Open Doors* includes the number of foreign students enrolled in United States colleges and universities, their native countries (proportions from each), distribution in the United States, percentage of students holding immigrant visas, students in two-year programs, length of students' stay and intent to remain in the United States, sources of support, male/female ratios, and fields of academic study. Some data also cover U.S. faculty teaching abroad.

Profiles: Detailed Analyses of the Foreign Student Population. New York: Institute of International Education, 1981- . Annual. $29.95pa. ISBN 0-87206-134-5.

This is a companion volume to the institute's publication, *Open Doors*, which provides annual census data on the foreign student population studying in American colleges and universities. *Profiles* gives more detailed information and analyzes foreign student enrollment by country of origin (e.g., how many students from a particular country are undertaking course work in a particular field of study) and gender composition.

17
Women's Studies and Feminist Education Reference Sources

GUIDES

Guide to Nonsexist Teaching Activities (K-12). Developed by Northwest Educational Laboratory Center for Sex Equity. Phoenix, Ariz.: Oryx Press, 1983. 99p. $27.00. LC 83-42515. ISBN 0-89774-100-5.

Classroom teachers who want to become familiar with lesson plans, teaching activities, and resources that have been identified as nonsexist can consult this guide. Information is organized in eight sections: (1) "General Awareness," (2) "Counseling and Career Guidance," (3) "Fine Arts," (4) "Health and Physical Education," (5) "Language Arts," (6) "Math and Science," (7) "Social Studies," and (8) "Sex Equity Organizations." Each subject area is subdivided into lesson plans, course outlines, and instructional resources, such as textbooks, periodicals, and multimedia and other audiovisual packages. In addition, there are bibliographies and other references which identify further resources. Items listed have a brief annotation and an indication of the grade level for which they are most appropriate. Other features include a model for developing equitable or nonsexist lesson plans, guidelines for instruction, and directions for obtaining materials described. A title index is included.

Wilkins, Kay S. **Women's Education in the United States: A Guide to Information Sources.** Detroit: Gale, 1979. 217p. (Education Information Guide Series, Vol. 4; Gale Information Guide Library). $65.00. LC 79-54691. ISBN 0-8103-1410-X.

Approximately 1,100 reference sources, general works, and periodical titles concerned with the education of girls and women in the United States are described in this guide. Materials are arranged by subject (e.g., historical accounts, education in the various professions, women's colleges) and each entry gives a complete bibliographic description and a brief annotation.

A related compilation is Esther Stineman and Catherine Loeb's *Women's Studies: A Recommended Core Bibliography* (Libraries Unlimited, 1979).

BIBLIOGRAPHIES

Bibliography of Nonsexist Supplementary Books (K-12). Northwest Regional Educational Laboratory Center for Sex Equity. Phoenix, Ariz.: Oryx Press, 1984. 108p. $27.00pa. LC 83-42838. ISBN 0-89774-101-3.

Developed by the Center for Sex Equity Programs at the Northwest Regional Educational Laboratory, the purpose of this bibliography is to allow educators to choose materials that present an image of girls and women that is not sex biased. They also portray them in a wide variety of careers and settings and with a wide range of interests and abilities. The work was first published as *BIAS (Building Instruction around Sex Equity: Bibliography of Non-Sexist Supplementary Books (K-12)* (Northwest Regional Educational Laboratory, 1982).

Some 595 titles are organized by reading level for grades 1 through 12. At each grade level section, the formula used to determine readability level is also provided. Each book is assigned an identification number, the first digit of which indicates readability level. Each entry includes complete bibliographic data and a brief annotation which summarizes the book and indicates the audience level for which it would be most appropriate. Appendix 1, "Resource Bibliographies," consists of lists of materials on sexism and women; appendix 2, "Analysis Procedures," includes a copy of the "Career, Race and Sex Bias Analysis Form" used in selection of books for inclusion in the bibliography. Appendix 3 is concerned with readability, and appendix 4 covers subject definitions. Title, author, and subject indexes conclude the work.

Chapman, Anne, comp., and ed. **Feminist Resources for Schools & Colleges: A Guide to Curricular Materials**. 3d ed. Old Westbury, N.Y.: Feminist Press, 1986. 190p. $12.95pa. LC 85-10110. ISBN 0-935312-35-8.

Curricular materials deemed free of sexual bias and discrimination are included in this list of print and nonprint resources appropriate for high school and college level. Various traditional subject areas plus women's studies and related topics, such as gender roles, and/or minority women are covered. Of the 445 entries, 310 are devoted to reference works, books and periodical articles; the remaining 135 are filmstrips, videos, films, sound recordings, slides, and other audiovisual programs.

Entries are arranged alphabetically by author in subject categories, and then by educational level. Attention is given to women's rights and legal issues related to women's studies, model programs, sex roles and sex-role socialization, women and career education, and others. An author/title and a subject index conclude the work.

Feinberg, Renee. **Women, Education and Employment: A Bibliography of Periodical Citations, Pamphlets, Newspapers, and Government Documents, 1970-1980**. Hamden, Conn.: Library Professional Publications, c1982. 274p. $27.50. LC 82-7816. ISBN 0-208-01967-7.

Opportunities in education and employment for women, with emphases on trends, policies, and programs are covered in this bibliography of references to the periodical literature from 1970 to 1980. Citations are limited to journal articles, pamphlets, newspaper items, government documents, and ERIC documents. Major databases and indexes were searched for all issues related to women, education, and employment. Topics in education address the educational status of women at all levels from K-12 to graduate study and professional schools, educational achievement, sex-role stereotyping, vocational and career training, vocational counseling, legal aspects and regulations, and women in specific categories, such as sports and physical education, returning women, rural women, gifted women, and minorities. Entries are not annotated, but educators studying patterns and trends in education of and for women will find this compilation very useful. A related title is *Women in Higher Education: A Contemporary Bibliography* by Kathryn W. Moore (National Association of Women Deans, Administrators and Counselors, 1979).

Parker, Franklin, and Betty June Parker, comps. and eds. **Women's Education – A World View: Annotated Bibliography of Books and Reports, Vol. 2**. Westport, Conn.: Greenwood, 1982. 689p. $39.95. LC 78-73791. ISBN 0-313-23206-7.

The second volume of this bibliography covers 3,942 books and reports on all aspects of education related to girls and women. It is international in scope. The Parkers examined resources in the major libraries of Washington, D.C., New York City, and London, as well as documents in the ERIC system, and made computer searches of major data bases to identify the items contained in them. Entries are arranged alphabetically by author, with comprehensive subject indexes provided in this volume, and volume 1. *Women's Education – A World View: Annotated Bibliography of Doctoral Dissertations* (Greenwood, 1979) which covers doctoral dissertations in the English language located in the United States and Canada. Related topics covered include feminism and the feminist and women's movement, suffrage, women's studies, and females in traditional or liberal arts education, as well as women in nursing, home economics education, physical education, vocational guidance, and career education.

INDEXES AND ABSTRACTS

Women Studies Abstracts. Rush, N.Y.: Rush Publishing, 1972- . Quarterly. $43.00/yr., individuals; $84.00/yr., institutions. ISSN 0049-7835.

This quarterly abstracting service covers all journal articles, reports, and papers published on issues related to women and the study of women. It is indexed annually; all fourth issues include the annual index. Abstract entries are arranged by subject, some of which include special issues and publications; education and socialization; sex roles, sex characteristics, differences, and similarities; society and government; literature and art; Women's Liberation Movement; and biography and criticism. Each entry includes a complete bibliographic citation and, in most cases, an abstract of approximately 100 to 200 words. Many of the latter have the indication *Journal Abstract* meaning they were provided by the periodical in which the articles were published.

HANDBOOKS AND YEARBOOKS

Beere, Carole A. **Women and Women's Issues: A Handbook of Tests and Measures**. San Francisco: Jossey-Bass, 1979. 550p. (Jossey-Bass Social and Behavioral Science Series). $45.00. LC 79-88106. ISBN 0-87589-418-6.

A compilation of 235 assessment instruments used in research regarding women and women's issues are contained in this handbook. Two chapters explain how the handbook is organized and discuss problems of measurement; eleven chapters describe instruments in a particular category. Tests are arranged alphabetically in the following subject categories: sex roles, sex stereotypes, sex-role prescriptions, children's sex roles, gender knowledge, marital and parental roles, employee roles, multiple roles, attitudes toward women's issues, somatic and sexual issues, and unclassified.

Entries include instrument number (sequence in book); title; author(s); date; variables measured; type of instrument (checklist, alternate choice, forced choice, adjective rating scales, etc.); description (item content, length, response options); previous administrations; persons appropriate for; administrational procedures; sample items; scoring; basis of development; reliability; validity; notes and comments; source; and bibliography (references to research studies in which the instrument was used). Access is further provided through three indexes: (1) instrument titles, (2) names of authors, or (3) variables measured, which greatly enhance facility in using this handbook.

Spencer, Mary L., Monika Kehoe, and Karen Speece. **Handbook for Women Scholars: Strategies for Success**. San Francisco: Center for Women Scholars, American Behavioral Research Corporation, 1982. 141p. LC 82-72317.

The purpose of this handbook is to provide, in one volume, information that will help women scholars overcome the handicaps resulting from sex discrimination. The first section documents cases of sex discrimination as revealed in a survey conducted by CFWS (Center for Women Scholars) in the San Francisco area. Sections are devoted to data on women's advocacy groups, caucuses and committees of professional organizations, women's research and resource centers, and career, financial, and legal aids.

Transcriptions of conversations with minority women and papers on discrimination submitted to a competition, including the winning entry, are presented. The two concluding sections, "Survival Aids and Information" and "Selected References," include strategies; the process for filing a faculty grievance, including a sample discrimination complaint form; career, financial, and legal resources; and a bibliography of reference tools, general works, and periodicals of interest to female scholars.

DIRECTORIES

Howe, Florence, Suzanne Howard, and Mary Jo Boehm Strauss, eds. **Everywoman's Guide to Colleges and Universities**. Old Westbury, N.Y.: Feminist Press, 1982. 512p. $4.95. LC 82-15402. ISBN 0-935312-09-9.

The 1970s and 1980s have seen changes in campus life with respect to opportunities for women. Stating their intention was to "report on the progress that institutions have made toward establishing a 'healthy' education environment for women" (p. xvii), the editors sent questionnaires to an unidentified number of college campuses to determine how they used resources in reponse to women's needs. Statistics are in three major areas: (1) enrollments by gender and race, (2) full-time faculty by gender, and (3) degrees awarded to students by gender, or the percentage of female students in nontraditional fields of study.

Nearly 600 schools were comparatively rated with respect to women in leadership positions (students, faculty, administrators); the curriculum; and athletics. Arrangement of entries is alphabetical by state and each entry provides name and address of institution; ratings that indicate whether an institution's progress is good, excellent, or outstanding, and how it compares to other schools; undergraduate enrollment; ethnic composition; availability of on-campus evening and/or weekend classes; off-campus classes; accessibility by public transportation; on-campus child-care facilities; women's studies programs; women holding faculty and administrative positions; intercollegiate sports for women; and an institutional self-description emphasizing features important for prospective women students.

A twenty-five page chart indicates schools and intercollegiate sports programs in which women can participate and a sample of the "Everywoman's questionnaire." An index of institution names concludes this work.

Schlachter, Gail Ann. **Directory of Financial Aids for Women**. 3d ed. Santa Barbara, Calif.: ABC-Clio, 1985. 370p. $40.00. LC 84-24582. ISBN 0-87436-374-8.

Approximately 1,500 financial aid programs designed primarily or exclusively for women are described in this directory, which is much expanded from earlier editions. Divided into four separate sections, the directory includes a descriptive list of financial aid programs, state sources of information on education benefits, an annotated bibliography of financial aid directories, and five indexes (program title, sponsoring organization, geographic, subject, and calendar index by filing dates).

Entries for program listings are grouped in subsections by type of assistance: scholarships, fellowships, loans, grants, awards, and internships. Information in each entry includes entry number and program title, sponsoring organization, availability, purpose, eligibility, financial data, duration, special features, limitations, number of awards, and application deadline.

18

Religion and Religious Education Reference Sources

BIBLIOGRAPHIES

Cheney, Ruth Gordon, ed. **The Christian Education Catalog**. New York: Seabury, 1981. 186p. $10.95. LC 81-8956. ISBN 0-8164-2328-8.

This annotated bibliography of print and nonprint materials was designed to provide teachers and librarians with a wide variety of resources in Christian education. Arrangement is by user group under subject categories. For example, resources included in the education category are as follows: children, youth, senior high school students, family/parents, vacation bible schools, curriculum series. Materials in a second section are arranged by different programs, ministries, and issues related to the church. Many sociological concerns are subjects as well, such as world hunger, homosexuality, crime, and divorce.

Day, Heather F. **Protestant Theological Education in America: A Bibliography**. Metuchen, N.J.: Scarecrow Press, 1985. 505p. (ATLA Bibliography Series, No. 15). $42.50. LC 85-18300. ISBN 0-8108-1842-6.

This bibliography of 5,249 entries is devoted to the history and development, as well as the current status of Protestant religious education in America at the postsecondary level. It includes references to the curricula of seminaries and theological schools. Access to specific categories of theological education is available in the subject indexes. While this work is comprehensive in coverage, its usefulness is limited by the lack of annotations.

Hunt, Thomas C., James C. Carper, and Charles R. Kniker. **Religious Schools in America: A Selected Bibliography**. New York: Garland, 1986. 391p. (Garland Reference Library of Social Science, Vol. 338). $47.00. LC 86-12118. ISBN 0-8240-8583-3.

Citations to 1,181 books, journals, and dissertations on private religious schools are provided in this comprehensive annotated bibliography. Arrangement of entries is in four sections. The first covers works on religion and schooling that are considered major treatises or pertinent general works; the second section covers court decisions related to religious schooling and the controversial questons of how much aid and how much control should be allowed by the government with respect to parochial schools. The third and largest section organizes materials under seventeen American religious groups, and citations in the fourth section are concerned with the evaluation of education in religious schools. Author and subject indexes are provided.

Menendez, Albert J. **School Prayer and Other Religious Issues in American Public Education: A Bibliography**. New York: Garland, 1985. 168p. (Garland Reference Library of Social Science, Vol. 29). $20.00. LC 84-48756. ISBN 0-8240-8775-5.

From the earliest days of public education in America, religion and religious issues have been of concern to a wide range of the population. Books, articles, dissertations, theses, newspaper articles, and reviews in law journals are listed in twenty-one subject chapters. Five of these are entirely concerned with the issue of prayer in schools, covering the history of school prayer, legal aspects, political issues, and pros and cons of the phenomenon. Other chapters cover related topics and centers of controversy; for example, Christian music and dramatizations for the Christmas season, religious teaching in the classroom, and Bible reading. Citations range from the mid-1800s to the mid-1980s. Entries include complete bibliographic description, but are not annotated. Author and subject indexes are provided, with access to states included through the latter index.

DIRECTORIES

A Guide to Christian Colleges. 3d ed. Christian College Coalition. Grand Rapids, Mich.: Eerdmans, 1984. 160p. $12.95pa. LC 84-13580. ISBN 0-8028-0010-6.

This college guide will be of interest to students wishing to attend a denominational or other religious school. A description is provided for each of sixty-three regionally accredited four-year liberal arts colleges which belong to the Christian College Coalition. Arrangement is alphabetical and entries provide information about the school's name, address, date of establishment, history, characteristics, religious affiliation, facilities, student life, denominational background of student body, expenses, academic courses, and degrees offered.

While this guide is similar to the information found in other standard guides, the compilation is very handy for those who want to attend a Christian college. The work is not indexed, but an alphabetical listing of colleges by state is helpful.

Guide to Schools and Departments of Religion and Seminaries in the United States and Canada: Degree Programs in Religious Studies. Compiled by Modoc Press. New York: Macmillan, 1987. 609p. $90.00. LC 88-121. ISBN 0-02-921650-8.

Prospective students interested in the study of religion, as well as counselors, the clergy, and librarians will find this guide helpful. Schools that have been recognized by six regional accrediting associations are listed, including those approved by the American Association of Bible Colleges and the Association of Theological Schools in the United States and Canada.

Arrangement of entries is geographical by state first, and then alphabetically. Information in each entry includes institution name, address, telephone number, key administrators, descriptions of major programs, community description, denominational affiliation, accreditation, enrollment, degree requirements, library facilities, tuition, financial aid opportunities, and housing facilities. The campus religious atmosphere and extracurricular activities are also described. Since information was provided by questionnaires sent to the schools, coverage is dependent on schools' responses to the survey.

NCEA/Ganley's Catholic Schools in America. Montrose, Colo.: Fisher Publishing, 1974- . Annual. $33.00. ISSN 0147-8044.

The National Catholic Educational Association has published an annual statistical report on Catholic elementary and secondary schools in the United States since the 1969-1970 school year. A database was established, with financial assistance from the Carnegie Corporation, and beginning with the 1974 annual publication, a report and directory of schools has been published. Each edition contains data related to enrollment, including minority and non-Catholic students and enrollment trends; faculty, staff, and pupil/teacher ratios; types and locations of schools; and the largest Catholic dioceses. Included as well is demographic information related to the U.S. school-age population in general, public and private school relations, and tax credits.

The directory section, the main body of the work, is arranged alphabetically by state. It includes for each diocese, the district/building name, address, telephone number, grades, enrollment, and principal. A section entitled "Historical Statistics" compares data for the past four years in Catholic elementary and secondary schools.

19

Research Centers and Organizations

DIRECTORIES

Directory of Educational Research Institutions. Prepared by the International Bureau of Education. 2d ed. Paris: United Nations Educational, Scientific and Cultural Organizations, 1986. 428p. (IBEdata Series). $19.00pa. LC 87-171164. ISBN 92-3-002405-8.

Scholars who wish to know what type of educational research has been done, by whom, and where, will find this directory useful. Since academic institutions and research centers are listed alphabetically by country, it is easy to get an idea of the types of educational research being conducted worldwide. Each entry includes official name of the research institution/center, address, year of establishment, parent organization (if any), staff, type and objectives of research, periodical publications, and research projects in progress.

This second edition represents a major update and expansion of the 1980 edition, actually doubling the size of the work. A main subject index and a keyword/phrase index in English, Spanish, and French conclude the work.

Lehming, Rolf, ed. **Directory of Research Organizations in Education: Research, Development, Dissemination, Evaluation and Policy Studies.** San Francisco: Far West Laboratory, 1982. 411p. ED 218271.

This publication is a camera-ready reproduction of a printed version of the computer files compiled by the ARROE (American Registry of Research and Research-Related Organizations in Education) project of the Far West Laboratory's Educational Dissemination Studies Program. The ARROE project involved a survey which served as a census of organizations performing research activities related to education in the areas of development, dissemination, evaluation, or policy studies.

A total of 2,418 organizations are arranged alphabetically by state, and information given includes organization name, address and telephone number, contact person, aims and purposes, focus of research activities, staffing and areas of specialization, funding sources, application of funds by research function and educational level, means of dissemination of research results, and availability of publications.

Indexes list organizations by subject area or by educational level to which the work is directed, a feature that increases flexibility in using this resource.

Research Centers Directory. 11th ed. Edited by Mary Michelle Watkins. Detroit: Gale 1986. 2v. $355.00. LC 60-14807. ISBN 0-8103-0472-4. ISSN 0080-1518.

This guide describes over 8,000 university-related and other nonprofit research organizations in the United States and Canada. Entries are arranged in subject categories, with over 400 entries listed under the section on education. Other subject categories include (volume 1) life sciences, physical sciences, and engineering; and (volume 2) private and public policy and affairs, social and cultural studies, and multidisciplinary and coordinating centers. The extensive indexes provide multiple means of access and are entitled "Alphabetic Index of Research Centers and Projects," "Acronyms Index of Research Centers," "Institutional Index," "Special Capabilities Index," and "Subject Index."

Each entry provides a sequential entry number, name of the sponsoring institution, research center name, acronym, address and telephone number, year founded, director (or head of center), governance/former names, sources of support, staff, volume and field of research, publications and services, conferences and seminars (etc.), and library facilities.

The educational researcher will find this an important tool in identifying major programs of educational research.

CENTERS AND ORGANIZATIONS

American Association for Adult and Continuing Education (AAACE). 1201 16th St., N.W., Suite 230, Washington, DC 20036. (202) 822-7866.

Formed in 1982 by the merger of the Adult Education Association of the USA and National Association for Public Continuing Adult Education, the purpose of this organization is to promote education as an ongoing learning process. It attempts to encourage continuing education programs and their support at various governmental levels. It publishes *AAACE Newsletter*, the monthly *Lifelong Learning*, and *Adult Education* (quarterly).

American Association of Colleges for Teacher Education (AACTE). One Dupont Circle, N.W., Suite 610, Washington, DC 20036. (202) 293-2450.

This higher education organization was founded in 1948 and has as its focus the training and development of teachers and other professionals in education. It maintains committees on accreditation, education, government relations, and research and information, as well as an Advisory Council of State Representatives. It publishes books, monographs, an annual directory and the bimonthly *Journal of Teacher Education*.

American Association of Community and Junior Colleges (AACJC). National Center for Higher Education, One Dupont Circle, N.W., Suite 410, Washington, DC 20036. (202) 293-7050.

This association's objectives are to promote the development of two-year colleges. It has an Office of Federal Relations which keeps track of federal court decisions and programs related to community, technical, and/or junior colleges; and it maintains a library of college catalogs and publishes a newsletter, the bimonthly *Community, Technical and Junior College Journal*, and two annuals, *Community, Technical and Junior College Directory*, and *Directory of Administrators*.

American Association of Special Educators (AASE). 107-20 125th St., Richmond Hill, NY 11419. (212) 641-1274.

The purpose of this organization is to provide assistance to educational, training, and recreational activities for special education students. It sponsors international conferences and has published *Dictionary of Special Education Terms* as well as other directories and newsletters.

American Association of State Colleges and Universities (AASCU). One Dupont Circle, N.W., Washington, DC 20036. (202) 293-7070.

State supported and controlled colleges and universities join the AASCU; associate members are state educational agencies involved with their administration. Founded in 1971, it maintains twenty-nine committees, sponsors several higher education awards, conducts national and regional workshops, and publishes an annual membership list, pamphlets, and proceedings of its annual convention. It also distributes films and other educational materials.

American Council on Education (ACE). One Dupont Circle, N.W., Washington, DC 20036. (202) 939-9300.

This council of institutions of higher education and educational organizations represents accredited colleges and universities and acts as their advocate before governmental bodies. It also promotes adult education and administers the GED high school equivalency exam on a national basis. It provides equivalency evaluation for course credit for courses taken through work or military experience. It publishes the biweekly *Higher Education and National Affairs*, the quarterly *Educational Record*, and other annual publications, including *A Fact Book of Higher Education*.

American Educational Research Association (AERA). 1230 17th St., N.W., Washington, DC 20036. (202) 223-9485.

The emphasis of the AERA is on educational research in the areas of learning and educational psychology, but it includes many other areas of research as reflected in its divisions in administration, counseling, curriculum, history, measurement, postsecondary education, evaluation, social context, teaching, and teacher education. It publishes the monthly *Educational Reseacher*, the quarterly *Review of Educational Research*, the annual *Review of Research in Education*, a biennial membership directory, and the *Encyclopedia of Educational Research*.

American School Counselor Association (ASCA). 5999 Stevenson Ave., Alexandria, VA 22304. (713) 823-9800.

Founded in 1953, the ASCA is a division of the American Association for Counseling and Development. It promotes the rights and welfare of children and the improvement of professional standards in school counseling. It disseminates materials related to school counseling and psychology. It publishes *The School Counselor* (5/year) and *Elementary School Guidance and Counseling* (quarterly), as well as various newsletters, manuals, and monographs.

American Vocational Association (AVA). 1410 King St., Alexandria, VA 22314. (703) 683-3111.

The aim of this association is to promote the development and improvement of vocational education at all levels: secondary, postsecondary, and adult. It works with the Office of Vocational Rehabilitation in the Department of Health and Human Services and has divisions related to agriculture, business, employment and training, guidance, health occupations, home economics, industrial arts, marketing and distributive education, trade, and technical education. Its publications include the monthly *Vocational Education Journal*, bimonthly *Update*, and semiannual *Job Market Update*. The AVA was established in 1925.

Council on International Educational Exchange (CIEE). 2505 E. 42nd St., New York, NY 10017. (212) 661-1414.

The CIEE was founded in 1947 for the purpose of facilitating educational international exchanges. It also promotes language study and study programs abroad, particularly in China, USSR, and other European countries. It cosponsors high school student exchange programs and provides services to students seeking overseas educational experiences. It sponsors a variety of publications, including *Monthly Campus Update*, *Student Travel Catalog* (annual), and various directories and brochures on foreign travel and study.

Far West Laboratory for Educational Research and Development. 1855 Folsom St., San Francisco, CA 94103. (415) 565-3000.

This laboratory is one of the major centers of educational research and development. It sponsors the Educational Computers Program dealing with the relationship of computers and education and is on the frontier of new trends and developments in curriculum and instruction. It publishes *ETC: Educational Technology and Communication* (monthly).

Institute of International Education (IIE). 809 United Nations Plaza, New York, NY 10017. (202) 883-8200.

The institute promotes crosscultural understandings through exchange programs of U.S. students, artists, researchers, and educators with those of other countries. It disseminates information on education in the United States and foreign countries, maintains offices in twenty-five cities abroad, and maintains a database that aids in matching international students' education in the United States with corporate employment needs. It publishes three volumes in the annual *Learning Traveler* series, an annual report, *Open Doors*, an annual census of foreign students in the United States, and *English Language and Orientation Programs in the United States* (biennial).

International Reading Association (IRA). P.O. Box 8139, 800 Barksdale Rd., Newark, DE 19714. (302) 731-1600.

Membership in the International Reading Association is comprised primarily of classroom teachers and teacher educators. Its purpose is to promote effective reading instruction at all levels. It maintains a placement service for members and publishes the *Reading Teacher* (9/year), *Journal of Reading* (8/year), *Lecturay Vida* (quarterly), *Reading Research* (quarterly), *IRA Desktop Reference* (annual), as well as books, monographs, and monthly newsletters. It was founded in 1956 by merger of the International Council for the Improvement of Reading Instruction and National Association for Remedial Teaching.

National Association for Bilingual Education (NABE). 1201 16th St., N.W., Rm. 407, Washington, DC 20036. (202) 822-7870.

The purpose of this association, founded in 1975, is to raise public consciousness of the need for bilingual education and then to promote its effective implementation. It also disseminates information about government decisions regarding bilingual instruction and encourages and publishes scholarly research in the field. It maintains special interest groups at all levels and categories of education, and publishes a newsletter and *Journal* (3/year).

Association for Childhood Education International (ACEI). 11141 Georgia Av_
200, Wheaton, MD 20902. (301) 942-2443.

Founded in 1931, the ACEI's membership supports sound education for, a_
human rights of, children from infancy through early adolescence. It conducts work_
and regional conferences, cooperates with government agencies and teaching institut_
and conducts activities through thirteen different committees. It publishes *ACEI Exch_*
(monthly), *Childhood Education* (5/year), *Journal of Research in Childhood Educat_*
and *Bibliography of Books for Children.*

Association for Educational Communications and Technology (AECT). 1126 16th St_
N.W., Washington, DC 20036. (202) 466-4780.

The AECT has had several name changes since 1923, the most recent in 1970 at which
time it was known as the Department of Audiovisual Instruction. Its objectives are to
promote learning through a systematic approach to instructional design. It maintains telecommunications services (electronic mail), twenty-three committees, and nine divisions. It
publishes *Tech Trends* (8/year), *Educational Communication and Technology Journal*
(quarterly), *Journal of Instructional Development* (quarterly), and an annual membership
directory.

Association for Supervision and Curriculum Development (ASCD). 125 N. West St.,
Alexandria, VA 22314. (703) 549-9110.

The ASCD was founded in 1921 and has fifty-three affiliated units. Teachers, principals, superintendents, curriculum personnel, parents, and others interested in school
supervision and curriculum development can join. It disseminates information, encourages
research, and conducts national curriculum study institutes. Publications include
Educational Leadership (8/year), *Journal of Curriculum Supervision* (quarterly), and
newsletters, booklets, and yearbooks.

Association of American Colleges (AAC). 1818 R. St., N.W., Washington, DC 20009.
(202) 387-3760.

The AAC supports (theoretically and financially) the attempts of American colleges
and unversities to provide academically outstanding curricula and instructional programs.
It also grants financial assistance to programs for minority students. Publications include
Liberal Education (5/year), *On Campus with Women* (quarterly), and reports and results
of funded projects.

Council for Exceptional Children (CEC). 1920 Association Dr., Reston, VA 22091.
(713) 620-3660.

This council promotes the educational rights of children who have instructional needs
that differ from the average because they are mentally or physically handicapped, learning
disabled, or gifted. It sponsors conferences and workshops and disseminates information
on the needs of, and opportunities for, exceptional children. It also maintains the ERIC
Clearinghouse on Handicapped and Gifted Children. It has divisions for different aspects
of special education and publishes *Exceptional Children* (bimonthly), *Exceptional Child
Education Resources* (quarterly), *Teaching Exceptional Children* (quarterly), and produces
print and nonprint materials related to special education.

National Association for the Education of Young Children (NAEYC). 1834 Connecticut Ave., N.W., Washington, DC 20009. (202) 232-8777.

Professionals and laypersons concerned with the education and development of preschool, kindergarten, and primary children are eligible for membership in this organization. It holds the annual "Week of the Young Child" to promote awareness of the rights and special needs of the very young, and provides accreditation through the National Academy of Early Childhood Programs. Its official publications include *Young Children* (bimonthly) and *Early Childhood Research* (quarterly), as well as various brochures, posters, and books.

National Associaton of State Universities and Land-Grant Colleges (NASULGC). One Dupont Circle, N.W., Suite 710, Washington, DC 20036. (202) 778-0818.

This association of the major U.S. public institutions of higher education includes seventy-two land-grant schools. Its objectives are to disseminate information about special needs and legislation related to these institutions. It sponsors the Office for Advancement of Public Black Colleges and maintains twenty Senate committees and various commissions and councils. It publishes *The Green Sheet* (20/year), *Appropriations of State Tax Refunds for Operating Expenses of Higher Education* (annual), *Enrollment at State and Land-Grant Universities* (annual), *Private Support for State and Land-Grant Universities, Student Changes at State and Land-Grant Universities* (annual), as well as conference proceedings and other periodical titles.

National Council for Accreditation of Teacher Education (NCATE). 1919 Pennsylvania Ave., N.W., Suite 202, Washington, DC 20006. (202) 466-7496.

This voluntary accrediting body is concerned with assessment and evaluation of teacher education programs at the K-12 levels. School services preparing personnel as principals, supervisors, superintendents, guidance counselors, school psychologists, and other specialists, are also included. It has committees on process and evaluation and professional standards. It publishes *Annual List of Accredited Institutions, Standards for Accreditation of Teacher Education,* and *Update.*

Phi Delta Kappa. Eighth and Union, Box 789, Bloomington, IN 47402. (812) 339-1156.

This professional honorary fraternity in education was founded in 1910. It publishes books, monographs, papers, proceedings of symposia, the monthly *Phi Delta Kappan*, and an ongoing series of booklets, each treating a current issue or topic in education, called *Fastbacks*.

Social Science Education Consortium (SSEC). 855 Broadway, Boulder, CO 80302. (303) 492-8154.

SSEC is a nonprofit organization established for the purpose of promoting social science education. It maintains a major multimedia library of textbooks and audiovisual instructional materials, and sponsors workshops to train educators in selection, evaluation, and utilization of materials for social studies instruction.

20

Periodical Literature

INDEXES AND ABSTRACTS

(See Chapter 4 "General Education Reference Sources").

DIRECTORIES

Dyer, Thomas and Margaret Davis. **Higher Education Periodicals: A Directory**. Athens, Ga.: Institute of Higher Education, University of Georgia, 1981. 148p. LC 81-621676.

This directory is a successor to an earlier 1969 title, *An Annotated Guide to Periodical Literature: Higher Education*. It provides information on 300 journals in various fields of education including periodical title (and former titles, if any), sponsoring agency/publisher, editor's name and mailing address, description (including frequency) of the publication, subscriptions rates and address to subscribe, circulation statistics, and manuscript information. The entries are arranged alphabetically by title and an index of titles concludes the listing. This work is helpful, but its usefulness would certainly be enhanced by a subject index. While *Education and Education-Related Serials: A Directory* by Wayne J. Krepel and Charles R. DuVall (Libraries Unlimited, 1977) is more comprehensive in scope, it is also more dated, as is *Guide to Periodicals in Education and its Academic Disciplines* by William L. Camp and Bryan L. Schwark (2d ed., Scarecrow Press, 1975).

Manera, Elizabeth S., and Robert E. Wright. **Annotated Writer's Guide to Professional Educational Journals**. Scottsdale, Ariz.: Bobets Publishing, 1982. 188p. $9.95pa. LC 82-141346. ISBN 0-9609782-0-8.

In addition to describing approximately 175 periodicals in the field of education, this guide is prefaced by several articles on writing. One of the articles particularly addresses manuscript writing, with tips for the prospective journal writer. Another is a study of publishing practices and provides information on who publishes what.

Entries are arranged alphabetically by title of the periodical and are divided into two main parts: publishing guide and manuscript guide. Information in the former includes editorial address, publisher's address, copyright, publishing date, and reading clientele. Information related to the manuscript is concerned with style, design (topics of concern and average number of articles per issue), length of manuscript, whether book reviews and abstracts accepted (etc.), rules for submission of manuscript, editorial policy, and author data. A brief annotated bibliography, "Books for Authors," and a "Periodical Title Index" conclude the work.

This inexpensive, spiral-bound guide provides a lot of useful information for the would-be published scholar in the field of education.

PERIODICALS

AACTE Bulletin. Washington, D.C.: American Association for Higher Education, 1947- . Monthly. $27.00/year. ISSN 0162-7910.
Articles are related to education at the college and university levels. Emphasis is given to new trends, developments, and academic programs.

Academe: Bulletin of the AAUP. Washington, D.C.: American Association of University Professors, 1915- . Bimonthly. $37.00/yr. ISSN 0190-2946.
Trends, developments, educators and scholars in higher education, and news of interest to members of the American Association of University Professors are covered in three or four major articles and brief items. Situations involving institutions censored by the AAUP are discussed.

Adult Education Quarterly. Washington, D.C.: American Association for Adult and Continuing Education, 1951- . Quarterly. $85.00/yr., nonmembers; $34.00/yr., members. ISSN 0001-8481.
Scholarly articles of interest to theorists and practitioners cover research, theory, and historical and empirical studies related to adult and continuing education. Its subtitle is *A Journal of Research and Theory*.

American Education. Washington, D.C.: U.S. Department of Education, 1965- . Monthly. $23.00/yr. ISSN 0002-8304.
This federal publication emphasizes outstanding educational programs, and provides federal perspectives on educational policy and practice at all levels. It also provides reviews of current books on education published by the Government Printing Office.

American Educational Research Journal. Washington, D.C.: American Educational Research Association, 1964- . Quarterly. $29.00/yr. ISSN 0002-8312.
Empirical and theoretical original research conducted in schools of education and institutions of higher education is reported in this scholarly research journal. Emphasis is given to investigations in educational psychology.

American Educator. Washington, D.C.: American Federation of Teachers, AFL-CIO, 1977- . Quarterly. $2.50/yr. ISSN 0148-432X.
Six or seven articles on current trends or issues in education are covered in each issue. The writing style is more popular than scholarly.

American Journal of Education. Chicago: University of Chicago Press, 1983- . Quarterly. $20.00/yr., individuals; $35.00/yr., institutions; $16.00/yr., students. ISSN 0195-6744.
Scholarly, well-documented articles on a variety of subjects related to education are written by experts at all levels of instruction. Reports both completed research and research in progress.

American School Board Journal. Alexandria, Va.: National School Boards Association, 1891- . Monthly. $38.00/yr. ISSN 0003-0953.
Perspectives on administering schools at the K-12 levels are given from the point of view of school board members. Each issue contains ten to twelve articles on aspects of school law, school administration, discipline, and evaluation of educational institutions.

American Teacher. Washington, D.C.: American Federation of Teachers, AFL/CIO, 1916- . Monthly (8/yr.). $7.00/yr. ISSN 0003-1380.

This official organ of the American Federation of Teachers emphasizes current union activities, negotiations, and legislation, but has selected coverage of topics related to general education.

Art Education. Reston, Va.: National Art Education Association, 1948- . Bimonthly. $50.00/yr. ISSN 0004-3125.

Teaching activities and strategies for art teachers from elementary through post-secondary levels are discussed and described.

Change. Washington, D.C.: Heldref, 1968- . Bimonthly. $40.00/yr., institutions; $20.00/yr., individuals. ISSN 0009-1383.

Subtitled *The Magazine of Higher Learning*, this publications describes and critically analyzes aspects of, and developments in, higher education on an international basis.

Childhood Education. Wheaton, Md.: Association for Childhood Education International, 1924. 5/yr. $32.00/yr., individuals; $40.00/yr., institutions. ISSN 0009-4056.

Subtitled *A Journal for Teachers, Teachers-in-Training, Teacher Educators, Parents, Day Care Workers, Librarians, Pediatricians and Other Child Caregivers*, this journal includes articles that emphasize instruction that corresponds to children's developmental abilities and their inductive thinking skills.

Chronicle of Higher Education. Washington, D.C.: Corbin Gwaltney, 1966- . Weekly. $50.00/yr. ISSN 0009-5982.

This important news source keeps college and university faculty and administrators aware of current trends, issues, and legislation related to education, as well as major reports, positions available, winners of grants and fellowships, conferences, and other events.

College Teaching. Washington, D.C.: Heldref, 1953- . Quarterly. $35.00/yr. ISSN 8756-7555.

Aimed at college faculty in graduate and undergraduate programs, articles emphasize strategies, techniques, and opinions related to improving instruction. Research and evaluation are also included, but emphasis is on practical application.

Comparative Education Review. Chicago: University of Chicago Press, 1956- . Quarterly. $53.00/yr. ISSN 0010-4086.

This international journal reports on educational developments, research, and trends in countries all over the world. Reviews of essays and books are also included.

The Computing Teacher. Eugene: International Council for Computers in Education, University of Oregon, 1979- . Monthly (9/yr.). $25.00/yr. ISSN 0278-9175.

Educators who are concerned about using computers in instruction will find short, practically oriented articles on a range of subjects from the impact of computers on education to specific applications in individual areas of the curriculum.

Curriculum Review. Chicago: Curriculum Advisory Service, 1962- . 5/yr. ISSN 0147-2453.

Curriculum Advisory Service has published this reviewing journal under varying titles—*CAS* (1962-1967), *CAS Bulletin* (1968-1975), and *Curriculum Review* (1976- .). It evaluates textbooks and other print and nonprint materials related to the K-12 school curricula. Feature articles are also included, which cover innovations in teaching methods, strategies and materials, recent trends in education in general, or specific curricular areas. In some cases, speaker referrals are also listed.

Early Years/K-8. Darien, Conn.: Allen Raymond, 1971- . Monthly (9/yr.). $15.00/yr. ISSN 0094-6532.

This popular periodical is "for teachers and by teachers" of children from preschool through fourth grade. Teaching activities, previews of print and nonprint materials, "how-to" articles, and discussions of new trends and issues comprise this publication.

EC & TJ (Educational Communications and Technology Journal). Bloomington, Ind.: Association for Educational Communications & Technology, 1953- . Quarterly. $24.00/yr. ISSN 0148-5806.

This periodical includes scholarly research articles, many of which are empirical investigations, and other articles of critical opinion, historical analysis, and new developments in educational technology. Major emphasis is given to mediated instruction and learning.

Education Daily. Arlington, Va.: Capitol Publications, 1968- . Daily. $429.95/yr. ISSN 0013-1261.

This daily newsletter emphasizes educational practices, conferences, financial status, research, and current issues in schools at the K-12 levels. Sources of news include the U.S. Department of Education, the U.S. Congress, and court decisions.

Education Digest. Ann Arbor, Mich.: Prakken Publications, 1935- . Monthly (9/yr.). $18.00/yr. ISSN 0013-127X.

Key articles on major educational trends and issues that have appeared in recent journals are reprinted or summarized. A variety of topics from preschool through higher education levels is available for the layperson and the professional scholar.

Education Week. Washington, D.C.: Editorial Projects in Education, 1981. 40/yr. $47.94/yr. ISSN 0277-4232.

This periodical is published weekly during the school year and is aimed at teachers and administrators in elementary and secondary schools. It has a wide scope with respect to coverage and articles could cover anything from items comparing education in other countries to technological innovations in education. A calendar of educational conferences, professional positions available, announcements of grants, and federal and state issues in education are also included.

Educational Administration Quarterly. Beverly Hills, Calif.: Sage, 1964- . Quarterly. $30.00/yr., individuals; $65.00/yr., institutions. ISSN 0013-161X.

Research and practice in educational administration at all levels and critical analyses of significant issues and problems of concern to school principals and higher education personnel are included in this scholarly, research-oriented periodical.

Educational Forum. West Lafayette, Ind.: Kappa Delta Pi, 1936- . Quarterly. $12.00/yr. ISSN 0013-1725.

Articles written by educators discuss education from preschool through higher education on a wide variety of topics. Emphasis is on current trends, issues, and problems. Some reports of original studies are included.

Educational Leadership. Alexandria, Va.: Association for Supervision and Curriculum Development, 1943- . Monthly (for 8 mo.). $48.00/yr, nonmembers; $24.00/yr., members. ISSN 0013-1784.

This journal provides thematic issues primarily aimed at school administrators at the K-12 levels, but a wide range of coverage is given to curriculum, instruction, and supervision.

Educational Record. Washington, D.C.: American Council on Education, 1920- . Quarterly. $20.00/yr. ISSN 0013-1873.

Articles in this periodical are written by and for college and university administrators. Focus of articles is on current issues and innovations in the field.

Educational Researcher. Washington, D.C.: American Educational Research Association, 1972- . Monthly. $19.00/yr., individuals; $23.00/yr., institutions. ISSN 0013-189X.

Trends in educational research conducted in American institutions are reported in this AERA publication. It also includes book reviews, editorials, and federal news related to education.

Electronic Learning. New York: Scholastic, 1981- . Monthly (8/yr.). $19.95/yr. ISSN 0278-3258.

Brief articles on new computer products and ideas related to using computers for instruction are included in this practically oriented periodical.

Elementary School Guidance & Counseling. Alexandria, Va.: American School Counselor Association, 1967- . Quarterly. $20.00/yr., nonmembers; $16.00/yr., members. ISSN 0013-5976.

Exceptional Children. Reston, Va.: Council for Exceptional Children, 1934- . 6/yr. $30.00/yr. ISSN 0014-4029.

All aspects of special education are covered in five major articles and book reviews per issue. Publishers considers unsolicited articles of interest to administrators, school psychologists, and speech therapists.

Harvard Educational Review. Cambridge, Mass.: Harvard University, Graduate School of Education, 1931- . Quarterly. $28.00/yr., individuals; $50.00/yr., institutions. ISSN 0017-8055.

Four major opinion articles and/or reports of scholarly research on all aspects of education, including historical, sociological, philosophical, and psychological perspectives are included in each issue. Readers can react via a "Letters to the Editors" column.

History of Education Quarterly. Bloomington: Indiana University, School of Education, 1961- . Quarterly. $25.00/yr., individuals; $47.00/yr., institutions. $15.00/yr., foreign. ISSN 0018-2680.

Instructor. Cleveland, Ohio: Harcourt Brace Jovanovich, 1981- . Monthly (10/yr). $20.00/yr. ISSN 0020-4285.

Teaching activities and ideas for practical application in all areas of the curriculum are provided, including stories, plays, arts and crafts projects, work units, and lesson plans for the elementary teacher.

International Bureau of Education Bulletin. Geneva, Switzerland: UNESCO, 1926- . Quarterly. 52 Fr./yr.

This international publication identifies information sources on various aspects of education and compiles annotated bibliographic guides on education in particular countries or on particular related topics. This publication incorporates three previous publications: *Educational Documentation and Information, Awareness List,* and *Cooperative Educational Abstracting Service.*

Journal of Educational Psychology. Washington, D.C.: American Psychological Association, 1910- . Bimonthly. $100.00/yr., nonmembers; $50.00/yr., individual members. ISSN 0022-0663.

This publication covers theoretical perspectives on teaching and learning. Original research covering all aspects of cognitive and psychological development, and learning behaviors are included.

Journal of Educational Research. Washington, D.C.: Heldref, 1920- . Bimonthly. $45.00/yr. ISSN 0022-0671.

Twelve articles per issue report experimental and other original educational research investigations. Topics covered are usually related to practice as opposed to theoretical development.

Journal of Higher Education. Columbus: Ohio State University Press, 1930- . Bimonthly. $20.00/yr., individuals; $30.00/yr., libraries. ISSN 0022-1546.

Five or six articles per issue analyze and discuss topics of interest to college and university faculty administrators. Emphasis is on current trends and issues related to educational psychology, educational technology, and administration.

Journal of Learning Disabilities. Cicero, Ill.: Gerald Serf, 1968- . Monthly. $40.00/yr., individuals; $50.00/yr., institutions; $60.00/yr., foreign. ISSN 0022-2194.

Educators involved with special education contribute eight to ten articles per issue presenting points of view, reporting research, or describing case studies related to learning disabilities.

Journal of Reading. Newark, Del.: International Reading Association, 1957- . Monthly (8/yr.). $30.00/yr. ISSN 0022-4103.

Articles in this publication of the International Reading Association that suggest strategies and techniques for teaching reading are predominant; others report research. Emphasis is on information for reading teachers at secondary, college, and adult levels.

Journal of Teacher Education. Washington, D.C.: American Association of Colleges for Teacher Education, 1950- . Bimonthly. $30.00/yr. ISSN 0022-4871.

Studies using experimental research and opinion articles, and those reporting trends and issues related to teacher education, comprise this journal.

Lifelong Learning: An Omnibus of Practice and Research. Washington, D.C.: American Association for Adult and Continuing Education, 1960- . Monthly (8/yr.). $32.00/yr. ISSN 0740-0578.

Research articles with findings applicable to practice in adult and community education are included. The orientation is half theoretical and half practical.

Peabody Journal of Education. Nashville, Tenn.: Vanderbilt University, George Peabody College for Teachers, 1923- . Quarterly. $18.00/yr., individuals; $28.50/yr., libraries and institutions. ISSN 0031-3432.

Thematic issues reflect topics of relevance to teachers, teacher-educators, faculty members in college level departments of education, and sociologists and psychologists concerned with learning and learning behaviors. George Peabody College for Teachers has a well-organized teacher education program.

Phi Delta Kappan. Bloomington, Ind.: Phi Delta Kappa, 1915- . Monthly (10/yr.). $25.00/yr. ISSN 0031-7217.

The publication of this national educational honorary society includes fifteen to twenty timely articles, with a large share of topical or thematic coverage. A combination of reported research, fact, opinion, and discussion.

Principal. Reston, Va.: National Association of Elementary School Principals, 1921- . 5/yr. $110.00/yr. ISSN 0271-6062.

Aimed at school administrators at the elementary and middle school levels, this publication covers brief articles related to discipline, evaluation, public relations, faculty management, scheduling, and other topics of relevance to school principals.

Reading Research Quarterly. Newark, Del.: International Reading Association, 1965- . Quarterly. $30.00/yr., members. ISSN 0034-0553

A scholarly research journal, this publication presents well-documented studies on all aspects of reading instruction and theories related to reading. It covers reading instruction at all levels.

The Reading Teacher. Newark, Del.: International Reading Association, 1947- . Monthly (9/yr.). $30.00/yr., members. ISSN 0034-0561.

While theory and research are covered, the emphasis is more on informative and practically oriented articles about the teaching of reading. Also included are evaluative reviews of instructional materials and news items related to the International Reading Association.

Review of Education. Bedford Hills, N.Y.: Redgrave Publishing, 1975- . Quarterly. $34.00/yr., institutions; $21.00/yr., individuals. ISSN 0098-5597.

This journal provides critical reviews of the most significant new titles published in all areas of education. Literature reviewed consists of teaching materials, scholarly works, and books on research. Some foreign language titles are included.

Review of Educational Research. Washington, D.C.: American Educational Research Association, 1931- . Quarterly. $23.00/yr., individuals; $29.00/yr., institutions. ISSN 0034-6543.

Critical and analytical summaries of major studies in the research literature are integrated in well-documented articles that attempt to relate research to practice.

Teachers College Record. New York: Columbia University, Teachers College, 1900- .
    Quarterly. $40.00/yr., institutions; $20.00/yr., individuals. ISSN 0161-4681.
    This is a scholarly periodical providing six to eight articles per issue that emphasize philosophical, historical, and practical concerns and issues in education. Authors are well-known educational scholars.

Theory into Practice. Columbus: Ohio State University, 1962- . Quarterly. $16.00/yr.,
    individuals; $30.00/yr., institutions. ISSN 0040-5841.
    Thematic issues include ten or twelve articles written from divergent perspectives. Content is of interest to all educators and is particularly useful in teacher education programs.

Index